An Introductory Course in Greek and Latin Grammar and Vocabulary Designed to Unlock the Romance Languages and English

A Comparative Approach to Learning Basic Language Skills

John R. Harris, Ph.D.

An Introductory Course in Greek and Latin Grammar and Vocabulary
Designed to Unlock the Romance Languages and English
John R. Harris

Bel Pianeta Series, Volume 2

Lo bel pianeta che d'amar conforta…

Works in this series represent the author's previously unpublished research primarily in the areas of classical antiquity and the European Middle Ages. His decision to bring them out through Amazon's self-publishing options reflects two motives: 1) the desire to leave behind the product of his labors now that his formal academic career has ended, and 2) the awareness that institutions in and around the academy are driven ever more by political calculation and tend to evaluate scholarship less on its intrinsic merits than on its service of trend. The freedom of the Internet, fortunately, has provided a timely and functional alternative to the tyranny of an intellectually inbred oligarchy. While not "peer reviewed", the titles in the Bel Pianeta Series offer their conclusions, translations, and speculations to the scrutiny of all educated, thoughtful people in full confidence that, with modest effort, they may reach a verdict quite as competent as that of a sinecured elite.

The cover art represents a slightly reduced version of Hubert Robert's canvas, *The Old Temple* (completed 1788). The evocative subject matter was selected for our purpose as an express reminder that Latin "decayed" into languages still vibrant today and, indeed (as this text often stresses), that historical Latin was itself clearly in decline from the rigors of a much more articulated system.

Acknowledgments

I should particularly like to recognize Savannah Blair for her assistance in proofreading the text's final version, proposing corrections and improvements, and completing the arduous labor of creating the glossaries. Though in the process of finishing her bachelor's degree and beginning a master's degree at the same time, Savannah somehow found the leisure to lend her considerable copy-editing skills to this ongoing project.

I must also thank Dr. Hui Wu of the Univeristy of Texas at Tyler for offering me the context of a college-level class within which to apply this book's contents and tweak them repeatedly after each semester. The indifference to classical learning that reigns in the conmporary academy sometimes borders on hostility, so enjoying the support of a department chair and established scholar like Dr. Wu was an unexpected benefit to my work.

Naturally, the remaining errors (of which there are likely more than a few, to judge by how many have surfaced at every new proofreading) are my sole responsibility.

IN MEMORY of

The Reverend Kenneth Arden Bentley Hinds

Contents

Chapter Three   Nouns Continued   93

Chapter Four   Verbs Continued   135

Introduction

This book is intended to guide the strongly motivated student along the path to superior language skills in numerous ways. The skills in question very much include a better understanding of and facility with English itself, but they are not confined within these limits. For instance, the program of study set forth here does not aim exclusively, or even primarily, at the narrow objective of enhancing the English-speaker's vocabulary by enriching it with Greek and Latin derivatives. That objective and similar ones, worthy though they are and courted by other books though they have been, do not satisfy the more complex ambitions of the present text.

To begin with, if the student has any plans of one day learning a foreign language, he or she is almost certain to run into some concepts that have no parallel in English. Greek and Latin display several of these "alien" qualities. Even tongues which are not related to or descended from the Western world's classical languages often possess many of the features so intimidating and strange to the young English-speaker struggling with Latin. Five such features receiving particular attention in this book may be singled out at once:

1) A system of variable spellings for nouns (usually affecting their final syllable or syllables) so as to designate *case*: i.e., the function which a given noun serves in a given sentence. English is among a very small minority of languages that have few or no cases.

2) The assignment of gender to all nouns. To the English-speaker, this convention may seem patent nonsense, since only living creatures can have gender; yet gender is grammatically ascribed to trees, stones, etc., in languages where it exists at all, and not just to sentient beings. Nonsensical or not, this practice is found in a great many languages around the world.

3) A system of indicators within the finite verb to show its exact person and number (again most often at the word's end). English has extremely few such indicators; in fact, only the third-person singular form ("he/she/it") ever alters its spelling in response to person and number, and then only in the present tense (and in compound constructions where the auxiliary verb is present tense).

4) A system of indicators within verbs (usually before the person/number indicators mentioned just above) to designate the verb's tense. Most English tenses are formed through the mediation of auxiliary verbs. This approach tends to be used much more sparingly in other languages.

5) The agreement of nouns and their adjectives in number and gender; though applying such tags to adjectives is both logical and helpful (inasmuch as it makes their misattribution very unlikely), English has abandoned the practice (still alive in its parent language, German). The English-speaker is thus likely to be very puzzled by yet another common convention in foreign languages.

Any experienced teacher of foreign language (where "foreign" is understood to mean "non-English," since this book is obviously written in English and intended for English-speakers) will have noticed that monolingual Anglophone students often have enormous difficulty with the grammatical concepts just listed. Some of them, very probably, never understand completely the ideas that are put before them during a brief classroom encounter with another tongue. Particularly when so much emphasis in contemporary pedagogy is placed on conversational speech, the student may endure two or four required semesters of French or Spanish or German without ever really grasping why adjectives change their spelling according to what they modify. This course aspires to reduce, if not eliminate, the months of misery suffered by such unhappy students.

The study of Latin and Greek also improves the English-speaker's general and technical vocabulary. This book seeks to advance both varieties of diction. English has a particular abundance of Latin words, many of them serving as roots from which perhaps a dozen derivatives may grow. Greek words are less common in general English speech; but in abundantly many the sciences, they turn out to be even more common than Latin derivatives.

(The word "dinosaur" is a Greek concoction, for instance, and most species of dinosaur were dubbed in Greek for some distinctive physical feature before paleontologists apparently gave up studying antiquity as it applies to human speech. Now hybrids as linguistically grotesque as the animals they name—e.g., "Spinops," a Latin/Greek concoction—are the norm.)

Latin and Greek also teach the Anglophone student a great deal about his or her grammar by forcing deliberate and repeated focus upon functions and ideas that are too often passed over in strictly English settings. The distinction between a perfect past tense, for example, and an imperfect past poses a formidable stumbling block for many English-speakers. "I came" can be either perfect or imperfect in English, depending on the setting (e.g., "I came at nine o'clock" versus "I came every Thursday throughout that year"). Even if the student has enjoyed an exceptionally thorough grounding in such distinctions, the English language itself does not draw attention to them, and precise usage is likely to erode into popular parlance as years of casual life outside the classroom mount. An encounter with even one language put together on radically different assumptions will most likely slow the rate of erosion. By way of analogy, one might say that an engineer who has designed only commercial jetliners for twenty years would be a less desirable choice for drawing up the blueprint of a wholly new aircraft (other things being equal) than a person with the same competency who had also flown helicopters and crop-dusters and had once built a small propeller-craft from scratch. Variety of experience feeds breadth of understanding.

Our culture's participants need the ability to understand complexity—to dissect ideas with accuracy and finesse—more, perhaps, than ever in Western history. The democratic republic has become the glistening model of that system which allows a maximum of freedom to individuals while assuring a maximum of efficiency in central government. The model only works, however, if animated by citizens who can think logically. As electronic means of communication undermine familiarity with the written word at an exponential rate, citizens grow more prone to respond unreflectively to manipulative images ("visual prompts," one may fairly call them) rather than pondering issues carefully. To equate the maintenance of literacy rates at certain levels with the very survival of our basic freedoms is not at all extravagant. To assert, of course, that civilization will perish if young students are not re-immersed in the classical languages is far closer to the ridiculous; but a sound introduction to one or two languages besides one's mother tongue is surely a tried-and-true means of building an analytical mind, and in light of the West's historical path of evolution, the classical languages seem a very good point of entry.

The kind of argument just presented for the "mission" of the liberal arts can scarcely be overdramatized, yet it is seldom heard even within the rooms where curricular decisions become final (let alone within public hearing). We may possibly be able to safeguard our individuality and creativity by developing a new fluency in icons and, perhaps, in mental telepathy. Much the most accessible approach to that destination, however, would be to maintain an acute sensitivity to words, such as is accomplished in an education where students speak *and* read *and* write, constantly and concertedly. The "quick fixes" of technology are really not fixing the existential crisis of the human adrift in a rootless environment at all: they are, instead, feeding that crisis. The kind of endeavor undertaken by this book is but one small way to upgrade our intellectual, political, and social prognosis... yet it is a *highly reliable* small way.

***

A few words of explanation—and perhaps apology—are owed to the devoted Hellenist: the Greek forms offered in this text are essentially Homeric. Since the course presented is introductory, a deliberate effort to avoid confusion whenever possible was made. This decision affected the kind of Greek represented in at least three major ways. First, words are unaccented (though breathing marks are supplied; in fact, these are printed *before* initial vowels, like the Arabic hamza, to highlight their importance). For students who are merely trying to grasp the rudiments of Greek, a treatment of the intricate rules for accenting would pose great difficulties but not promise matching rewards. Time is better spent tackling subjects more fundamental to the language's grammar and structure.

For similar reasons, Greek is described as resembling Latin in its lack of definite articles, though we stress as well that such usage is Homeric and quickly alters as Greek prose appears on the scene. A strong case could be made from the other direction that introducing the Latin demonstrative pronoun *ille/illa/illud* as a kind of proto-definite article would have created a platform for viewing the varieties of article in Italian, Spanish, and French. In an expanded version of this course, such a strategy would be very promising. Inasmuch as the book's material is intended for a single college semester, however—or two high school semesters—topics as intricate as demonstrative pronouns (and in Latin these little words, being extremely irregular, always vex students) do not seem a reasonable choice for inclusion.

Then, of course, there is the matter of spelling. Greek is much fonder than Latin of arranging vowels side by side. Having done so, however, it is in nowise resistant to the tendencies of erosion which usually work two vowels into a diphthong or into a single long vowel. Attic Greek, which has evolved much farther along these lines than Homeric Greek, is also far more widely represented in surviving classical texts. Many a Hellenist would therefore surely prefer that the more evolved forms be taught from the start. Yet these forms, as distortions of the original rules, also take more explaining, especially in an approach that seeks bare simplicity and stresses commonalities with Greek's close childhood friend, Latin. This is why we recur to forms which, in a few cases (always noted), do not even have example in recorded Greek.

Consolation for those students who continue in Greek and must learn more modern forms may be found in their deeper understanding of those forms. I recall being shocked as an undergraduate at the trouble my fellow students encountered in tracking backward from Attic Greek to Homer. I had experienced far less anguish in moving from Clyde Pharr's introductory *Homeric Greek* to Xenophon, Herodotus, and Plato. Working near to the language's earliest recognized forms, as well, must surely appeal to those with genuine intellectual curiosity. A truly committed classicist-in-the-making, it seems to me, should enjoy excavating the all-but-prehistoric roots of Greek. To this end, I have occasionally even drawn upon my limited knowledge of Sanskrit to speculate about the origin of certain structures in both Greek and Latin. I believe hat professional classicists of the highest rank might indeed be surprised and fascinated to learn of some of these connections, none of which my own formal education ever revealed to me.

The pronunciation guide usually offered with new Greek vocabulary may also require an apology. I chose not to employ phonetic symbols (including "œ," for which I substituted "ew"), for these would be unfamiliar to most of today's high school and undergraduate students. Instead, I simply (and sometimes crudely, I fear) transliterated sounds into approximate counterparts in American English. The strategy can most certainly create puzzlement, alas. Trying to mimic the *chi* with "hkh" was perhaps too daring. The dialects of some English-speakers, furthermore, may as readily induce an association of "ay" with the long "i" of "aye-aye" as with the long "a" of "day." Likewise, the long "o" (omega) is transliterated as "oe" in some places and "oew" in others, depending on which choice seemsed more likely to combine happily with surrounding consonants. All things considered, the want of rigor in my method can be painfully apparent, even though the beginning student may understand that method better than phonetic notation. Yet it is precisely such a student that the book seeks to serve; and in the classes I have so far taught with the aid of this text's earlier versions, students have indeed cried out for more of my facile transliterations.

Finally, many instructors will surely wonder why answers for most exercises appear at the end of each chapter. I offer two reasons for this. First, I anticipate the text's being used occasionally (and even predominantly) by home-educators who may not be as prepared to teach the subject as certified professionals. Secondly, whether or not the student enjoys the services of a teacher who correctly and meticulously grades papers, a lapse of time is necessarily involved between submitting any paper and receiving it back. Students struggling in new and alien material want and need instant feedback (and I speak from painful personal experience). I realize, of course, that making such feedback fully available would undermine the conventional method of assigning a grade for a homework submission. I added several "Solo Flight" exercises in afterthought to assist in this endeavor. Yet I would also encourage teachers to do what I do: be creative in assigning work for a grade. Require the student, for instance, to catalogue errors made before the answer key was consulted and to draw conclusions about the kind of error that he or she tends to commit. Another strategy—my favorite, in fact—is to have the student change all singulars to plurals and all plurals to singulars. "The boy saw red birds in the tree," must be rewritten, "The boys saw a red bird in the trees." One can add to this such further requirements as that all verbs must be shifted into a designated tense. Nonsense may sometimes result… but students enjoy a little deliberate nonsense when playing with words!

J. R. H.

Tyler, Texas

Dececmber, 2017

Chapter One: Introduction to Nouns

Topics Covered

Case

- Nominative, Genitive, and Accusative: Function
- Formation in Latin and Greek First and Second Declensions

Gender

- Masculine, Feminine, and Neuter in Latin and Greek
- Relation to Declensions
- Adaptation to Modern Romance Languages

Number

- Singular, Plural, and the Vestigial Dual
- Formation in Latin and Greek First and Second Declensions
- Formation of Singular and Plural in Romance Languages

Vocabulary

- Nouns of Latin and Greek First and Second Declensions
- Related Nouns of Modern Momance Languages

Alphabet

- Ancient Greek, All Upper and Lower Cases
- Comparison of Greek and Cyrillic (Russian) Alphabet

I. Case

Word order is absolutely critical in English. The only difference between "dog bites man" and "man bites dog" is a flip-flopping of the nouns; yet one sentence justifies a call to City Pest Control, while another strongly suggests that the local lunatic asylum should be contacted. This dependency upon word order actually makes English a very easy language to learn. The formula, *subject + verb + object*, is straightforward and inflexible, nor does it require that any supportive operations be performed upon individual words. Subject nouns, for instance, are a sentence's first nouns; they do not have the suffix "sub" added to them as a kind of flag. There is no need: the mere appearance of a noun at the sentence's beginning (unless it is preceded by a preposition, such as "in" or "by") designates it as the subject.

English spelling is quite another matter. Because English garners words from so many languages (especially German, Latin, and French), and because the Germanic contributions, in particular, have often seen faster changes in pronunciation than in spelling, those who grew up speaking other languages tend to find English words torturous to spell. (Try explaining to a Spaniard why "through" or "ought" has a *g* in it!) Spelling, of course, may adversely affect the English-learner's pronunciation if he or she is trying to model speech habits upon words printed in a book. How should one say, "Where is the nearest museum?" How does *wh* sound? What about the *ea* in "near" and the *eu* in "museum": are these diphthongs, combining two vowels in a gliding fashion, or does one vowel obliterate the other?

Pronunciation aside, however, a non-Anglophone (i.e., non-English-speaker) would really need little more than a dictionary and an awareness of the subject-verb-object formula to express simple observations. "Car hit tree" is an inelegant sentence, but no English speaker would have much doubt about its basic meaning.

Few other languages, it turns out, permit sentences to be built with such direct simplicity. In many, the subject would have to trail behind it a recognized subject ending, regardless of its order in the sentence. Likewise for the direct object: a special direct-object ending would override any clues implicit in word order. Whenever that ending popped up, the noun to which it was attached, infallibly, would be the verb's direct object. Many languages also have still more endings to designate functions which English identifies through prepositions. Some endings might tell the time, others the place, and others the kind of motion involved in a noun's vicinity. Perhaps the most common noun ending besides those designating subject and direct object is the possessive ending. In English, we in fact have this ending, though we use an apostrophe either before or after it: the *s*. This *s* is the relic of a Germanic possessive ending (where it was—and still is, in modern German—used without any apostrophe). Pronouns like "hers" and "its" come closest to illustrating how an English word might bear one of these ancient endings, for both words already have meaning without the *s*. The letter's addition does not change the pronoun's basic meaning, but it does tell us what the pronoun's function must be in a sentence.

At this point in our national history, most students who have taken any foreign language in high school will probably have studied Spanish or French. It so happens that neither of these two tongues has any system of case endings for its nouns. (We call "case" the function served by the noun in a given sentence, such as subject or direct object.) Italian, Portuguese, and Romanian—the remaining romance languages, or languages descended from the Roman tongue (i.e., Latin)—also have no case endings. This is entirely reasonable from a historical perspective. The Latin cases decayed away to nothing precisely because Romans in the Middle Ages started using prepositions instead of endings to express noun function. In ancient Latin, you might have said, "At Tarentum, the sons of fishermen (or fishermen's sons) eat crabs on holidays," something like this:

Tarenti filii pescatorum diebus festis acipenses edunt.

The same sentence in modern Italian would run close to the following (and note the intrusion of short new words all over the place: these are prepositions and articles).

A Tarento i figli degli pescatori mangiano degli storioni alle feste.

The good news, in short, is that one does not encounter the substantial challenge of mastering various case endings when trying to learn the modern romance languages. The bad news is that such endings are alive and well in a great many other tongues. German has four different cases; so do the surviving Celtic languages (Scots and Irish Gaelic, Welsh, and Breton). The Scandinavian languages have multiple case endings. Russian has six. Arabic has three, and other tongues of the Middle East typically have several. Sanskrit, the literary language of ancient India, had eight! Other than the languages of Western Europe, then, the world offers few safe refuges from this complex grammatical phenomenon.

To be sure, even ancient tongues like Latin and Greek that used distinct case endings also had a tendency to locate nouns in certain parts of the sentence when they were performing certain functions. You may have heard that word order is completely irrelevant in Latin. This is an exaggeration. The Romans *might* have jumbled their words without jumbling their meaning, thanks to case endings (and Roman poets often had to do such jumbling so that they might squeeze their ideas into intricate meters)... but the expectation of subject followed by object still existed. In many non-romance modern languages, likewise—say, Russian—you would usually be understood if you garbled a case ending now and then, thanks somewhat to expected word order. Yet the speaker who committed such errors routinely would probably not be listened to very closely, even if he or she could be understood. When you don't play by a language's rules, you risk not being taken seriously in that language.

Summary
"Case" refers to the noun's function (e.g., as a subject or direct object) in a given sentence. The complex system of suffixes used to identify such functions in many languages, both ancient and modern, does not exist in English or the modern romance languages; but in other tongues, even today, a noun may be given a specific ending that labels it as the sentence's subject, the verb's direct object, a preposition's object, and so forth.

Exercise Set 1.1

A. In the following sentences, identify whether the word "horse" functions as a subject, direct object, or possessive. Note that, even in English, standard word order can be relaxed.

1. We saw a horse in the field.
2. Far into the night, the horse was neighing.
3. The Highland pony is almost a dwarf horse.
4. A horse's hoof is really its fingernails.
5. A better horse I cannot imagine!
6. The life of a wild horse is a free one.
7. Does your horse count up to ten?
8. Seeing the horse, I ran from the barn.
9. A dog's eyesight is worse than a horse's.
10. Ride a horse if you want exercise!

B. What case is English able to express in two ways? Give an example.

II. Specific Cases Named and Defined

Latin cases carry Latin names, not surprisingly. The ambitious student of foreign languages would do well to learn these names even if he or she plans to concentrate on a non-classical language, because mainstream grammar books have embraced the convention of using Latin terms to discuss the case system in other tongues (such as Greek both ancient and modern, by the way).

> **nominative**: the case of the sentence's subject. (Example: "Rabbits are eating the farmer's carrots," where "rabbits" is the subject.) The term "nominative" is drawn from the Latin *nomen*, meaning "name." The nominative names the noun in that it posits a person, object, or quality without adding further subtleties of meaning (showing possession, telling where or when, etc.) as an oblique case does. Latin dictionaries always list nouns in the nominative case.

genitive: the case of possession. (Example: "Rabbits are eating the farmer's carrots," where "farmer's" is possessive.) Latin *gignere* means "to bear, give birth," and the adjective *genitivis* is directly related to this verb. A parent may be said in some ways to own his or her child—and in Roman law, these ways could be shockingly concrete (as in the father's right to end his son's life for filial impiety). The leap from creation to possession must have seemed quite short in such circumstances.

accusative: the case of the direct object, and also used with some prepositions. (Example: "Rabbits are eating the farmer's carrots," where "carrots" is the direct object.) The Latin *accusare* means (as you would expect) "to accuse, blame, reproach"—all words strongly implying a transfer of energy, as if through a pointing finger. The direct object receives the transfer of the verb's action if the verb is active in voice. (Much more on the active and passive voices of verbs may be found in Chapter Four.)

A special note about translating the genitive case into English: you may use either an apostrophe or the preposition "of" with the possessing noun as its object. *Spiritus mundi* may be rendered either "spirit of the world" or "world's spirit." Do not under any circumstances, in Latin or in any other language with a genitive case, seek to form such expressions by finding a preposition for "of" and then using the genitive case with it. *Spiritus de mundi* is untranslatable nonsense. The genitive ending, all by itself, conveys the idea of possession.

Some languages have only these three cases (e.g., Arabic); some (like classical Greek) have one more. Latin itself has two more, which will be presented later. For the time being, we shall focus on these three.

Summary
Five fully operational and identifiable cases survived in Latin, and four in Homeric Greek. (Meager relics of additional cases may enter ancient texts in rare circumstances.) We begin our study of the case system with the nominative, genitive, and accusative. Possessive phrases in English may use the preposition "of," but the Latin possessive case is never preceded by any preposition.

Exercise Set 1.2
Determine whether the words "apple" and "apples" are nominative, genitive, or accusative in the sentences below. You'll quickly realize that you are taking a crash course in English grammar!
1. An apple a day keeps the doctor away.
2. Apples' cores are said to be nutritional.
3. I never saw an apple I didn't like.
4. Why do apples have different colors?
5. Peel the apple before slicing it.
6. I always get the barrel's one rotten apple!
7. Organic apples may have spots on them.
8. Eating apples increases your sugar intake.
9. The price of apples is skyrocketing.
10. The forbidden fruit was not necessarily an apple.

Solo Flight: Write three sentences using the English word "friend" first as a subject, then as a possessive, and finally as a direct object. What would be this word's Latin case in each of the three instances? (No answers are provided in the key concluding this chapter. See if you can compose your sentences without external help.)

III. The Spelling of Latin Cases

It is time to turn to particulars: let us examine some actual Latin words and their cases. Many people are vaguely aware that *-us* is a frequent Latin ending. It figures in a lot of famous Roman names for men, such as Julius, Marcus, Lucius, and Titus. In fact, this is a nominative singular ending (the ending used for a sentence's subject). It appears on such ordinary Latin nouns as *taurus*, "a bull," and *digitus*, "a finger." Both of these nouns have transmitted cognate forms into modern Italian, Spanish, and French: in the former instance, *tauro*, *toro*, and *taure*; and in the latter, *digito*, *dedo*, and *doigt*. None of these modern languages, obviously, preserves the original Latin *-us*. Instead, Italian and Spanish have commemorated the very prominent *o* that appeared in most of the Latin endings. (As a matter of fact, *-os* [where the short *o* rhymes with "cot" or "lot"] was the pristine Latin *–us* nominative ending.) When the modern romance tongues discarded the old Latin cases, many of them (including Portuguese) held onto a final *o* to represent **all singular forms** of the nouns in question.

Likewise, the accusative and genitive endings of *–us* nouns once possessed a short *o*. (We'll deal with the accusative first here because its evolution from the *o* form is more transparent.) The direct object (accusative) form *taurum* would have been *taurom* in very early Latin. We have less evidence for the possessive (genitive) form, but the remarkable form *-oeo* instead of the classical *-i* crops up in the very ancient poet Ennius. Don't let this discussion complicate matters for you: rest assured that any Roman text you are ever likely to read will express "bull" (direct object) with *taurum* and "bull's" with *tauri*. Remember for the moment, however, that this set of endings was historically dominated by the *o*, because this will help us to make a connection with Greek very shortly. It will also prepare you to see a long *o* surviving in other case endings that we have not yet addressed.

Here, then, are three very common singular case endings in Latin:

nominative: for the subject, ends in *–us* as in *taurus* ("The bull sees me.")

genitive: for possession, ends in *–i* as in *tauri* ("bull's eye")

accusative: for the direct object, ends in *–um* as in *taurum* ("I see the bull.")

Now let us attempt a few simple sentences by adding more nouns to the two already named (i.e., *taurus* and *digitus*). The Latin word for "god" is *deus* (*deo*, *díos*, *dieu* in Italian, Spanish, and French); the word for "place" is *locus* (*loco*, *lugar*, *lieu*); and the word for "shoulder" is *umerus* (*ombro*, *hombro*, *omoplate*—but the far more common French word is *épaule*). With the aid of these endings, we might write the sentence, "The god touched the bull's shoulder," in any of these sequences:

Deus umerum tauri tetigit.

Umerum tauri deus tetigit.

Tauri umerum tetigit deus.

And still other orders are possible (with the verb *tetigit* also being able to change its position virtually without restriction). To be sure, when a noun other than the subject comes first, a hint of emphasis is bestowed upon that noun. For example, the final sentence above might justifiably be translated, "It was the bull's shoulder that the god touched." Putting *tauri* first would be odd enough to underscore its role in the expression. The fact remains, however, that case endings provide the real key to figuring out such sentences, and that word order is very much a secondary concern.

It needs to be said early on that the Latin language has no articles, either definite ("the") or indefinite ("a, an"). The sentence above, therefore, might be translated, "A god touched a bull's shoulder," or, "A god touched the bull's shoulder," or, "The god touched the shoulder of a bull"... and so forth. This seems very peculiar to us. Certainly we cannot omit articles in our English translations and produce smooth, proper sentences. How do you know when translating whether to insert an "a" or a "the" (or perhaps nothing at all)? Use your ear: the context will dictate to you what rendition sounds best.

Latin, by the way, is not unique in this regard. You would confront the same oddity if you were to study Russian, which also has no articles. Russian nationals who speak only broken English will often produce sentences like, "Meeting in afternoon is changed to bigger room on second floor."

Summary

In ancient Greek and Latin, the cases of nouns are indicated entirely by the spelling of the final one or two syllables: these endings are called case inflections. The modern romance languages, while having no case inflections themselves, have tended to preserve one or two letters common in the original Latin endings to cover all a noun's singular forms or all of its plural forms. Nouns in Latin and very early Greek also use no definite articles ("the") or indefinite articles ("a, an").

Exercise Set 1.3

A. Translate into English the five sentences below. Answers are given at the end of the chapter. Remember that the choice of whether to use "a," "the," or nothing before a noun is largely at the translator's discretion. The verbs have been translated for you, but you might note that they usually come at the sentence's end.

1. Deus locum tauri videt ("sees").
2. Locum dei taurus videt ("sees").
3. Dei digitus locum monstrat ("shows").
4. Taurum nutrit ("nourishes, feeds") locus dei.
5. Taurus videt ("sees") deum loci.

B. Now for a real challenge: try translating these English sentences into Latin. Again, verbs have been supplied and answers are at the chapter's end.

1. The place's god lifts (*levat*) a finger.
2. The bull of the god is devastating (*vastat*) the place.
3. The finger shows (*monstrat*) the god's place.

Solo Flight: No answers are provided. See if you can translate these sentences without external help. Given the words below, translate the following sentences.

avus—grandfather   *Rufus*—a male name   *Gallus*—a Gaul, resident of Gallia   *videt*—sees

1. The Gaul sees Rufus's grandfather.
2. The grandfather of the Gaul sees Rufus.
3. Rufus sees the grandfather and [et] the Gaul.

IV. Introduction to Greek

Part of this book's unique approach is to present Latin and Greek concurrently. The little bit that you have learned so far about Latin cases already has considerable "carry over" to Greek. We should note at once that this text's method of studying Latin first and then establishing parallels with Greek should not be understood as implying that the Latin language somehow preceded or influenced Greek. The great literature of the Greeks is in fact older—often by several centuries—than the classics of Rome, and most Roman authors deliberately copied their Greek predecessors in admiration. (Our modern notion of plagiarism would have made little sense to the ancient mind, which regarded an author's fitting his or her work clearly within a tradition as a requirement for great art.)

Yet we should not conclude from this that the Latin language grew out of Greek, either. A more correct conception would be to think of the two as first cousins. Their parentage is distinct, but they share a great amount of genetic material. Who were the parents, exactly? We don't know: the only historical record left by the common grandsire of Greek and Latin is the indirect testimony of his grandchildren. The "proto-language" that preceded these two can only be inferred through comparison of the two.

Latin is always given priority in this book, at any rate. Among other reasons for the preference is the Latin alphabet, which is far more familiar to us. Indeed, the first issue to address as we turn to Greek must be the slightly unfamiliar script. Let us begin with the vowels and with several consonants whose form is almost identical to Latin lettering.

Vowels

Roman/English:	Greek:
A, a	A, α alpha
E, e	E, ε (short) epsilon H, η (long) eta
I, i	I, ι iota
O, o	O, o (short) omicron Ω, ω (long) omega
U, u	Y, υ upsilon

You will notice immediately that Greek appears to have more vowels than Latin. This is a misconception caused by Greek's having more *letters* for vowels than Latin. The Romans (as well as English-speakers today) had both a short and long *e* sound, and also a short and long *o* sound. They simply lacked separate letters to designate these sounds.

The greatest contrast in pronunciation between Roman and Greek vowels is probably represented by upsilon, which we believe sounded like the French *œ* (as in *sœur*) rather than like the *u* in "put." Upsilon, iota, and alpha can all be either long or short, which is important for those who may one day read Greek poetry. We do not know why these vowels do not have two letters to represent long and short pronunciations, while such letters exist in other instances.

You will also notice that the characters for eta and omega have particularly alien forms. The English *w* looks like the lower-case omega (there is no *w* in Latin), and in fact the *w* sound is extremely close to being a vowel. (It is treated so in Arabic.) The upper-case omega is a jaunty horseshoe easily remembered. That leaves eta. The problem here is that its upper- and lower-case forms resemble two different English consonants—an *h* and an *n*—whose sounds are not remotely related to that of our Greek vowel. The culprit is pure historical accident. Watch out for the deceptive similarity.

Consonants

Roman/English:	Greek:
TH, th (no one-letter equivalent)	Θ, θ theta
M, m	M, μ mu
N, n	N, ν nu

20

P, p	Π, π pi
R, r	P, ρ rho
S, s	Σ, σ / ς sigma
T, t	T, τ tau

Most of these consonants at least bear a passing resemblance to their Roman/English cognates. The tau does not depart in any significant way from our "t." The letters mu and nu appear a little strange to us in lower case, the former looking more like an English "u" with curls extended on either side, the latter very hard for us to distinguish from our "v" (a letter which does not exist in Greek). Pi, though not at all like our "p," is familiar to many English-speakers who have run across it in their geometry books. (It begins the Greek word "perimeter," or the circle's "measure around.") The upper-case theta and sigma may also be familiar to many college students, for they figure prominently in the names of fraternities and sororities; but the lower-case form of sigma poses a unique difficulty (unlike the small theta, which its just a slimmer version of the upper case). The form that looks like our "s" with a bit of its tail cut off appears only at the end of a word: a sigma within a word, with letters on either side, looks more like an "o" with a curl to the upper right. No other Greek letter has two lower-case forms that respond to position within a given word.

That leaves rho, an especially confusing letter because it looks like the Roman/English "p" in both upper and lower case. (In some scripts, the lower-case rho's tail curls to the right rather than coming straight down.) This letter, like several others in Greek, preserves the same appearance in the Russian Cyrillic alphabet. Later on, you will see the two alphabets compared and realize that studying Greek, among other things, offers a shortcut to the study of Russian. For the serious linguist, then, taking the time to learn the oddities of the Greek alphabet as well as its more familiar characters is well worth the effort.

In closing, we should note that the so-called Erasmian System of pronouncing ancient Greek is followed in this text. Its practice differs from modern Greek pronunciation in several respects. Contemporary Greeks would find your speech very difficult to understand if you employed these Renaissance reconstructions of ancient usage (promoted by the great humanist Erasmus) in speaking today's language. That being said, all the evidence suggests that Erasmus was correct in his conclusions. His distance from antiquity, after all, was much less than ours!

Summary
Several vowels in ancient Greek use two distinct characters to designate their long and short versions. Hence there are more letters for vowels in Greek than in Latin (and its alphabetic descendent, English). Many Greek characters will be familiar to students associated with fraternities and sororities, and even more so to students who have some knowledge of the Russian Cyrillic alphabet.

Exercise Set 1.4

1. Try to record five phrases found in our culture today that employ Greek letters. These phrases might be the names of fraternities and sororities, scientific terms, and so forth.

2. Record all the Greek letters you know so far that are "false look-alikes" with English letters; that is, they appear to be almost identical to letters we use but are in fact not pronounced at all similarly.

Solo Flight: See how many English words you can "transliterate" with the few Greek characters available to you at this point. For instance, "spin" would be rendered σπιν. (Obviously, these will not be actual Greek words—just English ones written in Greek letters.)

V. Greek Cases

Let us return now to our analysis of the case system. Much of what we said earlier about Latin nouns can be applied directly to Greek ones. The three cases we have studied so far—nominative, genitive, and accusative—all exist in Greek, as well. Indeed, the actual spelling of these case endings in the two languages is often extremely close once we make allowance for the differing alphabets. (You may know that the very word "alphabet," by the way, is drawn from the first two Greek characters: alpha and beta.)

It so happens that the Latin word for "bull," *taurus*, is almost identical to the Greek word: ταυρος. In fact, the main difference between this noun in Greek and Latin as we follow it through various case endings is that the short "o" (omicron) tends to appear in Greek where Latin has a "u."

	Latin	Greek
nominative	taurus	ταυρος
genitive	tauri	ταυρου
accusative	taurum	ταυρον

You may recall an observation made earlier about the prominence of the "o" in original Latin case endings. If we were to juxtapose those very early Latin endings with their corresponding Greek ones, the similarity between the two would be almost perfect. The Greek accusative ending in "n" instead of "m" is not at all surprising. Related languages frequently differ in opting for one of these "nasal occlusive" consonants or the other in what is basically the same word. "M" and "n" are pronounced in the same part of the mouth, of course, and with the closing of the soft palate: the lips are touched to say the former, but otherwise no change occurs. We shall later observe other points where Greek favors "n" over the Latin "m."

The genitive endings, too, show a kinship—not only because both end in vowels, but also because the original Latin and Greek genitives were probably –eo and -oio, respectively (the latter occurring often in Homer's epics). Though these are archaic forms which need not be memorized, they serve to remind us that the two languages are close cousins.

We should be able to move directly to a few simple Greek sentences for practice once we have created a small stock of vocabulary words, for the cases are used almost identically to the Latin cases. Subjects have nominative endings, the genitive case shows possession, and direct objects have accusative endings. We will find later that the Greek genitive is also used with certain prepositions, whereas this is never true of the Latin genitive. For present purposes, however, we need observe no distinctions. In fact, even the conventions of word order, to the extent that they exist, are very similar in the two languages. Subjects tend to come first, then direct objects, then indirect objects and various prepositional phrases, and finally the main verb. As with Latin, though, these are only tendencies in Greek. Word order is very flexible in comparison to English.

You have just learned the word ταυρος. Using the Greek letters introduced above, we may add the following words to our list:

22

Greek	pronunciation	definition	English derivative
'ανεμος	AH-ne-moss	wind	anemometer
'εταιρος	he-TYE-ross	friend (male)	Hetaerist
θεος	theh-OSS	god	theism
'ιππος	HIP-poss	horse	hippodrome
κουρος	KOO-ross	boy, young man	-----
μαρτυρος	MAR-tur-oss	witness	martyr
νησος	NAY-soss	island	Peloponnese
πετρος	PET-ross	stone	petrify
ποντος	PON-toss	sea	pontoon
ποταμος	pot-ah-MOSS	river	hippopotamos
τοπος	TOH-poss	place	topic

Of course, the word 'ιππος also contributes to the word "hippopotamos." This compound word illustrates the universal human tendency to name something alien by associating it with something familiar. (The Irish Gaelic word for otter, by comparison, is *dobharchú*, "waterdog".) Another point raised by this word is that Greek has no letter for "h." In many languages, aspiration is not considered to be a distinct consonant, and is indicated whenever it occurs by a superscript something like our English apostrophe. (Once again, in medieval Irish the "h" was also non-existent as a discrete letter: aspiration was added in manuscripts by placing a dot above the letter most affected by the breathing.) Greek actually employs what we might call a reversed apostrophe to show aspiration at a word's beginning. When words begin with vowels but are not aspirated, the apostrophe is "correct," as it were (note 'ανεμος). Every word whose first letter is a vowel has either one or the other of these marks to indicate whether or not an "h" sound precedes the vowel.

The breathing marks just described are usually written more centrally over their vowels than the format of this book allows us to do. Greek words are also generally written with tonal accents over the vowels affected, like certain French words: an acute accent (*cliché*), a grave accent (*père*), or a circumflex (*bête*). Yet unlike accents in French, Greek accents often shift to different parts of the word in response to the cadence created by adjoining syllables. The rules affecting such shifts are not easily learned. We will not employ any accents in this book so as not to complicate learning the essentials here presented. The student should be aware, however, that he or she will surely run into such marks in a more advanced Greek course.

One more thing to be aware of: we shall not be using articles in this book when writing Greek sentences, for the sake of simplicity. Unlike Latin, ancient Greek does develop a definite article ("the") with time. Yet the Homeric epics and other early texts do not employ this article, which did not exist much before the fifth century (BC). If you take a more advanced Greek course some day and read prose authors, especially, you will encounter definite articles frequently.

Remember to use common sense when translating. If you saw this sentence, for example, it might theoretically have two translations since word order counts for little in Greek:

Ἵππος θεου τοπον ὁραει.

The god's horse sees the place OR *The horse sees the god's place.*

In general, genitives follow the word that they "own" rather than preceding it, in both Greek and Latin; hence "god's horse" is likely the better translation of the two above. Yet only context can determine with authority which of these two options makes better sense. Indeed, context may dictate that you write "a god's" instead of "the god's"; and although you have not yet studied verbs, you should also feel free to write "is seeing" instead of "sees" if your ear tells you that the former sounds better in English than the latter. Latin and Greek both have only one form for present-tense verbs.

Summary
Greek cases are used identically to Latin cases, with few and minor exceptions, and spelling confirms that they are first cousins. As in Latin, too, articles do not appear in early ancient Greek. An oddity of Greek spelling is the absence of a letter to represent "h" even though the sound exists. Words beginning in vowels have one of two small initial marks to indicate whether or not the "h" sound precedes the vowel.

Exercise Set 1.5

A. Translate into English the five sentences below. Answers are given at the end of the chapter. Let the case endings guide your translation exactly as you did with the Latin sentences earlier. Here as there, furthermore, the choice of whether to use "a," "the," or nothing before a noun is at the translator's discretion. Finally, remember that genitives usually *follow* the nouns they possess: moving them forward places emphasis on them.

1. Θεος ποταμου νησον ποιει ("makes").
2. Θεου πετρος ἱππον τυπτει ("strikes").
3. Ποντος τοπον νησου καλυπτει ("covers").
4. Ἀνεμον παυει ("stops, checks") θεος ποντου.
5. Ἀνεμος ποντον και ("and") ποταμον τυπτει ("strikes").

B. And now, try translating these two English sentences into Greek. Again, verbs have been supplied and answers are at the chapter's end.

1. The god of the wind makes/is making (ποιει) an island.
2. The witness sees (ὁραει) the bull of stone.

C. Memorize the ten words presented above: their Greek spelling, their pronunciation, their meaning, and an English derivative. In many cases, you can add several more derivatives to the one explicitly offered if you do a little research. This sort of exercise should be repeated throughout the book as you learn new vocabulary, especially if one of your goals is to strengthen your command of English.

Solo Flight: Make two Greek sentences of your own out of the few words you have been given so far, using all three cases (nominative, genitive, and accusative) in both. Borrow a couple of the verbs that appear above in parentheses. Your creations may sound nutty since you have few vocabulary options at this point—but don't let that concern you. Embrace the attitude that Henry Higgins takes (rather archly) of the French in *My Fair Lady*: "The French don't care what they do, actually, as long as they pronounce it properly." We're going for correct endings!

VI. Gender of Nouns

The notion that a certain few nouns should be male or female seems perfectly reasonable to English-speakers, although their own language never marks gender in nouns through any kind of grammatical convention.

(This is not entirely true: even in our era of political correctness, we still encounter words such as "count" and "countess" or "heir" and "heiress": nouns of the feminine -ess variety filtered into our language long ago through French.) Of course, we have several male and female names for animals of the same species, such as "stallion" and "mare." For some reason, we also frequently refer to a ship as "she," and pioneers and ballplayers were known to dub their favorite rifles or bats "Daisy" or "Betsy" in times gone by.

Yet the award of gender to nouns in most languages where a true gender system exists (and English is among a small minority of tongues that has no such system) does not involve the sort of calculation just described. Gender is often assigned inflexibly in Latin and Greek (and in their descendants) to nouns that appear to be neither male nor female. All of the words presented in both languages so far have been masculine. This makes sense for "god" and "bull"… but what about "finger" or "wind"? Though a neutral gender (simply called the neuter) exists in the classical tongues, a great many inanimate objects turn out to be masculine or feminine. Furthermore, even animals are sometimes locked into a single gender. The Latin word for fish, *piscis*, is masculine, as is the Greek words ʼιχθυς; the Latin word for a bird, *avis*, is just as arbitrarily feminine (though the Greek word, ʼορνις, is sometimes masculine and sometimes feminine, depending upon the author—*not* upon the particular bird). We can only imagine how determinations of gender were made historically. There seldom seems to be any broad generality guiding these decisions. Memorizing the gender of Latin and Greek nouns is hence an especially tedious chore for the poor English-speaker.

Yet it is a chore that must be taken seriously, because certain case endings are very often associated with nouns of a particular gender. As was just remarked, all the Latin and Greek nouns so far presented have been masculine. In Latin, the –us/-i/-um nominative/genitive/accusative set of endings is almost always confined to masculine words. The parallel set of endings in Greek (-ος/-ου/-ον) likewise belongs almost always to masculine nouns. If you try to think of a name for a typical Roman man, you will likely come up with "Marcus" or "Julius" or "Lucius." Notice that all of these end in –us. Ancient Greek names will probably require more effort for you to dredge up, and many of the male names will end in *on* (Agamemnon) or –es (Sophocles). Again, however, there is a class of male names—and a rather large class ending in –os, although these may be more familiar to you as –us names through Latin transliteration: Demetrios, Apollodoros, Heracleitos, etc.

A set of noun endings is called a **declension**. You have been studying several cases of the **second declension**, and we may reiterate that its nouns have an overwhelming tendency to be masculine.   We will soon see that the first declension, in both Latin and Greek, has an equally strong tendency to comprise feminine nouns. (The second declension was presented first, by the way, because it displays a slightly clearer resonance between Latin and Greek forms: no gender bias is concealed here!) To return to the second declension, the only set of nouns with –us endings which is feminine rather than masculine is—of all things—names of trees:

cupressus—cypress	*pinus*—pine
ficus—fig	*poplus*—poplar
laurus—laurel	*quercus*—oak
malus—apple	*ulmus*—elm

Unless you have intentions of studying botany (where these words are all used to designate the corresponding species of tree), you need not memorize the nouns above. They are offered only as the single curious exception to the second declension's rule of always containing masculine nouns when the nominative is -us. In Greek, for some reason, this curiosity is not routinely repeated. Though names of trees often have the nominative in -ος, these may be masculine or feminine (e.g., κυπαρισσος—almost exactly the same word as the Latin *cupressus*—is also feminine, but ʼολυνθος [a fig] is masculine). Otherwise, only a tiny fragment of second-declension Greek nouns possesses a feminine gender; and these, like the words βιβλος ("book"), νησος ("island"), and ʻοδος ("way, road"), do so for no imaginable reason. Incredibly, the word for "maiden"—παρθενος—also appears on the list!

Yet the second declension, in both Latin and Greek, is far from being owned by the masculine gender, even though almost its only feminine nouns (in Latin) are names of trees. The neuter gender is also prominently represented here. Neuter nouns have different endings from masculine ones in just a few cases: to be precise, in the nominative singular and in the nominative and accusative plural. (We will shortly take up the distinction between singular and plural: the spelling of any case ending always changes when it is made plural.) In a sense, this is convenient for the student: it means that neuter nouns do not have an utterly new set of endings to be learned. On the other hand, the nearly identical endings for the two groups make distinguishing their genders at a glance very difficult—and you will see later why the distinction can be important. Fortunately, the nominative singular endings for masculine and neuter words in this declension *do* differ. The nominative singular form is always that which is offered "up front" in any sort of word list or dictionary. Hence, when looking up one of these words, you can indeed tell at a glance if it is masculine or neuter.

We already know that the nominative masculine ending is *–us* in Latin and *–ος* in Greek. A neuter word will end in *–um* in Latin and in *–ov* in Greek. Said another way, the nominative singular ending for the neuter noun is the same as the accusative singular ending. As a matter of fact, this "twinning" is not unique to the second declension. We can state the following rule—again of both Latin and Greek nouns—without having to allow for a single exception:

Neuter nouns are always spelled the same way in the nominative and accusative cases, though the spelling of these two cases of course changes from singular to plural.

The same rule even applies to neuter nouns in Russian and Sanskrit—which may be rather more information than you desire at the moment; but the resonance again underscores how useful Latin is as a springboard for studying other languages.

In the second declension, therefore, the case endings of a neuter noun look like this:

	Latin	**Greek**
nominative	-um	-ov
genitive	-i	-ου
accusative	-um	-ov

With a little imagination, you may foresee how the identical formation of neuter nouns in the nominative and accusative could lead to confusion. Let us make a sentence with the neuter word for "stone" in Latin: *saxum*. *Lucius saxum videt* plainly means, "Lucius sees the stone." This is the only possible translation for two reasons. First, *Lucius* can only be nominative, and this sentence can only have one subject; second, common sense tells us that stones cannot see. Even though *saxum* is both the nominative and the accusative form, therefore, it must surely be the latter here.

Now suppose that we have a verb whose subject could be either an animate or an inanimate object: *Lucius saxum pulsat*. The sentence can still only mean, "Lucius strikes the stone," since the name *Lucius* continues to have an unequivocally nominative spelling—but we no longer have common sense as an additional argument, because a stone could potentially strike Lucius. That sentence would have to be written, *Saxum Lucium pulsat*, with *Lucium* now displaying the accusative ending. Though the form *saxum* could be either nominative or accusative, it would have to be the former because the masculine proper noun *Lucium* (thanks to the *–um*) would be disqualified as a subject. Please remember that word order, by the way, is a very treacherous clue to trust in when translating Latin. The last sentence above, where the stone strikes poor Lucius, might also be written *Lucium saxum pulsat*—or even

Lucium pulsat saxum.

Time to muddy the water just a bit further! Let us now create a sentence that has only neuter nouns. *Collum* is a second-declension noun meaning "neck": of course, our word "collar" derives from it. In the sentence, *Saxum collum pulsat*, both nouns could be either nominative or accusative. Word order and common sense would both incline us to translate, "The stone strikes the neck." Yet both of these reasons are rather weak, word order because it is very flexible in Latin and common sense because, after all, a neck might also strike a stone (as when someone trips and falls). Unless such a sentence as this has a broader context to give us more clues, we would have to keep an open mind about its translation, understanding that it might logically be taken in either of two opposing directions.

The potential confusion created by the neuter noun's nominative/accusative identity in Latin is every bit as much a hazard in Greek. Interestingly, we already know that "stone" in Greek is the masculine word πετρος. (Even more interesting, the common words for "stone" in French and Spanish—both thoroughly Latin-based tongues—are *pierre* and *piedra*: *saxum* only survives in the Italian *sasso*, for some reason.) If we choose the word ποτον, "drink," to help us generate an example, we shall still be using letters already introduced; so let this word represent a typical neuter noun, and let us create a situation with potential ambiguity. The sentence, "Kleitos wants a drink," might be rendered thus: Κλειτος ποτον βουλεται.* Realistically, we can be sure of the subject both because the masculine name's –ος ending can only be nominative and because the drink's wanting Kleitos would be nonsense!

Now let us substitute another neuter noun for Κλειτος. There are fewer of these second-declension neuters in Greek than in Latin, but the word for "work," 'εργον, is quite common. Our options for building sentences from so few words are severely limited, so some poetic license may be allowed. The sentence, "Work nourishes drink," might be offered in the metaphorical vein of Socrates' famous utterance (which quickly passed into proverb), "Hunger is a good seasoning." We could render this as 'εργον ποτον τρεφει. Now, how can we know that this does not mean, "A drink nourishes work"? That makes quite as much poetic sense, and we know that word order is an unreliable guide. The truth is that the sentence could be translated in either manner: either noun, that is, could be the subject, and the remaining one would become the object of "nourishes." So the moral of this story, once again, is that translation is as much art as science. Use context and common sense as well as standard grammatical clues.

* The beta and a few other new consonants which have slipped in will be formally introduced soon. It is worth noting that this verb equates with the Latin *volo*, the root of our "volition" and "voluntary." Greek has no "v," but "b" is very close to "v" phonetically and can sometimes help you to discover hidden links between the two languages. In Gaelic, which also has no "v," the "b" crops up in similar circumstances: e.g., the Latin *villa* lies at the root of the Gaelic *baile*, "town"; and in Spanish, the initial "v" in *vaquero* is virtually indistinguishable from a "b" sound.

Vocabulary

At this point, let us add a few words to our Latin and Greek vocabulary which belong to the neuter branch of the second declension, and also a few more masculine words in Latin.

Latin	definition	English derivative
auxilium	help, aid	auxiliary
bellum	war	belligerent
bracchium	arm	brachial
caelum	sky	celestial, ceiling

cerebrum	brain	cerebral
donum	gift	donation
dorsum	back	dorsal
folium	leaf	foliage, folio
periculum	danger	perilous
pretium	price	precious
regnum	kingdom	regnant
verbum	word	verbiage, verb

more masculine _–us_ words		
Latin	**definition**	**English derivative**
animus	inner life, spirit	animate
annus	year	annual
campus	field (unplowed)	campaign
filius	son	filial
modus	means, way	mode
mundus	world, universe	mundane
oculus	eye	ocular

If *animus* reminds you of the Greek 'ανεμος, your suspicions are well founded. The Latin word is used rather vaguely of an inner vitality that can cover everything from the soul to strong (generally noble) emotions; and the connection of such invigorating but invisible force with the wind has a lengthy history. In the Greek New Testament, the actual Greek word for "wind," πνευμα, doubles as the word for "soul," as in the grand verse, "The spirit [wind?] bloweth where it listeth."

Before adding a few Greek words to the list, we must first introduce six more consonants:

Greek Consonants

Roman/English:	**Greek:**
B, b	B, β beta
G, g	Γ, γ gamma
D, d	Δ, δ delta

K, k	Κ, κ kappa
L, l	Λ, λ lambda
PH, ph (no one-letter equivalent)	Φ, φ phi

Beta and kappa are very nearly identical to English in both their formation and their pronunciation. Gamma and lambda are pronounced as in English but have a slightly odd appearance, especially in the upper case. As for the upper-case delta, it is indeed a triangle. The Greeks were somehow aware, despite an absence of aircraft, that the silt deposits at the mouths of rivers formed triangular-shaped bodies of land, and they named these deltas after the letter (especially the one at the mouth of the Nile—the original Delta). Phi, though having no analogous letter in Roman/English script, is again very familiar to college students from "Greek" organizations. Actually, all words in Latin and virtually all in English that employ a –*ph* are directly transliterating a phi from Greek; so when you spot a word featuring these two consonants side by side ("graph," "trophy," "emphasis," etc.), you are very likely looking at a word borrowed from Greek.

Greek	**pronunciation**	**definition**	**English derivative**
δωρον	*DOE-ron*	gift	Dorothy (gift of God)
μεγαρον	*MEH-guh-ron*	main room	----
μετρον	*MEH-tron*	measure (of space or conduct)	meter
τεκνον	TEK-non	child	---- (*not* "technology")
φαρμακον	FAR-muh-kon	drug, medicine	pharmacy

It will no doubt strike any student as odd that the word for "child"—τεκνον—is neuter in Greek; but as a matter of fact, the Germans share this conception: *das Kind* is also a neuter noun. Though this word has no familiar English derivative, it is commonly used in ancient Greek texts, and should be learned for that reason. A μεγαρον is literally a big (*mega*) room. A large residence or palace in the ancient Greek world would often possess such a central room off of which smaller rooms would branch. The translation, "throne room," might work better in many circumstances, such as where the word appears in Homer's *Odyssey*. Again, no English derivative exists. Anyone interested in archeology or the history of architecture should probably know this word, however; and, to repeat a surprising fact, there simply are not many second-declension Greek neuter words, though a great many neuters appear in other declensions. These few words will give us enough to use in practice.

Summary
Every noun in Greek and Latin is inflexibly assigned to one of three genders: masculine, feminine, or neuter. While such assignments generally make sense, they can also be quite illogical (as when inanimate objects are masculine or feminine). Certain sets of case endings (called declensions) are often strongly associated with certain genders. For instance, the first declension overwhelmingly features feminine nouns, while the second is almost entirely masculine and neuter.

A. Translate the following Latin sentences into English (answers at end of chapter).
1. Mundus periculum belli timet ("fears").
2. Folium dorsum fili* tangit ("is touching").
3. Deus caeli mundum fecit ("made").
4. Modus belli campum vastat ("is devastating").
5. Auxilium cerebri vincit ("surpasses") auxilium bracchi.

Words ending in –ius or –ium simply drop the –us or –um to make a genitive: they do not double the –i in the best authors.

B. Translate these English sentences into Latin.
1. The spirit's eye sees (*videt*) heaven (= the sky).
2. A year of danger terrifies (*terret*) the son's spirit.

Exercise Set 1.6: Greek

C. Translate the following Greek sentences into English.
1. Μεγαρον δωρον τεκνου 'εχει ("holds").
2. Φαρμακον πετρον ποταμου 'ιαινει ("is melting").
3. Θεος μετρον ποντου καλυπτει ("conceals").
4. Τεκνον θεου 'ιππον βουλεται ("desires, wants").
5. 'Ανεμος και ("and") ποντος θεον φυουσι ("are producing").

D. Translate these English sentences into Greek.
1. The god's medicine is checking (παυει) the river.
2. A great room is not ('ουκ 'εστι) a horse's place.

Solo Flight: Again, no answers are provided later. You're on your own!
Given the words below, rewrite the following Latin sentences correctly. (Leave the verbs alone: all the mistakes are in the nouns.) Remember to check the gender of each noun and then be sure that ending and gender match!

    avus—grandfather   *Rufus*—a male name   *Gallus*—a Gaul   *Germanus*—a German

    regulus—prince, minor king   *miraculum*—marvel, miracle (neuter)   *praemium*—reward (neuter)

1. The miracle terrifies the Gaul's grandfather. ~ Miraculus avus Galli terret.
2. Rufus accepts the Gaul's reward. ~ Rufum praemii Galli accipit.
3. The prince's reward attracts the German. ~ Praemius regulum Germanus trahit.

VII. The First Declension

30.09.2019   _/

    That something labeled "first" should be postponed until after the introduction of something labeled "second" may stir suspicion—but, in this instance, there is no dark plot. Our objective, rather, was clarity. The Latin second declension scarcely differs from the Greek (the contrast involving mostly a shift from Greek omicron to the Latin *u*), and the two share letters that are easily identifiable to the English-speaker. Furthermore, the second declension comprises both masculine and neuter genders and is thus convenient for initiating the discussion of gender. Both the Latin and Greek first declensions, in contrast, overwhelmingly feature feminine nouns. Identification of letters is a little more challenging in Greek, as well, because eta (η) becomes the dominant vowel; and eta, since it looks so much like our "H" in upper case and our "n" in lower case, often poses problems to students. So much for the mystery of taking the second first!

    In Latin, a very assertive "a" forms the root to which case endings are added (we will see later that two plural forms absorb the "a"—but historically it occurred throughout the declension). A further aid to memorization is that this declension, like the second, has an accusative ending in –*m* and a genitive ending in a vowel.

Latin First Declension

nominative	a	*femina*
genitive	ae	*feminae*
accusative	am	*feminam*

In fact, a pre-classical genitive ended in –*ai* (*feminai*), creating yet another resemblance to the second declension; but you are unlikely to run across this ending in most ancient texts.

Once you accept that the Greek eta is *not* an "n" and that *η* is often the equivalent of a long alpha in Greek and a long "a" in Latin, you can readily apply the table above to the Greek first declension. Several of the more remote dialects in ancient Greece (e.g., Boeotian and Ionian) actually used the alpha instead of the eta for the endings below; some of these alpha-words entered ordinary usage, furthermore, and will strike you as looking very like Latin first-declension words. Yet you should stick with the eta as the basis of this declension in Greek, since it represents the mainstream.

Greek First Declension

nominative	η	κουρη
genitive	ης	κουρης
accusative	ην	κουρην

Again, the Greek second declension resonates with the first in that both have an accusative ending in –*v*. The genitive ending in –ς also enjoys a historical connection with a Latin pre-classical genitive ending (yes, yet another one: Latin's first-declension genitive appears to have had a colorful history). You may even have seen the phrase, *pater familias*, in some context: "father of the family" (where *familias*, of course, exemplifies the very old genitive with the sigma). To this day, Spanish-speakers keep the phrase alive in their *padre de familia*, a term of great honor as it was in ancient Rome. Yet the Latin –*as* genitive is no more common in mainstream classical Latin than the archaic –*ai*. You will probably just have to remember the Greek –*ης* as *sui generis* ("of its own kind," unique).

Be absolutely clear about one point, if you have retained any doubts up to now. *A word must use the endings of its proper declension: its classification among a certain set of endings is arbitrary and final.* Take the word for "life": *vita* in Latin, βιος in Greek. They are closely related (recall that Greek "beta" words are frequently first cousins to "v" words in Latin). Nevertheless, the Latin word is first-declension feminine, and the Greek word is second-declension masculine. Whether a man's life or a woman's life is under discussion makes no difference. These and other nouns must always retain the case endings peculiar to their declension and may never change gender. To write "the bull's life" as *vitus tauri* on the reasoning that a bull is male and that his life should therefore be a second-declension masculine noun would produce a nonsensical phrase—a Roman would not know what to make of it.

Just as the Latin second declension has a small group of feminine nouns—the trees—so the first declension has a tiny group of masculine nouns. (It contains no neuters whatever, by the way.) Though we do not know how the trees came to have both the *-us/-i/-um* endings and a feminine gender, we can be pretty sure that the first declension's masculine nouns simply took a wrong turn. Their nominative is a very peculiar *-ης* in Greek where a clear cognate exists: words like ποιητης, "a poet," and ναυτης, "a sailor." As these same words settled into Latin, their final sigma or "s" sound wore away, leaving the eta/alpha vowel that looks exactly like a standard first-declension nominative. As a result, *poeta* and *nauta* belong fully to Latin's first declension yet are masculine in gender, as are *agricola* ("a farmer") and *auriga* ("a charioteer"). Obviously, relegation to the first declension was in nowise meant to imply that the men described by these nouns were effeminate. The tradesmen and professionals at issue were often engaged in quite virile labors. The fusion of this group of nouns with the first declension, which otherwise accommodates only the feminine gender, was a pure accident of history.

In Greek, too, the first declension essentially belongs to the feminine gender—more so than in Latin, perhaps. Besides the tiny ποιητης set, the unusual group of proper nouns known as patronyms is treated as first declension by grammarians, even though such nouns are rather strangely improvised around the name of a given person's father. As with many tribal societies, ancient Greeks did not have surnames in our sense. The more aristocratic, especially, would carry a patronymic trailer to their name in order to keep their father's glory alive. Thus the *Iliad*'s Agamemnon is often called Atreides ("son of Atreus"), and Achilles Peleides ("son of Peleus"). We are very familiar with this kind of arrangement from Irish and Scots names that begin in "mc" or "mac" (MacCallum, for instance, meaning "son of William": forms like "Malcolm" and "Maholm" are somewhat garbled versions of the same name). The ancient Greek *-ides* suffix in these instances encounters the same problem as ποιητης: the genitive of both would end identically to the nominative (that is, in *-ης*) if not somehow altered. The patronyms therefore go with the archaic *-αο* in the genitive (e.g., Πηλειδαο) and sometimes keep the alpha in the accusative (Πηλειδαν and Πηλειδην are both found). The ποιητης group has a different strategy: its members simply pretend to be regular second-declension nouns throughout the rest of the singular (e.g., ποιητου, ποιητον).

This is certainly more than you need to know about masculine first-declension nouns at present. Be aware that such nouns do exist for both Latin and Greek, though only in very small numbers.

Latin Vocabulary

Since the rare masculine words of the first declension came up in the discussion above, the three most commonly used are listed below after the feminine nouns (whose membership in this declension is historically much more legitimate).

Latin	definition	English derivative
dea	goddess	deity
femina	woman	feminine
filia	daughter	filial
hora	hour	hour
ira	anger, wrath	ire
littera	letter (of alphabet)	literal, literature
puella	girl	-----

pugna	fight	pugnacious
regina	queen	regal
via	road, way, method	way, "via"
victoria	victory	victory
vita	life	vital
masculine nouns		
agricola	farmer	agriculture
nauta	sailor	nautical
poeta	poet	poet

For the most part, a single noun of a single gender exists even for life forms that have male and female sexes. In a few cases, though, alternate masculine and feminine forms are found. The two examples to which you have now been introduced are *deus/dea* and *filius/filia*. Don't expect this to happen very often!

Littera and *via* also have an unusual side to them. The former, when made plural (discussed soon hereafter), may mean either several letters of the alphabet or a written note (i.e., a collection of letters to make a message). As for *via*, it is used somewhat less abstractly than our word "way" and somewhat less often in a metaphorical sense than "way" in English. The second-declension noun *modus* remains a better choice for "way" in the sense of "means." In our expression "*via* satellite," the word does have a metaphorical turn. It appears in the ablative case (coming up in a later chapter) and literally means "by way of." Radio waves, one would have to say, are not actually moving along a road.

Greek Vocabulary

This time, we shall introduce two additional Greek consonants—the zeta and the chi—that will look very familiar; and also one whose form, if not its sound, appears rather bizarre: the xi.

Roman/English:	Greek:	
Z, z	Z, ζ	zeta
X, x	Ξ, ξ	xi
CH, ch (but no true equivalent)	X, χ	chi

All of these letters are more challenging to pronounce than they first appear. Zeta looks like our "z" in the upper case and somewhat in the lower case (no letter swirls more than little zeta except lower-case xi, about which more in a moment: writing these two by hand requires practice). Zeta seems to have been pronounced, however, as if a "d" were in front of a "z" (as in *Mazda*): it was not merely a voiced "s." As for chi, its pronunciation simply cannot be replicated by any sound in English (except, perhaps, a hearty "hah!" inaugurated with plenty of breathing). The "ch" combination in German is similar, and in Gaelic it is identical. If you have ever heard a Scotsman say the word *loch* (Gaelic for "lake," as in Loch Ness), then you should know what to aim for. We use a peculiar "hkh" notation in this book when trying to approximate the pronunciation of chi.

As for xi, you will probably struggle at first to remember that it is not chi. The latter looks just like our "x" in English but is pronounced quite differently; xi bears little resemblance to "x" when written in Greek yet is pronounced very closely to that letter in English. Just remember that the "x" sound, even in English, is actually a "ks." We tend to ignore this in words like "xylophone": we lazily transform the initial consonant into a "z." You should strive not to do this in Greek. The word for "wood," ξυλον (from which "xylophone" is derived), would best be transliterated as "ksulon."

And, yes, the actual writing of xi in both upper and lower case will require practice—but especially the lower-case letter. If you begin by thinking of that character as a reversed numeral 3, then all you really need to do is add a very short tail at the top and a long one at the bottom.

Greek	pronunciation	definition	English derivative
'αρχη	ar-HKHAY	beginning	archaic
'αταραξια	ah-tah-rak-SEE-ah	serenity, spiritual peace	ataraxy
γαια	GUY-ah	earth	geology
γνωμη	GNOE-may	knowledge	gnostic
'εταιρη	heh-TYE-ray	friend (female)	-----
ζωη	dzoe-AY	life (general)	zoology
θεα	theh-AH	goddess	theocracy
κουρη	KOO-ray	girl, young woman)	caryatid
ληθη	LAY-thay	forgetfulness	lethal
μνημη	MNAY-may	memory	mnemonic

The word "ataraxy" has vanished from modern usage, but it conveys a lofty idea. The state of "non-turbulence" (an initial Greek alpha is the equivalent of "non" or "dis": the rest of the Greek word means "stirred up") is absolutely central in much Greek philosophy. It corresponds to the Buddhist release from all passion and care for the material world.

Notice that the nominative forms of γαια and θεα belong to the not-insignificant group of first-declension nouns ending in an alpha rather than an eta. When this happens, the alpha usually switches back to an eta in other cases (*except* for nouns like θεα whose stem is an epsilon: θεας and θεαν are its genitive and accusative). The meaning of γαια, "earth," refers to the entire planet or to a great swathe of terrain rather than to dirt or soil.

Similarly, ζωη is a broad word for "life" (as in "existence" or "the spectrum of being") rather than the life of an individual (covered by the previously mentioned βιος, which will be added to a later vocabulary list). You can tell that the first declension features several abstract nouns (viz. ληθη and μνημη). We shall find in Latin, as well, a tendency for abstract nouns to be feminine, though not so often to belong to the first declension.

A caryatid, by the way, is a column sculpted in the figure of a maiden. Perhaps the most famous ones stand at one of the gates to the Parthenon in Athens. The Parthenon itself is in pretty bad shape these days, but the beautiful caryatids remain largely intact.

Summary

First-declension nouns, both Latin and Greek, are overwhelmingly feminine in gender. Their "a" (alpha) stem corresponds to the second declension's short "o" (omicron) stem. The pure alpha stem is more likely to survive in very ancient Greek words, however; in the majority, it has shifted to an eta.

Exercise Set 1.7: Latin

A. Translate the following Latin sentences into English (answers at chapter's end).
1. Ira reginae feminam terret ("is frightening").
2. Vita fili filiam terret ("frightens").
3. Bellum et campum et ("et… et" = "both… and") vitam vastet ("may destroy").
4. Pretium campi fecit ("caused") pugnam.
5. Cerebrum poetae deam concipit ("imagines").

B. Translate these English sentences into Latin.
1. The wrath of the god terrifies (*terret*) the kingdom.
2. The life of a farmer strengthens (*confirmat*) the back.
3. The sailor's son knows (*scit*) the way.

Exercise Set 1.7: Greek

C. Translate the following Greek sentences into English.
1. Θεα 'αρχην ζωης μανθανει ("understands").
2. Κουρη τεκνον 'εταιρης φιλεει ("likes").
3. Ποταμος ληθης μνημην και ("and") γνωμην 'αφαιρεει ("takes away").
4. Δωρον θεας ληθην διδωσι ("bestows").

D. Translate these English sentences into Greek.
1. The sea takes away ('αφαιρεει) the girl's memory.
2. The earth hides (καλυπτει) the place of the god and (και) the goddess.

Solo Flight: Translate these three sentences into Latin. Pay attention to each noun's declension.

    avus—grandfather   *regulus*—prince, minor king   *miraculum*—marvel, miracle (neuter)

    Drusilla—female name   *avaritia*—avarice, greed (feminine)   *fortuna*—good luck, fortune

1. The grandfather sees (*videt*) the goddess's miracle.
2. The goddess of victory gives (*dat*) good luck.
3. The prince does not like (*non amat*) the greed of Drusilla.

VIII. Number

Everyone knows that nouns can be either singular or plural. As a grammatical term, "number" refers to the quantity of a particular noun in particular circumstances. In English, we typically indicate a plural number of objects simply by adding an "s" to the relevant noun's singular form (e.g., "table… tables"). The situation in Latin and Greek resembles ours in that number is indicated by a final letter or letters. The second declension –*us* becomes –*i*, and the neuter –*um* becomes –*a*. (Actually, "a" is the nominative plural ending of every neuter word in Latin—

and alpha of every neuter word in Greek—regardless of its declension: no exceptions. This rule extends even to Russian and Sanskrit. The world's peoples can't agree about much, but they seem to agree about putting an "a" at the end of plural neuter subjects!) As for the first declension, its nominative plural ending is always *–ae*.

Students of Italian may recognize that the most common plural endings of that language preserve the imprint of these Latin forms: one *biscotto* (= "biscuit"), several *biscotti*; one *contessa*, many *contesse*. Speakers of French, joining the Spanish and following a practice which was passed along into English, simply add an "s" to make plural nouns.

Unfortunately, things grow much more complicated than this in Latin and Greek. The reason is that, unlike the modern romance languages, the ancient tongues employ several distinct case endings. *Each of these must have its own plural form: otherwise readers and hearers of Latin would recognize the noun's plurality but have no indication of its case.* The table below gives the singular and plural endings for all three cases that we have learned in the first two Latin declensions:

	1st **Declension**	2nd **Decl. Masc.**	2nd **Decl. Neuter**
nominative	*-ae*	*-i*	*-a*
genitive	*-arum*	*-orum*	*-orum*
accusative	*-as*	*-os*	*-a*

Several observations are worth making. 1) All nominative plurals in these two declensions end in vowels. 2) The neuter accusative, *as always*, is spelled identically to the nominative (which means, to repeat, that all neuter accusative plurals in Latin also end in "a"; and we may add that all neuter accusative plurals in Greek end in alpha). 3) The genitive plurals differ only in their vowel stem. In fact, every genitive plural ending in Latin features at least a *–um*: sometimes this is the ending in its entirety, but more often a vowel precedes it (with or without an "r").

In the masculine and feminine accusative plurals, you may recognize the plural endings used by Spanish. As the case system dissolved, the endings that survived in Spanish and Italian to represent a singular noun or a plural noun in all circumstances were among the most commonly used, most familiar endings. Spanish went with accusatives in the plural, Italian with nominatives. Both languages went with *–o* for all singulars that descended from the second declension and with *–a* for all that descended from the first; Spanish likely added the "s" to form plurals in a practice which (as has been noted) circulated throughout northwestern Europe. In particular, we see it affecting the French, who also (with their characteristic sense of economy) opted to shave away letters from inflections where possible. For instance, the Latin word *caballus*, a pack horse or nag, became (with an elevation in meaning) the Spanish *caballo*, the Italian *cavallo*, and the French *cheval*. Likewise, while the Spanish plural or this word became *caballos* and the Italian plural became *cavalli*, the French stayed minimalist and went with *chevals*— which modern French would phonetically streamline yet further into *chevaux*.

As a historical footnote, it should be observed that both Latin and Greek at one time possessed a set of endings for a *dual* number: i.e., for two things of a kind. One of these endings was a nominative in long "o" or omega. It survives in our English word "duo," which actually existed both in Latin and in Greek as the word for "two." Of course, the word for "two" would be dual if anything ever was! At any rate, dual endings are beginning to decay even in Homer, and in subsequent centuries they would be abandoned almost entirely. (Curiously, the Greek student of antiquities Pausanius often preserves a dual form when writing of two gods, as in chapters 34 and 38 of his comments on Athens—and this is the second century A.D. Apparently, keeping the time-honored form was a way of revering the divinities.) We may well have difficulty understanding why a language would ever designate any grammatical number other than singular and plural, but in the ancient tongues of pre-literate cultures such structures are quite common. The ancient Scandinavians seem to have had several endings for numbers beyond the dual which were yet not indiscriminately plural.

Since some of the plural endings in Latin are identical to singular endings for different cases, using common sense in your translations becomes more important than ever. For example, the second-declension nominative plural for masculine nouns like *digitus* is *–i*, yet this is also the genitive singular ending. Exactly the same ambiguity exists in the first declension between the genitive singular *–ae* and the nominative plural *–ae*. How do you reach a decision between the two options? Common sense and context are the answer. In the phrase *viae locus*, the former noun must be genitive singular rather than nominative plural because *locus* can only be nominative. In the complete sentence, *viae locus bellum incitat*, we know that we must translate, "The road's location is inciting a war," because there is no "and" (*et*) to indicate a compound subject and *locus* can be nothing but nominative, even though placing a genitive before it is oddly emphatic (viz., "It's *the road's* location—not the river's—that's starting a war").

Now, if we have the phrase *campi agricolae*, another source of confusion arises. Here we have two nouns whose ending could be either nominative plural or genitive singular: either "the field's farmers" or "the farmer's fields." The second option seems better simply on the basis of common sense, because a field is not usually spoken of as possessing farmers (especially several of them). Yet the expression could conceivably have that meaning, and the verb's ending would not help (even if we knew how to read its clues at this point in our book), because either possible subject will be plural. Hopefully, such a sentence would appear in a context which would make one choice or the other virtually certain.

Very little of what was just written about the Latin plural endings cannot be extended to Greek. In fact, the endings themselves are clearly akin to their Latin spelling once we make the kind of adjustment to which we have become accustomed. Remember that the Latin second declension once had an "o" (omicron) before all of its endings, and that the Latin first declension spelled the *–ae* ending as *–ai* in the language's infancy. That is, *tauri* would have been *tauroi* in early Latin, and *deae* would have been *deai*. These are the very nominative endings you will find in the chart below:

	1st Declension	2nd Decl. Masc.	2nd Decl. Neuter
nominative	-αι	-οι	-α
genitive	-αων	-ων	-ων
accusative	-ας	-ους	-α

The accusatives are also signaling us that Greek and Latin are first cousins. The endings of *feminas* and κουρας are identical except for slight variations in Greek and Roman script. As for the second declension, *tauros* is also no different from ταυρους if you reflect that two omicrons would naturally fuse into one long omega—which is just what happened in Latin—or into the *ou* sound. The Greek word for "mind" was originally νοος (cf. the English technical term "noetic"), for instance, but it very soon became νους.

Of course, the neuter nominative and accusative plural forms are again identical. You will recall that this is a hard and fast rule in both Latin and Greek. Though we shall see that other singular neuter endings exist for these two cases besides *um* and *–ov*, the plural neuter ending for both nominative and accusative is *always* an "a" for Latin and an alpha for Greek.

This leaves the genitive plural—a complicated matter. Latin genitive plurals always end in *-um*, as has been said; Greek genitive plurals, by the same token, always end in *-ων*. (The "n" and "m" sounds are very close linguistically, as we have also noticed before.) There may be another letter before these universal two, as in the case of the alpha for the first declension. Never, though, does a rho (the Greek "r") appear in any extant genitive plural. It would be impossible to say for certain whether an "r" sound once existed in Greek but eroded away or whether, on the other hand, the Romans' progenitors inserted an "r" to distinguish the two vowels on either side of it and halt the erosion. The latter option seems more probable, though, if only because "r" is introduced to separate vowels in many tongues. (In parts of the northeastern United States, for instance, people will say, "The law-r-is on his side"; and in certain British dialects which commonly ignore legitimate "r's," the consonant may mysteriously appear between two vowels to ensure that both are pronounced, as in, "The militia r-assisted local citizens.") The Greek omega could reasonably indicate that two vowels have indeed fused into one, because a long "o" is a common result of colliding vowels in any language. (In Irish, the "o" which begins surnames like "O'Neal" is the remnant of a very ancient word for "son": *ua*.) As a matter of fact, even the alpha of the first-declension *–αων* is confined to the Homeric epics and other early texts. Within a century, it has also been worn away! So the presence of the final omega may further imply that fusion was the fate awaiting vowels where the "r" wasn't artificially wedged in.

In short, Latin and Greek are really quite similar even in the genitive plural, but were simply codified in writing while at different phases of the same evolutionary process.

In the exercises below, pay particular attention to common sense, once again, for we now have several endings in Latin, especially, which might designate more than one case if viewed out of context.

Summary
As a grammatical term, "number" refers to the singular/plural distinction: a noun's number is either singular or plural. All Latin and Greek nouns have a distinct set of endings for the plural, whose spellings vary from case to case as do the singular endings.

Exercise Set 1.8: Latin

A. Translate the following Latin sentences into English (answers at end of chapter).
1. Filii villam agricolarum vident ("see").
2. Iram reginae poetae timent ("fear").
3. Ira deorum campos vastavit ("has destroyed").
4. Turba ("large group, crowd") nautarum et ("and") puellarum insulas spectat ("is looking at").
5. Anni belli dona vitae vastaverunt ("have destroyed").

B. Translate these English sentences into Latin.
1. The poet's words struck (*pulsaverunt*) the sailors like (*sicut*) stones.*
2. The arms of the gods touch (*tangunt*) the minds/brains of men (use *vir*, a regular second-declension masculine noun except for lacking the *–us* in its nominative singular).
3. The woman's daughters love (*amant*) the words of the poets.
*N.B.: Put "stones" in the same case as "words."

Exercise Set 1.8: Greek
C. Translate the following Greek sentences into English.
1. Δωρα θεαων ʽεταιρας ταρβεουσι ("dazzle").
2. Κουραι νησου ʼιππους φιλεουσι ("love").
3. Ληθη τεκνων κουρας φοβεει ("frightens").
4. Θεοι ποντων ʼανεμους λυουσι ("release").

D. Translate these English sentences into Greek.
1. The islands of the gods take away (’αφαιρεουσι) memories of life.
2. The gods know (γιγνωσκουσι) the beginning of the winds.

Solo Flight: Find and correct the errors in the Greek sentences, based on the English translations provided. Each sentence has only one error (always a noun).
1. ’Οδος ξενων νησους ’αποκαλυψε ("revealed"). ~ The stranger's journey revealed the islands.
2. Κουρη ’ιππου ‘εταιρης φιλεει ("loves"). ~ The girl loves the [her] friend's horse.
3. Ληθη ποιηταων μυθον φυει ("produces"). ~ The forgetfulness of the poets produces myths.
4. Θεος ’ανεμους νησου λυει ("releases"). ~ Λ god releases the winds of the islands.
5. Ψυχη μετρην ουκ ("not") ‘εχει ("have"). ~ The soul does not have a measure (i.e., "dimension").

IX. Tables of First- and Second-Declension Endings 01.10.2019

Here, then, are complete tables of the first two declensions based upon the endings that you know so far. (Yes, there are more coming.)

1st Declension (almost entirely feminine)				
case/function	LATIN		GREEK	
	singular	plural	singular	plural
nominative (subject of sentence)	-a femina	-ae feminae	-η κουρη	-αι κουραι
genitive (possessive, whole "owning" parts)	-ae feminae	-arum feminarum	-ης κουρης	-αων κουραων
accusative (direct object, motion toward)	-am feminam	-as feminas	-ην κουρην	-ας κουρας

2nd Declension (masculine)				
case/function	LATIN		GREEK	
	singular	plural	singular	plural
nominative (subject of sentence)	-us campus	-i campi	-ος ταυρος	-οι ταυροι
genitive (possessive, whole "owning" parts)	-i campi	-orum camporum	-ου ταυρου	-ων ταυρων
accusative (direct object, motion toward)	-um campum	-os campos	-ον ταυρον	-ους ταυρους

2nd Declension (neuter)				
case/function	LATIN		GREEK	
	singular	plural	singular	plural
nominative (subject of sentence)	-um bellum	-a bella	-ον τεκνον	-α τεκνα

39

genitive (possessive, whole "owning" parts)	-i belli	-orum bellorum	-ου τεκνου	-ων τεκνων
accusative (direct object, motion toward)	-um bellum	-a bella	-ον τεκνον	-α τεκνα

Exercise Set 1.9

Write out the general rules pertaining to both Latin and Greek for the following noun endings of the first and second declensions:

1. the nominative and accusative of all neuter nouns, both singular and plural (in all declensions)
2. the nominative and accusative of all neuter nouns (of all declensions) in the plural
3. the accusative singular of all masculine and feminine nouns in these declensions
4. the accusative plural of all masculine and feminine nouns in all declensions
5. the genitive plural of all nouns, regardless of gender (and declension)

Solo Flight: Create a grid for the two declensions in Greek and Latin and attempt to fill it out correctly. At first, you may wish to supply one or two answers beforehand in order to jog your memory. Take ten or fifteen minutes off between each attempt until you finally fill every slot perfectly.

X. Formation of Singular and Plural in Romance Languages

The preceding sections have already dropped a few hints about noun inflections in the romance languages. Naturally, one great convenience in memorizing Italian, Spanish, or French forms rather than Latin and Greek forms is the absence of any case system in the former, more modern tongues. Here prepositions have completely assumed the burden of expressing a noun's role as a possessor, an indirect object, a location, and so forth. The nouns of the romance languages do have distinct singular and plural forms, however; and, thanks to the survival of separate masculine and feminine genders, singular and plural forms also usually reflect the two genders. Now two endings (singular and plural) have become four (both numbers for both genders). At least the neuter gender has disappeared from all the romance languages! Because of its frequent near-identity of formation with the masculine gender in Latin (as we have observed in this chapter with the second declension), the neuter gender had a very strong tendency to bequeath its nouns to the masculine as the later languages took shape.

Latin is of further assistance to the Italian or Spanish student in that it gives useful clues to the origin and formation of the surviving noun inflections. One might assume that the nominative case dictates these forms. In Italian, it does... more or less. Consider the masculine and feminine forms of the word for "teacher."

	Latin	Italian
singular	*magister*	*maestro*
plural	*magistri*	*maestri*
singular	*magistra*	*maestra*
plural	*magistrae*	*maestre*

Of these four forms, three clearly come to Italian in direct descent from the corresponding Latin nominatives for masculine and feminine nouns of the first two declensions. The feminine plural form shifts from –ae to –e in a rather natural—even predictable—bit of compression from diphthong to long vowel. Only the masculine singular form utterly abandons the Latin –us (or –er in this case) for an –o. Since "o" is indeed the dominant vowel of the second declension, this, too, should not come as a great surprise.

Indeed, Spanish retains the "o" as the uniform masculine singular ending—and it also sticks with the "a" to designate a feminine singular noun. The departure from Italian comes in the plural, where an "s" appears:

	Latin	**Spanish**
singular	*magister*	*maestro*
plural	*magistri*	*maestros*
singular	*magistra*	*maestra*
plural	*magistrae*	*maestras*

An English-speaker is apt to respond that the Spanish alternative makes altogether more sense—plurals are supposed to end in an "s"! Interestingly, this "s = plural" association does not come to English from Germanic grammar (for the "s," while indicating possession in a German singular noun, never signifies a plural). The Spanish plurals, rather than staying with dominant Latin nominative forms, seem to have adopted the final consonant in three—or sometimes four—of the five Latin plural cases. (The genitive plural is the only case whose inflection never features an "s" in any declension: nominatives often do.) The "s/plural" notion is actually embedded so deeply in the history of European languages that English is tapping into that ancient fountain rather than into German in the formation of its plurals.

To be sure, it does so through the specific historical pipeline of French. All French plurals originally ended in "s." Singulars might end in practically any letter. This is somewhat unfortunate for the student, since most French nouns encode no obvious clues about their gender in the way their ending is spelled. Below are a few examples of the singular's diversity and the plural's regularity:

singular	**plural**
chien (dog)	*chiens*
arbre (tree)	*arbres*
soulier (shoe)	*souliers*
visage (face)	*visages*
mot (word)	*mots*

It is true that certain nouns have both masculine and feminine forms. A female dog, for instance, would be a *chienne*. We may easily discern this handy rule about doubling the final consonant and adding an "e" in a number of familiar proper names. "Michel" (Michael) becomes the feminine "Michelle," "Jean" (John) becomes "Jeanne," "Lucien" becomes "Lucienne," and so forth. For the most part, though, only a very accomplished French-speaker would not be reduced to guessing the gender (or looking it up in the dictionary) for the words above. Knowing Latin can help: *arbor* is feminine there as well as in French.

Problems can arise in forming French plurals when words of certain groups have undergone a historical transformation in how they are pronounced. The word for "horse" is *cheval*. Its plural was originally *chevals*, and would have been pronounced more or less as it looks. With time, however, the tongue flattened so that neither the "l" nor the "s" could be heard. A convention emerged which represented the sound of the result as *chevaux*. Now, in modern French, an entire class of words whose singular ends in *–au*, *–eau*, *-eu*, *-al*, *-ail*, or *-ou* has a plural ending in "x": e.g., *travail/travaux* (work/works), *gateau/gateaux* (cake/cakes), *neveu/neveux* (nephew/nephews), and *bijou/bijoux* (jewel/jewels). Again, all such plurals once featured a final "s": the paradigm simply eroded. It may be unfortunate from a learner's point of view—but language is always evolving, with new rules and new exceptions to rules ever rising to the surface.

There is another wrinkle to Italian and Spanish nouns, as well. This time, we are not dealing with evolutionary decay so much as with the persistence of the old Latin forms. You will find in Chapter Three that Latin and Greek both have a third declension (with Latin's fourth and fifth declensions really being mere spin-offs of this third one). Nouns from these declensions made the transition into the romance languages with vestiges of their distinct endings still very apparent. That is, this group of nouns does not end with "o" or "a" in the singular, and their plural forms tend to confuse the issue of gender for the beginner. We will save this subject, however, for the appropriate time. Just remember that a substantial group of nouns yet remains in Italian and Spanish whose singular and plural forms we have not yet adequately discussed.

Another important subject must also be withheld for a later day: articles. These seem like simple words to us—and, in English, they are. "The" is the all-purpose definite article (definite because it restricts the noun to a particular item), while the indefinite "a" does no further morphing than the addition of an "n" before vowels (though its plural form is in fact a little problematic). The articles of nouns in the romance languages, however, began life as adjectives. We shall see that this requires them to change their spelling in order to reflect the number and gender of the noun to which they are attached. The logically appropriate place for such a discussion is Chapter Five, where adjectives are the major focus. If you wish to peek ahead, feel free to do so.

Summary

Italian, Spanish, and French all possess a masculine and a feminine gender but have discarded Latin's neuter—every noun in these languages is one or the other of the former two. This means that formerly neuter words in Latin have been re-classified in the modern languages, usually as masculine. In these modern tongues, as well, the noun's termination will typically reflect its gender (though in French, gender-indexed endings are relatively rare). Furthermore, the modern nouns tend to have gender-specific plural endings (with French again the exception).

Exercise Set 1.10

A. Identify the following Italian nouns as singular or plural by using **S** or **P** and as masculine or feminine by using **M** or **F**. Then rewrite them in the opposite number (i.e., make singulars plural and plurals singular).

1. libro
2. sorelle
3. collina
4. ville
5. numeri
6. pagina
7. modi
8. scuso

B. Repeat the exercise above for the following Spanish nouns.

1. cuentos
2. hermana
3. muchachas
4. brazo
5. cielo
6. pueblos
7. casa
8. guerras

C. Once again, repeat the exercise above for the following French nouns—but this time, omit the notation of gender (which would have to be a guess unless you looked it up).

1. professeurs
2. chaises
3. plateau
4. armoire
5. chapeaux
6. homme
7. dent
8. bouteilles

Solo Flight: Of how many words in A, B, and C did you know the meaning? For those that utterly stump you, use a dictionary or go online to find an English definition.

XI. Complete Latin Vocabulary for First- and Second Declension Nouns

Below is a list of over a hundred nouns of the first and second declensions (with genders indicated in parentheses). Some were introduced to you earlier in this chapter: those with asterisks (about half) appear here for the first time. Whether you have seen the noun before now or not, however, you should know how to decline it, since all nouns stick to the basic rules. (In a few cases, explicitly noted, forms are always plural or switch gender or meaning in the plural—but the case endings will not vary from what you have learned.)

For the most part, these words have been chosen because they have English cognates and will thus help you to build your English vocabulary. The few which do not have cognates have been included either because the Romans used them often or because they have a certain resonance in the sciences even though they give us no particular word in English (e.g., the botanical employment of Latin tree names). You may wish to concentrate on special words—such as anatomical terms—or otherwise tailor your study to special objectives. Remember, in any event, that many of the words have more than one derivative in English and/or in the sciences. A helpful exercise might be to find additional derivatives for as many nouns as possible.

As far as other drills of the sort offered throughout this chapter, you should be able to devise several to give you practice with the new vocabulary below. Take the verb *videt* ("he, she, or it sees"), *pulsat* ("he, she, or it strikes), or one of the others used in exercises above and build a sentence around it by placing the subject noun in the nominative, the direct object in the accusative, and one or more possessive noun forms in the genitive: e.g., "The eagle's tail strikes the bear's nose"—*Cauda aquilae nasum ursae pulsat*). You can employ a plural subject, too, as long as you replace the verb's *–t* ending with an *–nt* (for reasons we shall study straightaway in the next chapter). Mix singulars and plurals in order to challenge yourself: for instance, "The men of the council see the queen's friends" (*Viri concili amicas reginae vident*). Test your translations by asking another student to render them back into English and comparing the result with your intent.

Of course, Latin has thousands of first- and second-declension nouns, not just a few hundred. We will be offering no more than these in the present text because it is introductory. Nevertheless, you should be able to acquire a Latin dictionary and add other words of these two declensions to your vocabulary without difficulty. Take heart in the Romans' rather rigorous and efficient mentality: they allowed very few exceptions to leak into their grammatical rules, as languages go. You can *always* be confident, therefore, that a second-declension masculine noun's accusative plural ends in *–os*, a first-declension noun's genitive plural in *–arum*, and so forth. The Romans were great engineers and administrators: they admired order, and they stuck to rules.

Latin (gender)	definition	English derivative
agricola (m)	farmer	agriculture

43

amica (f)*	friend (female)	amicable
amicus (m)*	friend (male)	amicable
animus (m)*	inner life, spirit	animate
anima (f)	(physical) breath	animal
annus (m)	year	annual
aqua (f)*	water	aquatic
aquila (f)*	eagle	aquiline
argentum (n)*	silver	argent
arma (n pl)*	arms, weapons	armor
auxilium (n)	help, aid	auxiliary
auxilia (pl)	reinforcements (military)	
aurum (n)*	gold	ore
avunculus (m)*	uncle	avuncular
avus (m)*	grandfather	atavism
bellum (n)	war	belligerent
bracchium (n)	arm	brachial
caelum (n)	sky	celestial, ceiling
campus (m)	field (unplowed)	campaign
castra (n pl)*	camp (military)	castle
cauda (f)*	tail	caudal
causa (f)*	cause, reason	cause
cerebrum (n)	brain	cerebral
cervus (m)*	stag, deer	-----
cetus (m)*	whale	cetacean
concilium (n)*	council, advisory body	council
consilium (n)*	counsel, advice	counsel
copia (f)*	abundance, wealth	copious

copiae (pl)	wealth, riches; also troops	
cumulus (m)*	heap, pile	cumulative
cupressus (f)	cypress tree	cypress
cura (f)*	care, concern	cure
dea (f)	goddess	deity
deus (m)	god	deity
digitus (m)	finger	digital
dominus (m)*	lord, master	dominion
donum (n)	gift	donation
dorsum (n)	back	dorsal
epistula (f)*	letter (mail)	epistolary
equus (m)*	horse	equine
fabula (f)*	story	fable
femina (f)	woman	feminine
ferrum (n)*	iron, weapon (of iron)	ferrous
ficus (f)	fig tree	fig
filia (f)	daughter	filial
filius (m)	son	filial
folium (n)	leaf	foliage, folio
hora (f)	hour	hour
impedimentum (n)*	obstacle	impediment
impedimenta (pl)	baggage	
imperium (n)*	power, authority, command	empire
iniuria (f)*	injury, hurt	injury
insidiae (f pl)*	ambush	insidious
insula (f)*	island	insular
ira (f)	anger, wrath	ire

laurus (f)	laurel tree	laurels
lingua (f)*	tongue, language	language
littera (f)	letter (of alphabet)	literal, literature
litterae (pl)	letter, note, missive	
locus (m in sing., n in pl)	place	location
ludus (m)*	game	ludic, interlude
luna (f)	moon	lunar
lupus (m)*	wolf	lupine
malus (f)	apple tree	-----
modus (m)	means, way	mode
mundus (m)	world, universe	mundane
murus (m)*	wall	immure
nasus (m)*	nose	nasal
nauta (m)	sailor	nautical
numerus (m)*	number	numerous
oculus (m)	eye	ocular
odium (n)*	hatred	odious
oppidum (n)*	town	-----
patria (f)*	fatherland, homeland	patriot
periculum (n)	danger	perilous
pinus (f)	pine tree	pine
poeta (m)	poet	poet
poplus (f)	poplar tree	poplar
populus (m)*	people, population	populace
pluvium (n)*	rain	alluvial
pretium (n)	price	precious
pugna (f)	fight	pugnacious

regina (f)	queen	regal
responsum (n)*	answer	response
saxum (n)	stone, rock	-----
silva (f)*	forest	sylvan
socius (m)*	comrade, ally	social
stella (f)*	star	constellation
taurus (m)	bull	taurine
tergum (n)*	back	tergiversation
terra (f)*	land, earth	terrestrial
turba (f)*	crowd, the masses	turbid
quercus (f)	oak tree	-----
ulmus (f)	elm tree	elm
ulna (f)*	elbow	ulnar
umerus (m)	shoulder	humeral
ursa (f)*	bear	ursine
venenum (n)*	poison	venom
ventus (m)*	wind	vent
verbum (n)	word	verbiage, verb
via (f)	road, way (also in metaphor)	via
victoria (f)	victory	victory
villa (f)*	house, country house	village
vinum (n)*	wine	vine
vita (f)	life	vital
vitium (n)*	flaw, weakness	vice

To this list should be added five very common second-declension masculine nouns with an odd nominative singular. As is often the case in language, commonly used words are more "eroded" than others and may endure some strange mutations. Suetonius tells us, for example (in the eighth section of his chapter on Caligula) that the obsolete forms *puellus* and *puera* for "boy" and "girl" both appeared in a certain ancient inscription. This strongly implies that *puerus* would also have existed. The characteristic –*us* of the nominative singular in such oft-used masculine words may have tended to wear off when it followed an "r." (The Romans would have pronounced this consonant with enough breath to trill it, like a modern Italian, so that the short "u" just after it could easily be lost.) In nouns where an –er was preceded by a consonant, furthermore, the short "e" would also disappear in all other cases and throughout the plural. "Teacher's" would be *magistri*, "of the fields" would be *agrorum*, and so forth; but the "e" remains in "boy's" (*pueri*).

ager	field (cultivated)	agriculture
liber	book	library
magister	teacher	master
puer	boy	puerile
vir	man, hero	virile

XII. Complete Greek Vocabulary for First- and Second-Declension Nouns

The formatting of this list is the same as the Latin list's above: Greek word with gender, English meaning, and an English derivative. The derivatives here are sometimes purely Greek words transported into English discussions of Greek myth and philosophy (e.g., "Centaur") rather than adaptations used in common English. Words not introduced earlier in the chapter are followed by an asterisk.

Note the number of scientific terms drawn from Greek: you can indeed find many in addition to the suggested derivatives. If you have a particular interest in the sciences, you should perhaps devote even more effort to memorizing Greek words than Latin words.

Greek	**definition**	**English derivative**
'αιτιον (n) *	cause	etiology
'ανεμος (m)	wind	anemometer
'ανθροπος (m)*	man, person	anthropology
'αριθμος (m) *	number, tally	arithmetic
'αρχη (f)	beginning	archaic
'αταραξια	serenity, spiritual peace	ataraxy
βιβλος (f)*	papyrus, book	Bible
βιος (m)	life (specific)	biology
βροντη*	thunder	brontosauros
γαια (f)	earth	geology
γνωμη (f)	knowledge	gnostic

48

δημος (m)*	citizenry, common people	democracy
δωρον (n)	gift	Dorothy (gift of God)
'ελευθερια (f)*	freedom	-----
'εργον (n)*	work, task	synergy
'εταιρος (m or f)	comrade, friend	Hetaerist
'ηλιος	sun	helium
ζωη (f)	life (general)	zoology
θανατος (m)*	death	euthanasia
θεα (f)	goddess	theology
θεος (m)	god	theology
'ιππος (m)	horse	hippodrome
κοσμος (m)*	world, arrangement, adornment	cosmology
κουρη (f)	girl, young woman	caryatid
κουρος (m)*	boy, young man	-----
κυβερνητης (m)*	pilot, helmsman	cybernetics
ληθη (f)	forgetfulness	lethal
λογος (m)*	word, pattern, order	logic
μαρτυρος (m)	witness	martyr
μεγαρον (n)	main room	-----
μετρον (n)	measure	meter
μνημη (f)	memory	mnemonic
μοιρα (f)*	fate, destiny	----- (name "Moira" is from Irish "Máire"))
μυθος (m)*	story, tale, order	myth
νησος (f)	island	Polynesia
ξενος (m.)*	stranger, foreigner	xenophobia
ξυλον (n)*	wood, wooden object	xylophone

'οδος (f)*	path, road, way	odometer
'οικος (m)*	home, domicile	economics
'οινος (m)*	wine	(equivalent of Latin *vinum*)
παρθενος (f)	maiden, virgin	Parthenon (temple dedicated to the virgin goddess Athena)
πετρος (m)	stone	petrify
ποιητης (m)	poet	poet
πολεμος (m)*	war	polemics
ποντος (m)	sea	pontoon
ποταμος (m)	river	hippopotamos
στρατηγος (m)*	commander, general	strategy
στρατος (m)*	army	strategy
'υπνος (m)*	sleep	hypnosis
ταυρος (m)	bull	Centaur
τοπος (m)	place	topic
τεκνον (n)	child	-----
τροπος (m)*	turn (in direction); manner	trope, tropic
τυραννος (m)*	ruler, autocrat	tyrant
φαρμακον (n)	drug, medicine	pharmacy
φοβος (m)*	fear, terror	phobia
χρονος (m)*	time	chronology
ψυχη (f)*	life, spirit, soul	psychology

XIII. Alphabets

The Complete Greek Alphabet

A, a	A, α alpha

50

B, b	B, β beta
G, g	Γ, γ gamma
D, d	Δ, δ delta
E, e	E, ε (short) epsilon
Z, z	Z, ζ zeta
E, e	H, η (long) eta
TH, th	Θ, θ theta
I, i	I, ι iota
K, k	K, κ kappa
L, l	Λ, λ lambda
M, m	M, μ mu
N, n	N, ν nu
X, x	Ξ, ξ xi
O, o	O, o (short) omicron
P, p	Π, π pi
R, r	P, ρ rho
S, s	Σ, σ / ς sigma
T, t	T, τ tau
U, u	Y, υ upsilon
PH, ph	Φ, φ phi
CH, ch	X, χ chi
PS, ps	Ψ, ψ psi
O, o	Ω, ω (long) omega

The Greek and Cyrillic Alphabets Juxtaposed

Because considerable correspondence exists between the Greek and Cyrillic (or Russian) alphabets, the two (along with the Roman alphabet) have been arranged comparatively below. You will not necessarily want to start learning Russian characters at this time unless you entertain a strong desire to pursue that language's study in the future; but at least you will appreciate, even from this cursory glance, that learning Greek makes the transition to studying Russian far easier than attempting the move from the Roman alphabet straight to Russian.

51

Roman/English	Greek	Cyrillic (Russian)
A, a	A, α alpha	A, a
B, b	B, β beta	Б, б
Z	z	В, в (pronounced "v")
G, g	Γ, γ gamma	Г, г
D, d	Δ, δ delta	Д, д
E, e	E, ε (short) epsilon	Е, е / Э, э (former preceded by consonantal but unwritten "y")
Z, z	Z, ζ zeta	Ж, ж / З, з (former pronounced "zh")
E, e	H, η (long) eta	И, и / Й, й (latter used in diphthongs)
TH, th	Θ, θ theta	
I, I	I, ι iota	Ы, ы
K, k	K, κ kappa	К, к
L. l	Λ, λ lambda	Л, л
M, m	M, μ mu	М, м
N, n	N, ν nu	Н, н
X, x	Ξ, ξ xi	[кс]
O, o	O, o (short) omicron	О, о
P. p	Π, π pi	П, п
R, r	P, ρ rho	Р, р
S, s	Σ, σ / ς sigma	С, с
T, t	T, τ tau	Т, т
U, u	Y, υ upsilon	У, у
PH, ph	Φ, φ phi	Ф, ф
CH, ch	X, χ chi	X, х

PS, ps	Ψ, ψ psi	Ч, ч
O, o	Ω, ω (long) omega	Ю / ю (approximate)

Several Cyrillic characters have no Greek equivalent: Ц / ц, Ш / ш, Щ / щ, Ъ / ъ, Ь / ь, and Я / я. (Of these, the two "b-looking" characters before Я do not actually designate a sound, but rather indicate how a previous consonant is to be pronounced.) Clearly, Greek and Russian letters are not exactly the same; nor, often, are the sounds represented by similar characters the same. Yet it should be just as apparent that learning the Cyrillic alphabet through Greek has considerable advantages.

X1V. The Romance Languages

Below are almost fifty Latin words which have cognates (or derivative forms) in all three of the romance languages most studied in the United States. Review this list and attempt to draw a few conclusions from it. Then compare your notes with the remarks below the list. Remember that Italian, Spanish, and French have only the masculine and feminine genders—not the neuter. Gender has only been given parenthetically where it wanders away from the Latin/Italian pattern. What *is* that pattern? (Think about it and then read the supplemental remarks.)

Latin	Italian	Spanish	French
amicus	amico	amigo	ami
aqua	aqua	agua	eau
aquila	aquila	águila	aigle
annus	anno	año	an
argentum	argento	argento (obs)	argent
aurum	auro	oro	ore
bracchium	braccio	brazo	bras
caelum	cielo	cielo	ciel
causa	causa	causa	cause
cerebrum	cerebro	cerebro	cerveau
deus	deo	dio	dieu
digitus	digito	dedo	doigt
donum	dono	don	don
femina	femina	hembra	femme
ferrum	ferro	hierro	ferre

ficus	fico	higo	figue (f)
filia	figlia	hija	fille
filius	figlio	hijo	fils
folium	foglio	hoja (f)	feuille (f)
hora	hora	hora	heure
insula	isola	isla	isle
ira	ira	ira	ire
lingua	lingua	lengua	langue
littera	lettera	letra	lettre
locus	loco	lugar	lieu
luna	luna	luna	lune
lupus	lupo	lobo	loup
magister	maestro	maistro	maître
mundus	mondo	mundo	monde
murus	muro	muro	mur
nasus	naso	nariz	nez
numerus	numero	número	nombre
periculum	pericolo	peligro	péril
populus	popolo	pueblo	peuple
pluvium	pluvio	lluvia (f)	pluie (f)
pretium	prezio	precio	prix
regina	regina	reina	reine
regnum	regno	reinado	règne
stella	stella	estrella	étoile
taurus	tauro	toro	taure
terra	terra	tierra	terre
ursa	orso	oso	ours

verbum	verbo	verbo	verbe
via	via	via	vie
villa	villa	villa	ville
vinum	vino	vino	vin
vita	vita	vida	vie
vitium	vizio	vicio	vice

You should notice, first of all, that Italian follows the Latin precedent more closely than any other romance language. This should hardly come as a surprise, since Italian *is* modern Latin, in effect (much to the frustration of those who wish to declare Latin dead). Sometimes, in first-declension nouns, the Latin and Italian spellings are indeed identical. Spanish is usually quite similar to Latin, as well. In a few cases, it blazes its own trail. The initial "f" of several Latin words, for instance, is transformed into an "h." (The familiar Spanish verb *hablar* is actually descended from the Latin *fabula*, thus equating "to speak" with "to tell a story.") The Latin "pl" is also rendered in Spanish by "ll" (pronounced more or less like consonantal "y": a *llano* is a "plain," from the Latin word *planus* for "flat.") Such cases aside, Spanish words often resemble their Latin progenitors very narrowly.

That leaves French. Through close contact with Germanic peoples during the Middle Ages (among others, the Franks), France drifted from its Roman linguistic heritage rather farther than the other two romance languages under our magnifying glass. (In chapter 3, section 21, of his classic *Historia de la Lengua Española*, Rafael Lapesa demonstrates that Gaul, being administratively tied much closer to Rome, mirrored more of the city's linguistic trends than remote, mountainous Spain; but for the same reason, Spain also held onto archaic Latin usage more faithfully.) You will notice, for example, that French words contain no vowel ending that betrays their gender. A singular ending in "o" always denotes a masculine noun in Italian and Spanish, and an ending in "a" can only belong to a feminine noun. Even the names of trees, since they acquire the "o" ending which Italian and Spanish bestow on all second-declension Latin words, are drawn into the masculine gender because of that "o"; yet French, having no gender-indexed noun endings (except for substantive adjectives—a special case), was free to preserve *figue* as a feminine noun while Italian and Spanish treated the "o" ending as requiring a masculine gender. (The names of other trees behave after the same fashion, by the way: *ficus* has been put on the list as a representative example.)

On the other hand, trees notwithstanding, French is more likely than either of the other two languages to assign a non-Latin gender to a noun. When Sir Thomas Mallory wrote his classic tale, *Le Morte Darthur* (*The Death of King Arthur*), in the late Middle Ages, he did not attribute the wrong gender to "death" because he was an ignorant Englishman, but rather because he was cleverly employing the masculine gender given to that noun by Norman French, the tongue of the greatest romances. Eventually the feminine gender prevailed in that particular instance (*la mort* is feminine in modern French, like *mors* in Latin)—but nouns in French generally traveled a rougher evolutionary road to their present form than did their cousins closer to the Mediterranean.

So what became of the Latin neuter gender, which has no parallel in any modern romance language? Almost universally, its nouns shifted directly into the masculine. A few exceptions exist in Spanish and French, such as the transformation of *folium* into *hoja* and *feuille*; but you may have figured out that Italian offers no exception at all to this neuter/masculine connection. Again, thanks to the similarity of second-declension masculine and neuter endings, history determined overwhelmingly that nouns whose singular form terminated in "o" would be masculine.

Finally, we should also remark a tendency in a few Spanish and French words to wander off their original

Latin target in meaning as well as spelling. *Villa* and *ville*, for example, are no longer large houses in these languages, but small townships. *Pueblo* in Spanish is often employed in a very similar way—i.e., to mean a certain place on the map rather than a somewhat abstracted collection of persons. Likewise, *mot* in French and *palabra* in Spanish are much more commonly used to mean "word" than any form of the Latin *verbum*. In this respect as in several others, Italian truly remains the modern incarnation of the tongue used by ancient Romans.

ANSWERS TO EXERCISES

Exercise Set 1.1

Answers to **A**: 1. direct object 2. subject 3. subject 4. possessive 5. direct object 6. possessive 7. subject 8. direct object 9. possessive 10. direct object

Answers to **B**: The genitive; it can be expressed either with an apostrophe or using the preposition "of" (e.g., "the horse's" or "of the horse").

Exercise Set 1.2

1. nom. 2. gen. 3. acc. 4. nom. 5. acc. 6. acc. 7. nom. 8. acc. 9. gen. 10. nom.

Exercise Set 1.3

Answers to **A**: 1. The god sees the place of the bull (or the bull's place). 2. The bull sees the place of the god (or the god's place). 3. The god's finger shows the place. 4. The place of the god nourishes the bull. 5. The bull sees the god of the place.

Answers to **B**: 1. Deus loci digitum levat. 2. Taurus dei locum vastat. 3. Digitus locum dei monstrat.

Exercise Set 1.4

1. For instance, the honorary fraternity Sigma Tau Delta, "alpha-male," "omega-3 fatty acids," and πr^2 (the formula for finding a circle's area). 2. Upper-case eta and "H," lower-case eta and "n," lower-case nu and "v," and both upper- and lower-case rho and "p." Upper-case upsilon and "y" are also a possibility, though many English words borrowed from Greek where the "y" is not a consonant (e.g., "oxygen") preserve something close to the Greek pronunciation.

Exercise Set 1.5

Answers to **A**: 1. The god of the river (the river's god) makes an island. 2. The god's stone strikes the horse (or, "It's the *god's* stone that strikes the horse," since the genitive acquires emphasis in the initial position). 3. The sea covers the island's place/location. 4. The god of the sea stops the wind. 5. The wind strikes the sea and the river.

Answers to **B**: 1. Θεος 'ανεμου νησον ποιει. 2. Μαρτυρος ταυρον πετρου 'οραει.

Exercise Set 1.6: Latin

Answers to **A**: 1. The world fears the danger of war. 2. A leaf is touching the son's back. 3. The sky's god made the universe. 4. The means of war is devastating the field. 5. The brain's help surpasses the arm's help.

Answers to **B**: 1. Oculus animi caelum videt. 2. Annus periculi animum fili terret.

Exercise Set 1.6: Greek

Answers to **C**: 1. The large room holds the child's gift. 2. The drug is melting the river's stone. 3. The god (or "God") conceals the measure (size, extent) of the sea. 4. The god's child desires a horse. 5. The wind and the sea are producing a god.

Answers to **D**: 1. Φαρμακον θεου ποταμον παυει. 2. Μεγαρον 'ουκ 'εστι τοπος 'ιππου.

Exercise Set 1.7: Latin

Answers to **A**: 1. The queen's anger is frightening the woman. 2. The son's life frightens the daughter. 3, War may destroy both a field and a life. 4. The price of the field caused a fight. 5. The poet's brain imagines a goddess.

Answers to **B**: 1. Ira dei regnum terret. 2. Vita agricolae dorsum confirmat. 3. Filius nautae viam scit.

Exercise Set 1.7: Greek

Answers to **C**: 1. The goddess understands the beginning of life. 2. The girl likes the friend's child. 3. The river of forgetfulness removes memory and knowledge. (We would probably want to use the genitive and say, "river of forgetfulness"; but the Lethe was visualized as an actual river in the mythological underworld, from which spirits drank to forget their past lives.) 4. The gift of the goddess bestows forgetfulness.

Answers to **D**: 1. Ποντος μνημην ʽεταιρης ʼαφαιρεει. 2. Γαια τοπον θεου και θεας καλυπτει.

Exercise Set 1.8: Latin

Answers to **A**: 1. The sons see the house of the farmers. 2. The poets fear the queen's anger OR The queens fear the poet's anger (but word order strongly favors the former). 3. The anger of the gods has destroyed the fields. 4. A crowd of sailors and girls is looking at the islands (N.B.: "crowd" is the subject, and is singular). 5. Years of war have destroyed the gifts of life. (If "dona" were the subject, no other word could be the direct object; and if "vitae" were the subject, what kind of sense would the sentence make?)

Answers to **B**: 1. Verba poetae nautas sicut saxa pulsaverunt. 2. Bracchia deorum cerebra virorum tangunt. 3. Filiae feminae verba poetae amant.

Exercise Set 1.8: Greek

Answers to **C**: 1. The gifts of the goddesses dazzle the friends. 2. The girls of the island love horses. 3. The children's forgetfulness frightens the girls. 4. The gods of the seas release the winds.

Answers to **D**: 1. Νησοι θεων μνημας ζωης ʼαφαιρεουσι . 2. Θεοι ʼαρχην ʼανεμων γιγνωσκουσι.

Exercise Set 1.9

1. Within a given number (singular or plural) their endings are always identical. 2. The ending is always a/α. 3. The ending's final letter is always "m." 4. The ending's final letter is always "s." 5. The ending's final letter is always a nasal consonant ("m" in Latin, "ν" in Greek).

Exercise Set 1.10

Answers to **A**: 1. SM libri 2. PF sorella 3. SF colline 4. PF villa 5. PM numero 6. SF pagine 7. PM modo 8. SM scusi

Answers to **B**: 1. PM cuento 2. SF hermanas 3. PF muchacha 4. SM brazos 5. SM cielos 6. PM pueblo 7. SF casas 8. PF guerra

Answers to **C**: 1. P professeur 2. P chaise 3. S plateaux 4. P armoires 5. P chapeau 6. S hommes 7. S dents 8. P bouteille

Chapter Two: Introduction to Verbs

Topics Covered

Basic Verbal Inflections in Latin and Greek

- The Three Persons
- Number (Singular and Plural)
- The Present System Active in Latin and Greek (Present, Imperfect, and Future Tenses)

Comparative Analysis of Italian, Spanish, and French

- Present Tense (All Persons) Compared to Latin and Greek
- Brief Comparison to Latin and Greek of Imperfect and Future Tenses

Vocabulary

- Verbs of Latin and Greek First and Second Conjugations
- Related Verbs of Modern Romance Languages

I. Person and Number

When grammarians use the word "person," they are often referring to that implicit quality in a verb which defines the subject's relation to the speaker. If you talk about yourself, you use the first person: "I see a train." You are both the sentence's subject and its speaker. If you say of another party in your presence, "You see a train," then the speaker is clearly no longer the subject of the sentence, but that subject is in the speaker's physical presence. The verb's subject is now second-person. Should the subject proceed to move to another room or out of earshot, you would amend your statement to, "He [or she] sees a train." This, of course, is a third-person statement.

All three of these persons have been employed in the singular number. They may be made plural by shifting from "I" to "we," from "you" to "you" (no shift at all, to be sure—but English would have observed a "thou/ye" distinction five hundred years ago), and from "he/she/it" to "they." A complete table of all three persons in both singular and plural, using the verb "see" as a paradigm for the present tense, would look like this:

	singular	plural
1st person	I see	we see
2nd person	you see	you see
3rd person	he, she, it sees	they see

You may find it quaintly unnecessary that the "see" is forced to take on a final "s" in the third-singular form in order to be perfectly grammatical. Indeed, this ending has failed to wear away over time as have others: the Germanic –st that once distinguished the second-singular form, for example (as in "thou seest"), is long gone. A hint is embedded in the archaic "seest," however, about the evolutionary path followed by verbs in many languages. Certainly in Latin and Greek, person could not simply be designated by dropping a pronoun in front of a changeless block of verbal meaning. *Every person was associated with a specific ending (or inflection) in Latin and Greek, and these endings were further articulated to express either a singular or a plural number.* "I see" in Latin would be *video*, whereas "we see" would be *videmus*. The different endings designate different persons and numbers.

In a way, this is equivalent to a verbal-block-of-meaning + pronoun. That is, you might think of *videmus* as "see we" turned into a single word. This explanation is somewhat misleading, for the classical Latin word for "we" is most definitely not *mus* (a suffix without any sense at all on its own). Yet the nominative pronoun for "we," *nos*, does possess a nasalized consonant (we have noted before how close "m" is to "n" linguistically) and an "s"; so in prehistory, the *–mus* inflection may indeed have conveyed "we" directly. In the same fashion, we can glimpse the pronoun for "I," *ego*, in the long "o" of *video*. It is not unlikely, therefore, that early Latin and Greek (for we shall see that all of this is fully true of Greek, as well) began quite as sensibly as English construction seems to us.

Before we go any farther, here are the essential person/number indicators at or near the end of all Latin finite verbs:

	singular	plural
1st person	*-o* ("I")	*-mus* ("we")
2nd person	*-s* ("you")	*-tis* ("you")
3rd person	*-t* ("he, she, it")	*-nt* ("they")

If you should wonder why the ancients had to make verbal meaning more difficult by fusing the "verbal block" with the pronoun, remember that these languages were spoken for centuries—perhaps millennia—before they were written. One cannot clearly perceive spaces between words when speaking or listening; or perhaps a better way of making this observation is that the very notion of "space between words" belongs to the textual universe. (A child of purely oral-traditional surroundings would understand that "John" and "James" are two different names, yet her favorite uncle is always, always "John-son-of-James.") Not surprisingly, then, entire sentences were written together as if they were a single word long after writing first made its appearance in the Greco-Roman world. Hence the fact that Latin and Greek verbs have latched onto some primitive remnant of a pronoun really tells us nothing more than that a convention eventually emerged which kept these elements together in written spelling.

Here's the long and the short of it: you must understand that verbal inflections in these ancient tongues have the full force of subject pronouns. This is proved by the typical absence of any more modern and recognized pronoun to accompany the verb. All by itself, *video* means "I see" in Latin. To write *ego video* would amount to stressing the first person heavily, as if to say, "I am the one who sees!" In the third person, of course, a noun will frequently define the subject further, but the particular ending for the third person must still be attached to the verb. You cannot grammatically compose a sentence on the order of *puella equum vid* ("The girl sees the horse"). The third-person singular inflection "t" must be affixed to the verb's vowel stem (producing *videt*, in this case). In effect, you say in Latin, "The girl she sees the horse."

From the exercises in the previous chapter, you may already have deduced that *videt* means "he, she, or it sees" and that *vident* (i.e., the same word with an "n" before the "t") means "they see" (all genders). This seems an appropriate time simply to offer the entire table of Latin verb inflections for the present tense:

	singular	plural
1st person	*video* ("I see")	*videmus* ("we see")
2nd person	*vides* ("you see")	*videtis* ("you see")
3rd person	*videt* ("he, she, it sees")	*vident* ("they see")

A little reflection may lead you to the insight that, since subject pronoun and verb are contained within a single word in Latin, some Latin sentences may indeed be a mere one word long. For this reason, verbs are the heart of Latin and Greek sentences. Even when confronted with quite lengthy sentences (especially then, really), you should locate the verb first and orient yourself to the rest of the sentence from its cues. If the verb is *videmus*, then any nominative noun will have to be plural. Say that the words *saxum* and *pueri* both precede the verb: either one could be a nominative. *Saxum* could also be accusative singular, and *pueri* could also be genitive singular. Only *pueri* could be nominative *plural*, however, so only that noun might correspond to the subject pronoun "we." *Saxum pueri videmus* may thus mean "we boys see a stone"—but be careful; it may also mean "we see the boy's stone"! Context would have to be the ultimate arbiter here.

As was mentioned in passing already, Latin verbs have vowel stems. The following stems exist: a long "a," a long "e," a short "e" (which is easily absorbed by or distorted into other vowels), and a long "i." These verbal groups are called **conjugations**, just as noun groups are called declensions. The table above conjugates *video* in the present tense, just as to give the different case endings of *femina* in order would be to decline that noun. We focused on the first two noun declensions in the previous chapter: in this one we shall undertake the first two verb conjugations. As you can tell, *video* adds inflections to an e-stem. It therefore belongs to the second conjugation.

This second group of verbs is not one of the larger ones, but it contains such common verbs as *teneo*, "I hold" (from which "contain" and a dozen other English verbs are derived, by the way), and *sedeo*, "I sit." All such words will and must have an "e" written before the inflection that indicates person and number. "They hold" is *tenent*. "Thou sittest" is *sedes*, an it please thee.

As luck would have it, the largest conjugation is the third, with its short "e" stem susceptible to many irksome transformations. The first conjugation, however (the "a" stems), claims almost as many verbs and is very nearly as orderly as the second. Below you find an a-stem verb declined beside an e-stem verb:

	singular	**plural**
1st person	amo / teneo	amamus / tenemus
2nd person	amas / tenes	amatis / tenetis
3rd person	amat / tenet	amant / tenent

Amo means "I like" or "I love." Other common first-conjugation verbs include *specto*, "I watch," and *voco*, "I call." You will immediately notice the single point where the first conjugation is just a bit tricky when compared to the second: the first-person singular form. Why does the a-stem disappear at that one place—why did the Romans not say *amao* and *spectao*? The truth is that they surely did, at one time. The long "a" is pronounced so closely to the position of the long "o" in the mouth, though, that the two must have fused early on. In every other respect, the first conjugation behaves precisely in the manner of the second.

Be very clear about the importance of observing conjugational boundaries. They cannot be crossed. Just as you cannot say *popula* instead of *populus* if a nation of people happens to consist mostly of women (the Amazons, perhaps), so you cannot write *amet* instead of *amat* or *vidat* instead of *videt*. (The word *amet* actually exists, but the change of vowels radically alters its meaning.)

Because vowel stems can occasionally be absorbed by other vowels, as in the case of *amo*, grammarians have established a convention of referring to verbs that avoids the unreliable first-person singular. They use what is called the infinitive: the form meaning "to see" or "to love" (termed "infinitive" because it is not limited, or "finite," by attachment to a particular person and number). In all regular verbs and almost all irregular ones, the infinitive is created simply by adding an –*re* to the verb's vowel stem. *Vide + re* yields *videre*, "to see." *Ama + re* gives us *amare*, or "to love." Most dictionaries will list the first-person singular form of a verb and then follow this with the infinitive so as to make the vowel stem and conjugation absolutely clear.

A word about pronunciation: all of the forms above receive the spoken accent on their penultimate (next-to-last) syllable except the second-conjugation first-person singulars (*video*, *teneo*, etc.). These examples reflect a rule that applies to Latin words generally. Unless the next-to-last syllable is short (and the long "e" becomes short through contact with the "o" in such forms as *video*) and is not followed by a consonant cluster, that syllable receives the stress. The noun *populus* is stressed on the first syllable (*POP-u-lus*) because the middle "u" is short and is followed by a single consonantal sound. On the other hand, *magister* is pronounced *ma-GIS-ter* because the next-to-last syllable is lengthened by the "s" and the "t."

Summary
When spelled out, finite Latin verbs have a root meaning, a vowel stem (sometimes absorbed into subsequent elements of the ending), and a suffix (inflection) that always indicates the subject's person and number. The single word that results may compose an entire clause when translated into English, since the inflection's indicated person and number always imply an English pronoun. If no nominative noun accompanies the verb in a given sentence, then this implied pronoun becomes the "default" subject in translation.

Vocabulary

Latin—1st Conjugation		
	meaning	English derivative
ambulo, ambulare	walk	ambulatory
amo, amare	like, love	amiable
do, dare	give, bestow	data
monstro, monstrare	show, point out	demonstrate
narro, narrare	tell, narrate	narrative
navigo, navigare	sail	navigate
porto, portare	carry	portable
pugno, pugnare	fight	pugnacity
specto, spectare	watch, observe	spectator
sto, stare	stand, be still	stationary
tempto, temptare	try, attempt	attempt
voco, vocare	call, summon	vocation

Latin—2nd Conjugation*		
	meaning	English derivative
debeo, debêre	ought (to), should; owe	debt
habeo, habêre	have, possess	habit
maneo, manêre	stay, remain	remain
moneo, monêre	warn	admonish
moveo, movêre	put in motion	move
sedeo, sedêre	sit	sedentary
teneo, tenêre	hold, restrain	retain
terreo, terrêre	frighten	terrify
timeo, timêre	fear, be afraid of	timid

*Second-conjugation infinitives on this and subsequent vocabulary lists are written with the -êre suffix (circumflex over the "e") to distinguish them very clearly from third-conjugation verbs; see Chapter Four.

A. Translate the following Latin verbs into English. Remember that each of these single words will yield at least a pronoun and one verbal form in English. They may also be translated with three words rather than two if you use the present tense of "to be" and a present participle: Latin draws no distinction between "I walk" and "I am walking."

1. amatis	3. terres	5. dat	7. movemus
2. habent	4. stamus	6. monstro	8. monet

B. Translate into Latin. Every answer will be a single word this time.

1. they remain	3. we are calling	5. you (pl.) fear, are afraid
2. you (sing.) stand	4. she is walking	6. we hold

C. Translate the following sentences into English. Remember that the subject indicated by the verb's ending and the noun in the nominative (if there is one) must be made one and the same: e.g., *Nautae insulas videmus* must be translated, "We sailors see the islands." Use the Latin word list from the previous chapter's end to find any unfamiliar vocabulary.

1. Filiae reginae dona amant.
2. Filii agricolae domi ("at home") manere temptamus.
3. Timent aquam pueri sed ("but") navigare amant viri.
4. Poeta copiam verborum habes.
5. Amicus reginae sedeo sed ("but") nautae stare debetis.

Query: Disregarding word order, what line of reasoning led you to decide upon the nouns that you chose as subjects of sentences 1 and 2 (both of which have more than one possible nominative)?

D. Translate the following sentences into Latin.
1. The god of the winds ought to warn the people.
2. As an uncle of twenty (viginti: not declinable) boys, I give piles of gold and (*et*) silver.

Solo Flight: Now that you know a little about verbs, you can correct from both directions a sentence whose subject and verb disagree. (For instance, in English, "He see the dog," might be changed either to, "He sees the dog," or, "They see the dog," without altering the third-person subject.) Each of the sentences below has an error in subject-verb agreement or some other fatal flaw that reduces it to nonsense. Rewrite each sentence in at least two ways that are coherent. Translate all of your changes.
1. Amici puerorum equos habet.
2. Nauta insulas amamus.
3. Filia reginae (gen.) Drusillam vocant.

II. Greek Verbal Inflections for Person and Number

The close similarity between Greek and Latin noun declensions is replicated as we focus on Greek conjugations. In fact, the Greek first-person hardly differs from its Latin counterpart, with the singular form ("I") ending in a long "o" and the plural ("we") in a syllable containing mu ("m") in the middle of things. The second-person singular has a final sigma ("s"), just like Latin, and the plural displays a central tau ("t"). At one time, the third-person singular ("he/she/it") ended in –τι and the plural ("they") finished in –ντι. (These very endings survived in Sanskrit, by the way—a distant cousin to Latin and Greek.) In the former case, the tau simply dropped out, leaving the two vowels beside it to merge; in the latter case, the –*nt* sound that we know from Latin eventually blended with the preceding vowel to lengthen that vowel and leave sigma as the only consonant. A complicated evolution! The connections with Latin, therefore, are not exactly transparent everywhere, but they certainly exist and would have been obvious in the very early history of Greek.

Below is a table that juxtaposes the Latin verbal inflections of Section 2.1 with corresponding Greek inflections and then, in the final column, the elements shared between the two:

Latin	Greek	Shared Elements
-o	-ω	-ω
-s	-εις	-ς
-t	- ει (once -τι)	(-τ)
-mus	-ομεν	-μ...
-tis	-ετε	-τ...
-nt	-ουσι (once -ντι)	(-ντ...)

Now let's look at a regular Greek verb featuring these inflections. We will use the word λυω, "I release," as a paradigm here and elsewhere.

	singular	plural
1st person	λυω (I release)	λυομεν (we release)
2nd person	λυεις (you release)	λυετε (you release)
3rd person	λυει (he/she/it releases)	λυουσι (they release)

It may be tempting to view Greek verbs as having an epsilon, or short "e," as a stem (-ε). If we removed the epsilon from the inflections running down the middle column of the comparative table (preceding the one just above), then we are left with endings even more like those in Latin. (The weak "e" could have been readily absorbed into an omega in the first-person singular and distorted into another vowel sound by nasalized consonants in the first- and third-person plural.) Yet the historical evidence for treating epsilon here as a transitional element from the root word to the actual ending is very sketchy. You should learn it, therefore, as part of the complete ending. Greek does not have several conjugations, so there is no advantage to viewing this intermediate epsilon as apt to change from one set of verbs to another. Only one set exists!

Now, a small number of Greek verbs retains the more primitive endings from which these evolved (e.g., διδωμι, "I give," and τιθημι, "I put"); and a much larger set of verbs does not have any active forms, and thus cannot be conjugated like λυω above. It would be wrong for you to take away the impression that Greek verbs are incredibly simple when compared to Latin ones, only to be shocked if you should pursue your Greek studies later. For the purposes of this book, however, we may indeed keep matters simple. All Greek verbs presented here will be treated as adding on the inflections given above to whatever form remains after the omega is removed from the first-person singular. Take the two verbs τευχω and ποιεω, both meaning "do" or "make." (The former seems to have been somewhat broader of scale, as in making a ship, while the latter was more often used of handicraft: both can mean "cause.") We shall write "he/she makes" as τευχει and ποιεει, even though the latter would only be found in very early authors like Homer. In later authors, the two short epsilons would fuse to form something like ποιηι (with the final iota usually all but disappearing as a subscript under the eta). This can get confusing—and such transformations are not rare as Greek evolves.

In fact, now is a good time to observe one of the major differences between Latin and Greek. Latin and its descendants have a distinct tendency to arrange sounds in chains of vowel + consonant + vowel + consonant. The decay of this tendency is most advanced in French, again thanks to the influence of German, no doubt (which frequently puts several consonants side by side); yet even in southern France, one notices a more or less Italian rhythm of alternation between consonant and vowel. In Greek, on the other hand, a tendency of several vowel sounds to come one after another may strike our ear as akin to the rhythm of many Eastern languages. The Greek language is not averse to vowel clusters, just as German and Russian do not shy away from consonant clusters. Greek therefore seems to have fragmented into far more dialects—and that within a relatively narrow geographical range—than Latin, since placing one vowel beside another is just asking for evolutionary change. (In different parts of the United States, for instance, the name "Wyatt" is very likely to come out sounding like "white," "watt," or even "wait.") The Greek of Homer reflects fewer of these changes than later Greek, naturally, so we shall stick with the Homeric precedent in spelling as well as in grammar. The earlier forms are the clearer forms.

The standard Greek infinitive ends in –ειν. "To release" would be λυειν, and "to make" would be τευχειν. We shall write the infinitive of the other word for "make" as ποιεειν (pronounced *po-YEH-ane*, with a glottal stop between the second and third syllables).

Since Greek verbs do not have various conjugations, we give only the first-person singular form in the vocabulary. Remember that you need only remove the omega from this form to build the verb with the specific ending that you require.

Vocabulary

Greek	pronunciation	definition	English derivative
’αγω	AH-goe	I lead, drive	agent
’ακουω	ah-KOO-oe	I hear, listen to	acoustic
βαλλω	BAHL-loe	I throw, cast	ball
δοκεω	doh-KEH-oe	I suppose, imagine	dogma
’εχω	EH-hkhoe	I hold, have; have ability(hence "am able")	-----
κρατεω	krah-TEH-oe	I rule, hold power	democratic
κρινω	KREE-noe	I judge	critic
λαμβανω	lahm-BAH-noe	I take, seize	syllabus
λυω	LEW-oe	I release, loosen	analysis
‘οραω	hoh-RAH-oe	I see	-----
πεμπω	PEM-poe	I send, escort	pomp
ποιεω	poh-YEH-oe	I make, fashion	poetic

πρασσω	PRAHSS-soe	I do, act, perform	practical
῾ρεω	HREH-oe	I run, flow	rheum
σκοπεω	skoh-PEH-oe	I watch, look at	scope
ταρβεω	tar-BEH-oe	I fear, dread	-----
τασσω	TOSS-oe	I arrange, organize	taxidermist
τευχω	TEUW-hkhoe	I make, cause; happen	technique
φιλεω	fi-LEH-oe	I like, love	philanthropy
φοβεω	foh-BEH-oe	I frighten	phobic
φυω	FEW-oe	I produce, bring forth	physics
φωνεω	foe-NEH-oe	I speak, give voice	phonics

Note that the small mark before ῾οραω is turned in the opposite direction of an apostrophe. This means that we must precede the vowel with breathing (an "h," in other words). Also note that the same mark precedes the rho of ῾ρεω. In fact, an initial rho always has breathing: the Greeks accurately perceived that they always inserted an "h" before this consonant when it began a word. (The standard American "r," pronounced with a much flatter tongue, has less noticeable aspiration.)

The "eu" sound in the middle of τευχω is also something new in our vocabulary lists. It should not be pronounced like our English word "you." In fact, no English word uses this exact diphthong—but it is not particularly hard to produce. Say the "e" in "get" and then rush it into the long "u" sound in "pool,'" and you will obtain the desired result.

In the word πρασσω, we have yet another option for saying "do" or "make." This verb, τευχω, and ποιεω are more or less interchangeable, but πρασσω seems to have been the most general of the three. Classical philosophers referred to ethics as "practical" knowledge because it deals with what people do (or ought to do).

You may have guessed that our adjective "physical" is related to the verb φυω—but you may find it easier to account for the word's meaning by learning a noun of this family, φυσις: "nature." The natural or physical world is thus identified in Greek with that which produces offspring (as opposed to that which has existed eternally—the spiritual).

Notice that the penultimate syllable of these verbs receives spoken stress whether or not it is long. Many other Greek words were not so predictable; and, indeed, this "rule" applies only to the singular forms of present-tense verbs. In the plural, the third-from-last syllable is stressed (e.g., λυομεν is pronounced LŒ-ah-men). The kind of stress placed on Greek words could be quite volatile, shifting sometimes according to their position in a sentence. Even under the simplest of conditions, Greek pronunciation was not as straightforward as Latin—or does not seem as much so to us. Certain Greek names like "Odysseus," for example, which have passed beyond familiarity to fame in our culture and which we therefore suppose ourselves to have mastered, were actually spoken in their native land with the stress on the *last* syllable! The accentuation of spoken Greek is thus another aspect of the language which seems rather alien to us as speakers of modern English.

Summary

Greek verbal inflections bear several obvious similarities to their Latin cousins. Yet Greek verbs are also susceptible to numerous peculiar mutations, due mostly to the frequency of adjoining vowels that fused as time passed. The forms used in this text are the minimally contracted Homeric ones. A compensating simplicity also exists in the Greek verbal system: despite odd morphs and lingering archaisms, there is only one true conjugation.

Exercise Set 2.2

A. Translate the following Greek verbs into English. As with Latin, each of these single words will yield at least a pronoun and one verbal form in English, and may also be translated with three words by using the present tense of "to be" and a present participle.

1. σκοπεουσι	3. πεμπει	5. βαλλω	7. 'εχετε
2. 'ακουετε	4. λαμβανουσι	6. κρινεις	8. φοβεομεν

B. Translate into Greek. Every answer will be a single word this time.

1. it flows	3. they act	5. she watches
2. we are ruling	4. you (pl.) are speaking	6. you (sing.) see

C. Translate the following sentences into English. As with the earlier Latin sentences in this chapter, you will find any unfamiliar vocabulary in the word list near Chapter One's end.

1. 'Εταιραι τεκνα 'Ερμιωνης (a woman's name) φιλεομεν.
2. Φοβος πολεμου δημον λαμβανει.
3. Ποταμοι 'ρεουσι και ("and") ποντον φυουσι.
4. 'Ανεμους χρονου 'ακουω, 'αλλα ("but") 'ανθροποι 'υπνον ληθης φιλεετε.

D. Translate the following sentences into Greek.

1. A man's soul rules over (use gen. rather than acc. with this verb) life and (και) death.
2. The gods of the universe make earth and (και) seas.
3. You generals are not ('ου) arranging the course (=path) of the war.

Solo Flight: Translate.

1. φοβεετε	3. τευχεις	5. λαμβανομεν	7. σκοπεω
2. κρινομεν	4. 'αγει	6. βαλλουσι	8. 'εχεις

III. Correspondences with the Romance Languages

The primary purpose of this book is to ground you in language study by focusing on classical Greek and Latin, so our discussion will dwell less on modern languages like French and Spanish. At this point, however, a stress of the similarities between the verbal inflections in modern romance tongues and those in Greek and Latin seems appropriate.

You may pass over this section if you are particularly intent upon the ancients: no new concepts will be introduced here. Yet when picking up a windfall of convenient information involves so little stooping over, why not gather what is in our path?

Everybody in our culture knows the word *rendezvous*, though not everybody can spell it; and most of us have heard the Spanish exhortation *vamos!* We are now in a position to understand where such words and phrases come from. The three romance languages which we have been tracking to some degree—Italian, Spanish, and French—all employ verbal inflections corresponding to the Latin ones given above. That is, in the present and other tenses, they designate the subject's person and number by a suffix added to the basic verb. Italian and Spanish are actually quite close to Latin. French, as we have come to expect, has evolved a little farther away from the ancient paradigm. In fact, although the French use *mandatory* verbal inflections, they alone of these three romance cultures also require a distinct subject pronoun. Thus French is like German and English in needing two separate words to say "I see"—a pronoun and a verb. This is just as well, because even though French verbs reinforce the subject by having a precise ending to designate it, *four of the six endings are pronounced the same!* (The French language offers several circumstances where consonants are to remain unpronounced.)

Recall the Latin inflections from above: *-o, -s, -t, -mus, -tis, -nt* ("I,' "you," "he/she/it," "we," "you," "they"). Observe how narrowly each of the romance languages sticks to the pattern:

Italian

	singular	plural
1st person	*amo* ("I love")	*amiamo* ("we love")
2nd person	*ami* ("you love")	*amate* ("you love")
3rd person	*ama* ("he, she, it loves")	*amano* ("they love")

Spanish

	singular	plural
1st person	*amo* ("I love")	*amamos* ("we love")
2nd person	*amas* ("you love")	*amaís* ("you love")*
3rd person	*ama* ("he, she, it loves")	*aman* ("they love")

* Limited mostly to Castellano today; demotic New World Spanish uses *ustedes* + third person for this form.

French

	singular	plural
1st person	*j'aime* ("I love")	*nous aimons* ("we love")
2nd person	*tu aimes* ("you love")	*vous aimez* ("you love")
3rd person	*il/elle aime* ("he/it, she loves")	*ils/elles aiment* ("they love")

In Italian and Spanish, at least, you can readily see the Latin/Greek long "o" in the first-person singular. Italian tends to discard any final "s," so the second-person singular and first-person plural of Spanish actually bear the closer resemblance to Latin. None of the three modern languages preserves an audible final "t" sound in any third-person form, either. (French has a "t" in the plural, but it isn't pronounced—and neither is the "n" preceding it.) The final "s" of *-tis* has dropped off the second-person plural form in Italian, while Spanish has preferred to discard the "t." (In the days of Cervantes, "you [pl.] love" would have been written *amadis*: the accented "i" tips us off that a consonant has been absorbed.) In medieval French, the same word would have resembled *aimats* (depending on the dialect). When the orthographical dust eventually settled, the *–ts* had turned into a "z" sound, naturally enough (which is also not pronounced, once again, in modern French).

We may say generally, then, that the "s" and "t" in various terminal positions have tended to erode as Latin has grown into the modern romance languages. This is by no means an unusual linguistic process. The former English word "relict" (drawn directly from Latin, where it means "something left") has long come to be spelled "relic"; and newscasters and politicians can often be trapped streamlining the word "district" in the coined verb "redistricting." It tends to come out "redistricking"!

Summary

Italian and Spanish add verbal inflections to indicate the subject's person and number that are spelled very similarly to the Latin prototypes. French inflections exist, as well, and must be spelled properly; but they are less close to Latin, are often not elocuted sufficiently to create audible distinctions corresponding to their differences in spelling, and must be accompanied by actual subject pronouns (as in English).

Exercise Set 2.3

A. Try your hand at translating these verbs into English. You are given the language of origin parenthetically only for the first half of the questions.

parlare—to speak (Italian   *hablar*—to speak (Spanish)   *parler*—to speak (French)

1. parliamo (It.)	4. tu parles (Fr.)	7. hablaís	10. hablamos
2. hablan (Sp.)	5. parlano (It.)	8. elles parlent	11. parlo
3. je parle (Fr.)	6. hablo (Sp.)	9. parli	12. nous parlons

B. Now try going from English into the romance language specified in parentheses. Remember that in French, a pronoun must be employed along with the verb (*je, tu, il/elle, nous, vous, ils/elles*: the *il/ils* is masculine or neuter in the third person and the *elle/elles* is strictly feminine).

First let us add one more verb to the two which have been introduced in the last couple of pages. (Not all verbs, by a long shot, have parallel forms in all three of these languages.)

cantare—to sing (Italian   *cantar*—to sing (Spanish)   *chanter*—to sing (French)

1. they sing (It.)	4. he speaks (Fr.)	7. she speaks (It.)	10. we are singing (Sp.)
2. you (s.) love (Sp.)	5. I love (It.)	8. you (pl.) love (Fr.)	11. I am speaking (It.)
3. we sing (Fr.)	6. you (pl.) sing (Sp.)	9. you (s.) sing (It.)	12. she is loving (Fr.)

Solo Flight: Be creative. Do exercise B above for the two languages not in parentheses, switch singulars to plurals and vice versa, translate the verbs in A into another of the three modern tongues, and so forth.

IV. The Future Tense: Latin

As Latin indicates the person and number of a verb by tacking on an inflection, so it can indicate several of the essential tenses through a syllable following the root word. The easiest of these add-ons to learn is the future inflection. Imagine, once again, that English had historically chosen to weld the subject pronoun together with the basic verb. "We call" might look something like "call-we," or even (once we had gotten used to the idea) "callwe." Why might not the future tense be expressed through the same technique? That is, using some few letters as the future indicator, we might insert these into the single word "callwe"—probably before the "we," since our linguistic tribe would have been conditioned to determine a verb's person and number by looking at the final suffix. Strictly speaking, the correct future of "call" in the first-person plural in English should employ the helping verb "shall": "we shall call." ("Will" is supposed to be used for the other two persons, though one must admit that the distinction is obsolete today.) We might therefore borrow the "sh" from "shall" and concoct the new word, "call + sh + we," or "callshwe." The pronunciation of such a word would cause several problems, and its form would no doubt decay quickly into an abbreviated version for that reason; but by using this technique, we should have done substantially what Latin does.

The explanation above is a bit flippant, to be sure, in that it invites us to believe that the ancient Romans had conceived of their language as separate words and then forged long single words of these. The historical process went in reverse. We cannot picture language in any other fashion than as individual units because we learn it through literate means—through writing. Yet recall that Latin and Greek, unlike English, both had a very lengthy prehistory when nothing was written down. If your culture possessed no documents or "letter-learning" at all, then "call shall we" might be viewed as three distinct words or as one distinct word with equal validity. The ear would hear the same thing, in either case. It so happens that, when Latin writing was finally broken into words, the verb came to include both tense and person/number indicators as suffixes. (As has been remarked already, this separation into words did not show up in written documents for several centuries: early manuscripts represented whole sentences as one block of letters without spaces.) The Roman system, then, is not really so very different from ours. We designate our indicators as pronouns and auxiliary verbs, while the Romans made suffixes out of their indicators and produced one big word. The distinction scarcely amounts to more than that.

For the first and second conjugations, at least, the future-tense indicator consists of the brief insertion –bi. (In the third and fourth conjugations, some erosion has taken place and the "b" no longer appears.) If we simply add the person/number inflections to this two-letter "marker," we can transform any first- or second-conjugation verb's present tense into the future tense, as follows:

(hypothetical—NOT historical)

voca + bi + o = vocabio	I shall call
voca + bi + s = vocabis	you (s.) will call
voca + bi + t = vocabit	he/she/it will call
voca + bi + mus = vocabimus	we shall call
voca + bi + tis = vocabitis	you (pl.) will call
voca + bi + nt = vocabint	they will call

Could it really be this easy? Alas, no—not quite. There are two complications, both involving points where the short "i" of –bi has interacted with ensuing sounds. The long "o" of the first-person singular has more or less swallowed the "i" by the time Latin comes to be recorded in writing, so that the correct form here must be learned as *vocabo*. Then, in a slightly different process, the third-person plural form has drawn the short "i" slightly forward in the mouth so that it resembles the "œ" (as in the French word for "sister," *sœur*). Historical Latin therefore shifted the spelling of this form to *vocabunt*. We have seen that the Greek upsilon—which should be identified with the Roman letter "u" in most cases—was pronounced in the same way. The change in spelling, then, actually reflects rather less of a change in pronunciation than modern English-speakers are likely to realize.

In the matter of pronunciation, furthermore, we might as well note that the first- and second-person plural forms are accented on the *third-to-last* syllable. Remember the rule: stress the penultimate syllable unless it is short and followed by no cluster of vowels. If either of these latter two conditions applies, shift the stress to the previous syllable. Since the "i" in –bi is short, it cannot bear the stress as a next-to-last syllable.

Here, then, is a slightly revised table of the future tense:

72

	singular	plural
1st person	-bo / vocabo	-bimus / vocabimus
2nd person	-bis / vocabis	-bitis / vocabitis
3rd person	-bit / vocabit	-bunt / vocabunt

For second-declension "e" stem verbs, the rules are entirely identical, even regarding pronunciation. The only difference is that the vowel stem now changes from "a" to "e":

	singular	plural
1st person	-bo / monebo	-bimus / monebimus
2nd person	-bis / monebis	-bitis / monebitis
3rd person	-bit / monebit	-bunt / monebunt

Though the vowel stem is only one letter, be sure to get it right. No such word as *monabit* exists: you must write *monebit*. Likewise, never write *amebimus* for *amabimus*.

Another brief word about translating: the future tense in English is relatively inflexible, being rendered typically by pronoun + shall/will + verb. However, one may say "she will be watching" as well as "she will watch." Latin very rarely draws this distinction. If a Roman used the future of "to be" followed by the present participle (our -ing word) as the former English option above does, a very heavy emphasis would settle upon the subject's watching, as if her gaze were uncommonly steady and intense. Such emphasis was almost never felt to be necessary. For our purposes, *spectabit* translates both phrases.

Summary
The future tense for the first two Latin conjugations is formed essentially by inserting –bi before the person/number inflection at the verb's end. However, the "i" is absorbed by the first-person singular "o" and mutates into "u" in the third-person plural form. An English translation may handle Latin's future forms by employing either a "you will see" or a "you will be seeing" template.

Exercise Set 2.4

A. Translate the following Latin verbs into English. Most are in the future tense, but several in the present tense (along with a couple of infinitives) have mixed in.

1. habebit
2. stabimus
3. times
4. portabunt
5. spectabitis
6. debebis
7. tempto
8. dare
9. manetis
10. pugnabo
11. videbunt
12. terrere

B. Translate into Latin.

1. they will sit
2. you (sing.) will give
3. I will show
4. we are holding
5. you (pl.) will walk
6. they will be afraid
7. we will narrate
8. she will be standing
9. to warn

C. Translate the following sentences into English. Remember that the subject indicated by the verb's ending and the noun in the nominative (if there is one) must be made one and the same: e.g., *Nautae insulas videmus* must be translated, "We sailors see the islands." Use the Latin word list from the previous chapter's end to find any unfamiliar vocabulary.

1. Equi puerorum puellas portabunt.
2. Bracchia viri ursam non ("not") tenebunt.
3. Venti folia movebunt sed ("but") ficus stabit.
4. Fabulam narrare temptabimus si ("if") amici reginae manebitis.
5. Puer linguam tenere debebis. (Try making "as" the first word of your translation.)
6. Oculi feminae iram monstrant sed ("but") lingua "auxilium dabo" narrat. (Use "says" for last verb.)

Query: Disregarding word order, what would indicate that only one of the two possible nominatives beginning sentences 2 and 3 can truly be the subject?

D. Translate the following sentences into Latin.
1. You (s.) will be obliged to watch the queen's gifts.
2. You sailors will not (*non*) see an abundance of victories.
3. As a (his) son, I will not look at Marcus's flaws.

Solo Flight: Return to Exercise Set 2.1 A above and shift the tense of every verb from present to future.

V. The Future Tense: Greek

In a way, the formation of the Greek future tense is supremely simple. Latin requires the insertion of a *–bi* before the person/number inflections: Greek merely requires the insertion of an "s" sound, or sigma. This strategy appears to be a prehistoric Indo-European one, for we also find it in Sanskrit. (For instance, *Kim bhavisyati?* means, "What will happen?" thanks to the "s" in the middle.) The word λυω means "I release"; to make "I will release," add sigma and create λυσω. The procedure works for each of the other five forms, as well.

	singular	**plural**
1st person	λυ + ς-+ ω = λυσω (I will loose)	λυ + ς-+ ομεν = λυσομεν (we will loose)
2nd person	λυ + ς-+ εις = λυσεις (you will loose)	λυ + ς-+ ετε = λυσετε (you will loose)
3rd person	λυ + ς-+ ει = λυσει (he/she/it will loose)	λυ + ς-+ ουσι = λυσουσι (they will loose)

For a few verbs, this delightfully easy formula works as shown above. For instance, φυω becomes φυσω in the manner modeled above. A great many snags start to occur, though, when the sound preceding the verb's person/number inflection is a consonant. In such cases, the sigma will often combine with this consonant to produce a new spelling. The resulting sound still amounts to no more than the introduction of an "s"—but the change in spelling, at least for beginners, can be a bit confusing. A verb whose stem ends in β, π, or φ, for example, will replace this letter with ψ (which in effect merges the original consonant with an "s" sound). A verb whose stem ends in γ, κ, or χ will replace the original consonant with ξ (the equivalent of "ks"). Since there is a certain regularity to such changes, you should be able to predict after a short while that πεμπω will become πεμψω, 'εχω will become 'εξω, and so forth.

Unfortunately, possible complications do not end there. We may generalize that verbs whose stem ends in τ, δ, or θ simply drop that letter and add the sigma, which historically appears to have won out in a struggle to be pronounced that didn't end in happy collaboration. Thus the verb πειθω, "I persuade," forms its future as πεισω. (You may have noticed that when languages with a "ts" consonant cluster wander into English, the "t" tends to disappear: cf. the German name "Franz," which is supposed to be pronounced "Frants" but which usually emerges with a simple "nz" at the end in English even when our countrymen are patiently corrected.)

Furthermore, verbs whose stem ends in a short vowel, like ποιεω and φωνεω, regularly lengthen that vowel under the influence of the future's added sigma (ποιησω and φωνησω). As our brief word list already suggests, such verbs are abundant in Greek, so *you should be especially aware of this alternative formation of the future tense.*

Then there are words ending in liquid or nasal consonants ("l" sounds and "m/n" sounds). Take βαλλω, which originally did as it was supposed to do, tacking on a short vowel so that it might flow smoothly into the sigma: βαλλεσω. Yet this form continued evolving until the added vowel was all that remained of the future indicator: βαλεω. This time the sigma lost the struggle for the tongue's attention!

Yet further permutations are found, and no productive end would be served by examining them all in this introductory setting. For our purposes, you should simply remember that an "s" sound (which will not necessarily be represented by the letter sigma in spelling) is the future tense's marker in Greek. If you should pursue your studies, you will eventually be able to spot all of the future's evolved forms in major verbs. You should also know that dictionaries typically list the future form immediately after the present, precisely because this transformation can be a little surprising.

If you have not already noticed, another significant difference between Greek and Latin is that the former has fewer, generally simpler rules of grammar than the latter—but it also has far more exceptions to those rules. Six of one, half-dozen of the other.

Summary
The future tense in Greek is basically formed by inserting an "s" sound between stem and person/number endings. Yet when spelled out, this sound may be represented by consonants other than sigma if some degree of consonantal merging takes place, and still further mutations are not uncommon. Remember as well that epsilon stems (very common in Greek verbs) lengthen to eta before adding the sigma ($\varepsilon > \eta + \sigma$).

Exercise Set 2.5

A. Translate the following Greek verbs into English. Most are future tense, but not quite all.

1. φιλησω	3. φοβησετε	5. βαλλουσι	7. ʽεξομεν*
2. πεμψεις	4. τευξει	6. κρατησεις	8. φυσετε

*The verb ʼεχω is practically unique in that its initial vowel has breathing (i.e., is said with an "h" sound) in the future tense but not in the present. This may have been a subconscious adjustment to the removal of breathing involved in changing chi to xi.

B. Translate into Greek. The future verbs will be a challenge—but stick to the tips given in the discussion above.

1. I will watch	3. she will lead	5. we will seize
2. they will judge	4. you (pl.) will speak	6. you (s.) will hear

C. Translate the following sentences into English. As with the earlier Latin sentences in this chapter, you will find any unfamiliar vocabulary in the word list near Chapter One's end.
1. Ποιηται μυθους φιλοσοφιης φωνησουσι.
2. Τεκνον θεου βιον ʼεργων ʼαξει.
3. Θεοι Μενελαον (a hero's name) κατα ("along, down through") ποταμον θανατου πεμψομεν.
4. ʽΙππους ʼανθρωπων ʽεξω ʼαλλα ("but") τεκνα λυσω.

D. Translate the following sentences into Latin.
1. Sleep will release memories and (και) build (=make) a road of forgetfulness.
2. You boys fear to observe the causes of the universe.

Solo Flight: Return to Exercise Set 2.5 A above and shift the tense of every verb from future to present. You should have only seven when you finish, because one is already present!

VI. The Imperfect Tense and the Progressive Aspect: Latin

The formation of the imperfect tense is even more regular than that of the future in Latin; and in Greek (if we may anticipate the next section), the imperfect is subject to none of the future's dizzying consonantal mutations. Yet this is one of the more difficult tenses for students to grasp. The reason has to do, not with structural formation, but with *meaning*.

Let us start with the tense's very name. You should rid yourself, immediately and permanently, of the notion that "perfect" has anything to do with excellence and "imperfect" anything to do with flaws in discussions of grammar. The Latin *perfectum* simply means "finished, completed"—and *imperfectum*, of course, negates this word: "not finished, incomplete." We will study the perfect tense later. For now, embrace thoroughly the idea that imperfect verbal action has something incomplete about it. Such action might have been interrupted. Its agent might have desisted after a long try or several tries—"tried to" is actually a common phrase used in translating imperfect verbs. The action might indeed have been completed but have needed repetition on another occasion, and another; that is, it might be routine or habitual. The Latin form *vocabam*, "I was calling," could be employed to translate all of the English verbal expressions below—not just their "call/calling" portion, but the entire main verb and pronoun:

> *I was calling* her when you tapped my shoulder.
> *I was trying to call* her when my drink choked me.
> *I used to call* her name first of all when, as children, we would run onto the playground.
> *I would call* her name whenever we would pass on the sidewalk.
> *I kept calling* her, but she gave no sign of having heard me.

In each of these sentences, a drawing out of the action is clearly expressed. The calling is never finished; or, if finished, it must be begun all over again.

Now, in proper grammatical terms, this "drawing out" effect is ascribed to what is called the verb's **aspect**, not its tense. Any tense may convey action in time that either crawls along without reaching the finish line or is treated as a tidy, completed unit. The term for the latter is our already introduced Latin derivative, *perfect*. The exclamation, "I see him," is perfect in aspect though present in tense because it emphasizes the instantaneous act of visual discovery (as if the speaker had been looking high and low for someone without spotting him until just now). We could transform this present-tense action into an imperfect—or, to use the more common term, a *progressive*—event by writing, "I am seeing him." Now the speaker appears to emphasize that the watched person is being steadily tracked throughout a sequence of motions, as if he were being tailed. Same tense... different aspect.

The Romans were not unaware of aspect. In fact, they considered all three tenses in the so-called present system (present, imperfect, and future) to be eligible for an imperfect—or progressive—interpretation in aspect. The reasoning of the Roman mind seems to have been that present action obviously lends itself to an "ongoing" perspective since it happens at this moment (a moment swelling steadily like a bubble until something breaks it off), and that future action also unfolds progressively because it has yet to "grow into" a current event and "reach completion" in the present. Such assumptions might readily be challenged, of course: to say, "She will wake up at noon," is rather different from saying, "She will be waking up at noon." (In the latter case, you'd probably be well advised to give her another ten minutes.) While the Romans were aware of aspect, then, we cannot claim that they awarded it as much importance as we do.

76

We now have a revised, grammatically more technical definition the Latin imperfect tense: it is the "simple past" tense (i.e., not distantly past or soon-to-be past: just a straight, unqualified past) when distinctly progressive in aspect. In the same way, we'll find later that the perfect tense is the simple past tense when perfect in aspect. In their use of the word *perfectum*, once again, the Romans extended the "over-and-done" quality to an entire system, or range of tenses, as well as to a single tense. The "perfect system" is considered to include the perfect tense itself, the pluperfect, and the future perfect. We will address all of those later.

One point of confusion, however, might as well be handled right now: the murkiness that we encounter in English over the tense/aspect distinction. If you were to say, "I saw her at the meeting," you might mean that you spotted her once as people were taking their seats. You might also mean that you saw her repeatedly within the meeting's hour of duration and can vouch that she stayed to the end. In Latin, *videbam* would plainly convey that you saw her and kept seeing her—not that you watched her steadily (for which we would use a verb like *spectabam*), but that you spotted her on more than one occasion within a certain window of time. To convey that you had seen her just the once as people were entering the meeting room, you would use the perfect form *vidi* (which will not concern us just yet).

So in this case, Latin would be less ambiguous than English. Our past tense can oversimplify events, lumping the two aspects together and leaving the listener to infer the proper aspect from context. "It rained for ten days," "It rained on the car," and, "It rained heavily in 1917," all employ a simple past tense. Latin and its heirs would express the ten-day weather event with the equivalent of "it was raining." The second and third cases would probably call for the perfect tense, the former because the car's getting soaked is viewed as one coherent and complete occurrence, the latter because 1917—even though it was an entire year—now lies in the distant past and can be treated as one "frame" in history's great film.

A second pitfall looms, then, to whose dangers you should also be alert: the imperfect/perfect option in choice of tense is not determined by the event's objective length, but by how the speaker regards it. A war might go on for years, yet a speaker might say, "I fought in the war," as simply as that, using the perfect tense to indicate the experience's completion. On the other hand, an event that lasted a mere five minutes might be drawn out with the imperfect if the narrator's further actions and observations should interrupt its completion or emphasize that those minutes seemed to drag on. Consider the sentence, "After I struck my head, I sat on the floor for five minutes before I heard knocking at the door." The verb "I sat" could be rendered *sedebam* in Latin ("I was sitting, I kept sitting") if the narrator wished to emphasize the degree of pain and disorientation experienced. The knocking on the door would then be understood as having interrupted an ongoing spell that might have dragged along many minutes more (and the word "when" would probably be used in Latin instead of "before"). A case could be made simply for using the perfect, however: blow to the head, period of semi-consciousness, knock on the door—three events following in "a, b, c" fashion. This style of narration would be less dramatic, since it would treat the period of sitting as a single complete event. Yet the event would be the same in both instances: the difference would reside in how the narrator viewed that event (or wants us to view it).

The "ongoing" or "drawn out" effect is implied in all three tenses presented by this chapter: i.e., we are covering the present system. You have noticed that *vocant* can mean either "they call" or "they are calling." It might also be translated, "they keep calling" or "they habitually call" (though Latin would probably devote further words to clarifying such an intent). Likewise for the future: *vocabis* can mean either "you will call" or "you will be calling." To reiterate an observation made above, Latin doesn't take the same trouble to distinguish aspect in present and future events as it does in past ones. One form conveys both "I wait" and "I am waiting," "she will rejoice" and "she will be rejoicing."

Thus the three tenses in the "present system" are not so called merely because the imperfect and future employ the stem of the present tense in their spelling (though that happens to be true, too). They also share the quality of suggesting action that may not be fully formed, not completed once and for all. The imperfect differs from the present and future in that such incompletion is more palpable within its time. While the exact stretch of time involved in "she walks" or "she will walk" remains to be determined, "she was walking" deals with an act whose measure we know in relation to surrounding events: it encompasses them, because it is ongoing. An imaginary stopwatch has already verified that her walking was very lengthy, or perhaps interrupted. In the previous two expressions, we cannot yet ascertain if her walking stretches around related events like a rubber band or comes and goes within those events like a firefly's twinkle.

Latin grammatical textbooks seldom use the word "aspect"; Greek grammars do so much more often because of the extraordinary Greek aorist tense (not presented in this volume). Yet aspect (or how an act's temporal wholeness is viewed) really lies at the heart of the distinction between the present system's three tenses and the perfect system's three tenses. When we arrive at this latter system in Chapter Four, we shall see that all actions therein expressed are viewed as *finished*. In languages like Russian, aspect even determines whether or not a verb has a special prefix. (In fact, this technique originated in the Latin/Greek family thousands of years earlier; but it had all but died out by the time those tongues came to be recorded, whereas it has survived more or less intact to this day in northeastern Europe.)

This matter of whether or not an act is viewed as completed must not be brushed aside lightly, then, even though it may seem tedious and pedantic. In fact, as just indicated, we will return to it in Chapter Four, where we will continue our discussion of the English language's aspectual troubles. Make the effort to understand aspect as well as you can, here and now; for you cannot travel very far into most other languages without confronting it.

Time for some good news: formation of the imperfect tense, as was promised, is extremely straightforward. Recall that the future tense involved placing a *–bi* after the verbal stem and before the person/number inflection. The imperfect indicator is a *–ba* which is inserted into just the same slot:

voca + ba + m = vocabam	I was calling
voca + ba + s = vocabas	you (s.) were calling
voca + ba + t = vocabat	he/she/it was calling
voca + ba + mus = vocabamus	we were calling
voca + ba + tis = vocabatis	you (pl.) were calling
voca + ba + nt = vocabant	they were calling

The single curiosity in this table is, of course, the first-person singular form. Why is "I" indicated by an "m" instead of an "o"? It would be tempting to conjecture that *–bao* coalesced into *–bam* through a kind of natural evolution; for if you say the former a little carelessly, you will note that your lips very nearly end up touching as they would do if pronouncing the latter. Yet a more likely line of historical development would have the touching lips carelessly withdrawing into an approximate "o" position. This is precisely what happened in Portuguese when "vowel + nasal" sounds like that in the first word of "San Paolo" ("Saint Paul") grew into "ão" (São Paolo). Indeed, the oldest surviving Greek inflection for the first-person singular is –μι, as in δίδωμι ("I give": this is also the ancient Sanskrit ending for "I")—and first-person "m" even appears in some tenses of such Celtic languages as Irish. So the "m" of *vocabam* most likely reflects a more pristine Latin from which forms like *voco* and *vocabo* "degenerated." All of this suggests that the imperfect might be the best preserved tense in the Latin language.

The second conjugation is just as orderly as the first: simply switch the vowel stem from a long "a" to a long "e".

	singular	plural
1st person	-bam / monebam	-bamus / monebamus
2nd person	-bas / monebas	-batis / monebatis
3rd person	-bat / monebat	-bant / monebant

Concerning pronunciation, the imperfect is also the most regular of tenses in this regard. Since the "a" is long in the *–ba* insertion, all of the plural forms are accented on the penultimate syllable, just as the singular forms. Always, therefore, stress the next-to-last syllable.

Summary

The endings of the imperfect tense are elegantly simple: a –ba indicator inserted between verb stem and person/number inflection. Note, however, that for the first-person singular, the inflection becomes -m instead of -o. The tense's meaning poses a greater challenge. Always remember that it implies incomplete action and often requires several helping verbs for adequate translation into English.

Exercise Set 2.6

A. Translate the following Latin verbs into English. Most are in the imperfect tense, but a few in the present- and future-tense forms are mixed in.

1. manebam	5. portabas	9. temptabunt	13. pugnabatis
2. sedebat	6. spectabitis	10. monebas	14. videbis
3. tenemus	7. timebamus	11. spectabam	15. monstrabas
4. narrant	8. habent	12. dabo	16. pugnabant

B. Translate into Latin.

1. she was obliged to
2. you (pl.) will be sitting
3. I would carry
4. we were standing
5. you (s.) were holding
6. he is staying
7. she will love
8. I used to call
9. you (pl.) tried to warn

C. Translate the following sentences into English. As before, use the Latin word list from the previous chapter's end to find any unfamiliar vocabulary.

1. Verba reginae turbam terrebant.
2. Timebamus propter quod ("because") digiti pueri non ("not") movebant.
3. Agricolae et terram et aquam (*et... et* = "both... and") habebatis.
4. Luna per ("through") stellas caeli navigare temptabat.
5. Si ("if") spectabis, caudas equorum et ("and") umeros virorum videbis.*
6. Venti puellas terrebant, sed ("but") dei auxilium dabunt.

*N.B.:** Latin typically uses the future tense with "if," as is entirely logical; so do the modern romance languages.

D. Translate the following sentences into Latin.

1. For three (*tres*) years (use accusative), the teachers were obliged to tell stories.
2. The whale's back would move, and (*et*) the sailors would watch the waves (use *unda*).
3. As a friend of the gods, you (s.) will see the means of victory.

Solo Flight: Choose a passage from a random document—a novel, an editorial, a textbook, etc. Assign an aspect (perfect or progressive) to each verb in the passage. Even if you cannot identify a particular tense, you should be able to determine whether its action is treated as complete or ongoing. Have another student check your answers, and discuss ant differences of opinion that arise.

VII. The Imperfect Tense: Greek

The Greek imperfect must be translated with just the same sensitivity as was recommended above for this tense in Latin. There are other tenses to express completed action in the past: the imperfect is strictly reserved for action that is unfinished, repeated, attempted, incipient, habitual, etc.

In compensation for the conceptual challenge of understanding this tense's meaning, its form is almost as easy to produce as in Latin—and this time (unlike the Greek future), the rules of formation have few significant exceptions. Distinctly different from Latin is the epsilon prefix (without breathing: always remember to insert to single "closed quote" or "reversed apostrophe" mark over the initial vowel). This prefix stays without any changes for all six verbal forms—and for the first- and second-person plural forms, it is the *only* change of any kind from the present tense. In the second- and third-person singular, the one additional change besides the epsilon prefix is a little vowel-shortening in the suffix: the iota drops out of both forms. (It was probably another epsilon in prehistoric Greek.)

That leaves the "I" and "they" forms. That they have evolved to be identical (as you see directly below) is entirely—and somewhat unfortunately—accidental. With a surrounding context, you should be able to distinguish them in the vast majority of cases. Even in a single sentence, the presence of a noun in the nominative plural will tip you off that 'ελυον (or the parallel form of any other Greek verb) is third-person plural; for a plural noun, obviously, cannot belong with the subject pronoun "I" except in very strange circumstances!

We have already noted that an early version of the first-person singular ending was –μι, and another for the third-person plural ending was –ντσι. How these morphed into –ω and –ουσι in the present tense is a long story; but in the imperfect tense, the pristine forms apparently decided to evolve in another direction which just happened to bring them to the same spot. The "n" sound (as we have seen so often already) is very close to "m," both being liquid nasal consonants; and as for the "they" form, the "n" already existed in its previous incarnation. No doubt, the Greeks would not have allowed both to settle in the same place if they had found that any practical confusion tended to follow. The good news is that both of these forms are more similar—or at least more clearly relatable—to Latin than their counterparts in the present tense (that is, -ον = -*bam* and –ον = -*bant*: a nasal all across the board).

	singular	plural
1st person	-ον / 'ελυον (I was releasing)	-ομεν / 'ελυομεν (we were releasing)
2nd person	-ες / 'ελυες (you were releasing)	-ετε / 'ελυετε (you were releasing)
3rd person	-ε / 'ελυε (he/she/it was releasing)	-ον / 'ελυον (they were releasing)

Naturally, other verbs follow the same pattern. The imperfect of τευχω proceeds thus: 'ετευχον, 'ετευχες, 'ετευχε. The imperfect of λαμβανω goes 'ελαμβανον, 'ελαμβανες, 'ελαμβανε. Yet there do exist two kinds of verb that can complicate the formation of the imperfect: those which begin in a vowel and those with a vowel stem to which endings must be added. Because the prefix (called an *augment* by grammarians) is a vowel—namely epsilon—we may expect some sort of mildly transformative collision when this epsilon is being added to a preexisting vowel. Seating two vowels side by side is asking for trouble! In this instance, though, the adjustment is both minor and regular: the verb's beginning vowel simply lengthens under the epsilon's influence. For instance, 'ακουω becomes 'ηκουον and 'εχω becomes 'ειχον. We need not go through the precise kind of transformation which each short vowel would typically pass through in becoming long. Most such changes are common sense (e.g., an omicron would become an omega, and a short iota or upsilon would become the same vowel pronounced

80

now as long). In any case, these augments are sometimes neglected by ancient writers. Homer will occasionally ignore one for the sake of making a word fit into his hexameter.

Then we have the similar case of verbs such as φιλεω. The first-person singular ’εφιλεον is apt to become ’εφιλων in later Greek, the omicron having merged with the epsilon precisely as it would in the augment of a verb beginning with omicron: say, ‘ομιλεω, “to keep company with, gather.” In fact, this verb would witness vowel-lengthening at either of its ends in later Greek, producing the form ‘ωμιλων for “I was keeping company with.” Yet in Nestor’s long speech after the fierce quarrel between Agamemnon and Achilles in the *Iliad*’s first book, the verb’s first-person singular imperfect form appears (though in slightly longer form: the prefix μετα has been added), and no lengthening has occurred at either point!

For the sake of simplicity, then, we will follow Homer and use forms such as ’εφιλεες and ’εφιλεε. Simply be advised that these will strike any true Greek scholar as very archaic: ’εφιλεις and ’εφιλει would look more “modern.”

Summary
The Greek imperfect is indistinguishable in meaning from the same tense in Latin. In form, it is constructed with an epsilon augment (not always used in poetry) and with person/number inflections very similar to the present tense’s. The first-singular and third-plural forms mutated to become identical and can potentially challenge the translator; context becomes very important in deciding between the two.

Exercise Set 2.7

A. Translate the following Greek verbs into English.

1. ’εβαλλες	4. φυσω	7. ’επεμπον (s.)
2. ’επρασσομεν	5. κρινειτε	8. ’εσκοπεετε (or ’εσκοπειτε)
3. ’ηγον (pl.)	6. ’ελαμβανε	9. ‘ωμιλεομεν

B. Translate into Greek. Every answer will be a single word this time.

1. we used to hear	3. she used to have	5. you (pl.) were afraid
2. they were ruling	4. you (pl.) will love	6. you (sing.) are judging

C. Translate the following sentences into English. As with the earlier Latin sentences in this chapter, you will find any unfamiliar vocabulary in the word list near Chapter One’s end as well as in the glossary.

1. ’Αρχη ποταμου κατα (“along, down”) πετρους ’ερρεε.*
2. Κυβερνηται μνημην μετρου ποντων ’ειχον.
3. Ποιηται ’αιτια πολεμων κρινειν ’εφιλεετε.
4. Κουραι ’αριθμον ‘ιππων ’ουκ (“not”) ‘ωραον.

* **N.B.**: Verbs beginning in rho typically double this consonant before the augment.

D. Translate the following sentences into Greek.

1. The words of the goddesses were frightening the people.
2. Memories of places produce stories (myths).
3. We were supposing the witness’s forgetfulness to be (’ειναι) the work of wine.

Solo Flight: Return to Exercise Set 2.5, Part A, above once more and see if you can transform all eight verbs into their correct imperfect forms. Don’t forget the epsilon augment!

VIII. The Imperfect and Future Tenses in the Romance Languages

We shall spend less space upon the imperfect tense in the modern romance languages than we did upon the present tense. Such "negligence" should not be interpreted as dismissing the importance of the imperfect. The formation of this tense is quite straightforward, however (as in Latin); and as for its meaning, everything said in our discussion of the Latin imperfect applies equally well in the more modern context. A major objective of our ongoing discussion is to highlight the connections between Latin, especially, and its progeny. The imperfect tense certainly sheds such light in abundance. With fine adjustments here and there, the student can readily see how the grandchildren resemble their grandfather.

The future tense in modern romance languages bears a rather less obvious resemblance to Latin. We will ponder the connection momentarily. Though this chapter presented the future tense before the imperfect (since the future's range of meanings is easier to grasp), most Latin grammar texts invert that order. We will fall into step with them now that we're addressing the three romance languages that we have been tracking: Italian, Spanish, and French. Below are their imperfect forms arranged beside Latin's:

English	**Latin**	**Italian**	**Spanish**	**French**
I was loving	amabam	amavo	amaba	j'aimais
you were loving	amabas	amavi	amabas	tu aimais
he/she/it was loving	amabat	amava	amaba	il/elle aimait
we were loving	amabamus	amavamo	amábamos	nous aimions
you were loving	amabatis	amavate	amabaís	vous aimiez
they were loving	amabant	amavano	amaban	ils/elles aimaient

You will quickly notice that Spanish looks a little more like Latin than does Italian. A "v," however, is simply a "b" with breathing, so the difference is not linguistically significant. Yet Spanish also seems to resemble Latin more closely in its endings, which depart from the ancient precedent mostly in dropping a final or intermediate "t" in three forms. This general impression would be reliable if Spanish adhered to the pattern in the table for all three of its conjugations. The truth is that only Spanish "a" stem verbs preserve Latin's –ba indicator. Other imperfects offer forms like *tenía* and *subía*, with the accented "i" indicating an absorbed consonant. Italian keeps the "v" stem in all three of its conjugations: on that basis, it might once again be said to remain closer to its Latin roots.

By the way, all three of these modern languages—Italian, Spanish, and French—have only three verb conjugations. The weak "e" stem of Latin's third conjugation (out of four) did not assert itself with sufficient strength to save its verbs from being taken over by conjugations with strong vowel stems. Even the –er verbs of French are really Latin's first conjugation –are verbs. As in nature, so in grammar: the weaker species perish!

1ˢᵗ conjugation example: Latin *fabulare*, "to tell a story," becomes Italian *parlare*, "to speak" (by way of medieval *favillare*), Spanish *hablar*, and French *parler*.

2ⁿᵈ conjugation example: Latin *monêre*, "to warn," becomes Italian *monêre*, Spanish *admonestar*, and French *admonir* (i.e., these verbs may end up in any conjugation, perhaps because the influx of Latin weak "e" stems confused the boundaries).

3rd conjugation example: Latin *vendere*, "to sell," becomes Italian *vendere* (considered second conjugation, even though "e" is unaccented), Spanish *vender*, and French *vendre* (both of last two treated as typical second-conjugation verbs).

4th conjugation example: Latin fourth-conjugation *dormire*, "to sleep," becomes Italian *dormire*, Spanish *dormir*, and French *dormir*; complete integrity of stem.

To return to the imperfect tense... is it any surprise that the French imperfect looks least like Latin's? We have begun to gather evidence that this tends to be the case throughout French grammar and spelling. Yet one can still see the "a" indicator that remains after "b/v" has eroded away; and the spelling of these French endings does not change according to conjugation, which makes memorizing them quite simple. Again characteristically, however, French has so streamlined pronunciation that all forms sound the same when spoken except for the first- and second-person plurals. This is undoubtedly why coupling subject pronouns with verbs became mandatory as French evolved.

Summary
The imperfect tense in the romance languages refers to past action not completed in some way, including repeated or habitual action (just as in Latin). Its formation is very straightforward, with standard endings being affixed to a vowel stem. The vowel stem varies according to conjugation in Italian and Spanish, however.

All three modern languages have strayed far indeed from Latin in the way that they form the future tense. You need not look for traces of a *–bi* insertion anywhere; you will find none. The later tongues all resorted to a strategy that we English-speakers know very well, though its logic has been thoroughly scuffed up over the centuries: they used "have" in an auxiliary capacity (i.e., as a helping verb). At some point in the early Middle Ages, as the regional spin-offs of Latin began to coalesce into the distinct tongues that we find today, expressions on the order of, "I have to repeat," became a common way of saying, "I will repeat." The intent of these expressions was not "have to" in our contemporary English sense of "must." Think of their signification, rather, as equivalent to our, "I have yet to repeat." In other words, to "have" the action expressed in the infinitive evokes the image of holding onto that action: it has not yet been released—that is, performed. If you "have" to eat in this metaphor (= "are holding on to eating"), then you have not yet eaten. Once your lunch is over, you will have "let go" of eating and will no longer have it to do.

This, then, is how speakers of Italian, Spanish, and French were apparently expressing their future tense toward the end of the Christian era's first millennium. All of these linguistically related peoples would say, in an inversion of our typical modern word order (but in standard Latin order), "to repeat I have." We would find in Italian, *ripetere ho*; in Spanish, *repetir hé*; and in French *répéter [je] ai*. The infinitive would recur unchanged as the verb "to have" was declined throughout its present tense to form different persons and numbers. Over time, the present tense of "have" was fully and permanently affixed to the infinitive, resulting in a single word... and a new future paradigm was born. (Sorry, *–bi* insertion!) The modern future tense in these languages is the direct product of that fusion. With very few exceptions (all occurring in the first and second persons of plurals), you can clearly see the present tense of "to have" by reversing the evolutionary process and subtracting the infinitive from these forms. (N.B.: In modern French, the subject pronoun must accompany the verb in the future as in all other tenses.)

English	**Italian**	**Spanish**	**French**
I shall love	amare + ho = amarò	amar + hé = amaré	aimer + ai = aimerai
you will love	amare + hai = amaraí	amar + has = amarás	aimer + as = aimeras
he/she/it will love	amare + ha = amarà	amar + ha = amará	aimer + a = aimera

we shall love	amare + aviamo = amaremo	amar + hemos = amaremos	aimer + avons = aimerons
you will love	amare + avete = amarete	amar + habéis = amaréis	aimer + avez = aimerez
they will love	amare + hanno = amaranno	amar + han = amarán	aimer + ont = aimeront

Since the regular Italian infinitive always has an "e" at the end, just as in Latin, this language actually drops a letter from the infinitive form before adding future inflections (*amare – e = amar*). Spanish and French, however, are making direct use of the present infinitive (*amar* and *aimer*) without any adjustments whatever. The same procedure is followed in all three languages for building any future. "They will sleep" in Spanish is *dormir + án*, or *dormirán*. "I shall sell" in Italian is *vendere – e + ò*, or *venderò*. "We shall show" in French is *pronoun + montrer + ons*, or *nous montrerons*. Few tenses are easier to form in the romance languages, once you understand infinitives.

Summary

The future tense of the romance languages is a compressed version of the medieval periphrasis, "to ___ I have." This tense is essentially formed, therefore, by adding the present tense of "to have" (slightly truncated in certain spots) onto the present infinitive.

Exercise Set 2.8

A. Translate the first five verbs from French into English and the second five from English into French. Use *aimer*, "to love"; *voler*, "to fly"; and *montrer*, "to show." All three tenses are represented.

1. elle montre
2. tu montreras
3. je volerai
4. vous montriez
5. ils aimaient

6. we will show
7. they are loving
8. I used to fly
9. she was showing
10. you (pl.) will love

B. Translate the first five verbs from Spanish into English and the second five from English into Spanish. Use *amar*, "to love"; *volar*, "to fly"; and *mostrar*, "to show." All three tenses are represented.

1. volarán
2. amarás
3. volamos
4. mostraba
5. mostraís

6. they were showing
7. you (s.) fly
8. I will love
9. we will show
10. she was loving

C. Translate the first five verbs from Italian into English and the second five from English into Italian. Use *amare*, "to love"; *volare*, "to fly"; and *monstrare*, "to show." All three tenses are represented.

1. volaranno
2. monstrate
3. amarò
4. volava
5. amiamo

6. you (s.) will fly
7. you (pl.) will show
8. I am showing
9. they were flying
10. we will love

D. Translate the following verbs (drawn from Italian, Spanish, and French) into English. The verb *ridere / reir / rire*, "to laugh" (second conjugation in Italian and French, third in Spanish), has been stirred in.

1. volavate
2. tenías

7. je pendais
8. mostraban

84

3. reiréis
4. penderé
5. monstraranno
6. nous aimerons

9. amarà
10. volaremos
11. ridevamo
12. tu tenais

IX. Complete Latin Vocabulary for First- and Second-Conjugation Verbs

Below is an ample list of first- and second-conjugation verbs following the format of the lists at Chapter One's end. That is, an English derivative has been supplied along with a basic definition. Many words can have more specific meanings in particular circumstances. The first-person singular form and the infinitive have been supplied for each listing, as is customary in Latin dictionaries. Remember that all of the second-conjugation verbs have a long "e" stem, so that their infinitive is pronounced AIR-reh. (Dictionaries will often simply print –*ère* after the first-person singular form.) This is important to understand, for we shall see that third-conjugation verbs have a short "e" stem which pushes the accent back another syllable.

As before, students and teachers are encouraged to devise their own exercises employing these words. If strengthening one's English vocabulary is a major objective, special effort should be given to tracking down further derivatives and to using those provided correctly in sentences. Those who wish to test their Latin competence further, on the other hand, would do well to repeat exercises earlier in this chapter after replacing the verbs first used with new ones. Of course, asterisks designate verbs that have not been introduced before this list.

Vocabulary

Latin—1st Conjugation	definition	English derivative
ambulo, ambulare	walk	ambulatory
amo, amare	like, love	amiable
celo, celare*	hide, obscure	conceal
clamo, clamare*	shout, cry out	exclaim
cogito, cogitare*	think, reflect	cogitate
curo, curare*	care for, look after	cure
desidero, desiderare*	want, crave	desire
do, dare	give, bestow	data
domino, dominare*	rule over	dominate
erro, errare*	wander, go astray	error
exspecto, exspectare*	wait for	expect
habito, habitare*	dwell or live in/at	inhabit
iuro, iurare*	swear, take an oath	jury

impero, imperare*	command (on broad scale)	imperial
laudo, laudare*	praise	laud
monstro, monstrare	show, point out	demonstrate
muto, mutare*	change, alter	mutate
neco, necare*	kill, slay	internecine
narro, narrare	tell, narrate	narrative
navigo, navigare	sail	navigate
nego, negare*	deny, refuse	negate
numero, numerare*	count	enumerate
nuntio, nuntiare*	report, bear a message	enunciate
occupo, occupare*	seize (town), attack	occupy
opto, optare*	choose, wish for	option
paro, parare*	prepare	preparation
porto, portare	carry	portable
pugno, pugnare	fight	pugnacity
puto, putare*	think, calculate	compute
pulso, pulsare*	hit, slap	pulse
rogo, rogare*	ask	interrogate
servo, servare*	save, keep	preserve
specto, spectare	watch, observe	spectator
spero, sperare*	hope for	despair
sto, stare	stand, be still	stationary
supero, superare*	conquer, prevail over	insuperable
tempto, temptare	try, attempt	attempt
vasto, vastare*	lay waste, raze	devastate
veto, vetare*	prohibit, forbid	veto
vito, vitare*	avoid	inevitable

voco, vocare	call, summon	vocation
volo, volare*	fly	volatile
vulnero, vulnerare*	wound	vulnerable

Latin—2nd Conjugation	definition	English derivative
debeo, debêre	ought (to), should; owe	debt
deleo, delêre *	efface, destroy	delete
doceo, docêre *	teach	doctor
gaudeo, gaudêre *	rejoice	gaudy
habeo, habêre	have, possess	habit
iaceo, iacêre *	lie (low, down, flat, etc.)	adjacent
iubeo, iubêre *	order, command	jussive
maneo, manêre	stay, remain	remain
misceo, miscêre *	mix, mingle	miscegenation
moneo, monêre	warn	admonish
moveo, movêre	put in motion	move
pendeo, pendêre *	hang/depend upon	dependency
placeo, placêre *	please, put at ease	complacent
pleo, plêre *	fill, fulfill (usually with prefix)	complete
rideo, ridêre *	laugh, smile	risible
sedeo, sedêre	sit	sedentary
splendeo, splendêre *	shine	splendid
taceo, tacêre *	be or remain silent	tacit
teneo, tenêre	hold, restrain	retain
terreo, terrêre	frighten	terrify
timeo, timêre	fear, be afraid of	timid
valeo, valêre *	be strong, healthy, of worth	valid

X. Complete Greek Vocabulary for First- and Second-Conjugation Verbs

The verbs below have been selected either because they are common in ancient Greek and will assist us in making sentences later or because they have useful derivatives in English. In several cases, we have already used the verb's noun form, so the English derivative offered may be the same as that given earlier for the noun. In a few cases (e.g., 'αγω and φερω), the verb has a parallel Latin form which might more properly be called the source of our derivatives.

Greek	definition	English derivative
'αγω	I lead, drive	agent
'ακουω	I hear, listen to	acoustic
'αμειβω*	I change, exchange	amoeba
βαινω*	I walk	binary
βαλλω	I throw, cast	ball
γιγνωσκω*	I come to know, learn	recognize
δοκεω	I suppose, imagine, believe	dogma
'εχω	I hold, have; be able	-----
ζωω*	I live, am alive	zoology
θνησκω*	I die, am killed	-----
καλεω	I call, name, summon	call
κρατεω	I rule, have power	democratic
κρινω	I judge	critic
λαμβανω	I take, seize	syllabus
λεγω*	I bring together, tell, say	dialect
λυω	I release, loosen	analysis
μιμνησκω*	I remember	mnemonic
νοεω*	I remark, notice, think	noetic
νομιζω*	I believe, accept as proper	anomic
'ομιλεω	I keep company with	homiletic
'οραω	I see	-----

πασχω*	I suffer	paschal
παυω*	I stop, cease	pause
πειθω*	I persuade	-----
πεμπω	I send, escort	pomp
ποιεω	I make, fashion	poetic
πρασσω	I do, act, perform	practical
῾ρεω	I run, flow	rheum
σημαινω*	I signal, mark out/off	semantic
σκοπεω	I watch, look at	scope
ταρβεω	I fear, dread	-----
τασσω	I arrange, organize	taxidermist
τελευταω*	I complete, bring to an end	-----
τευχω	I make, cause; happen	technique
τρεπω*	I turn, direct	entropy
φαινω*	I bring to light, show	phenomenon
φερω*	I bear, carry, bring	infer
φιλεω	I like, love	philanthropy
φοβεω	I frighten	phobic
φυω	I produce, bring forth	physics
φωνεω	I speak, give voice	phonics
χαιρω*	I rejoice, am glad (common greeting in imperative)	-----
χορεω*	I dance	chorus
χωρεω*	I make space, withdraw, move	-----
ψευδω*	I lie, tell a falsehood	pseudonym

XI. Comparative Latin and Romance Verbs: Vocabulary

Several derivative verbs in three major modern romance languages have been juxtaposed below with their Latin ancestor. Only the first two Latin conjugations are represented. The list is in nowise complete or exhaustive: the objective is merely to highlight the lineage of a few very common shared verbs. In the case of many Latin verbs introduced in this chapter, either no prominent modern derivative exists or it has survived only in Italian. *Stare*, for instance, produces the past participle for "to be" in Italian (*stato*) as well as meaning "to stand"; and by the time we reach Spanish and French, it means *only* "to be" (as in "to be in a state of") in all forms.

Latin	Italian	Spanish	French	English meaning
amare	amare	amar	aimer	to love
dare	dare	dar	donner	to give
debere	debere	deber	devoir	ought (to), should; owe
habere	avere	haber	avoir	have, possess
lavare	lavare	lavar	laver	wash, bathe
levare	levare	llevar	lever	raise, lift
monere	monere	amonestar	admonir	warn
monstrare	monstrare	mostrar	montrer	show
movere	movere	mover	mouvoir	put in motion
parare	parare	preparer	préparer	prepare
pendere	pendere	pender	pendre	hang/depend upon
placere	piacere	placer	plaire	please, put at ease
portare	portare	transportar	porter	carry
ridere	ridere	reir	rire	laugh, smile
sedere	sedere	sentar	asseyer	sit
spectare	spettare	espiar	épier	watch (spy)
sperare	sperare	esperar	espérer	hope
stare	stare	estar	être	to stand (= be in a state of)
tenere	tenere	tener	tenir	hold, restrain
valere	valere	valer	valoir	be strong, well, worthwhile
volare	volare	volar	voler	fly

ANSWERS TO EXERCISES

Exercise Set 2.1

Answers to **A**: 1. you (pl.) love, are loving 2. they have, are having 3. you (sing.) frighten 4. we stand 5. he (or she, or it) stands 6. I show 7. we move 8. he/she/it warns

Answers to **B**: 1. manent 2. stas 3. vocamus 4. ambulat 5. timetis 6. tenemus

Answers to **C**: 1. The queen's daughters love gifts. 2. We sons of the farmer try to remain at home. 3. Boys are afraid of water but men love to sail. 4. (As) a poet, you have an abundance of words. 5. (As) a friend of the queen, I sit, but you sailors ought to stand.

Answers to **D**: 1. Deus ventorum populum monere debet. 2. Avunculus viginti puerorum cumulos auri et argenti do.

Exercise Set 2.2

Answers to **A**: 1. they watch, are watching 2. you (pl.) hear, are hearing 3. he/she/it sends 4. they take 5. I throw 6. you (sing.) judge 7. you (pl.) hold 8. we frighten

Answers to **B**: 1. ῾ρεει 2. κρατεομεν 3. πρασσουσι 4. φωνεετε (When κρατεειν means "to rule over," it's followed by a genitive rather than an accusative.) 5. σκοπεει 6. ῾οραεις

Answers to **C**: 1. We (female) friends love the children of Hermione. 2. Fear of war is seizing the people. 3. Rivers flow and produce a sea. 4. I hear the winds of time, but you men like a sleep of forgetfulness.

Answers to **D**: 1. ψυχη ᾽ανθροπου βιου (or ζωης) και θανατου κρατεει. 2. Θεοι κοσμου γαιαν (better than γαιην) και ποντους ποιουσι (or τευχουσι). 3. Στρατηγοι ῾οδον πολεμου ῾ου τασσεετε (or τασσειτε).

Exercise Set 2.3

Answers to **A**: 1. we speak, are speaking 2. they speak, are speaking 3. I speak 4. you (s.) speak 5. they speak 6.. I speak 7. you (pl.) speak 8. they speak (females: French specifies gender with pronoun) 9. you (s.) speak 10. we speak 11. I speak 12. we speak

Answers to **B**: 1. cantano 2. amas s 3. nous chantons 4. il parle. 5. amo 6. cantaís 7. parla 8. vous aimez 9. canti 10. cantamos 11. parlo 12. elle aime

Exercise Set 2.4

Answers to **A**: 1. he/she/it will have 2. we will stand 3. you (s.) fear 4. they will carry 5. you (pl.) will watch 6. you (s.) will owe (or "will be obliged" in moral sense) 7. I try 8. to give 9. you (pl.) remain 10. I will fight 11. they will see 12. to frighten

Answers to **B**: 1. sedebunt 2. dabis s 3. monstrabo 4.   5. tenemus 6. ambulatbitis 6. timebunt 7. narrabimus 8. stabit 9. monere

Answers to **C**: 1. The boys' horses will carry the girls. 2. A man's arms will not hold (restrain) a bear. 3. The winds will move the leaves, but the fig tree will stand. 4. We will try to tell the story if you friends of the queen will remain. 5. (As) a boy, you will be obliged to hold your tongue. 6. The woman's eyes show anger, but her tongue says, "I will give help." **N.B.:** The placement of *femina* at the sentence's beginning suggests that it should be taken with both nominatives.

Answers to **D**: 1. Dona reginae spectare debebis. 2. Nautae copiam victoriarum non videbitis. #. Filius vitia Marci non spectabo.

Exercise Set 2.5

Answers to **A**: 1. I will love 2. you (s.) will send 3. you (pl.) will frighten 4. he/she/it will make 5. they throw, are throwing 6.. you (sing.) will rule 7. we will hold 8 you (pl.) will produce

Answers to **B**: 1. σκοπησω 2. κρινεουσι 3. ῾αξει 4. φωνησετε 5. λαμψομεν* 6. ᾽ακουσεις*

Answers to **C**: 1. The poets will speak words (tales) of philosophy. 2. The child of a god will lead a life of labors. 3. We gods will send Menelaos along the river of death. 4. I will keep (hold) the men's horses but release their children.

Answers to **D**: 1. Σομνος μνημας λυσει και 'οδον ληθης ποιησει. 2. Κουροι 'αιτια κοσμου σκοπτειν ταρβεετε (in later Greek, always ταρβειτε [φοβειτε, etc.] with the two adjacent vowels now an accented diphthong).

*For some reason, the forms in 5 and 6 never actually appear in any recorded Greek: the future tense of these verbs is only found in the middle voice, as if they were deponent. Furthermore, λαμψομαι has morphed into ληψομαι in Attic Greek, which thereby becomes the mainstream spelling.

Exercise Set 2.6

Answers to **A**: 1. I was staying 2. he/she was sitting 3. we hold/are holding 4. they tell 5. you (s.) were carrying 6. you (pl.) will watch 7. we were fearing 8. they have 9. they will try 10 you (s.) were warning 11. I was watching 12. I will give 13. you (pl.) were fighting 14. you (s.) will see 15. you (s.) were showing 16. they were fighting

Answers to **B**: 1. debebat 2. sedebitis s 3. portabam 4. stabamus 5. tenebas 6. manet 7. amabit 8. vocabam 9. monebatis

Answers to **C**: 1. The queen's words used to (would) terrify the crowd. 2. We were afraid because the boy's fingers were not moving. 3. You farmers used to have both land and water. 4. The moon was trying to sail through the stars of the sky. (Strictly speaking, "trying to sail" could also be rendered by putting *navigare* in the imperfect as the sole verb: *navigabat*. This would probably put too much strain on the imperfect, however; if unusual or important, as here, the "try" would be specified with its own verb.) 5. If you (s.) will watch, you will see the horses' tails and the men's shoulders. 6. The winds were terrifying the girls, but the gods will give help.

Answers to **D**: 1. Tres annos magistri fabulas narrare debebant. 2. Dorsum ceti movebat, et nautae undas spectabant. #. Amicus deorum modum victoriae videbis.

Exercise Set 2.7

Answers to **A**: 1. you (s.) were throwing 2. we were doing 3. they were leading 4. I will produce 5. you (pl.) are judging 6. He/she was seizing 7. I was sending 8. you (pl.) were watching 9. we were gathering

Answers to **B**: 1. 'ηκουομεν 2. 'εκρατεον 3. 'ειχε 4. φιλησετε 5. 'εφοβεετε (or 'εφοβειτε) 6. κρινεις

Answers to **C**: 1. The river's beginning was flowing down (or along) the rocks. 2. The pilots were retaining (holding/would retain/used to retain) the memory of the measure of the seas. (**N.B.**: The use of two genitives back to back in this manner can be a bit confusing but is not uncommon.) 3. You poets liked to judge the causes of wars. 4. The girls were not seeing (=did not see *for some time*) the number of the horses (=how many they were).

Answers to **D**: 1. Λογοι θεαων δημον 'εφοβεον. 2. Μνημαι τοπων μυθους φυουσι. 3. Ληθην μαρτυρου 'ειναι 'εργον 'οινου 'εδοκεομεν.

Exercise Set 2.8

Answers to **A**: 1. she shows/is showing 2. you (s.) will show 3. I will fly 4. you (pl.) were showing 5. they were loving (used to love) 6. nous montrerons 7. ils/elles aiment 8. je volais 9. elle montrait 10. vous aimerez

Answers to **B**: 1. they will fly 2. you (s.) will love 3. we fly/are flying 4. I (or he/she) was showing 5. you (pl.) show 6. mostraban 7. volas 8. amaré 9. mostraremos 10. amaba

Answers to **C**: 1. they will fly 2. you (pl.) are showing 3. I will love 4. he/she was flying/used to fly 5. we love 6. volaraí 7. monstrarete 8. monstro 9. volavano 10. amaremo

Answers to **D**: 1. you (pl.) were flying—IT 2. you (s.) were holding—SP 3. you (pl.) will laugh—SP 4. I will hang—SP 5. they will show—IT 6. we will love—FR 7. I was hanging—FR 8. they were showing—SP 9. he/she will love—IT 10. we will fly—SP 11. we were laughing—IT 12. you (s.) were holding--FR

Chapter Three: Nouns Continued

Topics Covered

Case

- dative and ablative: function
- formation of dative and ablative in Latin and Greek First and Second Declensions
- merging of Greek ablative with genitive and dative
- Latin Third, Fourth, and Fifth Declensions
- Greek Third Declension

Connections within and between Languages

- association between certain classes of Latin/Greek nouns and gender
- similarities between Latin and Greek noun inflections
- formation of English derivatives from third-declension noun bases
- typical transformations of third-declension nouns in romance languages

Vocabulary

- more nouns of Latin and Greek First and Second Declensions
- nouns of Latin and Greek Third Declensions

I. The Dative Case: Latin

Both Latin and Greek have an additional case besides the three already studied. For Greek, this is the last case of any importance to us, while for Latin there remains one more. (Both languages have relics of further cases whose forms occasionally appear in ancient recorded texts but nestle beneath the surface-level sweep of this introductory course.) As usual, the remarks made of the Latin dative's grammatical use in this section will apply fully to the Greek dative, with whose formation we shall deal in the next section.

The most obvious, easily remembered use of the dative case is for the indirect object. Verbs which transfer action to a direct object (called *transitive* verbs) may also steer some of the action indirectly to a noun or pronoun rather more loosely involved in the event; and intransitive verbs, as well, may take indirect objects (e.g., "For us, an apology will suffice"). In English, this indirect object is usually preceded by the preposition "to" or "for." You cannot buy a person, but you can buy a book *for* a person; and you may be praising Jack instead of Jill, but you can also praise Jack *to* Jill. The indirect object is thus somehow interested or implicated in the action without being its immediate target.

A couple of warnings must at once be sounded. We cannot assume 1) that the indirect object will always have "to" or "for" preceding it in English, or 2) that, where these prepositions occur in an English sentence, we will always place the ensuing noun in the dative case when translating to Latin. It is very common usage (probably more standard every day) for English-speakers to say, "Give me a chance!" The "to" has been dropped from before the "me" in such circumstances. The little preposition seems to serve no purpose: we all understand that the gift of a chance is being asked, not the gift of "me"! Yet when translating into another language, we sometimes grow confused by our own lack of precision; we're puzzled about what to do with words like "me" (in this instance). In Latin, no option would exist other than to put "me" (or any other noun or pronoun serving its function) into the dative case.

From the other direction, beware of assuming that "to" or "for" in English automatically signals a dative in Latin. The preposition "to" can also be employed in the physical sense of "toward"; and in such circumstances— that is, whenever a physical motion toward someone or something is involved—Latin and Greek both use the accusative case. Often, as we shall see later, a preposition precedes this accusative to distinguish it from a verbal direct object, but not always. When, in *Aeneid* 1.643-633, Queen Dido sends twenty bulls *to* the shore *to* (i.e., for) Aeneas's stranded comrades, the clause reads, *Sociîs ad litora mittit / Viginti tauros*, with *ad* stressing the "motion toward" idea. (You may also recall that the preposition κατα, meaning "along" or "down," cropped up in a Greek sentence earlier—and that an accusative followed it.)

The same thing may be said of "for": it has more than one sense in English, and not all of its dimensions suit the dative. You may actually know by heart the highly ironic verse of Horace's with which the short-lived poet Wilfred Owen ended his piece about World War One's gruesome trench combat: *dulce et decorum est pro patria mori* ("sweet and fitting it is to die for one's country"). The "for one's country" part of the verse does not use a dative, but rather the preposition *pro* with the remaining Latin case (the ablative) that we have not yet tackled. Deciding whether or not a sentence's action is happening "in someone's interest" (dative) or "in someone's behalf" (*pro* + ablative) can be the ultimate exercise in hair-splitting: the Romans themselves do not appear to have adhered strictly to whatever logical distinction exists here. In general, the dative is used more often of persons (e.g., "for my friends"), while the ablative is more common with things or abstract nouns (e.g., "for decency").

We might as well admit that the dative case can be used a bit sloppily in some classical texts. For instance, the historian Cornelius Nepos writes in his biographical sketch about Alcibiades, *Huic ergo renuntiat quae regi cum Lacedemoniîs essent*—"Therefore he renounced to him [= in his presence, to his dissatisfaction] the things which were for the king [= in the king's interest, agreed upon by the king] with the Lacedemonians" (7.10.2). "To him" and "for the king" (*huic* and *regi*) are both dative. Quite a mess! Frankly, Nepos, though among the earliest of those Roman historians whose works have partially survived (or perhaps for that very reason), was not a great stylist. His friend and contemporary, Cicero, would not likely have written such an unwieldy sentence for general consumption.

Yet a great many of Cicero's letters have been preserved; and we know from these that in private correspondence, the dative was tossed about quite freely. Frequent datives seem to have characterized a more relaxed vein of communication. Something analogous in colloquial English might be, "I'm going to take me three cookies for lunch"—the "me" (= "for myself") being entirely redundant, and the "for lunch" (= "as lunch") being a second dative.

Speaking of two datives... grammar texts often jauntily label a certain kind of construction a "double dative." The verb in these cases is always some form of "to be," and a dative used as a typical indirect object will represent one member of the double. The other dative is harder to explain. The textbooks call it a dative of purpose, as in the sentence, *Liber mihi auxilio est*: "The book is (as) a help to me." What's going on with *auxilio*? Why is it not the nominative form *auxilium*, balanced by the linking verb (or copula, as "to be" is often styled, since it couples things) with the sentence's subject? We would call "help" a predicate nominative in English grammar, and handling it hat way seems a perfectly logical way to think of the structure... but the Romans had other ideas. To say that "help" expresses a purpose or intent is really rather misleading, for our sentence merely declares that the book was a help—not that it was intended to be so. Besides, Latin actually has many ways of expressing purpose, and the dative is not among them. Perhaps we might better conceive of this dative as signaling something on the order of "like" or "functioning as": i.e., "The book was like a help/functioned as a help to me." Though the result strikes us as odd, the double-dative formula occurs often in Latin.

Since an unwelcome degree of confusion surrounds the dative, let us seek to cling confidently to a few solid observations. 1) Always remember that the dative is not used to express "motion toward"; 2) recall that the dative occurs especially often with verbs of giving (the word "dative" indeed comes from the Latin verb *dare*, "to give"); 3) think of the dative as somewhat informal ("for the public welfare" would involve the preposition *pro*, whereas "I'll get that for you" would clearly involve a dative); and finally, 4) NEVER use any sort of preposition in front of a dative in Latin. The case ending all by itself expresses the dative idea. In the same way, we have seen that the genitive case always translates the "of" idea of possession all by itself, without a preposition.

In Number 4 of the above observations and there only, Greek differs from Latin: Greek datives are sometimes accompanied by prepositions—as are Greek genitives. Yet this never occurs, even in Greek, when the dative noun is an indirect object or when the genitive noun is in possession of something. Because Greek has no ablative case, the dative and genitive cases came to be used for more than indirect objects and instances of possession. In other words, they were forced into double duty. More of that shortly.

Now let us consider the actual formation of the dative case in Latin's first and second declensions:

	1st Declension	2nd Decl. Masc.	2nd Decl. Neuter
singular	-ae / feminae	-o / tauro	-o / saxo
plural	-îs / feminîs	-îs / taurîs	-îs / saxîs

This table, one might say, contains good news and bad news. The good news is we see a substantial, almost complete overlap in spelling across the three genders. In fact, all dative plurals have identical endings within their declension, regardless of gender; and in these two closely related declensions, the common inflection is *–îs*. (The Romans would not have drawn a long mark over the "i" to indicate its "ee" pronunciation: we do so because the looming third declension has many words ending in short *–is*.) The first two declensions did not always have identical dative plural endings, by the way. The first declension would have used *–ais* in Latin's very early days, while the masculine and neuter second declension would have used *–ois*. This is worth knowing both because it reminds us of the dominant vowel in either declension and because, when transliterated, these earlier endings turn out to be the Greek dative in the plural. Yet after the two vowels (forming a diphthong) had fermented in each other's company for hundreds of years in Latin, they coalesced into the characteristic long "i."

The simplicity is not quite as severe in the singular, but still present. *All singular datives in Latin end in a vowel*—always. This vowel was once a short "i," so that the pristine inflections would have looked like *–ai* and *–oi*. In the first declension, the diphthong survives: indeed, *-ae* is just a Romanized spelling of *–ai*. In the second declension, however, the "o" absorbed the short "i" entirely, lengthening as it did so. Again, this process tips us off about what to expect from Greek, where the same decay had proceeded a little less far. A short iota (see the following section) remains alongside the Greek first declension's eta and the second's omega, but we have reason to doubt that it was audibly pronounced.

The bad news, of course, is that we have learned the first declension's dative singular *–ae* for two other case/number inflections in Latin—and the unwelcome recurrences will quickly grow worse once the ablative case's endings are unveiled in this chapter! If this plethora of different cases sharing the same ending seems to verge on an impossible complication, the historian might respond that the Greeks and Romans thought so, too. The redundancy that developed in their noun inflections as these decayed into closer and closer degrees of resemblance directly caused the birth of prepositions. That is, the case endings, finally, were undermined by so much ambiguity (thanks to shared spellings) that additional words came to be used with them in order to reinforce the intended meaning. Perhaps if the great-great-grandsires of our celebrated classical authors had pronounced their words more clearly, the preposition would never have been invented. The effective death of the case system is thus a kind of cautionary tale—a reminder to all young people to elocute their words precisely!

In classical Latin and Greek, however, the use of prepositions is still very occasional, as you know by now. This is an apt moment to repeat the exhortation that you rely on common sense in translating. When the word *feminae* appears, it will never have a preposition before it—but don't panic. Search the sentence for clues: create a context. *Puella dona feminae dat* clearly employs the word "woman" in the dative. The verb *dat* is singular, so *feminae* cannot be a nominative plural: only *puella* could provide the singular subject. The girl might be giving the woman's gifts—in which event *feminae* would be genitive singular. Yet this makes little sense when you ponder it. (If they are the woman's gifts, then how and why is the girl giving them?) In a complete paragraph, as well, such as you would be provided by an actual document from antiquity, we would surely have a broader context. We would know, for instance, if the girl were trying to please the woman with presents (by giving them *to her*)—or if, on the other hand, she were so displeased with the woman that she immediately passed along the "woman's gifts" (*dona feminae*) to some party not specified here.

Be patient in your translating, therefore; and when you think you have finished a translation, ask yourself if there might be another and more sensible way of interpreting the words.

Summary

The dative case governs the indirect object in Latin, and can often be translated into English with the prepositions "to" and "for." Never use a preposition with it in Latin, however—nor should you assume that the noun following "to" or "for" in English will always go into the dative in Latin. Datives are especially common in informal language. As for the actual inflection, all singular datives end in a vowel, and plural datives are always spelled the same in the first two declensions (and within other declension families) regardless of gender.

Latin Vocabulary

Below are the last nouns of the first and second declensions which will be introduced in this book. Several have no true English derivative, but were included because they are commonly used in Latin and helpful for creating sentences (e.g., *cena*). Others represent a much broader class of noun, such as the feminine –*tia* nouns like *amicitia* (often with English cognates ending in –*ty*) for abstract qualities. Of course, a Latin dictionary would be an excellent source for more of these and other nouns.

Let us precede the long list of nouns, however, with a much shorter one of Latin personal pronouns in the dative case. These little words are used even more often as indirect objects in Latin than in English. One of the reasons is that the Latin way of saying, "I have so-and-so…" is, "There is to me [dative] so-and-so." A person would also respond, if asked his or her name, "The name to me [dative] is…." These pronouns will crop up at several points in the exercises below with the verbs *est* and *sunt*, "is" and "are." Translate *equus est mihi*, for instance, as, "A horse is to me," if it helps you keep the issues clear in your head; but, "I have a horse," sounds much more sensible!

Personal Pronouns in Dative

	singular	**plural**
1st person	*mihi* (to me)	*nobîs* (to us)
2nd person	*tibi* (to you)	*vobîs* (to you)
3rd person	*ei* (to him/her/it)	*eîs* (to them)

New Nouns of the 1st and 2nd Declensions

Latin	**definition**	**English derivative**
amicitia (f)	friendship	amity
astrum (n)	constellation	astral
camera (f)	room	bicameral
cena (f)	meal	-----
corona (f)	crown	coronation
discipulus (m)	student	disciple
dolum (n)	trick, deceit	dolt
fumus (m)	smoke	fume
gaudium (n)	joy	gaudy
gladius (m)	sword	gladiator
gloria (f)	fame, glory	glory
gratia (f)	charm, kindness (used in plural to mean "thanks")	grace

iustitia (f)	justice	justice
lignum (n)	wood	lignite
membrum (n)	part, limb	member
mora (f)	delay	moratorium
pecunia (f)	money	pecuniary
praesidium (n)	outpost	president
saeculum (n)	century, age	secular
somnium (n)	dream	somnambulate
somnus (m)	sleep	insomnia

Exercise Set 3.1

A. Translate the following short sentences into English. All of them feature a noun in the dative. *Est* and *sunt*, by the way, are the third-person singular and plural of "to be": "he/she/it is" and "they are."

1. Corona est reginae.
2. Gladii virîs sunt.
3. Pecuniam puero dabam.
4. Femina cenam tibi dabit.
5. Amicitia nobîs gaudium dat.
6. Romani gloriam patriae dant.
7. Sunt mihi et filii et filiae.
8. Gloria Brittanorum* gaudio eîs est.

*N.B.: A *Britannus* is an inhabitant of ancient Britain, just as a *Romanus* is a Roman.

B. Now translate these English sentences into Latin. Again, each has a noun somewhere that should be rendered into the dative case.

1. I have (= there are to me) three (*tres*) horses.
2. Quintus is the boy's name (*nomen*).
3. We will give the queen's gifts to the teacher.
4. You (s.) used to give thanks to the gods. (What would "to God" be?)

Solo Flight: Select an English passage from a novel, an article, a historical document, or some other source. (The Pledge of Allegiance isn't a bad place to start.) Can you pick out all the dative phrases in the passages? Cross-check your answers with those of a classmate. (The Pledge, by the way, contains four dative phrases; and if you were actually translating it into Latin, several more words would go into the dative since they stand in apposition to those phrases.)

II. The Dative Case: Greek

The most challenging aspect of presenting the dative case in Greek may be the very verb for "give" in that language. It is one of a small but important group of verbs which retain several inflections from an earlier evolutionary period. The present tense ("I give," "you give," he/she/it gives," etc.) looks this way:

	singular	plural
1ˢᵗ person	διδωμι	διδομεν
2ⁿᵈ person	διδοις	διδοτε
3ʳᵈ person	διδωσι	διδουσι

If we confine ourselves to these present-tense forms, we should have sufficient verbal resources to forge a few examples of the dative case in action. The verb διδωμι doesn't really wander very far off the course of more mainstream verbs. The first- and third-person singular forms preserve a short syllable ending in iota: other than that, the conjugation should seem quite familiar. (Two other very common verbs in this same class—τιθημι ["I put"] and 'ιστημι ["I stand"]—have also been avoided up to now. We shall eventually work them in as we have διδωμι.)

At this point, little more need be said about translating the dative than what Section One offered. As in Latin, the Greek dative case is properly that of the indirect object. The dative has many other uses in Greek, as well—but these will be more easily understood after we consider Latin's ablative case. For the historical fact is that Greek's ablative endings came to resemble dative endings so closely that the two groups simply fused: by the time Greek came to be written down, its dative case *was* essentially the ablative, as well as being the continued repository of dative's own original function. As Section Four will reveal, Latin itself was already well along the same path to fusion when it came to be recorded.

Below are the dative inflections for the first two declensions:

	1ˢᵗ Declension	2ⁿᵈ Decl. Masc.	2ⁿᵈ Decl. Neuter
singular	-ηι / κουρηι	-ωι/ ταυρωι	-ωι / 'εργωι
plural	-ηις (ι) / κουρηις (ι)	-οις (ι) /ταυροις (ι)	-οις (ι) / 'εργοις (ι)

As mentioned in the previous section, these dative plural endings are merely Latin's without the merging of the vowel stem into an *–is* inflection. A diphthong remains instead of Latin's long "i" sound. You should also be aware, particularly since we have been following Homeric patterns, that all of these plurals may have an additional iota at the end (-ηισι, -οισι). Homer's choice of forms depended upon his metrical needs for a given verse: e.g., 'Αχαιοις ("for the Achaeans") appears in the *Iliad*'s second line, while 'οιωνοισι ("for the birds") follows in l. 5. Be that as it may, the inflection with the iota is, once again, clearly the more ancient form. (One eventually gets the impression that early Greek must have had a great many short iotas trailing after its words.) Furthermore, a nu would be appended to the iota (creating the inflection -οισιν) if the following word began in a vowel and the Homeric poet wanted to preserve the previous syllable from absorption (called elision). For instance, in the *Odyssey*'s opening invocation of the Muse, when Homer notes that the hero's men perished due to their own foolish deeds, the Greek runs, σφετερηισιν 'ατασθαλιηισιν 'ολοντο.

The final iota in the singular is not optional—but neither was it actually written as we represent it above. Apparently, it was elocuted so partially that the ear could hardly distinguish it. A late Greek in full possession of literacy would have written one of these dative singular inflections with a *iota subscript*: that is, with the tiniest of iotas inserted UNDER the eta or omega like a little comma reversed. (The first literate Greeks apparently wrote everything in capital letters.) This is equally true of the eta-iota pair in the feminine plural –ηισ. We have not followed the convention of the subscript simply to keep you more aware of the iota's presence. The subscript can be very easily missed in printed texts.

100

And one further alert. Remember that some feminine nouns prefer the alpha to the eta in all cases. The dative plural of θεα is always θεαις or θεαισιν, never θεης or θεηισιν.

Summary

The "true dative" in Greek functions exactly as its counterpart does in Latin; but the functions of several vanished cases were also absorbed into the dative. With these, a preposition is often used. With the indirect object, remember never to insert a Greek word to represent "to" or "for": the dative case conveys as much all by itself. The formation of the dative preserves the usual vowel stems and adds a iota, but it also historically involved a final iota in the plural. This unobtrusive vowel, however, soon disappeared in the plural's tail; and in the singular forms, it was eventually written as a subscript (suggesting that it was scarcely pronounced).

Greek Vocabulary

Here are a few more Greek nouns of the first and second declensions which will help to build easy sentences and also (in many cases) put you in mind of several English words you know from the sciences.

Again, let us begin with the Greek personal pronouns that are very frequent in dative expressions. Notice that all the forms beginning with a vowel except for 'εμοι have a breathing mark: i.e., their first sound is an "h."

Personal Pronouns in Dative

	singular	plural
1st person	'εμοι / μοι (to me)	'ημιν (to us)
2nd person	σοι / τοι (to you)	'υμιν (to you)
3rd person	'εοι / 'οι (to him/her/it)	σφισι (to them)

New Nouns of the 1st and 2nd Declensions

Greek	pronunciation	definition	English derivative
'αγορα (f)	ah-gor-AH	market/meeting place	agoraphobia
'αργυρος (m)	AR-gur-oss	silver	-----
βασίλεια (f),	bah-SEE-lay-ah	queen	basilica
βασιλεία (f)	bah-si-LAY-ah	kingdom	
βουλη (f)	boo-LAY	will, intent, plan	abulia
γλωσσα (f)	GLOE-sah	tongue, language	glottis
'ηλιος (m)	HEY-li-oss	sun	helium
κλεος (n)*	KLEH-oss	report (usually good; hence "fame, glory")	Herakles, Cletis
κομη (f)	koh-MAY	hair	comet

λαος (m)	LAH-oss	common people, mass	laity
λιθος (m)	LI-thoss	stone	monolithic
μαχη (f)	MAH-hkhay	battle	-----
'οπλον (n)	HOP-lon	weapon, tool	hoplite, panoply
'ορμη (f)	hor-MAY	attack, rush, passion	hormone
'ουρανος (m)	OO-rah-noss	universe, sky	Uranus
'οφθαλμος (m)	off-thal-MOSS	eye	ophthalmology
πυλη (f)	pew-LAY	gate	pylon
σαυρος (m)	SAUW-ross	lizard	dinosaur
στρατος (m)	STRAH-toss	army	strategy
'υλη (f)	HEW-lay	wood, forest	hylology
φαος (φως) (m)	FAH-oss	light (metaphor for "joy" and "eyes" [pl.])	phaeton
χαλκος (m)	HKHAL-koss	brass, copper	chalcid
χολος (m)	HKHOH-loss	bile, anger	choleric
χρυσος (m)	HKHREW-soss	gold	chrysalis
'ωμος (m)	OEW-moss	shoulder	homoplate

*Though frequently used by Homer and other early poets, κλεος only occurs in the nominative and accusative singular and plural. No other second-declension –ος word is neuter, although many are so in the third declension. Yet the plural form κλεα has to belong to the second declension since it lacks a proper third-declension stem change.

Exercise Set 3.2

A. Translate the following short sentences into English. All of them feature a noun in the dative.

  1. Βασιλεια λαωι φωνει.
  2. Δωρον σοι 'εχομεν.
  3. Κουροι 'ημιν 'οπλα διδουσι.
  4. Χαλκος 'οπλα 'ανθροποις ποιησει.
  5. Θεοι νομους 'εθνωι 'εποιεον.
  6. Κουραι τεκνοισι βουλην διδομεν.

N.B.: In Greek, the indirect object (dative) may appear either before or after the direct object (accusative). In English, likewise, we say both, "I gave [to] Janet the key," and, "I gave the key to Janet." There's no great difference in emphasis, either way.

B. Now translate these English sentences into Latin. Again, each has a noun somewhere that should be rendered into the dative case.

1. The gods will not release the soul to death for you (an emphatic way of saying "*your* soul to death": use two datives).

2. I will tell you the myth's words.

3. The sun's path was producing life for the earth.

Solo Flight: Translate, paying special attention to the datives.

1. Ειρηνη ‘υμιν (common in Greek New Testament: the first word means "peace" and gives us the name "Irene").

2. Αχιλλευς Αχαιοις πονους πολλους ’ετευχε (a paraphrase of the *Iliad* 's second line: Homer always refers to the Greeks as Achaians, in reference to the region ruled by the commander-in-chief, Agamemnon; the next-to-last word is an adjective meaning "many").

3. Φαινεται μοι κεινος ’ισος θεοισιν (the first words of Sappho's most famous love poem: the verb is passive, "is seen [= appears]"; the third word, having a nominative singular masculine ending, may be translated "that man"; and we know the adjective "equal" well from such words as "isosceles" and "isometric").

III. Phrases in the Romance Languages with a Dative Idea

The romance languages do not have cases: that point has been made before. It may not be inappropriate here, however, to point out a few of the ways in which they might be said to commemorate the dative case. This section will consume little space and may readily be bypassed. Yet for those who wish later to learn one of the modern descendants of Latin in greater depth, the discussion could be instructive, since the tendencies below often give English-speakers problems.

The Impersonal Expression: To be sure, English has its share of these. They are not unknown to any language. Yet the romance languages have a heavier density of them than do the Germanic languages. Such expressions are called impersonal because, taken quite literally, their subject is an abstract "it": for instance, the utterance, "It is necessary for me to buy groceries today." A born-and-bred English-speaker would be far more likely to say, "I have [or need] to get groceries today." Formulations like "it is necessary" are usually left for bureaucratic or scientific language, where a desire to conceal the party suffering the necessity is motivated by fear of blame, distaste for responsibility, attachment to objectivity, etc. We find such formulas stuffy. We are accustomed in common usage to bringing the person in question out from behind the smokescreen of the impersonal "it."

This is not so in the romance languages. Latin abounded in impersonal verbs that were seldom—or never—used in any other capacity: e.g., *libet* ("it is pleasing"), *licet* ("it is permitted"), and *paenitet* ("it causes regret"). A dative of the person involved typically occurs with these words. The arrangement carries over into modern Italian, especially, with expressions like the following:

> *mi bisogna*—"it's necessary for me, I must"
> *mi dispiace*—"it displeases me, I regret that…"
> *mi rincresce*—"it's distressing to me, I'm sorry that…"

To a lesser extent, French shares this fondness for the impersonal formulation. Phrases like *il me faut* ("it is necessary for me…") and *s'il vous plaît* ("if it pleases you") are part of ordinary conversation. The difference is precisely in the register. While the Anglophone world finds the impersonal stuffy, the world of romance culture finds it elegant and polite.

Possessive Expressions: We have seen how both Latin and Greek use the dative to signify possession. "I have a dream" might well be rendered *Est mihi somnium* or Εστι ’εμοι ’ονειρος in these ancient languages: i.e., "A dream is to me." The modern romance languages cling to this kind of expression. In French, you say *c'est à moi* to indicate personal possession ("it is to me")—never *c'est mien* ("it's mine"). French is also likely to use a dative expression as a way of reinforcing a possessive adjective. If in English you wished to distinguish your group of friends from someone else's, you would have little recourse other than to raise your voice: "*My* friends!" The more elegant French strategy would produce, *Mes amis à moi*—"My friends to me" (literally). About half a century ago, the French singer Yves Montand was well known for (among other things) a song titled *Mon manège à moi*. The word *manège* is slang for a head-spinning preoccupation, thanks to its appearance in the phrase designating a merry-go-round. Hence the translated title of Montand's popular number would be something like "My Personal Obsession" (= "my obsession *to me*").

As these examples indicate, French seems especially prone to embrace the *est mihi* possessive formulation, and the reason may have nothing to do with Latin, ironically. The Celtic past also influenced the formation of the French tongue; and with the Celts, this *it is + preposition +personal pronoun* structure is even more popular than it was with the Romans. "I have only one brother" might come out in Irish Gaelic as *níl agam ach aon bráthair amháin*—literally, "There is not to me but one brother only"; and "they have bad luck" might be phrased, *Tá an mí-ádh orra*—"The bad luck is upon them." French does not retain very many Celtic tendencies, to be sure, but they may crop up quite visibly at odd points. This is probably one of those points.

Shift of Direct to Indirect Object: This peculiarity attaches uniquely to Spanish. Verbs that normally take a direct object (i.e., transitive verbs) will treat their object as indirect if it happens to be a person. For instance, *matar los toros* means "to kill bulls" (a long-standing tradition in the Castilian world that has now become very controversial, for several reasons). Any English-speaker—and probably anyone at all who did not speak Spanish—would suppose that "bulls" could be replaced by "men" in the phrase above without any grammatical adjustment. If "kill" is a transitive verb for a bull, why would it not be so for a man? And yet, the phrase would indeed have to be adjusted to read *matar a los hombres*. This stunning oddity may very well be a relic of Latin grammar. Recall the Wilfred Owen example (drawn from Horace): *dulce et decorum est pro patriâ mori*. Though standard usage is rather sketchy here, it appears that the Romans would often shift a noun or pronoun normally in the ablative case (like *patriâ*) into the dative case when a warm-blooded human being was referred to. The ablative of personal agent (e.g., "by the soldiers") is even shifted into the dative frequently by poets like Virgil, so that the sentence, "He was seen by the soldiers," would in literal translation be closer to, "He was seen as for (= with respect to) the soldiers."

Is there a subtle kind of courtesy or delicacy involved in the Spanish convention? We can probably never collect the kind of evidence that would allow us to say confidently, one way or the other. Just don't be aghast if one day you discover that one kills (or loves) *to* someone in Spanish; or if you find the phrasing indefensible, you should probably blame Latin for it.

Exercise Set 3.3

Can you correct the following short sentences? You will probably find elements in all six that you do not understand: just remember that the "trick" in every case is drawn from the material discussed above.

1. The books are mine. ~ *Les livres sont miens.* (French)
2. I regret having abandoned you. ~ *Regretto d'averti abandonato.* (Italian)
3. We are helping your mother. ~ *Ayudamos tu madre.* (Spanish)
4. These are *my* friends [as distinct from *your* friends]. ~ *Ce sont MES amis.* (French)
5. I have to go now. ~ *Ora ho di partire.* (Italian)
6. We do not eat tortillas. *No comemos a las tortillas.* (Spanish)

IV. The Ablative Case: Latin

All of the cases bear Latin names, and these names, once translated, yield important clues about function. The word "ablative" literally means "borne away from" (the past participle of *aufero*), and the ablative case does indeed center upon movement away from a given point. This point may be temporal as well as physical. "From the third year onward" would be translated by an ablative phrase in Latin, *ê tertio anno*, just as would the spatial indentification, "down from the third town" (*de oppido tertio*). Sometimes such phrases communicate their meaning simply by being in the ablative, without the aid of any preposition (*tertio anno* all by itself would mean "in the third year")—but we may see in this case's complexities how the system is becoming overstrained, for prepositions also accompany the ablative case quite frequently.

This is because so many other functions have already been compressed under the ablative's aegis: the case has indeed become a kind of "grab bag" of functions in Latin. An ablative phrase can identify the "time when" something occurs as well as the "time from which." (One might argue that no real difference exists between these two: if Caesar departed at the third hour, did he not depart as clock time was moving away from the third-hour mark? Time always moves away from where it is "at"!) Similarly, an ablative may identify either the "place from where" action occurs or simply the "place where." Caesar might have moved his army *ex castrîs* ("from the camp") or he might have kept it *in castrîs* ("in the camp"). In this second pair of examples, you see clearly why the prepositions *ex* and *in* are needed with the case to underscore a critical distinction. Without them, we would not know if the army were leaving or staying.

In very early Latin, a distinct case called the *locative* existed whose inflection plainly communicated "in this place," without any implication of movement. We know of this case because it survives in very fragmentary form, sometimes looking like a genitive and sometimes like an ablative. The historical Romans used it only with the names of cities, towns, and small islands, and with a few very old nouns, however. Trying to memorize the locative form in these few instances would be wasted effort during an overview such as ours, so we shall treat the ablative case as having completely absorbed this function.

Furthermore, the ablative had taken on the function of expressing *means* and *manner*. Authors of so-called Golden Latin during the Late Republic (including prose masters like Cicero and Livy) used a preposition for neither of these functions. In later times, however, the "ablative of means or instrument" (which almost always involves some kind of material object) continued to use no preposition, whereas the "ablative of manner" (which often refers to an immaterial quality) followed *cum*. "The man was striking with a sword" would be written *vir gladiô pulsabat*, with the long "o" of *gladiô* expressing the sword's use as an instrument. (Some of these endings may be reminding you of the dative. They should! More of that momentarily.) If, on the other hand, a queen commands "with justice," you would find a later author writing *regina cum iustitiâ imperat*, the preposition *cum* clarifying how the ablative (signaled here by a long "a") is to be translated. Phrases known well to us today in academic settings such as *magnâ cum laude* ("with great praise") express an ablative of manner.

The preposition *cum* is also a common sight in the "ablative of accompaniment." An object such as a sword can serve as the means of a deed, but the Romans took care to distinguish human beings in situations which we English-speakers would handle indiscriminately through "with." The preposition, as we have seen, is not employed with an inanimate object: it IS employed with a person. *Iulia cum multîs amicîs villam spectat* means, "Julia is watching the house with many friends." To leave out the preposition *cum* would be bad form. The same treatment governs the use of the preposition *ab*, which corresponds to our English "by." If a window is broken "by a rock"—that is, by an inanimate object—then the ablative is used without any preposition: *saxô* (ablative of means). If the window is broken "by a boy," though, the preposition *ab* must precede the noun: *â puerô* (ablative of "personal agent": the "b" is dropped from *ab*, by the way, except when the following noun begins with a vowel.) The difference between instrumentality and agency is humanity. To compose the second window-breaking sentence without a preposition would imply that the poor boy had been picked up by a giant and swung like a hammer!

The Romans, in short, had developed an etiquette to restrain the ablative case from any further collapse. If you should ever study Russian, you will find (and we have found this before in another context) that some of its structures are better preserved than Latin's; regarding the ablative, specifically, Russian has separate "instrumental" and "prepositional" cases. The functions related to means, manner, and agency above would usually be governed by the Russian instrumental case. Other functions of the ablative would tend to fall somewhat more loosely into the prepositional case (whose inflection has in fact grown redundant in Russian, since a clarifying preposition *always* precedes it). This prepositional case is more closely associated with "place where" than anything else, so it obviously began as a Russian locative.

Ancient India's literary language, Sanskrit, also divides the case of instrumentality from that of "separation" (e.g., "place from which") and other ablative functions; and, besides having these two distinct cases, Sanskrit—unlike Russian—has not yet fused the ablative and the locative. You may know that linguists group together most European languages with several reaching across the Caucasus and into India: the so-called Indo-European family. In other words, Latin and Sanskrit do not resemble one another by chance, but rather share a common ancestor. Thus the multiplicity of cases performing Latin's ablative function in Sanskrit is yet more objective evidence that the tongue of the Romans had begun to decay grammatically (or, if you prefer, to become more "user-friendly") by the time it was written down.

The Romans had another reason for needing prepositions with the ablative besides its having soaked up so many archaic cases: it had also started to look very like the dative. The resemblance in the first and second declensions, in fact, is very nearly perfect:

	1st Declension	2nd Decl. Masc.	2nd Decl. Neuter
singular	-â / feminâ	-ô / taurô	-ô / saxô
plural	-îs / feminîs	-îs / taurîs	-îs / saxîs

Now, at last, you may appreciate the full impact of the "bad news" about the dative case: it really differs from the ablative at only one point! (Indeed, since the Romans did not draw accents over their words, an ancient manuscript would offer no obvious and immediate way of distinguishing *femina*, nominative singular, from *feminâ*, ablative singular.) The Greek language appears to have given up on policing such distinctions: we shall find soon that its ablative simply vanished into other cases like the dative. If only Latin had kept around its short iotas as Greek did, paradoxically, its own dative and ablative endings would not look so much alike. The dative singular of *puer*, for example, ought to be *pueroi*, with both vowels in the final diphthong being short; but they combined, instead, to form one long "o," which is exactly the true and proper form (from the historian's perspective) of the ablative *puerô* (omega). Nothing less than the oldest scrap of Latin in our possession—the inscription on an ancient bracelet—assures us that this distinction once existed. The inscription reads:

Manios med fefaked Numasioi. ~ "Manius made me for Numasius."

The short "o" (omicron) appears here both in the nominative form *Manios* and in the dative *Numasioi*, where the short "i" has not yet been absorbed. (There are also two instances of final "d" probably being pronounced as "t," as it would eventually be spelled… but that's another story.) The point is that the Romans did not create their language with the intent of inspiring consternation in their successors: most identical forms really were distinct at some point in history. The first-declension dative in *–ae* probably differed from the nominative plural in that the latter would once have been pronounced with two clearly long vowels. That is, *feminae* (nominative plural) would have come out *fem-in-AH-ee*. Apparently, a similar distinction was still operative between *femina* (nominative singular) and *feminâ* (ablative singular), the latter of which should properly have been drawn out to produce something almost like *fem-in-AH-ah*. Poetry may have aided the more educated Romans in preserving these differences; for once Latin adopted a more Hellenistic system of versifying, a premium was placed on making long vowels actually take longer to pronounce. The fate of any language, though, is eventually decided by the mass of people who speak it—and less educated Romans would have swept over these fine distinctions.

Here are some of the Latin prepositions most often used with the ablative case:

ab (*â* before consonants)—away from; by (personal agent)
cum—with (accompaniment, sometimes manner)
de—down from; also about, concerning; NEVER possessive "of"!
ex (*ê* before consonants)—out of, out from

106

in—in, at (only "into" with accusative)
sine—without

Much more about prepositions appears at the end of Chapter Five.

Summary
*The Latin ablative case, in both meaning and form, shows many signs of the earlier language's collapse. In general, the ablative tells where, when, how, and by whom. The Romans used prepositions with skillful selectivity to assist in separating some functions from others. In English translation, however, the ablative **must always be rendered with a preposition**. In form, the ablative came to be spelled (often in the singular and always in the plural) identically to the dative.*

Exercise Set 3.4

A. Translate the following short sentences into English. Remember always to use a preposition when putting an ablative phrase into English, whether the Latin uses one or not.

1. Debemus castra movêre sine morâ.
2. Equos in campîs non servabunt.
3. Nautae gladiô non pugnabunt.

4. Nuntii ex insulîs mox (soon) navigabitis.
5. Stellas in caelô spectabamus.
6. Sunt mihi libri de amicitiâ.

B. Now translate these English sentences into Latin. Remember not to use a preposition with the Ablative of Means.

1. You (pl.) will prevail over men with justice, not with swords.
2. The farmers will be walking from the town with money.
3. By a trick of the wine, he saw (kept seeing) his daughter in dreams.

Solo Flight: Repeat the exercise at the end of 3.1, substituting the ablative for the dative. That is, select an English passage from a novel, an article, a historical document, or some other source and pick out all the ablative phrases in the passages. Cross-check your answers with those of a classmate. (The Pledge of Allegiance is actually a bad choice in this instance, for it has very few ablative phrases.)

V. The Case of the Missing Case: Greek's Overworked Dative and Genitive

If we were now to begin a section on the Greek ablative, we would already be finished: it doesn't exist! Yet this is not entirely true. The Greek ablative does exist, but not as an independent case. Apparently gnawed away by the same processes which are clearly at work in recorded Latin, the formal ablative in Greek gradually disappeared. From another perspective, we could say that it always comes disguised as a dative but is often given away by the prepositions preceding it (or drifting around it as adverbs in Homer). This may be both the fairest and most useful way of stating the situation. Grammar books choose to ignore the Greek ablative as if it were non-existent because *in no single instance* is it spelled differently from a corresponding dative (matching first declension to first declension, singular to singular, plural to plural, etc.). Yet the true dative *never* has a preposition before it, whereas the ablative case, whose form has fused indistinguishably with the dative's, often does.

Or if we prefer to think of the evolutionary process as one of unloading ablative functions onto other cases... then the redistributing did not stop at the dative's boundary. As if keenly aware of that case's being burdened with too much new meaning, the Greeks occasionally shuffled formerly ablative meanings to the genitive. This explanation is more pleasantly graphic than historically certain, to be sure. We cannot know that the Greek genitive came to be populated with refugee ablative functions only because there was no more room at the Inn of the Dative. The supposition seems probable, but it remains a guess. For whatever reason, however, the Greek genitive case, like the dative, has a few functions beyond its proper one (i.e., possession), and with these are associated various helpful prepositions. An important instance would be the idea of "motion away." In Homer's *Iliad*, we encounter phrases like προ πυλαων ("before the gates") and πολεμου δ' 'αποπαυεο ("thou wert withdrawing from battle") where the movement away from something is implicit. This is perhaps less easy to see in the preposition προ, usually translated "before" and not clearly showing any kind of recoil; yet the Greeks felt that one object's being before another suggested a distancing in the mental process of measurement (which seems quite reasonable, after all). As for the preposition 'απο, which literally means "away from," it is actually prefixed to the verb παυω ("I cease") in the Homeric phrase above, but a movement *from* battle remains obvious. We speak of desisting or refraining *from* this or that act even in English.

The ablative of personal agent also becomes genitive with the help of 'υπο, which is translated "by" in such circumstances (and "under" in most others).

Remember, once again, that the proper genitive in Greek and Latin will *never* be preceded by a preposition. When we see certain Greek genitives, therefore, trailing after a preposition, we know that we are looking at a function originally allotted to some other case.

The dative remains the Greek case that absorbed most of the meanings associated with the Latin ablative. The Greek dative, often but *not always* with a preposition, is employed to express means or instrument, manner, and accompaniment—three of the most basic uses of the Latin ablative. It is also employed to express "where" if no motion away from the stated location is implied. It can even be used to express "time when," though the genitive more often takes on this function. Consider these illustrations from the *Iliad*'s first book:

'αμφω 'ομως **θυμωι** φιλεουσα ~ "she loved both equally **in/with her heart**..." (place where or means)

τοξ' **'ωμοισιν** 'εχων ~ "bearing arrows **upon his shoulders**..." (place where: and note that Homer has not only preserved the archaic iota on the dative plural ending, but has used poetic license to insert a nu so that the iota does not merge with the following epsilon and spoil his meter)

δεκατηι δ' 'αγορηνδε καλεσσατο λαον 'Αχιλλευς ~ "**On the tenth day**, Achilles called the masses to the meeting place." (time when)

It would be remiss not to add at some point that certain verbs in Greek—and in Latin, for that matter—evoked an indirect object (proper dative) or a partitive relationship (proper genitive) to the ancient ear where we see only a direct object. For example, ones trusts *as to/with respect to* someone in both ancient languages (indirect object—dative); and the Greek verb for "fight" also takes a dative, the Latin verb an ablative. Similarly, one hears or smells *of* something in both Greek and Latin, and one rules *of* a community, tribe, kingdom, etc., in Greek. The idea seems to be that an entire noise is not consumed by a single ear nor an entire smell by a single nose, and that not every aspect of every person's life is ruled even by a cruel despot (partitive genitive—a mere part of the whole is involved). Such precision has nothing to do with the collapsing of case functions one into another: the ancients appear truly to have conceived of reality in such a hair-splittingly sharp manner. (Americans from remote parts of Appalachia, by the way, can be heard to this day using phrases like "taste of" and "smell of," which also occur in the King James Bible; so the real force at work may be less some ancient ethnic admiration of precision than a broadly modern impatience with lingering over detail.)

The depth of analysis possible in an introductory course like this one is very limited, and exceptions must be neglected from time to time. Yet we may say strictly as a generality that Greek prepositions followed by the dative are taking over most of the functions associated with the Latin ablative. On the other hand, those prepositions which involve some notion of "motion away" tend to govern the genitive. The intricacies involved in this topic may indeed sometimes lead one to wonder if the Greeks themselves were always in full accord about which of the two cases to use when. The situation was a volatile one: let that be our last word here.

Summary

*The functions of the Latin ablative migrated mostly into the Greek dative, but a few flowed into the Greek genitive (such as "motion away"). Prepositions are often used with these cases to assist in unpacking the inflection's meaning, but are **never** used with the genitive's original possessive meaning or the dative proper's indirect object function.*

Exercise Set 3.5

A. Translate the following short sentences into English. Here are the prepositions used:

with genitive	
Greek	**English**
'απο	from, away from
'εκ / 'εξ (before vowel)	out of, from
προ	before, in front of
'υπο	by (personal agent, not space)
with dative	
'εν ('ενι / 'ειν in poetry)	in (static location)
συν	with (accompaniment; seldom means)

1. Στρατος 'εκ μαχης 'ερρεε.
2. Ποιηται μυθους λογοις τευχουσι.
3. Βασιλειαι λαον προ πυλης σκοπησουσι.

4. Βιος (here, "livelihood") 'εκ θαλασσης 'εμοι 'εστι.
5. Θεοι και θεαι 'εν ποντωι ζωουσι.
6. 'Οφθαλμους 'εξ 'ηλιου 'ετρεπετε.

B. Now translate these English sentences into Greek. Again, each has a noun somewhere that should be rendered into the dative case.
1. To poets, a goddess lives in the sea..
2. You men will produce weapons with brass.
3. From the sun's gate rushes (= runs) light for the earth.

Solo Flight: Translate. Follow patterns modeled in 3.5 A, and use the preceding table of prepositions.
1. We will make a room out of wood with the children.
2. The queen's army will not ('ου) retreat (use χωρεω) from battle.
3. Life for a queen (use dative) is with [her] people.

VI. Tables for the Entire First and Second Declensions, Latin and Greek

This section contains nothing completely new to you; rather, it synthesizes our growing information about the varying noun inflections of the first and second declensions in both Latin and Greek so that you may now see all endings together. You will notice that the tables below order the cases differently from the sequence in which this book introduced them. A longstanding pedagogical convention has always arranged the dative just after the genitive, even though the accusative is employed much more often than either of these (and the ablative, perhaps, more often than the accusative). We shall adhere to the convention from now on. Our book initially broke with it in the interest of making a more logical presentation.

LATIN

	1st Declension	2nd Decl. Masc.	2nd Decl. Neut.
SINGULAR			
nominative	-a / femina	-us / taurus	-um / saxum
genitive	-ae / feminae	-i / tauri	-i / saxi
dative	-ae / feminae	-o / tauro	-o / saxo
accusative	-am / feminam	-um / taurum	-um / saxum
ablative	-â / feminâ	-o / tauro	-o / saxo
PLURAL			
nominative	-ae / feminae	-i / tauri	-a / saxa
genitive	-arum / feminarum	-orum / taurorum	-orum / saxorum
dative	-îs / feminîs	-îs / taurîs	-îs / saxîs
accusative	-as / feminas	-os / tauros	-a / saxa
ablative	-îs / feminîs	-îs / taurîs	-îs / saxîs

GREEK

	1st Declension	2nd Decl. Masc.	2nd Decl. Neut.
SINGULAR			
nominative	-η / κουρη	-ος / ταυρος	-ον / 'εργον
genitive	-ης / κουρης	-ου / ταυρου	-ου / 'εργου
dative	-ηι / κουρηι	-ωι/ ταυρωι	-ωι / 'εργωι
accusative	-ην / κουρην	-ον / ταυρον	-ον / 'εργον
PLURAL			
nominative	-αι / κουραι	-οι / ταυροι	-α / 'εργα
genitive	-αων / κουραων	-ων / ταυρων	-ων / 'εργων
dative	-ηις / κουρηις	-οις /ταυροις	-οις / 'εργοις
accusative	-ας / κουρας	-ους / ταυρους	-α / 'εργα

(**N.B.**: You may recall that early Greek also has inflections for the dual number, as was mentioned briefly in Chapter One. We have not reproduced these because they are employed rarely even by Homer. The case inflections have already so decayed in

Homer's dual, furthermore, that the nominative is indistinguishable from the accusative and the genitive from the dative.)

Exercise Set 3.6

A. The Roman poet Horace arranged many profound thoughts in the intricate order required by classical versification. Here is one example: "Nullus argento color est avarîs abdito in terrîs." (The general idea is that human beings decide arbitrarily to confer great value on stones or minerals and then, in the height of folly, kill for them.) Translate the more prosaically organized sentence below, being mindful that it employs the "dative + 'to be'" construction to show possession:

Nullus (adj., "no") color est argento abdito ("hidden," dat. adj. that modifies preceding word) in terrîs avarîs ("miserly," adj. that modifies preceding word).

B. The following utterance was ascribed to Socrates. Translate. Notice that the verb governs a genitive in the same way as we would say "is deprived of."

Πασα ("every") ψυχη 'ακουσης ("unwilling," nom. adj. that modifies preceding word; we would use an adverb and say "unwillingly") στερεται (verb, "is deprived of") της 'αληθειας.

Solo Flight. Appendix C at the end of this book contains these two thoughtful sayings and many others. Test your competence with the first and second declensions by matching the Latin and Greek versions with the English translations beside them and then seeing how many noun inflections you can identify.

VII. The Third Declension: Latin

Most Latin textbooks undertake the third declension a little before midway and then devote three or four chapters to its vagaries. The fourth and fifth declensions make an appearance distinctly later, well into the second half of the text. This is a convention that has no apparent logic at all. In the first place, Latin, like Greek, has essentially three declensions *and no more*. The third declension's vowel stem, however, is a short "i"—and we have often had occasion to see how bullied that little vowel can be when it comes into contact with other vowels. As a result, competing vowels take over to varying degrees at various stages of the language's evolution. A few late nouns developed a "u" stem (fourth declension) or an "e" stem (fifth declension) after the "i" had been forced to retire almost entirely from the picture.

One can complicate this process of evolution if one enjoys complications. There is a worldly motive, certainly, for multiplying a single phenomenon into many phenomena. An abundance of medical disorders is good business for specialists, whereas the old country doctor's "aspirin and rest" approach is a recipe for poverty. To be sure, there's really no such thing as a panacea in medical science; but scholars in other disciplines also have a predisposition to make many things out of few, and they often do so with far less justification. (An old Sanskrit saying runs, "Learned men call one thing by many names.") Here we will strive to keep everything as simple as possible. Why take three pills for your grammatical health when you need only one?

Below are what would probably be the fundamental contents of those three or four intermediate chapters about the third declension. In fact, the "archaic" paradigm might well not even be presented; and if it were, it would come last of all, perhaps in a footnote. Yet if we view it first, we can see how "user-friendly" the third declension originally was. An "i" initiates almost every inflection: even the nominative plural in –es would have been –eis in the beginning (or perhaps –ies or –iis in the very beginning). For some reason, the forms of the word *turris*, "a tower," have preserved these primitive inflections. A tiny handful of other nouns may also be found with them. The great epic poet Vergil routinely uses the –îs form in the accusative plural for all third-declension masculine and feminine nouns, since his *Aeneid* is intended to evoke a spirit of glorious times past. (Milton employed archaisms for similar reasons in *Paradise Lost*, as did the King James Bible.)

The endings for nouns of this group, then, began life being supremely simple. Once again (as with the first and second declensions), the datives and ablatives within the singular and plural forms are identical; once again, the accusative singular ends in an "m"; once again, the genitive plural ends in a "um"; once again, the accusative plural is "dominant vowel + s"; and once again, the dative and ablative plurals contain an "i" and an "s." These endings should look very familiar! (The ones on the far right are bolded because, as the most common in ancient classical texts, they should be memorized.)

3rd Declension	archaic	i-stem	regular (for masc. & fem. nouns)
SINGULAR			
nominative	-is / turris	-is, etc. / finis	**-?? / mater**
genitive	-is / turris	-is / finis	**-is / matris**
dative	-i / turri	-i / fini	**-i / matri**
accusative	-im / turrim	-em / finem	**-em / matrem**
ablative	- i / turri	-e / fine	**-e / matre**
PLURAL			
nominative	-es / turres	-es / fines	**-es / matres**
genitive	-ium / turrium	-ium / finium	**-um / matrum**
dative	-ibus / turribus	-ibus / finibus	**-ibus / matribus**
accusative	-îs / turrîs	-es / fines	**-es / matres**
ablative	-ibus / turribus	-ibus / finibus	**-ibus / matribus**

The paradigm represented by *turris*, alas, is altogether too archaic to guide you through most classical texts. By historical times, the Romans had already begun either to drop the "i" entirely (as in the genitive plural) or to allow it to fade into an "e." The linguistic term for this latter process is *palatalization*, and it represents a universal tendency of human speech. Once the tongue grows a little lazy (people *always* seem to be fighting laziness), it starts to pronounce words with less curling and relaxes itself increasingly against the palate, or roof of the mouth, if no ensuing sound helps it to hold the tenser position. The vowel "i," for instance, lapses into "e" if followed by nothing or by certain consonants like "m." In other cases, the "i" might linger if the following consonant made it the easier option: *iss* is a little easier to say than *ess*, so the genitive singular always remained –*is*.

It is a great irony that in Latin's third declension, the second stage of evolution—where we now see far fewer "i" endings than in the *turris* stage—has been formally designated the i-stem group by grammarians. This is because nouns of the third evolutionary stage possessed still fewer endings with "i"; in fact, words like *mater* ("mother"), as has been noted above, typify written Latin's third declension.

Viewing the whole scene retrospectively, then, the linguistic historian really sees only two substantial groups of nouns, the *turris* group having left nothing but a few fossils like *turris* itself, *puppis* ("ship"—the source of our phrase "poop deck*"), sitis* ("thirst"), and the highly peculiar little noun *vis* ("force, strength").

Thus the word *mater* best represents the paradigm you should use for learning the third declension. The standard genitive plural ends merely in *–um* rather in *–ium*. Yet the class of nouns like *finis*—the so-called i-stems—remains a fairly large minority. Generally, any noun whose nominative singular ends in *–is* or *–es* and whose genitive has no more syllables than the nominative is an i-stem (meaning merely, in practical terms, that its genitive plural is *–ium*). Other nouns qualify for the i-stem distinction, as well, such as monosyllables whose nominative singular finishes in *–x*, *–ns*, *-rs*, or *–bs*. These rules can grow very tedious, and little would be gained by unveiling them all in an introductory setting like ours. Third-declension nouns (with the usual exceptions for neuter nouns) clearly share the same inflections most of the time; or, if you prefer this formulation, they share the same inflections almost all of the time except for the genitive plural.

It is not recommended that you preoccupy yourself with the rules for identifying an i-stem while working through this elementary course. You would be wasting your effort on what amounts to a rather trivial distinction. Just be aware that the genitive plural can sometimes be *–ium* instead of *–um*.

Well… and then there's the nominative singular. A third-declension noun's nominative can end in *almost anything*. The words *pax*, *soror*, *pes*, *dens*, and *homo* all belong to the third declension. Only *soror* ("sister") does not alter the consonants in its stem to form the ensuing cases. For this reason, you will have to memorize a third-declension word's genitive singular along with the nominative if you decide at a later to time to proceed with Latin studies: alterations in the stem are simply too numerous and unpredictable to follow any other procedure. Yet they *may* be somewhat predicted, after all, if you acquire a good English vocabulary, for our derivatives inevitably descend from the noun's stem rather than its nominative (e.g., "pacific," "dental," and "hominid").

The other trouble spot where endings are likely to shift is the ablative singular. Vergil and other poets will often use an "i" ending here where standard prose writers of the time will use an "e." (Horace, for instance, advises us stoically to keep a steady head in hard times and also to guard ourselves *ab insolenti… laetitiâ*—"from arrogant rejoicing"—in good times, *insolenti* being a third-declension adjective.) For neuter i-stems, the "i" in the ablative is indeed a hard and fast rule… and off we go into the third declension's Charybdis of fine distinctions. Again, in the present context, to remember simply that two possibilities exist for the ablative singular is quite sufficient.

Finally, we should address the subject of gender, for the first/second declension boundaries must now be largely erased. All three genders are heavily represented in the third declension. Masculine and feminine nouns usually bear no marks or clues whatever that give away their gender. A few exceptions mercifully exist. Nouns ending in a long "u" + s—e.g., *virtûs* ("virtue"), *iuventûs* ("youth"), and *senectûs* ("old age")—are always feminine; so are nouns ending in *–udo* (*multitudo*, "multitude," and *fortitudo*, "fortitude") and nouns ending in *–tas* (*libertas*, "liberty," and *felicitas*, "happiness"). The Romans clearly projected an idealized femininity onto abstract qualities!

One special group of neuter third-declension nouns just happens to end in short "u" + s, which is exactly the nominative singular ending of the *masculine* second declension. Be careful of these words. The genitive of *corpus* ("body") is not *corpi* but *corporis*, and it is neuter; the genitive of *genus* ("type") is not *geni* but *generis*, and it is also neuter. When we turn to Greek, indeed, we shall find an enormous volume of third-declension neuter nouns ending in –ος which reproduce this problem on a much grander scale. For example, the Greek word for "spoken word" or a tale created from spoken words, ΄επος (hence our word "epic"), does not have the genitive ΄επου but rather ΄επεος. So many Latin and Greek neuter words of this sort occupy the third declension that they must have arrived by the same evolutionary path (as opposed to what is called parallel evolution, where two similar structures develop independently of one another). There's a lot of shared DNA showing under the microscope here.

Again, do not be intimidated by look-alike endings in different declensions: simply be aware that they exist. You'll get the hang of the distinction with time and practice. In the meanwhile, consulting a dictionary frequently is a good idea; its entries will tell you which declension a given noun belongs to.

The normal idiosyncrasies of neuter nouns still apply in the third declension. That is, their nominatives and accusatives are always identical (though they change in response to number), and the plural ending for these two cases is always an "a." Below is the declension of a neuter i-stem beside that of a "regular" third-declension neuter noun, just so that you may see the whole picture in a single frame. As has been said, the neuter i-stem always has an ablative singular in –i instead of –e.

3rd Declension Neuter

	i-stem	regular (neuter)
SINGULAR		
nominative	-e,al,ar / mare	-?? / corpus
genitive	-is / maris	-is / corporis
dative	-i / mari	-i / corpori
accusative	-(see nom.) / mare	-(see nom.) / corpus
ablative	-i / mari	-e /corpore
PLURAL		
nominative	-ia / maria	-a / corpora
genitive	-ium / marium	-um / corporum
dative	-ibus / maribus	-ibus / corporibus
accusative	-ia / maria	-a / corpora
ablative	-ibus / maribus	-ibus / corporibus

Summary

The Latin third declension is a distinct set of noun inflections that historically began with a short "i." As time went on, the "i" was increasingly absorbed into other vowels (for example, when the so-called fourth and fifth declensions were formed) or became less assertive, vanishing from accusatives and often ablative singulars and genitive plurals. All three genders are represented in the third declension but are rarely indicated by the nominative singular's form, which is quite unpredictable. In fact, the nominative singular cannot be relied upon to give the noun's true stem; dictionaries therefore also supply the genitive.

Vocabulary

The lists below have been arranged so as to reduce the third declension's confusing diversity to a less imposing level. In the first two of these, genitives are not always spelled out in their entirety. All genitive inflections following a hyphen should be considered as beginning immediately after the last consonant that precedes a vowel in the nominative form.

i-stems

Latin (nom/gen)	meaning	derivative
auris, -is (f)	ear	aural

avis, -is (f)	bird	aviary
canis, -is (m/f)	dog	canine
civis, -is (m)	citizen	civil
dens, dentis (m)	tooth	dental
feles, -is (f)	cat	feline
fons, fontis (m)	fountain, spring	font
hostis, -is (m)	enemy (public)	hostile
ignis, -is (m)	fire	ignition
lex, legis (f)	law	legal
mens, mentis (f)	mind, intellect	mental
mons, montis (m)	mountain	mound
mors, mortis (f)	death	mortality
navis, -is (f)	ship	naval
nox, noctis (f)	night	nocturnal
nubes, -is (f)	cloud	nubid
os, ossis (n)	bone	ossify
ovis, -is (f)	sheep	ovine
pars, partis (f)	part, share	part
piscis, -is (m)	fish	piscine
pons, pontis (m)	bridge	pontoon
vulpes, -is (f)	fox	vulpine
urbs, urbis (f)	city	urban

regular

caput, capitis (n)	head (of body)	capital
caro, carnis (n)	flesh	carnal
cor, cordis (n)	heart	coronary
dux, ducis (m)	leader	ductile

flos, floris (m)	flower	floral
frater, fratris (m)	brother	fraternal
homo, hominis (m)	man, person	hominid
iter, itineris (n)	road, journey, way	itinerary
lac, lactis (n)	milk	lactose
leo, leonis (m)	lion	leonine
lux, lucis (f)	light	lucid
mater, matris (f)	mother	maternal
miles, militis (m)	soldier	military
ôs, ôris (n; not short "o" like os, "bone")	mouth, opening	oral
pater, patris (m)	father	paternal
pax, pacis (f)	peace	pacific
radix, radicis (f)	root	radish, radical
rex, regis (m)	king	regal
sol, -is (m)	sun	solar
soror, -is (f)	sister	sorority
vox, vocis (f)	voice	vocal

masculine (states of mind/spirit)

-or nom., -oris gen,

amor
candor
clamor
dolor
horror
pudor
terror
timor

Like some of the feminine nouns below, these words give obvious derivatives in most cases that also define them. *Pudor* is a sense of shame: modesty. *Dolor* is grief, pain (cf. the adjective "dolorous"). *Timor* is a word for "fear" bestowed as a name by European explorers upon an island near Australia. You should be able to figure out the rest.

feminine (qualities)

-tas, -tatis
antiquitas
celeritas
felicitas
ferocitas

The derivatives of these words ARE their meanings in most cases. Do you know the word "felicity"? What about "celerity" and "verity"? (The former is Einstein's "c" in

116

gravitas	"e = mc².") Only *potestas*, "power," has
libertas	no English equivalent.
potestas	
veritas	

-tudo, -tudinis

fortitudo	These nouns have also passed directly into
magnitudo	English—so much so that only the final "o"
multitudo	need be changed to "e" to produce their
pulchritudo	definition. Do you know the words "pulchritude"
servitudo	and "turpitude"?
turpitudo	

-tûs, -tûtis

iuventûs	youth
senectûs	old age
virtûs	virtue

feminine (abstract/intangible objects)

-tio nom., *-tionis* gen.

abrogation	repeal, annulment
admiratio	admiration (or act expressing it)
correctio	improvement
factio deed,	active group
indignatio	indignation (or matter producing it)
locutio	speech

The set of abstract nouns just above was created from verbs. The totality of such creations was very small in classical Latin; you can see in two cases, as well, that the Romans still tended to attach the abstraction to a concrete deed or occurrence associated with it. By the Middle Ages, however, this family of words would proliferate and give us one of the most voluminous groups of abstract nouns in modern English: nouns ending in *-tion*.

neuter

i-stems		
animal, -is	animate life form	animal
mare, -is	sea	marine
-*us* nom., *-oris/-eris* gen. (after dropping *-us*)		
corpus, -oris	body	corpse
genus, -eris	kind, type	generic
opus, -eris	work, task	operation
pectus, -oris	chest	pectoral
tempus, -oris	time, period	temporal
-*en* nom., *-inis* gen. ("e" in nom. becomes "i" in stem)		
crimen	accusation, fault	crime
flumen	river	flume

sanguen (also found as *sanguis*, m)	blood	sanguinary

Exercise Set 3.7

A. Translate the following phrases into Latin. You will find all the vocabulary you need in the lists directly above.

1. in the river
2. from fear of the lions
3. times (nom.) of grief and terror
4. in the light of the sun
5. the fishes (nom.) in the sea
6. for the citizens (dat.) of the city
7. the end (acc.) of virtue
8. with liberty and justice for people

B. Translate the following sentences into English.

1. Praemium turpitudinis odium hominum esse debet.
2. Amici libertatis, cum militibus tyranni (tyrannus, "tyrant") pugnabitis.
3. Ni piscibus ni avibus ("neither... nor") est ferocitas leonis.
4. Marcus puer sorores ab ore fluminis servabat.
5. Cum diligentiâ* et fortitudine trans pontem in monte ambulare temptabamus.
6. Opera poetae cor et mentem regis superabant.
7. Voces avium vitae pulchritudinem dant.
8. Crimina patrum contra ("against") virtutes filiorum non valebunt. (trans. verb as "weigh, prevail")
9. Caput est rex corpori: mens dux capiti esse debet.**
10. In duce desideramus gravitatem leonis, felicitatem felis, et intelligentiam vulpis.

* The –*entia* class of feminine noun (*diligentia*, "diligence"; *munificentia*, "munificence") is yet another specially designed to accommodate abstract ideas; of course, this time it pertains to the first declension, not the third.
** The dative instead of the genitive here signifies a somewhat figurative relationship.

C. Translate these sentences from English into Latin.

1. Fear of death and love of the laws were keeping the citizens away (use same verb and preposition as in B.4 above) from the city of the enemies.
2. We mothers of the soldiers will give flowers to the king.
3. Throughout (per + acc.) the night, we were watching the lights of the ships.
4. The power of youth ought to walk in peace with the wisdom (*sapientia*) of old age.
5. The dogs will frighten the lion with (by means of) their teeth and their uproar (use *clamor*).

Solo Flight: Take Numbers 2 and 6 from Exercise B above and change them in the following manner. Make every singular noun plural and every plural noun singular. Of course, having changed the subject's number, you will also have to make adjustments to the verb. Translate the results into English.

VIII. The Latin "Fourth" and "Fifth" Declensions

Are the Latin fourth and fifth declensions "real"? Of course... as grammatical constructs. But they are much less so as historical creations. All that has truly occurred in both instances is the emergence of a dominant vowel to govern what was originally the third declension. For the fourth declension, this vowel is a "u." It tends to lengthen in circumstances where it has absorbed the third declension's short vowel stem (the "i" that occasionally shifts to short "e"). For the fifth declension, the dominant vowel is a long "e" (eta) which is only shortened at one point—the accusative singular—through contact with an "m." As explained earlier, this text does not draw the long mark (or *circumflex*) over vowels except to emphasize some important distinction or other. The table below includes long marks by way of underscoring the intrusion of new, less easily altered vowels into the third declension to produce the fourth and fifth.

118

	3rd Declension	4th Declension	5th Declension
singular			
nominative	-is, etc. / finis	-us / exercitus	-ês / speciês
genitive	-is / finis	-ûs / exercitûs	-êi / speciêi
dative	-i / fini	-ui / exercitui	-êi / speciêi
accusative	-em / finem	-um / exercitum	-em / speciem
ablative	-e / fine	-û / exercitû	-ê / speciê
plural			
nominative	-es / fines	-ûs / exercitûs	-ês / speciês
genitive	-ium / finium	-uum / exercituum	-êrum / speciêrum
dative	-ibus / finibus	-ibus / exercitibus	-êbus / speciêbus
accusative	-es / fines	-ûs / exercitûs	-ês / speciês
ablative	-ibus / finibus	-ibus / exercitibus	-êbus / speciêbus

In the fourth declension, *-ubus* is actually found instead of *–ibus* for the dative and ablative plurals among the works of archaic authors. The epic poet Lucretius employs these forms regularly, whether because he knew them best or in order to create the hoary, reverend effect so prized by epic composers; for always remember that in classical culture, that which could lay a stronger claim to antiquity enjoyed a greater authority. Old was good in these societies, which regarded their distant past as eventually leading back to direct contact with the gods.

The attentive student, if he or she searches for discontinuity between the three declensions, will notice a single case where third-declension endings are altered by something more than a vowel: the genitives of the fifth declension. Why the genitive singular has come to be *speciêi* (like the dative singular) instead of *speciês* is not entirely clear, but the aberration is minor.

As for the "r" that intrudes into the genitive plural of this "new" declension (*speciêrum*), it harkens back to the *–arum* and *–orum* of the first and second declensions. Both vowels before the "r" happen to be long in these groups, too: the "r" was indeed probably inserted in all three cases as a kind of "glide" from a pronouncing position deep in the mouth to a very forward position against the lips. (Imagine a Boston cabbie saying, "I *sawr* it in the pahking lot.") An "i," on the other hand—even a long "i" (equivalent to our "ee")—is pronounced far forward in the mouth and would not pose any temptation to add an "r"; still less would a "u" do so. What this means, in straightforward terms, is that the third declension's *–ium* genitive plural and the fourth's *–uum* resisted a type of evolution that went on elsewhere for the genitive plural inflection.

Fourth-declension nouns are almost all masculine. Only *domus* ("home") and *manus* ("hand") are feminine. A few neuters exist, as well: their nominative singular—and indeed almost every case in their very odd singular—ends in –u, as in *cornu* ("horn") and *genu* ("knee"). Only the genitive differs, showing a -ûs ending (*cornûs*). This neuter group is not even numerous enough to make the study of its declensional paradigm worth a delay in our overview.

119

All fifth-declension nouns were originally feminine, though *dies* ("day") shifted to the masculine just after the heyday of classical Latin for some reason. In Vergil, *dies* is the former gender (feminine); and in Juvenal, about a century later, it is the latter. Most third-declension nouns ending in *–es*, by the way (such as *nubes*, "cloud," and *rupes*, "cliff"), are also feminine. One must wonder if these nouns were teetering right on the edge of a shift into the "new" declension!

The fourth and fifth declensions taken as one still do not produce nearly as many nouns as any of the first three declensions—not remotely. They give every sign of constituting small "eddies" along the third declension's vast mainstream.

Summary

*The fourth and fifth declensions are really not distinct groups of noun inflections at all, but rather branches of the third declension wherein the position of the vowel "i" has been largely usurped by "u" and "e," respectively. In the fourth, **-ubus** is often found for **-ibus** (the dative and ablative plural) in older texts, making the "u" substitution complete. In the fifth, only the genitives break from the third-declension paradigm, with the singular being **-ei** and the plural being **-erum**.*

Vocabulary

Nouns of the fourth declension are few and far between. They are overwhelmingly masculine (the two feminine and two of the few neuters are explicitly identified below), and most look exactly like second-declension nouns in the nominative singular. Dictionaries therefore usually append *–ûs*, the distinctive fourth declension genitive, to such entries.

Latin	meaning	derivative
adventus	arrival	advent
arcus	bow (weapon)	archery
cantus	song, music, poem	canto
casus	chance, accident	casual
cornu (n)	horn (animal's or instrument made from it)	coronet
cursus	running, race, track	course
domus (f)	home, residence	domestic
exercitus	army (trained)	exercise
fructus	fruit	fructose
genu (n)	knee	genuflect
ictus	blow, slap	ictus (medical term for seizure)
impetus	attack, rush	impetuous

lacus	lake	lake
manus (f)	hand	manual
portus	seaport	port
sinus	hollow, cavity, bay	sinus
tumultus	uproar, bedlam	tumult

Nouns of the fifth declension are all feminine, *dies* being a late and occasional exception that continued into the romance tongues as masculine (cf. *buenos dias!*). In their entirety (and these pages offer only samplings), they number even fewer than fourth-declension nouns.

acies	straight line (of sight, of blade, etc.)	no derivative, but common in Latin
dies	day	diurnal
facies	face, surface	superficial
fides	faith, trust	fidelity
glacies	ice, hard texture	glacier
res	matter, affair	*in re* ("concerning")
species	type, kind	species
spes	hope	despair

Exercise Set 3.8

A. Translate the following phrases into Latin. You will find all the vocabulary you need in the lists directly above.

1. on the day of the crime
2. with (by) a blow of the knee
3. in the uproar of the attack
4. songs (nom.) of hope
5. the types (nom.) of fruits
6. We will see the bays of the lakes.
7. on the surfaces of the ice
8. by an accident of the hands

B. Translate the following sentences into English.

1. Acies militum cum fortitudine impetum hostium sustenebat (from *sustenêre*, "sustain, withstand").
2. Fructûs ex arbore ictibus saxorum obtinebimus (from *obtenêre*, "obtain").
3. Hieme (from *hiems*, "winter") cumulos glaciei seneces (from *senex*, "old man") vitare debent.
4. Si ("if") spem fidemque non servabitis, amici pacis domum non habebitis.
5. Videbas-ne,* soror, dentes in facie leonis et cornua in capite tauri?
6. Agricola in genibus flores puerîs manu monstrabat.

*The particle *ne* (short "e"), when added to the end of a clause's first word, forewarns the audience that a question is being asked. There was actually no hyphen inserted: the little suffix was fully attached.

C. Translate these sentences from English into Latin.

121

1. The army's horns will create (use *creare*) an uproar.
2. We were singing songs for the girls on the mother's knee.
3. In the matter of the race, I will preserve (use *servare*) faith in the horses of the king.
4. The leaders of the armies by chance (=accidentally) gave burial (use *sepultura*, 1st decl) to (their) enemies.
5. Home was standing in the (our) line of sight when (use *ubi*) blows began to hit the ship.

Solo Flight: Translate the following sentence based upon Cicero's *De Divinatione* 24.53: "Responsa haruspicum [*responsum*—just what it looks like, 2nd decl. neuter; *haruspex*—prophet, 3rd decl. masculine] nobîs [from pronoun *nos*, 'we'; take an educated guess at the case] in Graeciam Româ missa sunt [last two words: 'were sent']." Identify the case of each noun or pronoun, and also explain the logic behind the two proper nouns' having the cases they do. When you have finished, you should be staring at a brilliant example of the two distinct senses in which something may be "sent to."

IX. The Third Declension: Greek

Ancient Greek has but one more declension—the third. The number of nouns that it represents is huge, so it must not be neglected. Roughly half the nouns on any page of Homer will be drawn from this group. At least we may be comforted that grammarians have not carved up this final declension into two or three more. There are other reasons to take heart, as well. Only two case-endings out of eight present much of a challenge to the learner by assuming strange forms, and one of these is the nominative singular. As with Latin third-declension nouns, Greek nouns of this group may start out with practically any spelling under the sun.

Nevertheless, a few general nominative-singular formations occur in the vast majority of nouns to be found. Below, along with the table of inflections for masculine and feminine nouns (these two genders share all non-nominative endings, again as in Latin's third declension), are three "sample" nouns whose nominative singular's last syllable is quite common:

	3rd **Declension masc./fem.**	-ευς	-ηρ	-ων
singular				
nominative	-ευς/-ηρ/-ων, etc.	βασιλευς	μητηρ	δαιμων
genitive	-ος	βασιληος	μητερος	δαιμονος
dative	-ι	βασιληι	μητερι	δαιμονι
accusative	-α	βασιληα	μητερα	δαιμονα
plural				
nominative	-ες	βασιληες	μητερες	δαιμονες
genitive	-ων	βασιληων	μητερων	δαιμονων
dative	-εσσι	βασιληεσσι	μητερεσσι	δαιμονεσσι
accusative	-ες	βασιληες	μητερες	δαιμονες

Several connections are worth drawing: 1) the dative singular in iota is the same vowel sound we find concluding the dative singular of Latin's third, fourth, and fifth declensions; 2) the nominative and accusative plural endings are again identical to the standard Latin endings for the third declension, and more or less to those for the fifth (although the "e" here is an epsilon, not an eta or long "e"); and 3) the genitive plural ending is the same that you have learned for the other Greek declensions (though, in the first, an alpha precedes this syllable).

The –ος in the genitive singular may seem like trouble at first, for it is indistinguishable from the second declension's nominative singular masculine inflection. In fact, it *is* trouble in the beginning: hence the importance of knowing what declension a noun belongs to. The accusative singular, too (as long as we are anticipating how wires may get crossed with other declensions), is a short alpha rather than the long alpha in many first-declension nominatives—but long marks are never added to Greek texts by editors to avoid this problem, since they would interfere with the system of tonal accents already present in those texts. Once again, the student simply has to memorize which noun belongs to which declension. (The short "a" accusative singular, by the way, is the standard one for Russian masculine and feminine nouns in that case/number slot; once you learn the ending, then, you will enjoy another small headstart into a very difficult modern language.)

Then we come to the dative plural: an epsilon, two sigmas (which may be reduced to one), and little iota— all the letters, it seems, that most easily lend themselves to complex transformations. In fact, the form given for μητηρ is not actually found in any extant text: what we have, rather, is usually μητρασι. Similarly, βασιληεσσι is much more commonly βασιλευσι, while δαιμονεσσι typically becomes δαιμοσι. The sigma and the iota are not really condensing into another form in these examples, but the unstressed syllable composed by them seems to create an added inducement to absorb the epsilon into a previous vowel. Thus the dative inflection we offer will often be changed: the later the texts you study, the more extreme the variety of absorption performed upon the epsilon. In our overview of Greek, to list all the mutations possible with this dative plural ending would be neither useful nor feasible. Do not be surprised to see the –εσσι inflection contracted with the previous syllable: that modest warning should suffice for an introductory exposure.

The truth is that neither the nominative singular ending nor the dative plural ending represents the exact "problem point" faced by the learner. That problem may be restated, now that we have examined it, as the *transformation of the word's stem* in front of the endings. Remembering the word βασιλευς ("king") is probably no more difficult than remembering any other new word—but remembering the lengthening of the epsilon to eta is indeed taxing. The ending of δαιμοσι ("spirits") could scarcely be anything but a dative plural, even though its contracted form may seem troublesome… but what happened to the nu which appears just before all the word's other inflections? A very general tendency (somewhere close to a rule) is that long vowels occupying the nominative's final syllable tend to shorten in the base's formation (μητηρ > μητερος, δαιμων > δαιμονος). The tendency is strong enough to keep in mind; and while it doesn't hold the key to all possible dative plural contractions, it turns one of the locks.

As with the Latin third declension, yet again, our greatest task here is probably to recognize the metamorphosis that occurs from the nominative singular to the other cases: i.e., the formation of the stem. If you should devote yourself to studying Greek some day, this labor will be no minor undertaking. Yet the Latin/Greek resemblance holds true on one more level that will prove helpful: English derivatives drawn from these third-declension Greek nouns are almost always built from the *oblique* (or non-nominative) cases: e.g., "gerontology" from the root of γερων. You can't tell there that the omega has shortened into an omicron, since English has just one "o"—but you *can* tell that a tau has been added to the root.

Let us add just a few more observations about the third declension's neuter nouns. All of the usual rules about the neuter gender's declension continue to apply. Nominative and accusative forms are identical. In the plural, these two forms end in an alpha (short "a"). Otherwise, the neuter form follows the masculine within its declension with very rare exceptions; and in this declension, masculine never veers from feminine, so an impressive uniformity emerges.

One particular category of neuter nouns bears emphasis: those ending in –ος in the nominative singular, corresponding to Latin's third-declension –us neuters like *corpus*. In Greek, this set of nouns is truly vast and includes several words often used in English derivatives. Because they can be so easily confused with second-declension –ος masculine words, they pose a formidable challenge to the student. The genitive in –εος, furthermore, is a volatile mix with its two short vowels side by side: it becomes the diphthong -ους in later texts. Likewise, the nominative and accusative plural in –εα turns to –η by the time we reach Plato. Thus, many more opportunities for confusion lurk down the historical road… but we're not going there, fortunately!

For the sake of reference, two neuter nouns have been declined below:

singular		
nominative	σωμα	τελος
genitive	σωματος	τελεος
dative	σωματι	τελει
accusative	σωμα	τελος
plural		
nominative	σωματα	τελεα
genitive	σωματων	τελεων
dative	σωματεσσι (σωμασι)	τελεεσσι (τελεισι)
accusative	σωματα	τελεα

Summary
*The Greek and Latin third declensions are very similar, the major differences being -**α** for -**em** in the masculine/feminine accusative singular and -**εσσι** for -**ibus** in the dative plural of all genders. As in Latin, too, learning the difference in spelling between nominative singulars and the stem to which those endings are added can be arduous; and in post-Homeric texts, the -**εσσι** dative and any case where two short vowels stand side by side may be contracted.*

Vocabulary
As with the Latin list above, genitives are seldom spelled out in their entirety. All genitive inflections following a hyphen should be considered as beginning immediately after the last consonant that precedes a vowel in the nominative form.

Greek	pronunciation	meaning	derivative
'ανηρ, 'ανδρος (m)	AH-nair	man (praiseful)	Andrew
'αστηρ, -ερος (m)	AH-stair	star, constellation	astral

βασιλευς, -ηος (m)	bah-si-LEUWS	king	basilica
γερων, -οντος (m)	GEH-roewn	old man	gerontology
γυνη, -αικος (f)	GEW-nay	woman	gynecology
δαιμων, -ονος (m)	DYE-moewn	lesser god, fate, genius (=inspiration)	demon
'ερως, -ωτος (m)	EH-roews	love	erotic
'ημαρ, 'ηματος (n); also 'ημερα (f. 1st decl.)	HAY-mar	day	ephemeral
'ηρως, -ωος (m)	HAY-roews	hero, champion	hero
'ηως, 'ηοος (f)	AY-oews	dawn	-----
θυγατηρ, -ερος (f)	thew-GAH-tair	daughter	-----
'ιχθυς, -υος (m)	IHKH-thewss	fish	ichthyosaurus
κυων, κυνος (m/f)	KEW-oewn	dog	cynic, cynosure
λεων, λεοντος (m)	LEH-oewn	lion	leonine
μην, μηνος (m)	MAYN	moon	month
μητηρ, -ερος (f)	MAY-tair	mother	maternal
νυξ, νυκτος (f)	NEWKS	night	(equivalent of Latin *nox*)
'οπλης, 'οπλιτις (m)	HOP-layss	armed footsoldier	hoplite
'ορνις, -ιθος (m/f)	OR-niss	bird	ornithology
πατηρ, -ερος (m)	PAH-tair	father	paternal
παις, παιδος (m/f)	PYEss	child	pedagogy
πυρ, πυρος (m)	PEWR	fire	pyromania
'υβρις. –ιδος (f)	HEW-briss	arrogance	hubris
'υδωρ, 'υδατος (m)	HEW-door	water	hydrogen
'υιος, gen. both 'υιου and 'υιεος (m)	HWEE-oss	son	(related to Irish "uí" that became "o" beginning names: e.g., O'Toole)
χαος, χαεος (n)	HKHAH-oss	wild disorder, bedlam	chaos
χειρ, χειρος (n)	HKHAIR	hand	chiropractor

χθων. –ονος (f)	HKHTHOEWN	earth, soil	chthonic

Feminine: nom. -ις, gen. -ιος /-εως

γενεσις	GEH-neh-siss	origin, birth	genesis
δοσις	DOH-siss	gift, portion	dose
κρισις	KRISS-iss	judgment, determination	crisis
λυσις	LEW-siss	loosing, release	analysis
μαντις (also m)	MAHN-tiss	prophetess (prophet)	mantic
μηνις	MAY-niss	anger, rage	mania
πολις	POH-liss	city (organized)	politics
ποσις (also m)	POH-siss	wife, husband	spouse
φυσις	FEW-siss	nature, Creation	physics

Neuter: nom. –ος, gen. -εος

’αλγος	AL-goss	hurt, pain	analgesic
γενος	GEH-noss	race, descent	gene
δενδρος	DEN-dross	tree	dendrite
’εθνος	ETH-noss	race, tribe, nation	ethnic
’εθος (also’ηθος)	ETH-oss	custom, habit	ethics
’επος	EH-poss	word, story	epic
κρατος	KRAH-toss	power, rule	democracy
κυδος	KEW-doss	honor, glory	(popular parlance for "honor"—often misused as plural)
μισος	MISS-oss	hatred	misanthropy
νεφος	NEH-foss	cloud, cludbank	-----
παθος	PAH-thoss	anguish, suffering	pathetic
πελαγος	PEH-lah-goss	open sea	archipelago
πενθος	PEN-thoss	grief, mourning	nepenthe
στηθος	STAY-thoss	chest, breast	stethoscope

τελος	TELL-oss	end, purpose	teleology
φαος	FAH-oss	light	Phaeton

nom. -α, gen. -ατος

‘αιμα	HYE-muh	blood	hemophilia
δερμα	DAIR-muh	skin, hide	dermatology
δογμα	DOG-muh	opinion, decree	dogma
δραμα	DRAH-muh	deed, action (on stage)	drama
’ονομα	ON-oh-muh	name	onomatopoeia
σπερμα	SPAIR-muh	seed	sperm
στομα	STOH-muh	mouth, face, front	stomach
σχημα	SuHKHAY-muh	arrangement, plan	scheme
σωμα	SOE-muh	body	somatic
χαρμα	HKHAR-muh	joy, delight	charm
χασμα	HKHASS-muh	empty space, gulf	chasm
χρημα	HKHRAY-muh	thing needed (goods, money)	chrematist
χρωμα	HKHROE-muh	color	chromatic

Exercise Set 3.9

A. Translate the following Greek sentences into English.
1. Φαος μηνος χρωματα ’αστερων καλυπτει.
2. Πενθος χασμα ’εν στηθεσι (= στηθεεσσι) μητερων ’εφυε.
3. Ποιηται ’επεα εξ ’εργων ‘ηρωων ’επρασσον.
4. Γεροντες δοσεις βασιληος ’ουκ ("not") ’ελαμβανον.
5. Χρωματα δερματος ‘ιππου ’εγω ’ουκ ’εσκοπεον.
6. ‘Υιες ’ανθρωπων ’επι χθονι ’αλλ’ ("but") ’ουκ ’εν ‘υδατι ζωουσι.

B. Now translate these English sentences into Greek. Most of the vocabulary you need is in the word lists above.
1. I do not fear words from the mouth of a tyrant.
2. The prophet's love is holding (back) the king's army.
3. Children love birds with colors.

Solo Flight: Give the case and number of all nouns; then translate. The third-declension nouns can be tricky!
1. Καρη σωμα σαωσει (Delphic Oracle's advice to the Argives, who were reluctant to join their old enemies, the Spartans, against the invading Persians; first word is a third-declension neuter for "head," and last one is a future-

127

tense form of verb meaning "save").

2. Μηνις ᾿Αχιλληος ᾿Αχαιοις ᾿αλγεα ποιησει (paraphrase of *Iliad*'s first two lines; we get "mania" from the first word, the second is the genitive of "Achilles," and an Achaean is a Homeric Greek; do you know what an analgesic is?).

3. ᾿Ανδρα μοι ῾εννεπε, Μουσα (first four words of the *Odyssey*: the imperative verb, "speak of, tell of," takes a direct object in Greek).

X. Odds and Ends About Cases

In both Latin and Greek, you should know that the accusative case has also absorbed functions beyond its original and "proper" one of indicating the direct object. Primarily, these functions involve some sort of "motion toward" an object or idea. (You *can* move toward an idea, figuratively.) A preposition usually precedes this kind of accusative: *ad* in Latin, for instance, and ᾿επι in Greek. The conceptual leap from direct object to destination of a movement is not difficult, fortunately. Seeing a tree and walking toward it are both acts which point their spotlight on the tree.

The visualization may become a little more challenging when the movement involved is less clearly polarized (as when proceeding from A to B becomes moving *around* B)—or when it turns from spatial to temporal. If you move *through* a meadow toward a tree, for example, the tree is obviously your destination; but as you walk, are you moving *toward* or *away from* the meadow? The Romans and Greeks opted for the former. Prepositions like *per* and δια (both translated "through") are followed by the accusative case. Even the prepositions *circum* and περι, meaning "around," govern the accusative case. Why would "motion around" appear more similar to "motion toward" than to "motion away"? The question is unanswerable: we simply have to accept the convention.

Likewise for time: when one reads a phrase like *multos annos* in Latin or πολλους ᾿ενιαυτους in Greek, one must picture oneself passing *through* many years on a journey to their far side—which would yield a translation like "for many years" or "during many years." The ancients, again, placed the emphasis on moving forward rather than moving away. This, no doubt, is logically defensible, since we live by advancing into new days rather than by backing away from old ones. A preposition was typically not used to express "for" or "during" in such circumstances. Grammar books refer to this structure as the "accusative of duration."

As we shall find in the final chapter, the accusative had a few other chores to perform, as well, through particular prepositions. The notion of cause—"because," "on account of" (expressed by the prepositions *ob* and *propter*, without any real distinction)—drew the accusative since. Once again, an image of "motion toward" seemed to be involved. If you stay home because of rain (*propter pluvium*), it might be said that your decision was made "facing" or "in regard to" the rain.

Even the nominative—the case for designating a sentence's subject—was not entirely excused from the double duty visited upon other cases by the gradual decay of the system. A special case once existed for persons or things addressed directly. (Though addressing things directly seems rather pointless, it happens: one of Horace's odes begins, *O fons Bandusiae*... "Oh, thou fountain of Bandusia!") The case of direct address, or the *vocative* (from *voco*, "I call"), was originally distinct in spelling. One can readily imagine how it came to fuse with the nominative; for when you say a person's name aloud, that person is often also likely to be the subject of a second-person verb. ("Bill, you left the door open.") Very occasionally in Latin and Greek, we find vocative forms that have not quite merged with the nominative—which is indeed our main evidence that this separate case ever existed. If you were to tell a woman, "Julia, you are in error," the proper noun would keep its nominative form: *Iulia, erras* (or perhaps *O Iulia*; the interjection "Oh" seems melodramatic to us, but it was standard among the ancients). If you were to tell Marcus the same thing, however, the sentence would emerge, *Marce, erras*. Second-declension Greek names observed just the same change. "Phaidros, you are wrong," would be written, ᾿Ω Φαιδρε, ῾αμαρτανεις.

Vocatives are not uncommon in more ancient languages. To this day, Gaelic-speakers aspirate the proper noun's first letter when addressing a person by name: e.g., *A Sheáin* (the "sh" pronounced more like "h" than "s," like a Welsh -*ll*) to get Sean's attention. Notice the initial "a" corresponding to the Latin/Greek "o." Is not our "hey" in utterances like, "Hey Cindy, your friend is calling," very close to a vocative-case indicator?

A final note about cases: an epitaph, you may say. As has been suggested elsewhere in this book, case endings would eventually become so dependent upon prepositions to clarify their intent that they would erode to nothing, surrendering their nuances entirely to those little words preceding nouns. One can sense the urgent need for such an adaptation in late Roman authors like the soldier-historian Aemilianus, who often places such terrific strain upon case inflections that he surely could not have spoken Latin as he writes it. Brace yourself for this description of Musonianus: … *in totum* (acc.) *lucrandi* (gen.) *aviditate* (abl.) *sordescens* (nom.) *ut inter alia* (acc.) *multa* (acc.) *evidenter apparuit in questionibus* (abl.) *agitatîs* (abl.) *super morte* (abl.) *Theophilî* (gen.), *Syriae* (gen.) *consularis* (gen.), *proditione* (abl.) *Caesaris* (gen.) *Gallî* (gen.) *impetû* (abl.) *plebis* (gen.) *promiscuae* (gen.) *discerptî* (gen.): "[a man] wallowing altogether in the lust of profiteering, as appeared, among other things, in the inquiries stirred up about the death—through the betrayal of Gallus Caesar—of Theophilus, governor of Syria, torn to pieces by the assault of a promiscuous rabble." Gone is any Ciceronian sense of cadence, any feel for the restraint needed to avoid mixing genitives and ablatives (as here) that have entirely different antecedents or functions.

Cicero, let us remember, may be assumed to have spoken in the forum or at court in much the same way as he wrote. Now Latin has become a thousand-piece jigsaw puzzle that can only be assembled in meditative silence. We have reached the early Middle Ages. The language is a highly artificial literary medium—and not a very elegant one, at that. It's time for the modern romance languages to begin pecking their way out of the egg.

Summary
Besides its original designation of the direct object, the accusative case has also assumed the task from vanished cases of expressing "motion toward or through" and "time during which" in both Latin and ancient Greek, usually with the help of a preposition. The case of direct address, called the vocative, has furthermore been all but absorbed by the nominative. Only second-declension singular nouns preserve an identifiably distinct vocative (e.g., Marce/Μαρκε for, "Hey, Marcus!").

Exercise Set 3.10

A. Translate the following Latin sentences into English.
1. Equites (from *eques*, "horsesoldier, cavalryman") per glaciem ad montem paene ("almost") non movebant.
2. Imperator praesidia circum fines hostium ponebat ("was placing").
3. Quinte, pedes manûsque ob nivem celare debes.

B. Now translate these English sentences into Latin.
1. Gallus, will you show the road to the fountain to father? (Place *ne* after first word essential to clause [i.e., not "Gallus"] to make question.)
2. The journey was taking (*ducebat*) the messengers around the mountains for the sake of safety (use *salûs, salutis*).

C. Translate the following short sentences into English.
1. Γλαυκε, νοματα παισι (= παιδεσσι) διδωμι.
2. Κουρη πυρες 'επι ("on") γαιηι (or χθωνι) και περι 'υδατα 'εσκωπεε.
3. Περι νυκτα κυνες 'επι ("toward") πολιν 'ερρεον.

D. Now translate these English sentences into Greek.
1. Philippos and Chloe, you are giving opinions to the king about (use περι) the city.
2. For three (use τρια) days, we moved through the vast spaces of Anatolia ('Ανατολια [modern Turkey], 1st decl.).

Solo Flight: Take Sentence A.2 above and change all singulars to plurals and all plurals to singulars in Latin; then translate the result into English. Do the same thing in Greek for Sentence C.3 above.

XI. Typical Transformations of Third-Declension Latin Nouns in Romance Languages

To draw up a list of the various cognates that have kept alive Latin third-declension nouns in the romance languages would be time-consuming, though not unprofitable. We can take a short-cut to just about the same destination if we simply frame some generalizations. Below are a few patterns and tendencies that emerge when one studies the course followed by this group of nouns through Latin's inheritor-languages. These principles could potentially turn up hundreds of modern relations and descendants.

Latin	Italian	Spanish	French	English
Masculine Nouns from Latin				
-or	**-ore**	**-or**	**-eur**	**-or**
horror	horrore	horror	horreur	horror
Endings of Feminine Nouns (Abstract)				
-tas	**-tate**	**-dad**	**-té**	**-ty**
gravitas	gravitate	gravidad	gravité	gravity
-tio	**-zione**	**-ción**	**-tion**	**-tion**
correctio	correzione	corrección	correction	correction
-tudo	**-tudine**	**-tud**	**-tude**	**-tude**
multitude	multitudine	multitud	multitude	multitude
-ura	**-ura**	**-ura**	**-ure**	**-ure**
cultura	cultura	cultura	culture	culture
Many Romance Nouns Drawn Straight from Latin Base				
leo, leonis	leone	león	lion	lion
genus, generis	genere	género	genre	general, etc.
mons, montis	monte	monte	mont	mountain
mors, mortis	morte	muerte	mort	mortal, etc.

130

... BUT Certain Groups (-x) Create Odd Patterns				
pax, pacis	pace	paz	paix	peace
vox, vocis	voce	voz	voix	voice
Adverbs Formed from Ablative of Means				
mente (abl)	**-mente**	**-mente**	**-ment**	**"with a ___ mind"**
dulci mente	dulcemente	dulcemente	doucement	with gentle intent, gently

Exercise Set 3.11

A. Using the tips just above, adapt each Latin noun below to the form that it would assume in the modern romance language given parenthetically. If you do not know what the word means in English, be sure to look it up in a dictionary!

1. pudor (Fr.)
2. servitudo (It.)
3. serpens (Fr.)
4. serenitas (Sp.)
5. langor (It.)
6. tigris (Sp.)
7. approbatio (It.)
8. ardor (Sp.)
9. natura (Sp.)
10. lux (It.)
11. urbanitas (Fr.)
12. magnitudo (Fr.)

B. From the following Latin adjectives, make adverbs appropriate for the modern romance languages given parenthetically. Refer to the last expansion above, "Adverbs Formed from the Ablative of Means." Then find an English adverb to translate each word you have created.

1. tristis (Sp.)
2. superbus (Fr.)
3. fidelis ((It.)
4. completus (Fr.)
5. utilis (It.)
6. subitus (Sp.)

Solo Flight: Go through the table above and see if you can supply a new example for each category of ending in all five of the language-brackets. Try creating a row of adverbs at the bottom, as well.

ANSWERS TO EXERCISES

Exercise Set 3.1
Answers to **A**: 1. The queen has a crown (= a crown is to the queen). 2. The men have swords. 3. I used to give money to the boy. 4. The woman will give a meal to you (= will give you a meal). 5. Friendship gives joy to us. 6. The Romans are giving glory to the (their) country. 7. There are to me (= I have) both sons and daughters. 9. The glory of the Britons is (as) a joy to them.
Answers to **B**: 1. Tres equi mihi sunt. 2. Quintus puero est nomen (word order not important here). 3. Dona reginae magistro dabimus. 4. Gratias deîs (usually contracted as dîs or spelled divîs) dabas; the singular form "to God" would be Deo.

Exercise Set 3.2
Answers to **A**: 1. The queen is speaking to the people. 2. We are bringing a gift for you (s.). 3. The boys are giving (to) us weapons. 4. Brass will make weapons for the men. 5. Gods were making/used to make laws for the tribe. 6. We girls give advice to the children.
Answers to **B**: 1. Θεοι σοι θανατωι ψυχην ουκ λυσουσι. 2. Λογους μυθου 'υμιν λεξω (φωνησω). 3. 'Οδος 'ηλιου γαιηι βιον 'εφυε.

Exercise Set 3.3
Answers: *Les livres sont **à moi**. 2. **Mi rincresce** d'averti abandonato. 3. Ayudamos **a** tu madre. 4. Ce sont mes amis **à moi** (and you would add **pas à toi** to emphasize "not yours"). 5. Ora **mi bisogna** di partire. 6. No comemos las tortillas (just remove the a).*

Exercise Set 3.4
Answers to **A**: 1. We ought to move camp without delay. 2. They will not keep the horses in the fields. 3. Sailors will not fight with a sword. 4. You messengers will soon sail from the islands. 5. We were watching the stars in the sky. 6. There are to me (= I have) books about friendship.
Answers to **B**: 1. Iustitiâ non gladiîs viros superabitis. 2. Agricolae ex oppidô cum pecuniâ ambulabunt. 3. Filiam in somniîs dolô vini videbat.

Exercise Set 3.5
Answers to **A**: 1. The army was running from the battle. 2. Poets make stories with words. 3. The queens will watch the people before/in front of the gate. 4. I have (there is to me) a livelihood (or "My livelihood is") from the sea. 5. Gods and goddesses live in the sea. 6. You (pl.) were turning/kept turning (your) eyes away from the sun.
*That is, "by means of words": the tendency is to use the case alone without a preposition to designate means, as in Latin.
Answers to **B**: 1. Μεγαρον 'εξ 'υλης συν τεκνοις ποιησομεν / τευξομεν. 2. 'Ανθροποι 'οπλα χαλκωι φυσειτε (see note to A.2 above). 3. Φαος 'εκ πυλης 'ηλιου γαιηι (also γαιαι) 'ρεει.

Exercise Set 3.6
Answers to **A**: "No color is to the silver hidden in the miserly earth" (last word is a poetic plural, best translated in singular); or, "There is no color to…" or, "The silver hidden in the miserly earth has no color."
Answers to **B**: "Every soul is unwilling[ly] deprived of truth," or, "No soul is willingly deprived of truth."

Exercise Set 3.7
Answers to **A**: 1. in flumine 2. ê timopre leonum 3. tempora doloris et terroris 4. in luce solis 5. pisces ê (or â) mari 6. civibus urbis 7. finem virtutis 8. cum libertate et iustitiâ hominibus

Answers to **B**: 1. The reward of (for) wickedness ought to be the hatred of men. 2. Friends of liberty, you will fight with (= against) the tyrant's soldiers. 3. Neither to fish nor to birds is the ferocity of a lion (i.e., neither fish nor birds have...). 4. (As) a boy, Quintus would keep (his) sisters from the river's mouth. 5. With diligence and courage, we tried to walk across the bridge in the mountain. 6. The poetr's works used to/would overcome the king's heart and mind. 7. The voices of birds give beauty to life. 8. The crimes of the fathers will not prevail (= hold up, be a match) against the virtues of the sons. 9. King to (= of) the body is the head: to the head, the mind ought to be leader. *(In proper classical Latin, **dux** would probably become **duci**, forming a "double dative": i.e., "The mind is **as** a leader to the head....".)* 10. In a leader we desire the gravity of a lion, the luckiness of a cat, and the intelligence of a fox.

Answers to **C**: 1. Timor mortis et amor legium civibus ab urbe hostium servabant. 2. Matres militum regi flores dabimus. 3. Per noctem luces navium spectabamus. 4. Potestas iuventutis in pace cum sapientiâ senectutis ambulare debet. 5. Canes leonem dentibus et clamore terrebunt.

Exercise Set 3.8

Answers to **A**: 1. die criminis 2. ictu genûs 3. in tumultu impetûs 4. cantûs spei 5. species fructuum 6. Sinûs lacuum videbimus. 7. in faciebus glaciei 8. casû manuum

Answers to **B**: 1. The battleline of soldiers was sustaining the attack of the enemies with fortitude. 2. We will obtain fruits from the tree with the blows of stones. 3. In winter, the old men ought to avoid heaps of ice. 4. If you (pl.) do not (= "will not") preserve hope and faith, you friends of peace will not have a home. 5. Did you see, sister, the teeth in the lion's face and the horns on the bull's head? 6. On (his) knees, the farmer was showing the flowers by hand (= with his hand) to the girls.

Answers to **C**: 1. Cornua exercitûs tumultum creabunt. 2. Cantûs puellîs in genû matris cantabimus. 3. In re cursûs, fidem in equîs regis servabo. 4. Duces exercituum sepulturam hostibus casû dabant. 5. Domus in acie stabat ubi ictûs navem pulsabant.

Exercise Set 3.9

Answers to **A**: 1. The light of the Moon is covering (= dimming) the clolors of the stars. 2. Grief was producing a chasm in the chests of the mothers. 3. Poets were making (used to make) stories out of heroes' deeds. 4. The old men did not take the king's gifts. 5. I did not see the colors of the horse's hide. 6. The sons of men live on the earth but not in the water.

Answers to **B**: 1. ’Επεα ’εκ στοματος τυραννου ’ου φωβεω. 2. ’Ερως μαντεος στρατον βασιληος ’εχει. 3. Παιδες ’ορνιθες συν χρωμασι χρωματεσσι φιλεουσι

Exercise Set 3.10

Answers to **A**: 1. The cavalrymen were almost not moving through the ice to (= in the direction of, toward) the mountain). 2. The general was placing outposts around the boundaries of the enemies. 3. Gallus, you ought to cover (your) feet and hands because of the snow.

Answers to **B**: 1. Galle, monstrabisne viam ad fontem patri? 2. Iter nuntios circum montes ob/propter salutem ducebat.

Answers to **C**: 1. Glaukos, I am giving names to the children. 2. The girl was watching fires on land and around the water. 3. Around nightfall, the dogs were running toward the city.

Answers to **D**: 1. Φιλιππε και Χλωη, δογματα βασιληι περι πολιν διδοτε. 2. Τρια ‘ηματα, δια χασματα ’Ανατολης ’εχωρεομεν.

Exercise Set 3.11

Answers to **A**: 1. pudeur 2. servitudine 3. serpent 4. serenidad 5. langore 6. tigre 7. approbazione 8. ardor 9. natura 10. luce (English adj. "lucid") 11. urbanité 12. magnitude

Answers to **B**: 1. tristamente 2. superbement 3. fidelmente 4. complètement 5. utilmente 6. Subitamente

Chapter Four: Verbs Continued

Topics Covered

Tense

- Perfect System: Perfect, Pluperfect, Future Perfect
- Greek Aorist Tense
- Perfect Tenses of Romance Languages

Voice

- Contrastive Meanings of Active and Passive
- Passive Formation of All Tenses in Latin and Greek
- Formation of Passive with Auxiliary Verbs in English

Participles

- Meaning and Formation of Perfect Passive Participle in Latin and Greek
- Ambiguity of Perfect Participle's Voice in English and Romance Languages
- Participles as Adjectives: Agreement with Subject

Vocabulary

- Formation of English Words from Latin and Greek Participles
- Verbs of Latin Third and Fourth Conjugations

I. The Perfect System: Meaning

We left off our discussion of verbs by noting the critical distinction between action that is incomplete, ongoing, habitual, etc., and action that is over and done with. The Latin word *perfectum* literally means "thoroughly done, finished": hence its use to designate completed verbal action.

This designation, though, is properly one of aspect rather than tense: that is, any tense may suffer its action to be stretched out like a rubber band or compressed like a spring. We can say "he drops" or "he is dropping," "we will close" or "we will be closing." Yet Latin treats all of the tenses in the present system (present, imperfect, and future) as suited to emphasizing a protracted rather than a completed act. With the same somewhat flawed decisiveness, it treats all of the tenses in the perfect system as suited to complete rather than ongoing action. They are listed below:

Perfect Tense: sometimes called the "present perfect" in English. If, in the course of taking a test, you were asked by a teacher how far you had advanced, you might declare as you placed the last period on the last sentence, "I've finished." You are *right now* in the state of being done: the act is part of the past as of this moment, or as of a very recent moment. Indeed, we shall see when the *passive voice* is considered later in this chapter that the Romans would literally say, "I am called" (using the word for "I am" and then the past participle for "summoned"), rather than, "I have been called."

Pluperfect Tense: used to describe very distant past action, as its name—"more than perfect"—suggests. English fortunately has one and only one way of rendering such an idea: the helping verb "had" + a past participle. Past action must be shifted to the pluperfect when it is mentioned in the context of more recent past action. For instance, in the sentence, "**I had seen** him every day that year before the relapse forced him to stop receiving visitors," the seeing is clearly ended by the relapse and must be treated as pluperfect, whether or not the writer wishes to emphasize that it was habitual. The verb "forced" (or "it forced" in Latin: subject, "relapse") would be perfect, and its temporal influence would thrust the seeing into a more distant past. Alternatively, the sentence, "I was seeing him daily when my first child was born," does not plainly represent the seeing as interrupted by the child's birth. The former would remain imperfect even though the latter is obviously perfect (few actions are more definitely completed than childbirth!), since "seeing him daily" may well have continued.

Future Perfect Tense: again arranged in English through helping verbs in one and only one way. We use the future auxiliary "shall/will" followed always by "have" and then the past participle. As with the pluperfect, the future perfect occurs when another action is expressed or implied which serves as a reference point. The future perfect event has not yet occurred—but at a certain point not yet reached, it *will have* occurred: it will be done and finished. The human colonization of the Moon may be well in the future. When men and women are scurrying about the lunar landscape, however, we *will have solved* the challenge of existing for weeks at a time in low-gravity environments.

Note that this tense is indeed perfect in a way that the future cannot be. The future, by definition, is unfinished: the future perfect, by definition, portrays an act which is completely past when regarded from a certain temporal vantage point.

Nevertheless, all of these tenses are capable of being progressive in aspect (as opposed to perfect). A century from now, perhaps human beings *will have been raising* children on the Moon for a generation (and raising children takes a lot longer than giving birth to them). Likewise, perhaps our visitor in the pluperfect example *had been recording* the sick man's life story before the unfortunate relapse. In both cases, a progressive aspect is introduced in English by shifting from a simple past participle to "been + present participle." The Romans almost never adopted any such strategy as writing *fuerant scribentes*—"they had been writing." Instead, they allowed the perfect system's progressive aspect to fade away until it all but disappeared. The historian Cornelius Nepos offers a few phrases like *Corinthii saepe adiuti fuerant*—"The Corinthians had often been helped" ("Timoleon," 20.2.2); and the much later historian Suetonius, when referring to one of Claudius's many unhappy brides, writes *nupta fuerat*— "she had been married (26). At its peak, however, classical Latin avoided such constructions as clumsily redundant.

Other problems exist with the "perfect tense" specifically (as indicated at the end of Chapter Two) that have as much to do with English as with Latin. "I have seen," "I did see," and "I saw" are all acceptable ways of translating the Latin perfect-tense verb, *vidi*. Yet do these three forms really mean the same thing in English? "I have seen" probably comes closest to the perfect sense: it puts the action recently but firmly in the past. English grammarians, as noted, call this the "present perfect" because—so they say—it is present in tense but perfect in aspect. Not true. "I see" is the present tense with a perfect aspect: "I am seeing" is the present tense with a progressive (or imperfect) aspect. We Anglophones cannot call "I have seen" the past perfect, however, because we have bestowed that honor upon the Latin pluperfect; and, to be fair, "I had seen" does seem to differ from "I have seen" only in having been nudged one stage farther into the past.

But that leaves us with a problem. We now have a past tense called the present perfect which is certainly perfect in aspect but certainly not present in tense; and we can't simply call this tense the past, because then what would we do with forms like "I saw"? ("I did see" may be ignored as a peculiar case: the verb "do" is used as a kind of "phony helping verb" in English to create emphasis or to facilitate questions and negatives.) The grammarians tell us that the "I saw" form is the plain, vanilla past tense of our language. So that seat is taken; and remember that the true present perfect is "I see" (as opposed to "I am seeing").

The classical precedent, far from being any help here, is probably responsible for rendering the conceptual water so muddy, to begin with. For the Romans, no distinction existed between "I have seen" and "I saw." This is surely why we moderns use very clumsy terminology to designate the former. Forgive the emphasis… but to say it one more time, "I have seen" is not present in tense and perfect in aspect: it describes a past act. What appears needed is a new tense name—something like the "immediate past". If Latin scuffs up the distinction between "I have seen" and "I saw," English doesn't exactly sweep away all the dust, but our extensive use of helping verbs at least makes the task of clarification a little less formidable.

Our English past tense is so sloppily used, as well, that our fuzziness in categorizing past action has obviously worked its way from grammar book to daily usage. Many times we inject a blunt past tense into a situation whose circumstances would justify an imperfect verb in Latin or the romance tongues. "I saw him every day of that year" certainly sounds repeated or habitual. "I edited my three book manuscripts as summer drew on" sounds like a protracted labor. Though both of these drawn-out activities are treated as a completed unit and thus placed in the perfect (or past) tense, they could more logically be handled with the imperfect.

The modern romance languages actually do the best job of all here, for they all possess a tense for events neither immediately past nor distantly past (as in the pluperfect). This tense is variously called the preterite, the narrative, or the historic. It is used almost exclusively to refer to events and occurrences that have settled (so to speak) into the past's fixity, yet not into a relative remoteness. The perfect tense in Italian, Spanish, and their cousins (the exact equivalent of our "I have seen") is a rather late creation that takes the place left by the old Latin perfect, now become the preterite. If you were telling a friend about a shouting-and-shoving match that you witnessed five minutes earlier, you would employ the newly modeled perfect; if you were giving testimony about the fight before a judge in court, you would shift to the historic/preterite tense.

When we apply them to the "past present" controversy, the modern romance languages again do a better clean-up job than English. In particular, they don't advance the outrageous claim that "I have seen" is present in tense. Yet by preserving the word "perfect" to designate this tense, they do indeed continue the grand old tradition of blurring the line between tense and aspect. What has been needed for all these years is simply a new name, and a

138

sensible one. "Immediate past" doesn't sound like a very exotic solution to a mystery as ancient as the Sphinx's riddle… but it fits every piece into the proper place, and for that we should be grateful.

Here, then, is a suggested revision of how we view tenses in English, with fully adequate attention devoted to aspect:

CHART OF TENSES AND ASPECTS

TENSE	ASPECT	
	Perfect (completed, viewed as "done" even if much time spent in doing)	Progressive (unfinished, repeated, ongoing, habitual, etc.; all forms use some form of auxiliary "be" + present participle)
present	I call	I am calling
immediate past*	I have called	I have been calling
preterite	I called	I was calling
distant past**	I had called	I had been calling
future	I will call	I will be calling
future past***	I will have called	I will have been calling

*Called the perfect tense in Latin and the romance languages; Latin has no preterite, however, and thus allows this tense to "bleed" into the preterite's perfect aspect.
**Called the pluperfect tense in Latin and the romance languages.
***Called the future perfect tense in Latin and the romance languages.

A warning as we conclude this introduction: NEVER use a form of the verb *habere* ("to have") in seeking to translate any of the tenses above. For that matter, do not use *desiderare*, *volle*, or any other verb that you might find in a Latin dictionary under "will" when translating the future perfect. Any Latin verb belonging to any of these tenses will be a single word as long as it remains in the active voice: that is, as long as the subject is initiating the verb's action rather than receiving it. Later in this chapter, we shall see that the perfect system's passive voice (where the subject receives the verb's action rather than initiating it) does indeed employ two verbal forms. Neither of these, though, is connected to *habere*. That manner of expression enters English through the romance tongues. As noted above, it is a relatively late development in linguistic history.

Summary
All of the perfect system's tenses refer primarily to completed action (though context may imply a progressive aspect). These tenses are the perfect (for just completed action), the pluperfect (for long-completed action), and the future perfect (for action likely to be completed in the future). No helping verbs are ever used in Latin for an active verb; but "had" is always the English helping verb employed in building the pluperfect, and "shall/will + have" must appear when building the future perfect. The English language itself sometimes draws only sketchy distinctions between past tenses. The romance languages typically show greater accuracy.

Exercise Set 4.1

A. Identify the tense employed by each verb below. Not all examples belong to the perfect system.

1. they had been calling
2. we shall have discussed
3. you had forgotten
4. he will have fallen
5. she was selling
6. you are leaving
7. I used to know
8. she has told
9. you will be following
10. they won
11. we had been having
12. he had

B. Design two English sentences for No. 10 above that, while using the same verb, would be translated by different tenses in Latin. Repeat this exercise with No. 12. What two Latin tenses are involved?

139

C. Supply the tense of the English verb that makes most sense in the given context. Specify the tense as well as writing in the verb.

    1. While you _____ (to sleep), a stranger came to the door.
    2. The polls _____ (to close) by the time we learn the election results.
    3. I _____ (to swim) in that river often when we were children.
    4. Now that we _____ (to complete) every item on the questionnaire, we can compare responses.
    5. The weatherman _____ (to warn) of the risk long before the hurricane made landfall.
    6. When they _____ (to visit) California, they experienced an earthquake.

Solo Flight: Though Latin places less emphasis on aspect than English, the concept remains an important one. Return to the twelve verbs in 4.1.A and assign each of them an aspect (i.e., progressive or perfect). Then see if you can shift the aspect of each without changing its tense (e.g., "I am calling" would become "I call").

II. The Perfect System in Latin: Formation

Believe it or not, this section will undertake to familiarize you with all three tenses of the perfect system at once: they are easy enough to inspire great optimism in any lesson-planner! While handling the present system, we had to tread more warily. In fact, you may have noticed that very little has been said so far about the third and fourth conjugations. The main reason for that calculated negligence was because the present and future tenses both feature several aberrations from the paradigms that you learned for the well-behaved first and second conjugations. Such intricacies are best left for a more advanced course in Latin, though we shall glance over them in passing (just for the curious) toward the end of this chapter.

All verbs, however, use the same inflections of tense, person, and number in the perfect system: all four conjugations, for all three of the tenses. These inflections, besides, follow a very straightforward sequence in their spelling, especially in the pluperfect and future perfect. But before commenting on any more specifics, let us simply chart the inflections of all three tenses at once in synoptic fashion.

PERFECT TENSE		
	singular	**plural**
1st person	-i (amavi, tenui)	-imus (amavimus, tenuimus)
2nd person	-isti (amavisti, tenuisti)	-istis (amavistis, tenuistis)
3rd person	-it (amavit, tenuit)	-erunt (amaverunt, tenuerunt)
PLUPERFECT TENSE		
	singular	**plural**
1st person	-eram (amaveram, tenueram)	-eramus (amaveramus, tenueramus)
2nd person	-eras (amaveras, tenueras)	-eratis (amaveratis, tenueratis)
3rd person	-erat (amaverat, tenuerat)	-erant (amaverant, tenuerant)

FUTURE PERFECT TENSE		
	singular	**plural**
1ˢᵗ person	**-ero** (amavero, tenuero)	**-erimus** (amaverimus, tenuerimus)
2ⁿᵈ person	**-eris** (amaveris, tenueris)	**-eritis** (amaveritis, tenueritis)
3ʳᵈ person	**-erit** (amaverit, tenuerit)	**-erint** (amaverint, tenuerint)

Now that these tenses have been laid out graphically, we may reason our way carefully through their formation, tense by tense:

Perfect: very nearly the same as present, with an "i" added before each inflection. To be sure, this holds strictly true only of *–it* and *–imus*; but it is almost true of *–istis*. The second-person singular *–isti* ending has the archaic look of certain Greek verbs like διδωμι where the iota frequently produces a short tail (a feature of Sanskrit, as well); and perhaps the same dynamic was at work in the first-singular (*amavimi* could easily decay into *amavi*). The third-plural suffix *–erunt* poses the most puzzling case. We would have expected a simple *–int*. Ancient texts do little to enlighten us as to how this odd fruit could grow on the same branch as the other five forms. Just remember that these inflections hold true for ALL Latin verbs in the perfect tense. Once memorized, they will be universally employed.

Pluperfect: nothing easier—simply precede the usual person-number inflections (and "m" is historically as common for the first-singular as "o") with the tense indicator *–era*.

Future Perfect: almost as simple as the pluperfect—replace *–era* with *–eri*. This fails to work only in the first-singular form, where we shift back from "m" to "o." It is entirely possible (even probable) that the pristine form in this slot was *–erio* and that the "i" was absorbed into the "o."

You may have remarked that all of the forms using *amare* ("to love") display a "v" in their mid-section, and that all of those using the second-conjugation verb *tenere* ("to hold") display at the same point a "u." These are the indicators of the perfect system for regular verbs: they form the completed stem. That is, every first-conjugation verb, if one removes the *–re* from its infinitive, will add a "v" at that position to signal its entry into the perfect system before it also adds the specific ending of a specific tense, person, and number. This is a bit redundant (since the endings themselves are not duplicated in the present system), but not unhelpful. Only the remarkable verbs *dare* and *stare* do not morph into *davi* and *stavi* according to the rule, but rather assume the irregular forms *dedi* ("I gave") and *steti* ("I stood").

The Romans pronounced "v" and "u" almost identically (indeed, when chiseling letters in stone, they wrote both as "v," since curves are highly labor-intensive when cutting marble), so we should not be surprised to find the "u" supplanting the "v" in the second conjugation. A linguistic historian would probably prefer the explanation that there *was* a "v" at first—*tenevi* for "I held"—and that the "ev" degenerated into "u" as it was casually uttered thousands of times. In any case, far fewer second-conjugation verbs have this "u" indicator in the stem than first-conjugation verbs have the "v." Exceptions to the "u" indicator fall into no particular pattern: hence several irregular perfect-system stems in this second group must be learned. To one of them—the *vid-* of *vidi* ("I saw")—you have already been exposed. This is really the only hard part about learning the perfect system: i.e., remembering the irregular stems of what are often otherwise regular verbs. A dictionary will assist you greatly here. It will give the *video* or *amo* form, then the infinitve (probably abbreviated as *–are* or *–ēre*); and then, if the perfect stem is at all irregular, the first-person singular of the perfect: *vidi*, in this case.

Below are some examples, first of second-conjugation verbs with regular *principle parts* (the forms listed in the dictionary from which stems may be drawn), then of several verbs where the "u" does not appear in the perfect stem:

"regular" perfect stem ("u")

moneo, monêre, monui	teneo, tenêre, tenui
habeo, habêre, habui	terreo, terrêre, terrui
placeo, placere, placui	timeo, timêre, timui

irregular perfect stem

deleo, delêre, delêvi	moveo, movêre, movi
iubeo, iubêre, iussi	sedeo, sedêre, sêdi
maneo, manêre, mansi	video, vidêre, vidi

With the chart above as your guide, test yourself now to see how well you can translate in the following exercises. Always remember that Latin does not use an auxiliary verb like "have" in any such circumstances as these. All of the English-to-Latin exercises will be answered by a single word.

Summary
The three tenses of the perfect system are formed with strict adherence to a single set of endings, used by all four conjugations. The verbal stem to which these inflections are added, however, may be irregular, especially in conjugations subsequent to the first (where the stem is almost always -av). The third principle part given in any dictionary will confirm the proper perfect stem.

Exercise Set 4.2

A. Translate into English:

1.	monueras	7.	timuerint
2.	vocaverunt	8.	clamavimus
3.	tenuistis	9.	habuero
4.	spectabam	10.	vidisti
5.	laudaverimus	11.	vocabis
6.	pulsaveram	12.	manserint

B. Translate into Latin:

1.	he has sailed	6.	you (s.) had watched
2.	you (pl.) had announced	7.	they will have sat
3.	we will have pleased	8.	you (pl.) have terrified
4.	you (pl.) have praised	9.	we have seen
5.	I will have warned	10.	she was carrying

Solo Flight: Return to Exercise 4.2.A above and transform all singular forms into corresponding plurals, all plurals into singulars (e.g., the "I" form should become "we" and the "they" form should become "he/she/it"). Translate your results into English as you go.

III. The Latin Verb "To Be"

For reasons both obvious and yet to be revealed, knowledge of the forms of the verb "to be" is essential. Of course, among the most obvious reasons is the frequency of simple sentences that couple one noun with another or with an adjective (to be studied further in Chapter Five). Despite the incessant efforts of English teachers to eradicate such sentences from our writing, we use them all the time. "Marcus is a sailor. His son will be a farmer." All four nouns in these two sentences fall into the nominative case, since "to be" merely couples them (and hence is often called the *copula*) rather than transferring any action from one to the other. "Sailor" and "farmer" are called *predicate nominatives*. The adjective in the sentence, *Villa est alta* ("The house is tall"), is also nominative.

As you look at the present system of "to be," you will probably be surprised to find some very familiar forms, especially in the imperfect and future tenses:

PRESENT TENSE

	singular	plural
1st person	sum	sumus
2nd person	es	estis
3rd person	est	sunt

IMPERFECT TENSE

	singular	plural
1st person	eram	eramus
2nd person	eras	eratis
3rd person	erat	erant

FUTURE TENSE

	singular	plural
1st person	ero	erimus
2nd person	eris	eritis
3rd person	erit	erunt

The imperfect forms of "to be" ("I was, you were, he/she/it was…") and the future forms ("I will be, you will be, he/she/it will be…") are, in Latin, the *endings of the pluperfect and future perfect*. The only point at which this is not true is the "they will be" form, which shifts to -*erint* as a future-perfect ending because *erunt* has already been used by the perfect tense. (This, at least, is a convenient explanation: the truth may have more to do with the almost identical pronunciation of short "u" and short "i" in Latin, which could easily have caused confusion about spelling.)

So how would we make the perfect system of "to be," since the present system is already employing several perfect-tense endings? Nothing could be simpler: we take the perfect stem of *esse* (the irregular infinitive of "to be"—originally *essere*, no doubt, as it is in modern Italian), which is *fu-*; then we proceed to add the regular endings. This means that, in the pluperfect and future perfect, you are putting one form of "to be" together with another!

PERFECT TENSE

	singular	plural
1st person	fui	fuimus
2nd person	fuisti	fuistis
3rd person	fuit	fuerunt

PLUPERFECT TENSE

	singular	plural
1st person	fueram	fueramus
2nd person	fueras	fueratis
3rd person	fuerat	fuerant

FUTURE PERFECT TENSE

	singular	plural
1st person	fuero	fuerimus
2nd person	fueris	fueritis
3rd person	fuerit	fuerint

Is it mere accident that so much of *esse*'s present system also constitutes the endings for the perfect system? The odds are against it: that is, in these perfect-system inflections we probably *do* see the present system of "to be" collaborating with a verbal form whose original, distinct meaning has long been lost and can only be guessed at. Never forget that Latin was once an exclusively spoken language. The eventual carving up of Latin sentences into discrete words as the written language evolved was a somewhat arbitrary process. Most documents even from late antiquity and the Middle Ages, in fact, had no such separation at all: entire sentences were written in one word, as it were. We may speculate that the forms of *esse* were never teased out of the preceding word in these perfect-system verbs because that first "word" no longer had an independent meaning. It was likely the relic of a Latin *active past participle*: e.g., a form that would mean "having loved." Greek indeed has this kind of participle, but Latin as we have received it possesses only a *passive* version of the perfect participle ("having been loved").

Thus the word *amavi* may have meant "I am having loved" in our sometimes unwieldy English system of helping verbs. It perhaps would originally have consisted of the two elements, *amavus* (or *amava*, for a woman) and something like the Sanskrit *asmi* (=*sum*). Indeed, speaking of Latin's ancient Indo-European cousin, consider this. Sanskrit offers some very likely cognates of our missing participle. It possesses two forms of a perfect active participle, specifically, that both display a "v" stem. Our hypothetical *amavus* might once have been used like either one of the second words in these sentences: *Rāmam drishthavatī Sitā gacchati* ("Having seen Rama, Sita goes"), and *Rāvanam jigīvān Rāmah Ayodhyām gacchati* ("Having conquered Ravana, Rama goes to Ayodhya"). If you guessed that the nouns ending in "m," by the way, are accusative, give yourself a star!

This defunct perfect active participle could account for perfect-system indicators like the first-conjugation "v" and the second-conjugation "u." We remarked before that such indicators seem redundant with the perfect system's distinct endings. Why say "the pizzeria on Main Street" when there's only one pizzeria in town? Why designate the perfect system with a unique stem when the following inflections will designate a precise tense of that system? The answer may be that these stray intermediate letters were actually an integral part of some lost form like the perfect active participle.

Yes, but why are the perfect tense's endings not therefore *sum, es, est* just as the pluperfect's are *eram, eras, erat*: why is some form of *esse* not clearly the standard ending throughout the perfect system? Perhaps it is. The perfect tense's endings in fact resemble the present tense of the Greek "to be" fairly closely. The first-person *–i* could be the remnant of a form very like 'ειμι, "I am." (In Sanskrit, *asmi*: you may have gathered by now that Greek—and even Sanskrit—often give us a window into the prehistory of Latin.) Certainly *–istis* is very nearly *estis*, and the *–erunt* inflection which appeared so puzzling before would make sense as *sunt* interacting with the worn-down hulk of a lost participle.

All of this is more than you need to know about Latin's history to proceed in this book. It is unquestionably more than you will find on the subject in most formal Latin textbooks. Developing a taste for the mysteries that guide a language's evolution, though, is an important part of truly understanding language—any language. Besides… when we turn shortly to the passive voice later in this chapter, all of the discussion about *esse*'s role in building the perfect system will grow much less speculative. At that point, we really do have a form of "to be" plus a participle appearing as two separate words.

Summary
Though a highly irregular verb, "to be" (esse) in Latin follows the normal rules in forming its perfect system (the perfect stem being fu-). In fact, the regular endings for that system are almost certainly the verb's three present-system tenses appended to the relic of a perfect active participle with a v/u stem.

Exercise Set 4.3

A. Translate these forms of "to be" into Latin:

1.	you (pl.) used to be	6.	she will have been
2.	we had been	7.	I have been
3.	they will be	8.	they will have been
4.	you (s.) are	9.	we were being
5.	I will be	10.	you (s.) have been

B. Translate these forms of *esse* into English:

1.	eritis	6.	eras
2.	sumus	7.	fueris
3.	fuerunt	8.	fuero
4.	fueram	9.	sunt
5.	est	10.	erit

C. Translate the following sentences into English.
1. Ante adventum hostium, filius imperatoris dux populi fuerat.
2. Ubi ("when") Ariovistus (name) erit rex, Britannîs spes auxili non erit.
3. Fueras-ne, Luci,* in Marsiliâ ante bellum Gallicum?
4. Dies hiemis brevissimae ("very short") sunt, sed dies proeli militibus longissima ("very long") est.
5. Liberi sumus, cives! Gaius tyrannus in vitâ erat, nunc ("now") non est.

*The vocative of names ending in *–ius* simply drops the *–us* and adds nothing.

D. Translate the following sentences into Latin:
1. The forests around the mountain did not belong to the farmer (= were not "to him").
2. You sisters of the teacher had not been in the city on the holiday (use *dies festa*).
3. Marcus, I had been a leader: now you are a king.

Solo Flight: In Exercise 4.3.C above, four of the five sentences have at least one predicate nominative. List each pair (remembering that adjectives qualify: e.g., "Roses are red"). Why does Number 3 have none at all, even though it uses a form of "to be"?

IV. The Perfect System: Greek

A few pages back, did you memorize the oldest words of Latin in our possession—the dedication found engraved inside a bracelet? They are *Manios med fefaked Numasioi*—"Manius made me for Numasius." Every one of these four words gives fascinating testimony about Latin's pristine form. The word for "made"—*fefaked*—is actually perfect tense. It belongs to the confusing, often-morphing third conjugation, which we have largely avoided in this introductory study. What renders the word especially significant as we turn to Greek, however, is its *reduplicative* spelling. That is, the first syllable of *facere*, "to make," has been more or less reproduced, as if employing the formula "2 x *fa* + perfect inflection." (One would think that true *reduplication* would yield *fa*^{2}, since a double would be *re*-doubled… but classicists apparently are not sticklers for mathematical logic.)

This formula is used in extremely few Latin words by the time of Cicero. (Even *facere* has dropped it: the mainstream spelling of "he made" would be *fecit*.) In Greek, though—yes, and also in Sanskrit—duplication was the standard manner of turning a present-system stem into a perfect-system stem. The doubling is often not precise. The perfect stem of our paradigm-word λυω, for instance, is not λυλυ- (as irresistibly festive as that may sound) but λελυ- with a kappa added afterward to keep the vowels of stem and inflection from merging (verbs without a stem ending in a vowel do not pick up this kappa). As in Latin, the actual endings of the perfect mirror the present tense in several ways, with the major difference being an alpha's presence in five out of six forms. The following paradigm results:

PERFECT TENSE

	singular	plural
1st person	-α / λελυκα	-αμεν / λελυκαμεν
2nd person	-ας / λελυκας	-ατε / λελυκατε
3rd person	-ε / λελυκε	-ασι / λελυκασι

The pluperfect tense essentially makes two adjustments to the forms of the perfect. First, it adds an initial epsilon (called an *augment*, if you recall—also employed in Sanskrit past tenses). The imperfect tense made this addition, as we noted earlier, in transforming the present tense. Secondly, the pluperfect inserts another epsilon where the inflection begins. In recorded Greek, the resulting two short vowels merge into an eta; and the pluperfect is used so seldom in Homer that, frankly, the forms given below have little textual reality. For some reason, the alpha does *not* interact with the epsilon in plural forms: it simply disappears—an unusual development, since epsilon is not known for triumphing in clashes with other vowels. It probably didn't do so here, either: its "triumph" is surely owed, rather, to the surrounding consonants, all pronounced close to the teeth.

146

PLUPERFECT

	singular	**plural**
1st person	-εα (η) / ’ελελυκεα	-εμεν / ’ελελυκεμεν
2nd person	-εας (ης) / ’ελελυκεας	-ετε / ’ελελυκετε
3rd person	-εε (ει) / ’ελελυκεε	-εσαν / ’ελελυκεσαν

The forms above are surprisingly rare, even in historians who write about the distant past routinely. Herodotus reports of Sparta's early run-ins with the city of Tegea (in *Histories* 1.67.1) that the Spartans *had been* the underdogs in war: ’εγεγονεσαν. Yet it appears that the Greeks grew rather lazy about resorting to the pluperfect's acute specificity as they became enamored of a "grab bag" past tense called the aorist. More on that later.

The future perfect would perhaps be the easiest and most sensible tense of all within the perfect system—if only it existed as we have represented it below. The future tense's stem would simply be "reduplicated," yielding the following paradigm:

FUTURE PERFECT

	singular	**plural**
1st person	λε + λυσω = λελυσω	λε + λυσομεν = λελυσομεν
2nd person	λε + λυσεις = λελυσεις	λε + λυσετε = λελυσετε
3rd person	λε + λυσει = λελυσει	λε + λυσουσι = λελυσουσι

The problem is that the forms immediately above are rarely used—even more rarely than the pluperfect, occurring in trace amounts just sufficient to justify the inferences that have produced the table above. The perfect tense itself is well documented. Plato, when recording Socrates' defense in the *Apology*, uses two examples of the perfect in fairly close proximity (20.D and 21.A): ’εσχηκα from ’εχω ("I have held": see Vocabulary below) and τετελευτηκε from τελευω ("it has ended"). Not infrequently, however, we must guess at forms of the pluperfect and future perfect for particular verbs, for we cannot find any confirmation in a known text.

How, then, did the Greeks commonly make a future perfect? They used their perfect active participle with the future of "to be." "I will have released" would literally become, in two Greek words, "I will be (in a state of) having released." We will not delay over the grammar necessary actually to generate these two Greek words, for our discussion would become quite involved. Yet the mere fact that the Greeks were performing this operation with their active past participle makes one wonder all the more if the Latin future perfect is a fusion of *esse*'s future and a disused active participle.

No more of that, however! We have gone far enough to establish that the Greek perfect system once had a principle of organization very similar to Latin's.

Summary
The three tenses of the Greek perfect system were formed originally by doubling the verb's first syllable and then adding a fixed set of endings (with an epsilon augment in the pluperfect). The perfect system's tenses have the same

meanings as they do in Latin; but in surviving texts from antiquity, only the perfect tense itself is relatively easy to find, the pluperfect and future perfect being much less used than their Latin counterparts.

Vocabulary

Before we proceed to exercises, let us ponder in their reduplicative form some of the Greek verbs that we already know; for it is this form that we must use to make the perfect system's tenses.

1ˢᵗ s. present	1ˢᵗ s. perf.	English perf.
’αγω	’αγηοχα (later ηχα)	I have led
’ακουω	’ακηκοα	I have heard
βαινω	βεβηκα	I have walked
βαλλω	βεβληκα	I have thrown
’εχω	’εσχηκα	I have held
κρινω	κεκρινα*	I have judged
λαμβανω	λεληθα	I have taken
λυω	λελυκα	I have released
‘οραω	‘εορακα	I have seen
πεμπω	πεπομφα	I have sent
ποιεω	πεποιηκα	I have made
πρασσω	πεπραχα	I have done
τευχω	τετευχα	I have made
φιλεω	πεφιληκα*	I have loved
φυω	πεφυκα*	I have produced
φωνεω	πεφωνηκα*	I have spoken

*These forms are likely but not documented in actual Greek texts.

Exercise Set 4.4

A. Translate these verbs into English.

1. ‘επεφωνηκετε
2. πεπραχεσαν
3. ‘εορακας
4. ’επεπομφεμεν
5. λελυσω
6. πεφιληκα
7. τευχουσι
8. πεμψεις
9. ’εκεκρινεσαν
10. ’ακηκοε

B. Translate these verbs into Greek.

1. you (pl.) have done
2. I was taking (or they
3. you (s.) will have produced
4. he/she/it has taken
5. he/she/it had thrown were taking)
6. we were throwing
7. I have released
8. they had loved

C. Translate the following sentences into English.

1. Δια νεφεα φαος μηνος 'εορακαμεν.
2. Ιχθυες εν ποντωι δια νυκτα 'ουκ 'ελεληθεμεν.
3. 'Επι τελεος 'ενιαυτου τειχεα πολεος 'ηροες τετευξουσι.
4. Στρατηγε, βασιλεια 'οινον 'οπλισι (= 'οπλιτεσσι) πεπομφε.
5. Θεος κερδεα 'ανθρωποισι πεφυκε, 'αλλ' 'εργα 'ανθρωπων 'ου φυει.

D. Translate the following sentences into Greek:

1. We sailors threw the things (= possessions) of the commander into the sea.
2. When ('Επει) you hear the words of the poet, you have not heard the truth.

Solo Flight: This exercise is a kind of "linguistic musical chairs." Imagine a small circle moving from the perfect tense to the pluperfect to the future perfect and then to the perfect again. Rotate each of the verbs in 4.4.A by one "chair." Write the new form with its English translation. Which two verbs are not in the perfect system and, thus, cannot play in the game?

V. The Greek Aorist

There is another reason for why the future perfect's original form so very rarely appears in Greek. It is the reason, as well, for why the Greek pluperfect is so rare compared to Latin; and, indeed, the Greek perfect tense itself is used probably not one tenth as much by most Greek authors as their Roman counterparts employed the Latin perfect.

The reason behind all of these curiosities is the *aorist* tense. This odd word has nothing to do with the heart's aorta. The second-declension Greek noun 'ορος means "limit, boundary"; and in Greek (and Sanskrit), the prefix used for negating a word's meaning—the way *in-* does in Latin and *un-* does in English—is the "privative a" (so called because it deprives the following word of its force). Hence "aorist" literally means "unlimited." In fact, the aorist tense is decidedly past, so it is not unlimited without limits! Yet in the hands of an ancient Greek writer, it seems to have conveniently communicated all of those temporal relationships about which Latin's perfect gave us pause. We pondered, for example, how a sentence such as, "The Romans fought the Parthians for centuries," could be perfect tense, since the action is represented as now complete yet was ongoing for an extremely long time. Why should such sentences be cast in the same tense as a child's announcing, "I've finished my milk"?

In effect, the aorist became the Greek historic/narrative tense. The perfect was more or less reserved for "I've finished my milk" utterances, where the action is over but just recently so. You can detect the difference very clearly at the beginning of Plato's *Phaedo*. Cebes remarks to Socrates that people are asking why "you have composed" (πεποιηκας) poems in prison when "you composed" ('εποιησας) no poems before arrest and trial. The former verb is perfect in tense, the latter aorist. Cebes is saying, in effect, "You have just now written several poems—putting your stylus down, perhaps, right before I walked into your cell. A few weeks ago, or a year ago, or twenty years ago, you were never known to have produced a single one." The time period covered by the aorist is distinctly less confined.

Cebes could even be referring to the very distant past in noting all the foregoing occasions when Socrates

149

has declined to compose verse; for the Greek pluperfect was also somewhat usurped by this roving past tense. In English, we frequently shade the pluperfect into a vaguer past significance in just this way, as when someone says, "I finished my course work before I started on my thesis." Since both events occurred in the past but the former explicitly preceded the latter, shouldn't this student say, "I **had** finished my course work"? Yet we decline to worry over such hair-splitting, and so did the Greeks… thanks to the aorist.

This book will *not* introduce you to any forms of the aorist tense. A sigh of relief is well justified, because the aorist's form has a multitude of idiosyncratic guises. One steadily recurrent quality that it possesses, though, is a sigma ("s") preceding the person-number endings. (Very broadly speaking, the aorist's stem is often the same as the future's, but with an epsilon augment leading the way.) Is it just a coincidence that the Latin third conjugation, which we are evading because its forms also tend to grow very peculiar, typically features an "s" sound in the perfect stem? The other three conjugations use the "u/v" stem very consistently in their perfect system. Latin's unique third conjugation may just be some sort of response or distant relation to the Greek aorist. On occasion, the Latin third's perfect stems also, for good measure, don't look remotely like any other form of the verb (e.g., *fero, ferre, **tuli***… "I bear, to bear, I have borne"). Similarly, in its Greek incarnation, the aorist is sometimes spelled so differently from other forms of its verb that we can recognize in it the single descendant of a completely distinct verb, apparently long dead in all other tenses. (For instance, the aorist of a verb we learned in Chapter Two, ‘οραω—"I see"—is ’ειδον: clearly these two forms did NOT spring from the same original source.)

So, you see, not only the spelling and the meaning, but (especially) the historical evolution of the aorist is just too dense a mystery to tackle here. The main purpose served in bringing up this odd tense—other than to explain why competing past tenses suffer neglect in Greek—is to prepare you for an adaptation made by the modern romance languages, which will be this chapter's final topic of discussion. These languages, too, were evidently uncomfortable with their Latin grandsire's inability to distinguish between a hundred years' war and a finished glass of milk. We shall find that they essentially transformed the Latin perfect tense into something very like a Greek aorist and created a system of helping verbs to express the true perfect—a system which closely resembles the German approach (and the English one).

Summary
The Greek aorist tense broadly expresses past action. Its indulgent imprecision made it so popular that more explicit tenses (like the pluperfect and future perfect) fell into disuse.

Exercise Set 4.5
Revisit the sentences in Exercise Set 4.1 C. Identify the five that make most sense with a past tense; then, instead of using the strictly proper tense (as you did when first completing the exercise), use a vague past that would correspond to the Greek aorist.

VI. The Passive Voice
As a grammatical category, "voice" is either active or passive. Ancient Greek persistently nursed along a "middle" voice; but its forms had all but merged with those of the passive by historical times, so we shall not be exploring that option in this book. The "middle" idea had become obscure to the ancients, as well: it requires that the subject both direct the action elsewhere and, paradoxically, receive that same action. Something like the contemporary colloquialism, "I got me some new shoes," comes close to the middle voice, since "I" did the getting but "I" also received, indirectly. We are more inclined, however, to understand the "me" (the "I" at the receiving end) as "for me"—i.e., as a dative expression. It's difficult to grasp how the middle voice would have differed from or improved upon a normal "dative of interest" (or "ethical dative").

The distinction between active and passive is already more than enough of a challenge for most students without our trying to resurrect the defunct middle voice. Explanations usually stress the contrast just hinted at in the previous paragraph. That is, the active verb features a subject producing action aimed at some other entity (a person or object affected either directly or indirectly by that action). The passive voice, continues this reasoning, has the subject now receiving the action produced by the verb.

Such a view is not inaccurate, but its terms leave students confused sometimes. If a hiker **is struck by** a falling stone, is he not the direct object in painful receipt of the action, and is the stone not the action's author? Does that mean, then, that "stone" is the sentence's subject? You must always be alert to the presence of prepositions in English, since we do not have case inflections to indicate any noun's function. "Stone" is the object of the preposition "by," and therefore cannot be the sentence's subject. The hiker is the subject—and yet he does indeed also bear the brunt of the action expressed. This forces us to conclude (if we do not otherwise know how to tell) that the verb "is struck" has a passive voice.

Students are also befuddled by certain verbs which appear to thrust action upon the subject even when their voice is active. The sentences, "I am ailing," "I am suffering," and "I am dying," all seem to cast the lamentable subject in a role that receives rather than initiates some sort of activity. Yet verbs of this sort are usually *intransitive*: that is, they cannot take a direct object. Their subject may seem to have a more passive than active relation to them because the essential action they convey puts the subject in this recipient posture. You cannot "ail" or "die" someone else (though you can "suffer" someone in the sense of enduring that person's presence—a meaning of the verb that has grown rare). Intransitive verbs do not have passive forms. If a verb cannot take a direct object—i.e., if it is not transitive—then it cannot be turned around so that the subject receives its action.

English expresses the passive voice by using some form of "to be" with the *past participle* (typically ending in –*ed*, though English has many irregular past participles: "said," "seen," "got" or "gotten," the word "struck" used above, etc.). Even a present- or future-tense verb must use a past participle in our language to become passive: e.g., "I am (being) called" or "you will be praised." The logic of this arrangement begins to fall apart if you think about it for too long, since a perfect participle—as the term implies—is supposed to convey completed action. What is the difference between "you will be praised" and "you will be having been praised" (i.e., "you will be someone who has been praised")? Are we not properly dealing with a future perfect in both instances? The convention in English, of course, is to let such trivial discrepancies slip by without notice. We'll find out in a few sections that Latin's logic is more punctilious here.

In both Latin and Greek, passive forms are created in the present system by a process fundamentally different from that used in the perfect system. Present-system tenses (present, imperfect, and future) have standard inflections at the very end—after the person-number indicators—that designate the passive voice. In the perfect system (perfect, pluperfect, and future perfect), "to be" is employed as an auxiliary verb along with a participle: an approach much closer to our way of doing things in English. (This helping-verb method is standard operating procedure in the Latin perfect system, but Greek occasionally uses it, too.)

Because Latin and Greek form passives in the present system by employing the same general technique, we shall take the two languages together in the next section.

Summary
Transitive verbs have a passive as well as an active voice: e.g., their subjects can "make" or "be made." The passive may generally be said to express verbal action in such a way that the subject is receiving that action. Intransitive verbs (e.g., "flow," "reek," "arise") cannot take a direct object and hence cannot transmit action back to the subject in a passive construction.

Exercise Set 4.6

A. Decide whether the following English verbs are active or passive.

1. you have fallen	6. it was long thought
2. we will be perceived	7. they used to brood
3. they used to know	8. he had been warned
4. I will have been appointed	9. we were rejoicing
5. were you convicted?	10. she is being pressured

B. Parse the preceding English verbs from Section A: that is, give their person, number, tense, and voice. Example: "they will be honored"—3rd person plural, future, passive (because they will not be honoring someone else).

Solo Flight: Now take the verbs in Exercise 4.6.A above and reverse their voice: i.e., make the actives passive and the passives active. (N.B.: This will change the verbs' basic sense, as when "we were chasing" becomes "we were being chased.") There are three intransitive verbs that cannot be "flipped" in this manner, and also an impersonal expression that doesn't make a lot of sense if you flip it. Which are these four?

VII. Formation of Present-System Passives in Latin

The Latin language forms passives in the present system by adding an "r" to the verb's active ending: the situation is almost as simple as this. In the first-person singular of the present and future tenses, the operation is indeed as was just described, since the active forms *voco* and *vocabo* end in a vowel. In other forms, an accommodation must be made so that smooth transition may be achieved from the active form's final consonant to the passive "r" (for Latin avoids consonant clusters). The third person forms, both singular and plural, toss in the least intrusive of vowels between their final "t" and the "r": a short "u" (what linguists call a *schwa*). First-person plural forms ("we") sooner or later must have dropped their final "s" rather than attempt to sustain something like *vocamusur*. Yet the second-person singular form ("thou") could not take this short-cut, which would have led it from *vocasur* to *vocur*: the result would have sounded confusingly similar to *vocor*, "I am being called." Whether by accident or design, then, the "s" and the "r" were inverted, creating a form that preserved them both: *vocaris*.

Such decisions, frankly, are seldom made by design in the history of any language. The "r" has a natural tendency to "leap-frog" other consonants: e.g., the shift of the Greek verb ‘ερπω (cf. "herpes") to ‘ρεπω (cf. "reptile"), which two verbs have a meaning within the range of "crawl, slide, sink" (hence their Latin cognate, *serpo*, from which we get "serpent"). A more colorful and homespun example might be the case of the Pedernales River in southern Texas, which is pronounced "Perdenales" by most of the locals, both Anglo and Hispanic.

That leaves the second-person plural form. The suffix *–mini* lacks the faintest hint of an "r" and resembles, instead, several Greek endings as well as certain archaic inflections from proto-Latin. It is apparently a dinosaur that forgot to become extinct. Its main advantage is that, being unique, it poses few problems to memorization.

Below is the present system's passive voice. **N.B.:** NEVER confuse the word "passive" with the word "past." In grammar, they are entirely distinct. All transitive verbs have a passive voice even in their present and future tenses. If you take care to understand this clearly right now, you will spare yourself much anguish later.

PRESENT TENSE

	singular	**plural**
1st person	vocor (I am being called)	vocamur (we are being called)
2nd person	vocaris (you are being called)	vocamini (you are being called)
3rd person	vocatur (he/she/it is being called)	vocantur (they are being called)

152

IMPERFECT TENSE

	singular	**plural**
1st person	vocabar (I was being called)	vocabamur (we were being called)
2nd person	vocabaris (you were being called)	vocabamini (you were being called)
3rd person	(he/she/it was being called) vocabatur	vocabantur (they were being called)

FUTURE TENSE

	singular	**plural**
1st person	vocabor (I will be called)	vocabimur (we will be called)
2nd person	vocaberis (you will be called)	vocabimini (you will be called)
3rd person	vocabitur (he/she/it will be called)	vocabuntur (they will be called)

Note that "you (singular) will be called" is spelled *vocaberis* rather than *vocabiris*. Since the "i" is short throughout the future, the spoken accent is thrust back to the preceding syllable. (The "b" syllable is never accented except in *vocabimini*, where the accent has already moved back the maximum three syllables possible, and *vocabuntur*, where the penultimate syllable ends in a consonant cluster). This means that *-biris* and *–beris* would have no detectible difference in pronunciation. The Romans must have taken to spelling the word the way it sounded rather than preserving the integrity of the *-bi* future indicator. Their culture was still much more oral than written, no doubt, as such forms were crystallizing.

Summary
*In the present system (present, imperfect, and future) of Latin, the passive voice is formed essentially by adding an "r" inflection to the appropriate active verb. Minor changes in preceding vowels and consonants have resulted from this suffix's addition in several instances. Only the second-person plural form does not feature any trace of the "r" (adding **-mini** instead).*

Exercise Set 4.7

A. Translate these verbs into English.

1.	iuvabamini	6.	pulsaberis
2.	moneris	7.	videmini
3.	laudatur	8.	servabunt
4.	tenentur	9.	spectabor
5.	terrebimus	10.	movebar

B. Translate these verbs into Latin.

1.	we were being praised	5.	we used to be afraid
2.	they are being watched	6.	she will be helped
3.	you (s.) will be seen	7.	you (pl.) are being frightened
4.	I am being held	8.	I used to be called

Solo Flight: Switch the singular verbs in Exercise 4.7.A above to plural and the plurals to singular. Supply the English meanings of the resulting Latin verbs.

VIII. Formation of Present-System Passives in Greek

We have seen that the Latin passive throughout the present system does little more than work an "r" onto the appropriate active endings. As usual, the situation with Greek is somewhat more complicated. Roman culture radiated from a single great population center—that being Rome, of course (known among Romans simply as *urbs*, or "the city"). The arbitration of various issues concerning grammar and orthography was therefore more orderly and rigid. Greek culture swirled around several competing focal points, from Thebes to Athens to Sparta to the prosperous ports of Ionia: hence we are less likely to find streamlined or uniform solutions to grammatical issues among these rival dialects.

Nevertheless, we can discern a convergence upon the notion that final –αι and -ο designate the passive voice. Starting with the present tense, you will see—in four out of six instances—that an –αι inflection has attached itself to relics of the active person-number endings, with small changes having occurred due to the attachment (shortened vowels, a dropped sigma, etc.). Consider these transformations:

λυομι (hypothetical ancient first-person s. form, like 'ιστημι): integrate –αι suffix to yield λυομαι
λυεις (second person s.): drop sigma and shorten -ει diphthong to -ε, then add –αι suffix to yield λυεαι
λυει (third-person s.): shorten -ει diphthong to -ε, then add tau as a glide into –αι suffix to yield λυεται
λυοντσι (hypothetical third-person pl. form): integrate –αι suffix to yield λυονται

This pattern recurs in the future tense. In the imperfect, all bets are off for the final –αι diphthong, but -ο takes its place in precisely the same positions.

PRESENT TENSE

	singular	plural
1st person	λυομαι (I am being loosed)	λυομεσθα (we are being loosed)
2nd person	λυεαι (you are being loosed)	λυεσθε (you are being loosed)
3rd person	λυεται (he/she/it is being loosed)	λυονται (they are being loosed)

IMPERFECT TENSE

	singular	plural
1st person	'ελυομην (I was being loosed)	'ελυομεσθα (we were being loosed)
2nd person	'ελυεο (you were being loosed)	'ελυεσθε (you were being loosed)
3rd person	'ελυετο (he/she/it was being loosed)	'ελυοντο (they were being loosed)

FUTURE TENSE

	singular	plural
1st person	λυσομαι (I will be loosed)	λυσομεσθα (we will be loosed)
2nd person	λυσεαι (you will be loosed)	λυσεσθε (you will be loosed)
3rd person	λυσεται (he/she/it will be loosed)	λυσονται (they will be loosed)

The first- and second-person plural endings are rather like the Latin –*mini* in that they hearken to an earlier era. In fact, the single set of distinctly passive inflections that survived into recorded Greek—the aorist endings (which we will *not* study)—uses the letter theta as the passive voice's primary indicator. If we pause to reflect that our table's other endings *historically belonged to Greek's middle voice*, and only came to represent the passive as the middle lost its force, then the two theta endings are probably original inhabitants rather than squatters on the passive's territory (if you'll pardon the metaphor). Both –σθα and –σθε, that is, are likely the closest to historical authenticity, if you are at all curious about how things must have looked at the very beginning. As for the forms that Greek authors actually used in their texts, it should be noted in passing that the λυομεσθα ("we are being loosed") of the first-person plural has already further degraded to λυομεθα in most works: the sigma has quietly slipped overboard.

Take all of these present-tense forms, add a sigma just before the person-number inflections to indicate the future, and you have just made the future passive—a veritable walk in the park!

The imperfect makes up for the future's ease, however. You may already have suspected that an epsilon augment will be required. If Greek had done no more than that—in other words, had merely slipped the epsilon augment before the present-tense forms—it would have displayed a logical efficiency rivaling Latin's. But the Greeks also messed around with most of the inflections in the imperfect's passive voice, basically altering the –αι ending to an omicron. The adjustment is not major, but it does constitute one more detail necessary to memorize.

Your instructor will probably not require that you add all of the forms above to your vast store of knowledge unless you are using this book with the specific intention of preparing for further study in the classics. We have included some exercises with passive forms below, as usual, but it is not necessarily recommended that you be able to create such forms from memory, without the aid of your textbook. At this point, the primary objective is merely that you should understand the concept of the passive voice.

Summary
In the present system of Greek, the passive voice is formed essentially by adding the diphthong –αι to the proper active forms (though such adaptations as vowel shortening occur in the process). The imperfect is more complex. Its passive form includes both an epsilon augment and an omicron ending. First- and second-person plural endings in all three tenses also employ a theta, the likely remnant of Greek's pristine passive indicator.

Exercise Set 4.8

A. Translate these verbs into English.

1.	’επεμπεσθε	6.	’εφυομην
2.	φοβησομαι	7.	’εκρατεετο
3.	’εβαλλετο	8.	’ακουονται
4.	‘οραομεσθα	9.	‘εξομαι
5.	φιλησονται	10.	’ελυομεσθα

B. Translate these verbs into Greek.

1.	you (s.) will be loved	5.	they are being thrown
2.	she was being watched	6.	it will be made
3.	you (pl.) will produce	7.	you (pl.) were being seized
4.	we are being led	8.	I used to be sent

Solo Flight: Take each verb in Exercise 4.8.A above and shift its number from plural to singular or singular to plural. Write out both the new Greek form and its English translation.

IX. The Perfect Passive Participle in Latin and Greek: "To Be" in Greek

Participles are verbal adjectives. In English, strictly speaking, we have only two. We form *present participles* by adding *–ing* to the root word, as in "the running horse." We generally form *past* or *perfect participles* usually by adding *–ed* to this root... but not always. Unlike the present form, the past participle has a great many irregular versions: "led," "fallen," "sung," and so on through dozens of variations. (The *–ed* forms descend from the regular German past participle ending in "t" [*gestellt, gestimmt*], whereas our many irregular forms ending in *–en*, or once ending in that syllable, descend from German participles with the same suffix [*gefallen, gesungen*].) We use these two participles ingeniously with auxiliary words to create other participles and, indeed, different verb tenses. "About to be seen" is considered an English future passive participle, even though "seen" on its own is perfect tense; "I was seeing" represents an imperfect active form, even though "seeing" alone is a present participle.

As has already been remarked, some of these structures—perhaps most of them—do not withstand intense logical scrutiny. Is "I am called" really a present-tense verb? Does the phrase not say, rather, that I am in a state of having been called... which should be equivalent to "I have been called"? By the same token, "I was called" could arguably be parsed as pluperfect; for my state of having been called, already indicating a completed action, has now been thrust even farther back into the past by the use of "was" rather than "am"!

Though we do not ponder such questions in English unless we relish headaches, they are worth weighing in the present context, because their answer—the strictly logical answer which English-speakers brush aside—explains precisely what the Romans and Greeks did to form the passive voice of their perfect-system verbs. A Roman would take the word for "I am"—*sum*—and add the past participle "called" or "having been called" to it—*vocatus*—to say in two words, "I have been called": *vocatus sum*. Yet the phrase quite literally means "I am called." We must not allow our own cultural sense that such expressions are present in tense (though perfect in aspect) to blind us to their Latin significance. These passive formations in the perfect, pluperfect, and future perfect are among the very few situations where Latin employs helping verbs more or less in the English fashion. The result can be that the perfect system is very easy for us to learn in the passive voice—but only if we understand (as we often do not in our own tongue) that the idea of completed action is *built into the participle*, not conveyed by the helping verb.

The same goes for Greek, to some extent: "I have been released" may be translated into Greek as "I am released"—λελυμενος 'ειμι. (There is an alternate and more mainstream way of making perfect passives in Greek: more of that anon.) The old Latin liturgy of the Christian church heralds Easter with the short sentence, *Est orsus*. Since the days of King James, this has been translated, "He is risen"—and that is quite literally what it says (or, "He is having risen / having been raised"). Yet today we would unfailingly render the same two words, "He has risen," or, "He has been raised." As much as Latin and Greek appear—for once—to be doing the same thing as English does, then, we must realize that it is not *quite* the same thing, or our translating may lurch down a wrong path.

Before we apply ourselves to completing the formation of the perfect system's passive voice in these tongues, we must learn a little more about how to build a perfect passive participle in both of them. We shall only occupy ourselves with that participle in this book—not the present participle (or the future, for which Latin and Greek have a single-word paradigm)—since they are not directly involved in the formulation of main verbs.

Latin is again delightfully simple. If you take a verb's present stem (i.e., what remains after you remove the *–re* from infinitives like *vocare* and *amare*), then add a mere "t," and finally include a nominative ending (about that, too, more shortly), then you have the perfect passive participle. This is the component used with some form of *esse* to make a passive verb in the perfect system. Here are a few examples of the participles by themselves:

amare – re + t + us = *amatus*, "the loved (boy, man, etc.)"
vocare – re + t + ae = *vocatae*, "the called (girls, women, etc.)"
dare – re + t + um = *datum*, "the given (gift, stone, etc.)"

This procedure is incredibly widespread in the Indo-European languages. The German "t" in regular past participles, mentioned above parenthetically as the source of our English *–ed*, reflects the same process. Sanskrit perfect participles show the same tendency: the "t" forms the root of this verbal adjective in words like *kriyatah* ("done") and *hatah* ("killed"). Even Gaelic preserves this "t" (e.g., *duinte*, "closed"). Almost every Latin perfect participle, including some of the highly irregular samples from the ever-troublesome third conjugation, possesses either a "t" or the remnant of a "t" in its stem.

We shall see in Chapter Five that adjectives are declined like nouns in Greek and Latin, and that—unlike nouns—they can change genders. They make this latter alteration, reasonably enough, to reflect the gender of the word they modify; and to the same end, they also change number. Since participles are verbal adjectives, they abide by these adjectival rules of operation. In forming part of a main verb, they will *only change gender and number*—never case, which will always be nominative. Why is this so? If you reflect upon the situation for a moment, you will understand why. A participle forming part of a main verb must be nominative because it will *necessarily and always be modifying the sentence's subject*.

All transitive verbs in Latin have a past participle. (Since this participle is usually passive in Latin—there are a few exceptions—it does not exist for intransitive verbs.) As shown above, first-conjugation verbs (i.e., those with infinitives in *–are*) have an extremely reliable tendency to form participles in *–atus/a/um*. Even *dare* produces the regular form *datus*, and its fellow first-conjugation rebel *stare* obediently produces *status* (which is practically non-existent in classical Latin, however, since "stand" is intransitive: you cannot "stand" something" in the sense of "make stand" when using the language of Virgil and Horace). Our word "datum," the plural of which is "data," comes from *datum*, which means "thing (having been) given," its "thingness" implied by the neuter gender; and our word "status" exists because the participle *status* would eventually produce in later Latin a fourth-declension noun— "how something has been stood, fixed, or arranged."

The second conjugation's perfect participles are a little less predictable. These *–ēre* verbs typically acquire a short "i" in the past participle—and we know all too well by now that a short "i" can lend itself to all sorts of mutation. Several second-conjugation participles, to be sure, play by the rules, such as these:

> habêre, habitus—*Concilium habitum est*: "A council was held."
> monêre, monitus—*Puella monita est*: "The girl was warned."
> terrêre, territus—*Nautae territi* sunt*: "The sailors were terrified"

*Notice that *territi* is masculine in inflection because *nautae* is masculine, despite its extraordinary ending.

On the other hand, the past participle of *movêre* is *motus*, and *vidêre* produces *visus*. The verb *manêre* does not have a past participle, because you cannot *be remained*.

The Greek method of building the perfect participle passive is also straightforward, and the formation of participles generally may be the most rigorously followed procedure in the Greek language's whole verbal system. There are three passive participles in Greek, all told—actually four: but we are going to pretend that the troublesome aorist tense doesn't exist. This tally has Latin beat at the starting gate, for only the perfect participle is a true passive in that tongue. (Many Latin grammars treat the gerundive as a future passive participle, but the association is careless: see Appendix B.) All three of the Greek passive participles—present, perfect, and future—end in –μενος. This suffix is added to the relevant stem (i.e., the present, perfect, or future stem) to create the desired verbal adjective. The word 'αγομενος (present passive participle) means "being led, driven"; the word βαλησομενος (future passive participle) means "about to be thrown."

These are not the forms that interest us, however. We seek a parallel for the *vocatus/monitus* paradigm in Latin. What, then, would be the form of a Greek word that means "having been released"? Let us first shift λυω to the perfect tense: λελυκα. Now we will cut off the first-person singular alpha (for the subject "I") and also as much of the stem as we need to until we find a vowel—for we cannot attach our –μενος smoothly to a consonant. In this case, we would end up deleting –κα, which would leave us with λελυ. At last we may add our participial suffix… and we have λελυμενος: "released."

The only real hitch in this operation is that some perfect stems in Greek assume rather surprising shapes. Usually the verb's first syllable is duplicated (more or less), but some contraction and/or vowel lengthening may take place at the other end, as well. The verb φυω yields the perfect participle πεφυμενος ("produced") without too much confusion. The verb φιλεω is a little more complicated: its perfect passive participle is πεφιλημενος ("beloved"), thanks to the epsilon in the original stem that lengthens throughout the perfect system. And since the perfect active of the verb βαλλω morphs off of βεβληκα, we emerge with a perfect passive participle of βεβλημενος ("thrown"). The more you repeat this operation, the more you acquire a kind of "feel" for it.

The single most famous Greek passive participle in our language is bound to be "phenomenon," from φαινω, "I bring to light, show." It's a present participle—not perfect—as you may quickly discern by the absence of any duplication at its beginning. Note that our word φαινομενον has a neuter ending. This word therefore signifies a "thing being brought to light"; and its plural, signifying "things being brought to light," would have to end in the neuter gender's universal nominative plural, alpha: φαινομενα. Many a television announcer apparently has not the remotest idea of how to distinguish this word's singular form from its plural.

Since we have not yet formally presented the conjugation of the Greek verb "to be" ('ειναι), now seems an ideal time to do so. Let us confine ourselves to the present tense. Other tenses are not as relevant to the tasks ahead of us as they are in Latin.

	singular	**plural**
1st person	'ειμι ("I am")	'εσμεν ("we are")
2nd person	'ει ("you are")	'εστε ("you are")
3rd person	'εστι ("he/she/it is")	'εισι ("they are")

With these forms, you can build some elementary Greek sentences involving predicate nominatives (e.g., "The girls are goddesses") as well as construct perfect-system passives.

Summary
Both Latin and Greek use perfect participles frequently, especially when forming verbs in the passive voice. These participles are regular adjectives that change their inflections to agree in case, number, and gender with the nouns they modify. (The case will always be nominative when the participle contributes to a main verb's formation.) Their stems in Latin have a characteristic "t" sound (which on occasion merges with another consonant), and in Greek they show a –μεν stem, as in "phenomenon."

Exercise Set 4.9

A. Create these perfect passive participles in Latin and Greek, using the root word in parentheses. (The gender of the ending doesn't matter, but the answer key will use the masculine singular.)

1. shouted (clamo)
2. shown (monstro)
3. ruled (domino)
4. awaited (exspecto)
5. held (habeo)

6. called (καλεω)
7. believed (νομιζω)
8. made (τευχω)
9. turned (τρεπω)
10. judged (κρινω)

B. Translate the following phrases that employ participles into English. Latin and Greek have been mixed together, obviously! Furthermore, be aware that a few phrases are not nominative.

1. filiae laudatae
2. populus monitus
3. ’ανηρ κεκλημενος ‘Εκτωρ
4. corpus vulneratum
5. ’αστερα ‘εοραμενα
6. reginarum laudatarum
7. cum amicîs amatîs
8. βασιλεια πεπειμενη/α*
9. aurum datum
10. ’επου πεφωνημενου
11. litterae non visae
12. θυγατερες πεφιλημεναι

*In post-Homeric Greek, participles often employ an alpha instead of an eta for the feminine nominative singular form.

C. Translate into English these simple sentences that use past participles:

1. Fabulam narratam amavimus.
2. Κυων κεκλημενος ’Αργος ’εστι.
3. Κουραι, ‘υπο θεων ’εστε πεπεμμεναι!
4. Marce, ad regem vocatus es.
5. ’Αλγεα πεπομμενα (πασχω) ‘υμιν ’εστι.
6. Magister docta* libri laudati servabit.

*It's very common in Latin for a neuter plural participle to become a noun that refers to "things" having the verbal quality described (e.g., data = "things given" and correcta = "things corrected").

D. Translate into English:
1. Equi in castrîs tenti non curabantur.
2. Πολεμον πεπαυμενον γεροντες τελευτησομεν.
3. Fructûs patri dati filiîs amatîs (dative with "placeo") placebunt.
4. Φαος ’απο μηνος φυομενον* ’εις ’αγορην ’ερρει (ending = -εε).
5. ‘Ιπποι πεφοβημενοι ‘υπο λεοντος** ’επι νησον ’αγηομενοι ’εισι.
6. Milites civesque portati in nave urbem occupatam spectabant.

*Note that this is a *present* passive participle (no reduplication): the light was being produced *during* the main verb's time frame.
**Recall that the genitive, usually with ’απο, is the standard Greek way of expressing agency (e.g., "it was done BY so-and-so").

Solo Flight: In Book 3 of Virgil's *Aeneid*, the hero describes to Queen Dido a typical night during his tireless travels. The fleet's pilot Palinurus is said the rise early in the verse, *Necdum* ("not yet") *orbem medium nox horîs acta subibat* (from *sub + ire*, "to approach from under"). Can you decipher the hour of the night? The pilot immediately observes the position of the stars, taking special note of the constellation Orion: *Armatum-que* ("and") *auro circumspicit* (related to *spectare*) *Oriona* (Virgil preserves the name "Orion" as a Greek third-declension noun in spelling its case). Translate this line.

X. Formation of Perfect-System Passives in Latin

You may well have divined by now that the way to form the passive voice of the perfect system is to use the past participles just introduced in conjunction with a form of "to be": this technique was employed by the Romans far more than by the Greeks, but the latter did not wholly avoid it. Just remember that "we have been praised" is NOT EVER *sumus habiti laudati*. In other words, do not try to turn English helping verbs directly into Latin or Greek, even though these languages are indeed using an auxiliary-verb method similar to what we know so well. Do not even write "we have been" and then tack on a participle. The result of such endeavor might be *fuimus laudati*, which is indeed possible in classical Latin but very rare—and it does *not* mean "we have been praised." The participle *laudati* is viewed as having already provided the perfect-tense element of the expression. The perfect-tense verb *fuimus* would double up on this element and convey something like, "We have been in the positon of already having been praised." Such a wistful, elusive idea flowed from an ancient author's stylus occasionally (cf. Cornelius Nepos, *Alcibiades* 6.4, *pulsus fuerat*), but it is plainly not an effective way of communicating routine perfect-tense action.

We may as well use *laudare* for our table this time, since it is completely regular. Look carefully at the third-person singular translation and try to figure out how it differs from those given previously for this position. Why do you think the difference has appeared?

PERFECT

	singular	plural
1st person	laudatus sum (I have been praised)	laudati sumus (we have been praised)
2nd person	laudatus es (you have been praised)	laudati estis (you have been praised)
3rd person	laudatus est (he has been praised)	laudati sunt (they have been praised)

PLUPPERFECT

	singular	plural
1st person	laudatus eram (I had been praised)	laudati eramus (we had been praised)
2nd person	laudatus eras (you had been praised)	laudati eratis (you had been praised)
3rd person	laudatus erat (he had been praised)	laudati erant (they had been praised)

FUTURE PERFET

	singular	plural
1st person	laudatus ero (I will have been praised)	laudati erimus (we will have been praised)
2nd person	laudatus eris (you will have been praised)	laudati eritis (you will have been praised)
3rd person	laudatus erit (he will have been praised)	laudati erunt (they will have been praised)

Answer to the foregoing question: third-person singulars can no longer be annotated "he/she/it" because the past participle preceding *est*, etc., is an adjective. This means that its ending designates a gender. "She had been praised" would have to be written *laudata erat*, with a first-declension nominative "a" ending on the participle. To save space, we did not print *laudatus/laudata/laudatum* (or *laudatus-a-um*, as the abbreviated notation runs) and then "he/she/it." Of course, the English "they" does not specify a gender, so women may feel no less included than men when they read "they will have been praised." Yet remember that Latin *is* exclusive in this way: *laudati erunt* applies only to males—just as *laudatae erunt* would apply only to females.

Also note, by the way, that the *erunt* of the example just given is indeed the third-person plural of *esse*'s future—not the future-perfect ending which would be attached at this point to an active verb. Literally, the two words translate, "They will be (people) having been praised."

In the exercises below, the female gender will be represented quite as much as the male—and even a few neuter inflections will be appropriate. Bear in mind that what was just said about the third person really applies to all three persons, both singular and plural; that is, if we know that *you* are female and we write "you had been called" in Latin, then the participle must have a feminine ending: *vocata eras*. Likewise, if the "I" uttering 'I have been warned' is someone named Julia, then the verb must be written *monita sum*.

160

Once again, Greek uses this method of composing the passive rather sparingly. It isn't completely alien to Homer. In *Iliad* 13.764, for instance, we find ‘οι δ’ ’εν τειχει ’εσαν βεβλημενοι ’ουταμενοι τε: "those who were on the wall were struck and wounded." The imperfect-tense ’εσαν, however, is not the present-tense ’εισι. That is, Homer is not literally saying, "They are [having been] struck." Eventually, one finds a βαλλομενον ’εστι kind of structure with the signification of "it has been thrown" more regularly in ancient texts. The strategy even appears to gain considerable ground in later Greek. That second-century (A.D.) connoisseur of interesting places, Pausanius, uses ’επεργασμενοι ’εισι ("they have been wrought"—of a frieze's figures) and λεγομενον ’εστι ("it has been said") within a few dozen words when describing the isle of Aegina (29-7-8). The standard practice in Homer, however, fundamentally differs. We shall look briefly at the earlier alternative in the next section.

Summary

The tenses of Latin's perfect system are always formed by using the perfect passive participle with a present, imperfect, or future form of "to be." This method is less favored in ancient Greek, though it is occasionally employed and grows more popular in later authors. In both languages, the participle's nominative ending must reflect the subject's number and gender.

Exercise Set 4.10

A. Translate into English. Specify the subject's gender by writing "m," "f," or "n" after your translation.

1. amata erit
2. dati sumus
3. monitae estis
4. visum erit
5. monstratus sum
6. territi eramus
7. mota erunt
8. spectata erit

B. Now translate from English to Latin:

1. they (f.) had been called
2. we (m.) will have been shown
3. you (pl. f.) have been watched
4. they (n.) have been given
5. she had been seen
6. you (s. m.) have been moved
7. I (f.) will have been frightened
8. it had been seen

C. These Latin verbs are drawn from all six tenses and represent both the active and passive voices. Translate.

1. monstraverint
2. stabitis
3. monueras
4. portatum est
5. daris
6. temptavistis
7. manebamus
8. spector
9. sedebit
10. narratum erat
11. iuvamini
12. videbuntur
13. vocaberis
14. moverat
15. monêris
16. terrebar

D. Translate the following sentences into Latin. Remember the *ablative of personal agent*, which appears frequently with passive verbs and is preceded by the preposition *â* (*ab* before a vowel), meaning "by." The ablative of means, used more generally, does not employ this preposition.

1. The kings had not been warned by the messenger's brother.
2. The stories were being told to the populace with ill will (use *malevolentia*) by the old men.
3. You soldiers have been wounded neither by sword nor arrow.
4. We sisters will have been taught (use *doceo, docêre, docui, doctus*) with diligence by wise men (use *sapiens, sapientis*).
5. I will be frightened neither by the lion's face (use *facies*, 5th decl.) nor by its attack (use *impetus*, 4th decl.).

Solo Flight: Translate these slightly rewritten lines opening Julius Caesar's *De Bello Gallico*:

Gallia omnis ("all") *in tres* ("three") *partes divisa est. Belgae unam partem habitant, Aquitani secundam, tertiam populus linguâ propiâ* ("their own") *Celtae appellatus sed nobîs Galli scitus* ("known as").

The verb *habitant* extends to all nominative nouns, by the way, the two participles in the final phrase being completely adjectival and not part of a main verb. Be aware, as well, that many tribal names are first-declension masculine, like the noun *nauta*.

XI. The Greek Perfect-System Passive

Latin students often ask why, since the Romans used an "r" suffix to create passives in the present system, they didn't continue the same thing in the perfect system. If *vocor* means "I am being called," then what about *vocavir* for "I have been called"? A code being rationally designed for use by a select few might very well employ principles as consistently as this; but, of course, languages are not mere codes devised like a system of semaphore flags. They often have a vast history, littered with incident and accident. There is much of the arbitrary in their mainstream form at any given historical moment.

Nevertheless, ancient Greek, which often seems to border on chaos in comparison to Latin due to the straining of a dozen major dialects against each other, actually adopts something like the "r" solution for its perfect system's passive. That is, it takes the passive forms already used in the present system and renders them perfect with little more than the help of reduplication. The result turns out to be fairly orderly. At any rate, if you have memorized the somewhat complex forms of the passive inflections in the present system, you need make only faint adjustments to the verb now in order to arrive at a passive perfect form.

For the sake of emphasizing this point, the table below does not simply give perfect passive forms: it first reminds you of the corresponding passive from the present system which you have already studied, and then—on the right side—gives you a passive within the perfect system.

PRESENT VS. PERFECT

	singular		
1st	λυομαι (I am being loosed)		λελυμαι (I have been loosed)
2nd	λυεαι (you are being loosed)		λελυσαι (you have been loosed)
3rd	λυεται (he/she/it is being loosed)		λελυται (he/she/it has been loosed)
	plural		
1st	λυομεσθα (we are being loosed)		λελυμεσθα (we have been loosed)
2nd	λυεσθε (you are being loosed)		λελυσθε (you have been loosed)
3rd	λυονται (they are being loosed)		λελυνται (they have been loosed)

IMPERFECT VS. PLUPERFECT

singular		
1ˢᵗ	’ελυομην (I was being loosed)	’ελελυμην (I had been loosed)
2ⁿᵈ	’ελυεο (you were being loosed)	’ελελυσο (you had been loosed)
3ʳᵈ	’ελυετο (he/she/it was being loosed)	’ελελυτο (he/she/it had been loosed)
plural		
1ˢᵗ	’ελυομεσθα (we were being loosed)	’ελελυμεσθα (we had been loosed)
2ⁿᵈ	’ελυεσθε (you were being loosed)	’ελελυσθε (you had been loosed)
3ʳᵈ	’ελυοντο (they were being loosed)	’ελελυντο (they had been loosed)

FUTURE VS. FUTURE PERFECT

singular		
1ˢᵗ	λυσομαι (I will be loosed)	λελυσομαι (I will have been loosed)
2ⁿᵈ	λυσεαι (you will be loosed)	λελυσεαι (you will have been loosed)
3ʳᵈ	λυσεται (he/she/it will be loosed)	λελυσεται (he/she/it will have been loosed)
plural		
1ˢᵗ	λυσομεσθα (we will be loosed)	λελυσομεσθα (we will have been loosed)
2ⁿᵈ	λυσεσθε (you will be loosed)	λελυσεσθε (you will have been loosed)
3ʳᵈ	λυσονται (they will be loosed)	λελυσονται (they will have been loosed)

The table should make clear that the perfect-system passives are also those of the present system with just a little window-dressing. The omicron or epsilon that complicated the present passive's stem with vowel shortening disappears, and the first syllable is doubled: so much for the perfect tense's passive. For the pluperfect's, similarly, the "glide" vowel of the imperfect is again removed, the reduplication continued, and the imperfect's epsilon augment preserved. As for the future, because it already has a sigma separating the stem vowel from the inflection's first vowel, nothing is dropped at all—only the reduplication is performed.

There are two problems, alas, with the argument above that Greek suddenly becomes easy in the passive of the perfect system. The main problem is that finding the proper perfect stems can be a chore in specific cases. Though some verbs like λυω do indeed simply take their present-system passives and double the first syllable, more than a few do not. Often the stem will be a blend of the present-system form and the perfect active stem. For example, the verb βαλλω, "I throw," turns into βεβληκα ("I have thrown") when it shifts to the perfect active. Its perfect passive form ("I have been thrown") appears to have been βεβλημαι instead of βεβαλλομαι. The eta from the perfect active form has been retained. Such scuffing of the boundaries is fairly common.

The other problem is perhaps also a great blessing. We have had occasion to stress already that the aorist tense reduced Greek's use of its perfect system well below the levels found in Latin. This continues when the voice

163

shifts from active to passive: in fact, it's more valid than ever now. So while we sometimes have to conjecture about the forms of rarely used perfect-system passives in Greek, we can console ourselves with the knowledge that they are rarely used!

The only purpose served by conjecturing at all, really, is to reach a deeper understanding of the logic of language. For instance, consider what reduplication does for Greek verbs in a very general sense: by adding a little something extra to the verb's beginning, you shift its aspect. Modern Russian indicates the difference between action of unspecified duration and action soon finished (i.e., the progressive and perfect aspects) by adding a Greek-like prefix to its verbs (though not exactly duplicating their first syllable). The verb читатъ means "to read", without any particular limit placed upon the length of the reading. To express that something was read within a certain rather narrow length of time, the verb почитатъ would be used. Though you're probably not familiar with the Cyrillic alphabet, you can tell that a little syllable consisting of something like a pi and an omicron has been inserted at the second word's beginning. This designates it as quickly done.

Such is the technique that the ancient Greeks also must have used heavily at one time to designate the perfect system (called the "perfective aspect" in Russian grammar books), as we see clearly in this lesson even though the strategy has already started to decay. While the patterns presented here in Section XI will seldom crop up in Homer and even less often in Plato or any latter classical author, therefore, they have far-reaching resonance.

Curiously, a post-classical form of Greek came to be in very wide circulation throughout the non-Hellenic Eastern Mediterranean region (Russian would descend from this process of diffusion), thanks largely to the conquests of Alexander the Great and their subsequent political influence; and in this "koinê" or "commonly used" Greek, the perfect-system passives more or less ignored in classical texts appear to make a comeback. Many, many early Christian documents are written in such Greek, including the most broadly disseminated versions of the Gospels themselves. The fourth-century (AD) author Eusebius, born in Palestine, puts the word δεδιδαγμεθα ("we have been taught") in the mouth of the martyr Polycarpus as he makes his last defense (4.15.22), and then a few lines later (4.15.30) describes his preparation to be burned alive with 'εκεκοσμητο ("he had been handled"). Not the pleasantest of subjects… but the passage offers us two brilliant examples of perfect-system passives constructed just as they should be! Sometimes those who acquire a language as their second tongue pay more attention to its grammar than those who absorbed it more casually as their mother tongue.

As we struggle toward the end of a very difficult chapter, perhaps the instructor should simply consider not making a major issue of having the inflections above memorized. They are offered more in the spirit of tracing linguistic evolution than with the intent of giving beginners further material to master. One may sample an exotic dish and be the wiser for it without wanting or needing to retreat to the kitchen and cook a fresh batch from scratch. View this section as a mere sampling, and try the exercise below only if you enjoy a challenge.

Also remember that you can use a perfect passive participle and a form of "to be" to create these passives, just as Latin does. That is, you can write λελυμενος 'ειμι as well as λελυμαι.

Summary
The passive voice of Greek's perfect system is almost identical to the present system's passive forms, with a reduplicated syllable added at the verb's beginning (or near it, preceded by an augment, in the pluperfect). In literary texts that have actually been preserved from antiquity, these forms are quite rare.

Exercise Set 4.11

A. Translate these verbs into English. Both active and passive are represented, and also both the present and perfect systems.

1.	'ακουεται	6.	πεπεισομαι (from πειθω)
2.	'εκεκλομεσθα (from καλεω)	7.	'εφιλεομην

3. λελεξονται   (from λεγω)   8. θνησκουσι

4. βεβληκασι   (from βαλλω)   9. 'εχεαι

5. πεπραχεσθε   10. 'εδεδοικεας (from δοκεω)

B. Give the active AND passive of these forms in Greek. Try your best. The perfect stems of some of these words not only morph surprisingly, but are even somewhat conjectural in places. Recall that the Greeks made very sparing use of the pluperfect and future perfect, especially in the passive. Numbers 6 and 7, in particular, involve guesswork. Use the practice to stretch your mind, and don't worry over the results.

1. you (pl.) will call/be called
2. you (s.) were leading/being led
3. they have/have been produced
4. I had/had been sent
5. we have/have been thrown
6. it will have/have been made
7. they had/had been shown
8. he was recognizing/was being recognized

Solo Flight: Return to Exercise 4.11.A above and rewrite every verb after shifting its number, changing singulars to plurals and plurals to singulars. If you really want a challenge, you might also try changing each verb in voice: i.e., make the passives active and the actives passive.

XII. Latin's Fourth Conjugation

It's time to do a bit of "mopping up" as we conclude our discussion of verbs. Chapter Two noted that the modern romance languages all have only three verb conjugations to Latin's four, and that the "missing conjugation"—the third in Latin—was easily absorbed by others because its short "e" stem was so unassertive. We have given virtually no attention, however, to Latin's fourth conjugation, which would become the third in Italian, Spanish, and French. This conjugation, whose infinitive ends in *–ire*, has a long "i" stem and forms various tenses in a remarkably straightforward manner. The verb *audire* is often chosen by grammar books as a paradigm; but the truth is that we could use almost any fourth-conjugation verb, for as a group they are extremely regular

PRESENT TENSE (ACTIVE/PASSIVE)

	singular	**plural**
1st person	audio/audior	audimus/audimur
2nd person	audis/audiris	auditis/audimini
3rd person	audit/auditur	audiunt/audiuntur

IMPERFECT TENSE (ACTIVE/PASSIVE)

	singular	**plural**
1st person	audiebam/audiebar	audiebamus/audiebamur
2nd person	audiebas/audiebaris	audiebatis/audiebamini
3rd person	audiebat/audiebatur	audiebant/audiebantur

Throughout the present tense, the strong "i" does not merge with any other vowel at any point, though in the third persons and the first-person singular it becomes a short "i" sound. Indeed, the strange "u' in *audiunt* ("they hear")

probably represents no more than a kind of time-lapse portrait of what happens when you say *au-deent* several times; that is, the long "i" is shortened as the tongue's tip is drawn into the forward position necessary to make an "n."

The imperfect tense is just as orderly. Nothing more has happened here than the insertion of an *–eba* into every position. The long "e" of this insertion is a new development, to be sure. It may have evolved so as to keep the conjugation's distinctive "i" from eroding into a schwa, or short "e" sound (which is just what occurs if you repeat *audibam* casually). The eventual effect of that process would be *audebam*—and then there would be no distinction between the fourth and the third conjugations. The verb *ducere* of the third conjugation ("to lead") proceeds thus in the imperfect: *ducebam, ducebas, ducebat*, etc. The Latin-speaker, as you can see, would have ended up on a slippery slope, and at the bottom of that slope, he or she would have had no fourth conjugation at all!

Let us skip the future tense for the moment and turn to the perfect system. Here the fourth conjugation looks exactly like the first, except that the *-av* stem has shifted to an *–iv*.

PERFECT TENSE

	singular	**plural**
1st person	audivi	audivimus
2nd person	audivisti	audivistis
3rd person	audivit	audiverunt

PLUPERFECT TENSE

	singular	**plural**
1st person	audiveram	audiveramus
2nd person	audiveras	audiveratis
3rd person	audiverat	audiverant

FUTURE PERFECT TENSE

	singular	**plural**
1st person	audivero	audiverimus
2nd person	audiveris	audiveritis
3rd person	audiverit	audiverint

What could be easier? As for forming the passive voice, you can always do this—even for a third-conjugation word—by finding out its past participle and then supplying the correct tense of *esse*, "to be." As was observed in Section IX above, these participles have a characteristic "t" in the stem. "I have been heard" would be translated *auditus* (or *audita*) *sum*. Using the third-declension verb *ducere*, we would write "it had been led" as *ductum erat*. Dictionaries will typically give this participle as the fourth and last of a transitive verb's principle parts because it was so frequently employed by the Romans.

And the future tense? It is the one point where the fourth conjugation turns inscrutable (and where the third, following the same route, grows even more curious). The first two conjugations have a distinctive, perfectly functional –*bi* indicator for the future tense. The last two conjugations ignore this indicator and retreat to a messy system of vowels which invites misidentification with other verbal forms at several points.

FUTURE TENSE (ACTIVE/PASSIVE)

	singular	**plural**
1st person	audiam/audiar	audiemus/audiemur
2nd person	audies/audieris	audietis/audiemini
3rd person	audiet/audietur	audient/audientur

The interactions of the long "e" with the original "b" of a –*bi* future inflection may be somewhere at the bottom of this metamorphosis. The "alternative formation" of the future in the third and fourth conjugations, at any rate, doesn't bear further exploration here. If you persist in Latin studies, you will eventually master all such forms; but in an introductory course, we might as well save our energy for more important battles.

Summary
In both active and passive voices and in both present and perfect systems, the fourth conjugation behaves very like the first except for the suppression of the –bi inflection in the future. The essential difference is that it features a long "i" stem instead of a long "a" stem.

Exercise Set 4.12

A. Translate these verbs into English. All are from the fourth declension. For vocabulary, refer to the list in the next section.

1. puniam
2. audivistis
3. custodiverint
4. sentimus
5. custodiris

6. finitum erat
7. audiebamini
8. munientur
9. punitae sunt
10. scitum erit

B. Translate these verbs into Latin.

1. they will feel
2. I (m.) had been punished
3. they are fortifying
4. you (pl.) know

5. we shall have finished
6. you (s.) used to be guarded
7. it will be known
8. I have slept

Solo Flight: Go to Appendix C at the end of this book—"Maxims and Proverbs"—and conduct a "verb hunt." Parse six verbs from these sayings: that is, give each verb's person, number, tense, and voice.

Alternatively, go back to Exercise 4.12.A above and perform one of our "flipping" drills: that is, turn actives into passives and passives into actives, or make singulars of plurals and plurals of singulars.

XIII. Vocabulary from Latin's Third and Fourth Conjugations

Lest we ignore some of the very influential verbs of the last two conjugations simply because we have avoided emphasizing their grammatical mutations, the following list supplies several transitive third- and fourth-conjugation Latin verbs that have many derivatives in English and other languages. These words are presented much as you would find them in a dictionary: i.e., listed with their principle parts. An English derivative has been placed in parentheses at the end of each listing, but—as usual—you should be able to think of more in several cases. Notice that all of the fourth-conjugation verbs have regular, fully predictable perfect forms except for *sentire* (and, of course, the two very common intransitive verbs—*eo, ire* and *venio, venire* ["go" and "come"]—that are displayed afterward in full tables). Of the third-conjugation words, in contrast, every one has a surprising twist.

ago, -ere, egi, actus—do, perform (agent)

audio, -ire, -ivi, -itus—hear (auditory)

capio, capere, cepi, captus—take, seize (capture)

custodio, -ire, -ivi, -itus—guard, watch over (custodian)

dico, -ere, dixi, dictus—say, speak (dictophone)

dormio, -ire, -ivi, ___—sleep (dormitory: no participle because intransitive)

duco, -ere, duxi, ductus—lead, bring (deduce)

facio, facere, feci, factus—do, make, accomplish (affect)

finio, -ire, -ivi, -itus—bring to an end (finish)

frango, -ere, fregi, fractus—shatter (fracture)

iungo, -ere, iunxi, iunctus—put together (junction)

mitto, -ere, misi, missus—send (transmit)

munio, -ire, -ivi, -itus—fortify (munition)

perdo, -ere, perdidi, perditus—lose, misplace (perdition)

peto, -ere, petivi, petitus—seek, attempt (petition)

pono, -ere, posui, positus—put (position)

primo, -ere, pressi, pressus—hold tightly, squeeze (compress)

punio, -ire, -ivi, -itus—punish (punishment)

relinquo, -ere, reliqui, relictus—leave, depart (relinquish)

rumpo, -ere, rupi, ruptus—break (rupture)

scribo, -ere, scripsi, scriptus—write (scribe)

scio, -ire, -ivi, -itus—know as fact, be certain of (science)

sentio, -ire, sensi, sensum—feel, perceive (sentiment)

traho, -ere, traxi, tractus—draw, pull, drag (contract)

vinco, -ere, vici, victus—conquer (victor)

For the record, here are the two heavily used, much eroded verbs for "go" and "come." Notice that neither of these is transitive, yet the fourth part (the perfect participle) is given in the neuter. This is because the idiomatic expressions *itum est* and *ventum est* are frequently found: "it was gone" and "it was come" (that is, "they went," "we came," etc.: the subject is always to be inferred from the context). *Itur* in the present tense is also common.

eo, ire, ivi, itum	
Present	
eo (I go)	imus (we go)
is (you go)	itis (you go)
it (s/he/it goes)	eunt (they go)
Imperfect	
ibam, ibas, etc.	
Future	
ibo ((I will go)	ibimus (we will go)
ibis (you will go)	ibitis (you will go)
ibit (s/he/it will go)	ibunt (they will go)
venio, venire, vêni, ventum	
Present	
venio (I come)	venimus (we come)
venis (you come)	venitis (you come)
venit (s/he/it comes)	veniunt (they come)
Imperfect	
veniebam, veniebas, etc.	
Future	
veniam (I shall come)	veniemus (we shall come)
venies (you will come)	venietis (you will gcome)
veniet (s/he/it will come)	venient (they will come)

Now consider the next list, which specifically juxtaposes past participles **from all four conjugations** with English words directly and obviously derived from them. Some of these verbs are on the previous list, as well. The point being stressed below is that knowledge of past participles is an important aid to building your English vocabulary. Not included are a great many English words ending in -*ate* and derived from the first conjugation. The reason for the omission is that few such words preserve their true Latin meaning. The noun "precipitate" does (i.e., "something rushed forward"—e.g., the salt left in a beaker after a liquid is boiled off); but "cogitate," "demonstrate," "devastate," and other verbs of this sort do not carry the original Latin sense of an event "having **been** done"—that is, of the passive voice.

169

infinitive	derivative from past participle	literal (not always usual) meaning in English
abrumpere	abrupt	broken away
adiungere	adjunct	joined to
agere	act	done, performed
cadere	case	fallen (out, down, etc.)
complêre	complete	wholly filled
*credere	credit	trusted in, believed
cumburere	combust	wholly burned up
dare	datum, -a	thing(s) given
*debêre	debit	owed
dicere	dictum	thing said
docêre	doctor	someone (having been) taught
ducere	duct	thing led
erigere	erect	straightened
facere	fact	accomplished
habêre	habit	thing held (onto)
mittere	missive	sent
mutare	mutate	changed
praecipitare	precipitate	rushed forward
refrangere	refract	broken back
relinquere	relict (relic)	thing left
scribere	script	thing written
*stare	state	thing stood (=made to stand)
*tacêre	tacit	quieted
trahere	tract	drawn out (=treated)
vidêre	visa	seen

*These verbs are not transitive—but their participles were nevertheless sometimes given a passive sense by Romans.

Summary

Past participles from all four Latin conjugations are a major source of English vocabulary. These participles will be the fourth element listed by any dictionary in a transitive verb's principle parts. English derivatives from other verbal parts (all of them active) are far less common.

Exercise Set 4.13

A. We haven't studied present participles, but they are treated as third-declension adjectives, always have a stem ending in *-nt*, and naturally give us English derivatives that preserve an active sense. The word "present" is itself built upon the present participle of *praesens*, "being at hand, being on the spot" (genitive *praesentis*). Such adjectives often have a noun form in English ending in *-nce*, such as "presence." How many English derivatives, either adjectives or nouns, can you ferret out from words on the list above that descend from the present participle?

B. Can you think of another English word like "precipitate" above that is based upon a first-conjugation verb's truly passive sense—that is, an English word ending in *-ate* that projects the passive voice in its meaning? There aren't many! They will probably be nouns before which we usually place an article ("a" or "the").

Solo Flight: See how many past-participle derivatives you can think of from Latin verbs not on the list above. Use your imagination—they're all around you. For instance, a cantata is a "sung" piece of music (from *cantare*).

XIV. Past Tenses in the Romance Languages

If you have studied one of Latin's modern descendants, then you know that learning the forms of the preterite tense is one of the hardest tasks you ever have to perform in that endeavor. This is also called the historic tense (especially in French) and the past absolute (especially in Italian). It may roughly correspond to the Greek aorist tense, since sometimes it can obscure the interrelationship of past events in a generalized aura of "pastness"; yet its historical pedigree leads much more directly to the Latin perfect tense, with respect both to meaning and to form. The Latin perfect signifies *things done*. Its emphasis is on completion, on once-and-for-all accomplishment (i.e., on the perfective *aspect*). The preterite of the romance languages is so congenial to this usage that it is the preferred tense in testimonials about long-finished events, in nostalgic stories about bygone days, in quasi-historical accounts or narratives of times several years or centuries past, and so forth. If you intend to study the literature of such languages, you cannot avoid the preterite, because—as you can readily infer—it is a highly "literary" tense.

This is bad news to many students, because the preterite, being the Latin perfect's grandchild, has inherited all of that old man's peculiar qualities. No conjugation in Latin has as many verbs as the third (only the first comes anywhere close)—and no conjugation, likewise, has so many bizarre perfect stems. (Some of these, as we noted earlier, may have rooted in the same prehistoric phase of Indo-European as Greek's aorist tense.) Furthermore, since verbs of the Latin third conjugation melt away into one of the remaining three conjugations—"a" stem, "e" stem, or "i" stem—in the romance languages, they often carry their odd forms into circumstances which seem wholly unsuited to them. For instance, *facere*, "to do, make," becomes a second-conjugation *-re* verb in French (*faire*), where its preterite form, *je fis*, is predictable from none of that group's precedents. Take another example: the Latin verb *dicere* has the perfect active stem *dix-* (i.e., *dixi* means "I have said"). In Italian, you would write the words "I said" in a short story with the word *dissi*, from the third-conjugation verb *dire*; in Spanish, you would write *dije*, from *dir*; and in French, you would write *je dis*, from *dire*. All of these forms use a stem from which nothing else is built but the preterite tense (and, in the case of French, a rare subjunctive).

On a more optimistic note, the preterite stem is not used for building any other tense! Italian, Spanish, and French all evolved in the direction to which German and (through German) English have shown a special attraction: the employment of auxiliary verbs. If you were chatting with a friend in French about something, and your friend remarked, "I've already told you that," he or she might say, *Je te l'ai dit déjà*. The notation of *pronoun + finite form of "have" + past participle* has long been the preferred method in all three languages of handling completed actions that are not formally commemorated in some kind of literature. Even if the described action shifts back to the pluperfect or "ahead and back" into the future perfect, helping verbs are still awarded the task of description. The Latin perfect-active stem remains confined to the preterite tense. If an Italian were to remark, "I told you that before I heard otherwise," he or she might say, *Te l'avevo detto prima che abbia sentito altra cosa.* The "I had said" part of the sentence (*avevo detto*), being pluperfect, would actually state the temporal relations involved more precisely than we would in English—but it would continue using our *have + participle* formula. The perfect stem would be of no relevance whatever in the communication.

In short, all of the perfect tenses except the notorious preterite are built in these tongues after the fashion that we know so well in English. Since a little demonstration is superior to a great deal of narration, perhaps a comparative table would make this point best of all:

PERFECT TENSE

English	*Italian*	*Spanish*	*French*
singular			
I have slept	ho dormito	he dormido	j'ai dormi
you have slept	hai dormito	has dormido	tu as dormi
he/she/it has slept	ha dormito	ha dormido	il/elle a dormi
plural			
we have slept	abbiamo dormito	hemos dormido	nous avons dormi
you have slept	avete dormito	habéis dormido	vous avez dormi
they have slept	hanno dormito	han dormido	ils/elles ont dormi

PLUPERFECT TENSE

singular			
I had slept	avevo dormito	había dormido	j'avais dormi
you had slept	avevi dormito	habías dormido	tu avais dormi
he/she/it had slept	aveva dormito	había dormido	il/elle avait dormi
plural			
we had slept	avevamo dormito	habíamos dormido	nous avions dormi
you had slept	avevate dormito	habíais dormido	vous aviez dormi
they had slept	avevano dormito	habían dormido	ils/elles avaient dormi

singular			
I will have slept	avrò dormito	habré dormido	j'aurai dormi
you will have slept	avrai dormito	habrás dormido	tu auras dormi
he, etc. will have slept	avrà dormito	habrá dormido	il/elle aura dormi
plural			
we will have slept	avremo dormito	habremos dormido	nous aurons dormi
you will have slept	avrete dormito	habréis dormido	vous aureez dormi
they will have slept	avranno dormito	habrán dormido	ils/elles auront dormi

Of course, the fourth-conjugation Latin verb *dormire* is used in our paradigm above in its various modern transformations. In all three of these romance tongues, its perfect-system tenses follow a regular pattern. Notice that in no instance does the past participle change to reflect the subject's gender or number, unlike the Latin precedent. (This happens with a few verbs in Italian and French that conjugate their perfect tenses with "to be" rather than "to have," but it never occurs in Spanish.) You will most likely also have figured out that the helping verb in all three modern languages is "to have," just as it is in English. (The forms in the future perfect employ the future of "to have": the romance languages do not use an additional helping verb equivalent to "will.")

Hence the old Latin formula of "you are having been called" has been fully discarded. Now we confront something that is really quite idiomatic—for what, after all, would be the strict logical sense of "you have… having been slept"? "To sleep," being intransitive, cannot even create a past participle in Latin. And indeed, if you wished to make any of the above expressions passive, you could not do so with this verb, for it remains intransitive in all the romance languages. (How could it be otherwise, since you can't "be slept"?) The point is, though, that these tongues can give a Latin-derived verb a Latin-style perfect participle yet have that participle behave *actively*, as it could never have done in Latin (except for a few odd verbs, called deponents, which this book does not discuss).

The formation of perfect participles in our three romance languages, by the way, is pretty straightforward. Only the second conjugation shows significant divergence among the three:

First Conjugation		
Italian	*Spanish*	*French*
change *–are* of infinitive to *–ato*	change *–ar* of infinitive to *–ado*	change *–er* of infinitive to *–é*
parlare > parlato	*hablar > hablado*	*parler > parlé*
Second Conjugation		
Italian	*Spanish*	*French*
change *–ere* of infinitive to *–uto*	change *–er* of infinitive to *–ido*	change *–re* of infinitive to *–u*
rendere > renduto	*render > rendido*	*vendre > vendu*

Third Conjugation		
Italian	*Spanish*	*French*
change –*ire* of infinitive to –*ito*	change –*ir* of infinitive to –*ido*	change –*er* of infinitive to –*i*
dormire > dormito	*dormir > dormido*	*dormir > dormi*

To pursue a final issue… if you *did* want to place a romance-language verb in (say) the pluperfect passive, you would simply deploy the past participle of "to be" along with the imperfect of "have." Let's use *haber* from Spanish: "You had been called" would be *habías sido llamado*. In Italian, "they will have been praised" would similarly produce *avranno stato laudato*; and the same transformation would work for French. What this shows us is that the perfect participle *passive* is consistently used in the romance languages as a perfect participle *active* when combined with auxiliary verbs. We do the same thing in English. "She will have led" quietly transforms a word— "led"—that is always understood as passive when by itself into a word with an active sense. The oddity of the shift easily escapes the notice of native speakers, but it's quite peculiar. Of all of these languages, Latin has the most logic on its side.

Past Participle of "To Be"		
Italian	*Spanish*	*French*
essere >stato	*ser > sido*	*être > été*

Whether there is a lesson in the most logical language's having lost history's battle while its less logical inheritors thrive is a topic for the moralist to ponder. We will allow that issue to rest.

Summary
The Latin model of forming perfect-system active expressions in one word based on a unique stem is almost lost in the modern romance tongues, surviving only as a preterite or historic tense. Otherwise, these languages follow the Anglo-Germanic model: they use "to have" as an auxiliary verb in the proper tense and add the past participle, here understood in an active sense (with the past participle of "to be" inserted to create the passive voice).

Exercise Set 4.14

A. Create past participles for the following romance verbs:

1. mangiare (It.)
2. demonstrar (Sp.)
3. corriger (Fr.)
4. vendere (It.)
5. studiare (It.)
6. repeter (Sp.)
7. utiliser (Fr.)
8. amare (It.)
9. recibir (Sp.)
10. finir (Fr.)

B. Translate these perfect-tense verbs into English: note their original language in parentheses.

1. hemos repetido
2. j'ai fini
3. abbiamo studiato
4. elle a corrigé
5. vous avez vendu
6. ils ont mangé
7. he amado
8. hanno demostrato
9. tu as utilisé
10. habéis recibido*

*New World Spanish has all but discarded the second-person plural form *habéis* in favor of the third-person *hanno* used with *ustedes*.

C. Translate these perfect-tense English verbs into the language parenthetically indicated.

1. I have received (*ricevere*, It.)
2. she has studied (*estudiar*, Sp.)
3. you (pl.) have used (*usare*, It.)
4. we have loved (*aimer*, Fr.)
5. you (s.) have shown (*demonstrar*, Sp.)
6. they (f.) have repeated (*répéter*, Fr.)
7. you (s.) have corrected (*corrigere*, It.)
8. we have eaten (*mangiare*, It.)
9. I have sold (*vender*, Sp.)
10. they have eaten (*comer*, Sp.)

D. These verbs are drawn from all three perfect tenses: perfect, pluperfect, and future perfect. They also include a few passives. See how many you can translate into English. The verbs are the same as were used above in C.

1. habré demonstrado
2. avete stato ricevuto
3. ils auront répété
4. habíamos vendido
5. tu avais aimé
6. avranno mangiato
7. habrán estudiato
8. había sido demonstrado
9. ha stato usato
10. avremo corretto

Solo Flight: Log onto the Internet and find a text in one of the three romance languages studied here. (Wikipedia, for instance, can readily be shifted into different tongues.) See how many examples of the perfect tenses you can find, and identify each by person, number, exact tense, and voice. Repeat the exercise for the other two modern languages, if you wish.

ANSWERS TO EXERCISES

Exercise Set 4.1

Answers to **A**: 1. pluperfect 2. future perfect 3. pluperfect 4. future perfect 5. imperfect 6. present 7. imperfect 8. perfect 9. future 10. perfect (or imperfect) 11. pluperfect 12. perfect (or imperfect)

Answers to **B**: For instance, "They won every game they played throughout the summer as long as Trevor was on the team," vs., "They won the championship game in their senior year." Also, "He had sickness on board to complicate matters during the entire voyage," vs., "He had just enough money to pay for passage." The Latin tenses at issue are the perfect and the imperfect (though the distinction is truly a matter of aspect).

Answers to **C**: 1. were sleeping (imp.) 2. will have closed (fut. perf.) 3. swam/used to swim (imp.) 4. have completed (perf.) 5. had warned (plup.) 6. visited (perf.)

Exercise Set 4.2

Answers to **A**: 1. you (s.) had warned 2. they called/have called 3. you (pl.) held/have held 4. I was watching 5. we shall (will) have praised 6. I had struck 7. they will have feared 8. we shouted/have shouted 9. I shall (will) have had 10. you (s.) saw/have seen 11. you (s.) will call 12. they will have remained

Answers to **B**: 1. navigavit 2. nuntiaveratis 3. placuerimus 4. laudavistis 5. monuero 6. spectaveras 7. sederint 8. terruistis 9. vidimus 10. portabat

Exercise Set 4.3

Answers to **A**: 1. eratis 2. fueramus 3. erunt 4. es 5. ero 6. fuerit 7. fui 8. fuerint 9. eramus 10. Fuisti

Answers to **B**: 1. you (pl.) will be 2. we are 3. they will have been 4. I had been 5. he/she/it is 6. you (s.) were/used to be 7. you (s.) will have been 8. I will have been 9. they are 10. he/she/it will be

Answers to **C**: 1. Before the arrival of the enemies, the general's son had been the leader of the people. 2. When Ariovistus will be (= is) king, there will be no hope of help for the Britons (= they will have no hope…). 3. Had you been in Marsilia (Marseilles), Lucius, before the Gallic War? 4. The days of winter are very short, but the day of a battle is very long for soldiers. 5. We are free, citizens! The tyrant Gaius was in life (= alive), but now is not.

Answers to **D**: 1. Silvae circum monetm agricolae non erant. 2. Sorores magistri die festâ in urbe non fueratis. 3. Marce, dux fueram: nunc rex es.

Exercise Set 4.4

Answers to **A**: 1. you (pl.) had spoken 2. they have done 3. you (s.) have seen 4. we had sent 5. I will have released 6. I have loved 7. they are making 8. you (s.) will send 9. they had judged 10. he/she/it has heard

Answers for **B**: 1. πεπραχατε 2. 'ελαμβανον 3. πεφυσεις 4. λεληθε 5. 'εβεβηκεε 6. 'εβαλλομεν 7. λελυκα 8. 'επεφιληκεσαν

Answers for **C**: 1. We saw the light of the moon through the clouds. 2. We had not caught fish in the sea throughout the night. 3. At the end of the year, the heroes will have built the city's walls. 4. Commander, the queen has sent wine to the hoplites. 5. God has produced useful things (= advantages) for men, but he does not produce the works of men.

Answers for **D**: 1. Ναυται χρηματα στρατηγου 'εν θαλασσαν βεβηκαμεν. 2. 'Επει 'επεα ποιητου 'ακουεις, 'αληθειαν 'ουκ 'ακηκοας.

Exercise Set 4.5

Answers: the affected sentences are 1, 3, 4, 5, and 6. In 1, "were sleeping" becomes "slept"; in 3, "used to swim" becomes "swam"; in 4, "have completed" becomes "completed"; in 5, "had warned" becomes "warned"; and in 6, "visited" remains "visited." Notice that 2 cannot use an aorist even though its verb is future perfect and hence in the perfect system. The aorist cannot be made to stretch that far conceptually.

Exercise Set 4.6
Answers to **A**: 1. active 2. passive 3. active 4. passive 5. passive 6. passive (but the impersonal "it" makes an active form unlikely; can "it" think?) 7. active 8. passive 9. active 10. passive

Answers to **B**: 1. 2nd s./pl. perfect active 2. 1st pl. future passive 3. 3rd pl. imperfect active 4. 1st s. future perfect passive 5. 2nd s./pl. imperfect (possibly perfect) passive 6. 3rd s. ("it" is impersonal subject) imperfect (possibly perfect) passive 7. 3rd pl. imperfect active 8. 3rd s. pluperfect passive 9. 1st pl. imperfect active 10. 3rd s. present passive

Exercise Set 4.7
Answers to **A**: 1. you (pl.) were being helped 2. you (s.) are being warned 3. he/she/it is being praised 4. they are being held 5. we will frighten 6. you (s.) will be struck 7. you (pl.) are being seen 8. they will keep 9. I will be watched 10. I was being moved

Answers to **B**: 1. laudabamur 2. spectantur 3. videberis 4. teneor 5. timebamus (NOT passive, despite English translation) 6. iuvabitur 7. terremini 8. vocabar

Exercise Set 4.8
Answers to **A**: 1. you (pl.) were being sent 2. I will be feared 3. he/she/it was being thrown 4. we are being seen 5. they will be loved 6. I was being produced 7. he/she/it was being ruled 8. they are being heard 9. I will be held 10. we were being released

Answers to **B**: 1. φιλησεαι 2. ’εσκωπειτο (= -εετο) 3. φυσεσθε 4. ’αγομεσθα 5. βαλλονται 6. τευξεται (or πραξεται) 7. ’ελαμβανεσθε 8. ’επεμπον

Exercise Set 4.9
Answers to **A**: 1. clamatus 2. monstratus 3. dominatus 4. exspectatus 5. habitus 6. κεκλημενος 7. νενομενος 8. τετευμενος 9. τετρομενος 10. κεκριμενος

Answers to **B**: 1. the praised daughters 2. the warned people 3. a man called Hector 4. the wounded body 5. seen stars 6. of the praised queens 7. with beloved friends 8. the persuaded queen 9. the given gold 10. of the spoken word 11. letters not seen 12. beloved daughters

Answers to **C**: 1. We loved the narrated story. 2. The dog was called Argus. 3. Girls, you are (= "have been") sent by the gods! 4. Marcus, you are (= "have been") summoned to the king. 5. Pains are (= "have been") suffered by you (dative: "with respect to you"). 6. The teacher will conserve the teachings (lit., "things taught") of the praised book.

Answers to **D**: 1. The horses held in the camp were not being cared for. 2. We old men will end the suspended (paused, checked) war. 3. The fruits given to the father will please the beloved sons. 4. The light produced (and continually produced as it streamed—present) by the moon was streaming into the agora. 5. The horses frightened by the lion have been led (are having-been-led) to the island. 6. The soldiers and citizens transported in the ship were watching (kept watching) the seized city.

Exercise Set 4.10
Answers to **A**: 1. she will have been loved (f) 2. we have been given (m) 3. you have been warned (f) 4. it will have been seen (n) 5. I have been shown (m) 6. we had been frightened (m) 7. they will have been moved (n) 8. she will have been seen (f)

Answers to **B**: 1. vocatae erant 2. monstrati erimus 3. spectatae estis 4. data sunt 5. visa erat 6. motus es 7. territa ero 8. visum erat

Answers to **C**: 1. they will have shown 2. you (pl) will stand 3. you (s) had warned 4. it has been carried 5. you (s) are being given 6. you (pl) have attempted 7. we were remaining 8. I am being watched 9. he/she/it will sit 10.

it had been told 11. you (pl) are being helped 12. they will be seen 13. you (s) will be called 14. he/she/it had moved 15. you (s) are being warned 16. I was being frightened

Answers to **D**: 1. Reges â fratre nunti moniti non erant.* 2. Fabulae populo cum malevolentiâ â senibus narrabantur. 3. Milites ni gladio ni sagittâ vulnerati estis. 4. Sorores (cum) diligentiâ â sapientibus doctae erimus. 5. Ni faciê ni impetû leonis terrebor.

*Note that *non* is placed between the participle and the "to be" form. This practice underscores to us that the Romans actually conceived of the participle as an adjective in the passive construction and not as the first stage of an inseparable—though two-stage—verb.

Exercise Set 4.11
Answers to **A**: 1. he/she/it is being heard 2. we had been called 3. they will have been said 4. they have thrown 5. you (pl.) have been made 6. I will have been persuaded 7. I was being loved 8. they are dying 9. you (s.) are being held 10. you (s.) had thought likely

Answers to **B**: 1. καλησετε/καλησεσθε 2. ’ηγες/’ηγεο 3. πεφυκασι/πεφυονται 4. πεπομφα/’επεπομφομην* 5. βεβληκαμεν/βεβλημεσθα 6. τετευξει*/τετευξεται* 7. ’επεφηνεσαν*/’επεφαινοντο (logically—but ’επεφασοντο is better attested)* 8. ’εγιγνωσκε/’εγιγνωσκετο

*These forms are somewhat conjectural.

Exercise Set 4.12
Answers to **A**: 1. I will punish 2. you (pl.) have heard 3. they will have guarded 4. we feel 5. you (s.) are being guarded 6. it had been finished 7. you (pl.) were being heard 8. they will be fortified 9. they (f.) have been punished 10. it will have been known

Answers to **B**: 1. sentient 2. punitus eram 3. muniunt 4. scitis 5. finiverimus 6. custodiebaris 7. scietur 8. dormivi

Exercise Set 4.13
Answers to **A**: "Agent," "cadence," "credence," "docent," and "mutant" are five that might occur to you. With further thought or some research, you might also come up with words like "delinquent" and "immunofacient."

Answers to **B**: One of the few in common usage is "mandate," "a thing ordered or commanded" (from *mandare*).

Exercise Set 4.14
Answers to **A**: 1. mangiato 2. demonstrado 3. corrigé 4. venduto 5. studiato 6. repetido 7. utilisé 8. amato 9. recibido 10. fini

Answers to **B**: 1. we have repeated (Sp.) 2. I have finished (Fr.) 3. we have studied (It.) 4. she has corrected (Fr.) 5. you (pl.) have sold (Fr.) 6. they (m.) have eaten (Fr.) 7. I have loved (Sp.) 8. they have shown (It.) 9. you (s.) have used (Fr.) 10. you (pl.) have received (Sp.)

Answers to **C**: 1. ho ricevuto 2. ha estudiato 3. avete usato 4. nous avons aimé 5. has demonstrado 6. elles ont répété 7. hai corretto (for *corrigetto*: the irregularity descends straight from the Latin third-conjugation *regere*— perfect participle *rectus*) 8. abbiamo mangiato 9. he venduto 10. han comido

Answers to **D**: 1. I will have shown 2. you (pl.) have been received 3. they (m.) will have repeated 4. we had sold 5. you (s.) had loved 6. they will have eaten 7. they will have studied 8. he/she/it had been shown 9. he/she/it has been used 10. we will have corrected

Chapter Five: Adjectives and Prepositions

Topics Covered

Adjective/Noun Agreement

- related to case, number, and gender
- distinguished from identical spelling
- connected to modern Italian, Spanish, and French

Adjective Classification

- different adjectival declensions in Latin and Greek
- consequences of distinction to modern romance languages
- articles in the romance languages

Substantives

- evolution and meaning in Latin and Greek
- relative scarcity in modern languages

Vocabulary

- Latin and Greek adjectives
- Latin and Greek numbers (cardinal and ordinal)
- Latin and Greek Prepositions

I. Agreement of Adjectives and Nouns

When you select a pair of shoes, you do so with the intent of having them fit your feet and also suit your taste. When you decorate the walls of a room or private space, you choose pictures, posters, banners, and other items of display that reflect your special interests. Many other of the inanimate objects on or around you (rings, furniture, vehicles) express some part of your character: you own them, and because of that ownership you may speak through them.

The notion, therefore, that nouns own their descriptors, while requiring a degree of personification, should not be hard to grasp. It is so to English-speakers sometimes only because the concept of inflections in general is largely alien to us. For any language that makes ample and frequent use of word endings, however, having an adjective wear the livery or hoist the flag (or fulfill whatever personifying metaphor you prefer) of its possessing noun must seem an obvious strategy for improving clarity. After all, inflections historically came into existence in circumstances where word order had little importance in determining function. As word order assumed a greater role in determining meaning, endings grew more redundant; but when they were still vital to clear expression, a noun might have been separated from its adjective by several words. If the two had corresponding inflections, then the reader or listener could remain in no doubt about their relationship.

Even in a system like ours, wherein word order is rigidly indexed to word function, troublesome ambiguity can surround a drifting adjective—*especially* in such a system. In the sentence, "I hate to talk to strangers eating finger-food," the speaker's precise connection to the hors-d'oeuvres at issue fails to come clear. Who is doing the objectionable eating? Languages which affix inflections to their nouns and adjectives avoid such problems. The word "eating" in our example, as a present participle, is a verbal adjective; and as an adjective, it would carry an ending which would connect it either to the speaker or to other guests if the sentence were put in Italian, Spanish, French, or—of course—Latin or Greek. In the modern languages, the adjective would be helpfully restricted by the number and gender of its ending. (A number indication alone would suffice to distinguish between "I" and "strangers.") In Latin and Greek, the adjective would be further limited by bearing an inflection with the same case as its governing noun's.

Hopefully, you understand some of these principles from the previous chapter, where noun-adjective agreement had to be addressed during the discussion of participles. In the sentence, "Drusilla has been asked," we would literally be writing in Latin, "Drusilla is (someone) having been asked," or *Drusilla rogata est.* The participle *rogata* ends in an "a" because it describes Drusilla, a noun which is feminine, nominative, and singular. Now, if Drusilla and Julia were both asked, we would have to alter the verbal adjective in number: its inflection would still be feminine and nominative, but *two* women are involved in the query. The sentence would be rewritten, *Drusilla et Iulia rogatae sunt.*

To use first-declension endings on adjectives when they describe feminine nouns seems obvious enough, since most nouns of that declension are indeed feminine. By the same reasoning, we should use the second declension for masculine nouns and that declension's neuter forms for neuter nouns, since those two genders account for almost all second-declension words. This is precisely what happens. Say that we had the more complex sentence, "Drusilla has been asked about the lost stone, and Titus has been detained." Each of the three nouns in the sentence would then have a perfect participle depending upon it, and each participle's inflection would have to be spelled accordingly. The result would be as follows: *Drusilla de saxo perdito rogata est, et Titus retentus est.* A neuter descriptor and a masculine one could potentially be confused because these two genders share so many of the second declension's forms; but there would really be no way around this, because no distinctly neuter declension exists.

Greek operates after the same fashion. When Odysseus is rebuking Thersites in the council of *Iliad* 2, he begins a vow to thrash Thersites for speaking out of turn with these words: μηδ' 'ετι Τηλεμαχοιο πατηρ κεκλημενος

’ειην… ("May I never again **be called** the father of Telemachus"). The second-declension -ος ending of κεκλημενος designates it as belonging to a masculine singular subject—in this case, πατηρ (i.e., Odysseus). Similarly, when Hera sends Athena down to mediate the quarrel between Achilles and Agamemnon in Book 1, the queen goddess is described as κηδομενη: "concerned, preoccupied." The eta inflection (which becomes alpha in later Greek) locates the subject in the predominantly feminine first declension and further shows that the subject is singular.

Yet it would be disingenuous to leave the impression that a noun's endings and its adjective's *are spelled the same*. This happens sometimes, naturally—even often. Yet if the first declension is to be dedicated to signifying an adjective as feminine in all circumstances, no exception can be made for second-declension feminine words. A tall laurel tree would be a *laurus alta* in Latin, because *laurus* is a rare second-declension feminine noun. *Alta* agrees with it by being spelled differently from it—by using the first-declension endings reserved for adjectives marked as feminine. In the same manner, the way to say "a good farmer" is *agricola bonus*, since the word *agricola* is considered masculine in Latin and the adjective "good," to agree with it, must apply those second-declension endings reserved for masculine adjectives. Furthermore, an adjective that uses only first- and second-declension endings cannot become third-declension just because its noun may be. A bad king is a *rex malus* (and cf. πατηρ κεκλημενος just above). Do not under any circumstances try to invent some form of *malus* that will mimic the spelling of *rex*, such as *malux*. No such word exists—you will create mere nonsense by being thus creative!

As a matter of fact, third-declension adjectives do exist; and, as with first/second declension adjectives, they may employ only endings drawn from their declension. *Brevis*, "short," is such an adjective. You cannot write the phrase "short story" with *fabula breva* on the rationale that the noun ends in an "a," so the adjective should, as well. The phrase *fabula brevis* is correctly spelled and in complete agreement, because *–is* is a standard third-declension nominative singular feminine ending. End of story.

Third-declension adjectives, like the nouns of that group, actually have a variety of possible nominative singulars. We shall reserve that topic until after some new vocabulary has been introduced and some exercises offered to give you practice. This broad area of noun/adjective agreement often seems dizzyingly complex to students; but if you review the introductory section carefully and then work the drills below, you should find things starting to fall into place. The essential concepts are quite simple.

Summary

In Latin and Greek (and the modern languages descended from them), adjectives and nouns "agree." This does not necessarily mean that they possess the same endings, but rather that the adjective assumes the case/number/gender ending dictated by its noun BUT ALSO appropriate to its proper declension. Both classical languages have a first/second declension group of adjectives and a third-declension group; and the adjectives from one group must not be given endings from the other, regardless of their governing noun's declension.

Vocabulary: Latin

The following list of Latin adjectives only includes those of the first/second declension variety. Words are listed here as they would appear in a dictionary: i.e., with the *–us-a-um* notation that signals the three possible nominative singular endings for such an adjective. A few words with *–er* in the masculine form drop the "e" to create subsequent forms (like the nouns *ager* and *magister*). One of these words, we should acknowledge—*niger*— has acquired unfortunate associations in the post-Renaissance West, but most definitely had no such baggage in antiquity.

Adjectives both Latin and Greek are especially fertile in the production of English words. If there were ever a set of word lists in this book that you should memorize for vocabulary-building, here would be that set. You can think of additional derivatives (especially from scientific terminology) for most words with little effort.

Latin	meaning	derivative
aeger-gra-grum	ill, sick	vinegar
albus-a-um	white	albino
altus-a-um	high, deep	alitude
bonus-a-um	good, moral	bounty
calidus-a-um	hot, warm	calorie
candidus-a-um	bright, shining	candid
ceterus-a-um	the other, the rest	*et cetera*
clarus-a-um	famous, bright	clear
dexter-tra-trum	right (side), propitious	dexterity
dignus-a-um	worthy, noble	dignity
durus-a-um	hard, tough	durable
frigidus-a-um	cold	frigid
latus-a-um	broad, wide	latitude
liber-a-um (*e* not dropped)	free, independent	liberty
longus-a-um	long, extensive	longitude
magnus-a-um	big, great	magnitude
malus-a-um	bad, wicked	malice
medius-a-um	mid-, in the middle	median
meus-a-um	my, mine	*mea culpa*
miser-a-um (*e* not dropped)	sad, wretched	miserable
multus-a-um	many, much	multitude
niger-gra-grum	black, dark	negritude
noster-tra-trum	our	*Nostra Dama* (medieval: "Our Lady")
novus-a-um	new	novel
pallidus-a-um	pale	pallid

parvus-a-um	small	parvulus
paucus-a-um	few	paucity
plenus-a-um	full, filled, whole	pleniary
pulcher-chra-chrum	beautiful, handsome	pulchritude
quantus-a-um	how much, how many	quantity
rapidus-a-um	fast, swift	rapid
rufus-a-um	red	rufous
sanus-a-um	healthy, wholesome	sane
sinister-tra-trum	left (side), ill-omened	sinister
splendidus-a-um	shining, brilliant	splendid
suus-a-um	his/her/their own	*sui generis*
tantus-a-um	so much, so many	tantamount
tardus-a-um	slow, late	tardy
tuus-a-um	your (singular)	-----
verus-a-um	true, genuine	veritable
vester-tra-trum	your (plural)	-----

Not given are several very common adjectives—such as *nullus*, *ullus*, *totus*, and *alter*—which have irregularities in their declension (gen. in –*ius*, dat. in –*i*).

Vocabulary: Greek

Once again, we have followed the dictionary convention of listing adjectives with their three possible nominative singular inflections in notation (since each gender does have a distinct form in first/second declension adjectives). The convention is especially useful for Greek modifiers, for you will notice that the two masculine forms ending in -ας (μεγας and μελας) radically alter their stem thereafter; and you may also observe that the feminine nominative is alpha rather than eta when the adjective's stem ends in a vowel (e.g., παλαιος-α-ον).

Greek	pronunciation	meaning	derivative
’ατοπος-η-ον	AH-top-oss	foolish, stupid	atopical (= off topic, wandering)
’αλλος-η-ον	AH-loss	other	allegory
’αυτος -η-ον	AOW-toss	self, same	autonomy

184

γεραιος-η-ον	ger-AYE-yoss	old, aged	geriatric
δεινος-η-ον	DAY-noss	frightening, "terrific" (two senses, as in Engish)	dinosaur
δηλος-η-ον	DAY-loss	clear, obvious	adelopod
'ελευθερος-η-ον	eh-LEOUW-theh-ross	free, independent	eleuthero
'ερυθρος -η-ον	eh-rew-THROSS	red	erythroderma
'ετυμος -η-ον (and 'ετητυμος)	EH-tew-moss	true, real, genuine	etymology
'εχθρος-η-ον	ehkh-THROSS	hated, hostile ("enemy" as substantive)	_____
ζωος-η-ον	DZOEW-oss	alive, living	protozoa
'ιερος-η-ον	hee-eh-ROSS	holy, sacred	hierarchy
'ισος -η-ον	ISS-oss	equal, even, level	isosceles
κακος-η-ον	KAH-koss	bad, wicked, inferior	cacophony
καλος-η-ον	KAH-loss	good, beautiful, right	caligraphy
λευκος-η-ον	leuw-KOSS	white, bright	leucocyte
μακρος-η-ον	MACK-ross	long, tall, deep	macroeconomic
μεγας, -γαλα, -γαλον	MEH-gass	big, great, mighty	megalomania
μελας, -λαινα, -λαινον	MEH-lass	black, dark	melanoma
μικρος-η-ον	MICK-ross	small, paltry	microscope
μονος-η-ον	MON-oss	one, lone, single	monochrome
νεος-α-ον	NEH-oss	new, raw, young	neophyte
'ολιγος -η-ον	oh-LEE-goss	few	oligarchy
'ομοιος-α-ον	hoh-MOY-oss	similar, alike	homogeneity
'ορθος -η-ον	or-THOSS	straight, proper, correct	orthography
παλαιος-α-ον	pah-LYE-oss	ancient, aged	paleontology

185

σοφος-η-ον	SOFF-oss	wise	philosopher
φιλος-η-ον	FILL-oss	fond, beloved, friendly	philanthropy

Just to be sure that we're on the same page, here follow two tables that match up a first/second-declension adjective with a third-declension noun, in both Latin and Greek. Only the feminine form is declined fully in both numbers; you should be able to infer how the masculine and neuter forms would be completed.

	singular		plural	
	M	F	F	N
nom.	rex bonus	nox longa	noctes longae	maria alta
gen.	regis boni	noctis longae	noctium longarum	marium altorum
dat.	regi bono	nocti longae	nocibus longîs	maribus altîs
acc.	regem bonum	noctem longam	noctes longas	maria alta
abl.	rege bono	nocte longâ	noctibus longîs	maribus altîs

	singular		plural	
	M	F	F	N
nom.	δαιμων δεινος	μητηρ καλη	μητηρες καλαι	σωματα μικρα
gen.	δαιμονος δεινου	μητερος καλης	μητηρων καλαων	σωματων μικρων
dat.	δαιμονι δεινωι	μητερι καληι	μητηρεσσι καλαις	σωματεσσι μικροις
acc.	δαιμονα δεινον	μητερα καλην	μητηρες καλας	σωματα μικρα

Exercise Set 5.1

A. Translate the following noun/adjective phrases into Latin. Make them nominative unless they are preceded by a preposition. You may need to look up some of the nouns (especially the third-declension ones) to ascertain their gender before choosing an ending for the adjective in question. Also remember that adjectives typically follow nouns in Greek and Latin (and in the romance languages): only the really common ones like "good" and "bad" do not.

1. the beautiful trees
2. the tall women
3. of the little boys
4. with the good king
5. the wicked wars
6. for the miserable farmer (dat.)
7. warm days
8. many armies
9. on a cold night
10. of our soldiers

B. Now translate these phrases into Greek. Remember to keep them in the nominative unless a preposition precedes them, and also bear in mind the other advice given for Exercise A.

1. the frightening war
2. the black horses
3. of the other queen
4. in an ancient city (dat.)
5. the young daughters

6. great sorrows
7. from the bright star (gen.)
8. for living prophets (dat.)
9. of the wicked tyrants
10. toward the free poet (acc.)

C. Translate into Latin.

1. (Though) wounded, we were holding the white lion with our hands.
2. Of the many stars in the sky, red Antares (m.) has always (semper) seemed* to me a good sign.
3. A great heap of leaves had been carried into the city's wide streets by the swift wind.

* "To seem" in Latin is expressed by the passive of *videre* (= "is seen"). Use a dative with it just as we does with "seems" in English.

D. Translate into Greek.

1. Many woes will appear (use passive of φαινω) in the lands of the great king.*
2. The holy gods, though (και) not feared, have spoken to the foolish boys.
3. Beloved Kleitos,** you are being kept (= held) from terrible deeds by a kind (= good) fate.

*The word you choose for "woes" will be a neuter plural—and such nouns, when the sentence's subject, always use *singular* verbs in the pre-Christian era. (Things are changing by Quintus of Smyrna's day [fourth century A.D.], whose would-be epic supplement to the *Iliad* lets several plural verbs leak in around plural neuter subjects).

**Remember that the vocative of –ος names, like that of –*us* names in Latin, has a special form: -ε.

Solo Flight: Make ten noun/adjective phrases of your own, using A above as a model, and then translate them into Latin. Use both singular and plural expressions, and represent at least four of the five cases.

II. Third Declension Adjectives: Latin and Greek

Just as every noun in Latin and Greek has its own declension and cannot assume the endings of any other, so every adjective is either first/second in its range of possible endings or strictly third. An adjective from one group, as has already been explained, cannot shift to the other under any circumstances. Such a shift might seem entirely harmless, and even very helpful and reasonable: why not write *fabula breva* for "short story" and *rex brevex* for "short king"? As we have often had occasion to note, however, language is something of a human institution as well as a system of communication. It differs from Morse Code or semaphore in that it has reverend traditions to accommodate along with basic logic—and sometimes the two conflict.

Mere common sense, then, is seldom enough to cause a culture to overhaul an entire linguistic tradition. This means, in the matter under discussion, that we must accustom ourselves to using certain adjectives only with third-declension endings. It would be more sensible to make all adjectives in both Latin and Greek into the first/second declension variety, since we would then a) have only one set of inflections to remember, and b) profit from using inflections whose masculine and feminine forms are almost always distinct. In the third declension, all three genders can often look alike. The dative and ablative plural will always end in –*ibus* (though these cases are also indistinguishable in first/second declension adjectives, ending always in –*îs*); the genitive singulars always end in –*is*; the dative singulars always end in –*i*; and even the ablative singulars and genitive plurals declare no difference from gender to gender (-*i* or -*e* and –*ium*, respectively), for third-declension adjectives are all i-stems.

A few of these adjectives do have three distinct forms in the nominative singular—the one case/number slot of which this may be said sometimes; yet the differences there do not follow a rigid pattern, especially for the masculine form. Below are some examples of Latin third-declension adjectives. The final ending given is always the neuter. Sometimes only one form serves all three genders in the nominative, sometimes the masculine and feminine forms are the same, and sometimes all three are different... thoroughly disorganized! Dictionaries will usually give the genitive when the nominative has a single form, for otherwise we could not be sure of the stem.

Latin	meaning	derivative
acer-acris-acre	sharp, bitter	acrid
atrox (gen. atrocis)	cruel, horrible	atrocious
audax (gen. audacis)	bold, rash, daring	audacious
brevis-e	short (in size or time)	brief
celer-is-e	swift	celerity
difficilis-e	hard (to do or grasp)	difficult
dives (gen. divitis)	rich, wealthy, fertile	-----
felix (gen. felicis)	happy, joyful	felicity
facilis-e	easy, effortless	facility
ferox (gen. ferocis)	fierce, ruthless	ferocious
fidelis-e	faithful, trusty	fidelity
fortis, -e	strong, brave	fortitude
gravis, -e	heavy (of weight or mood)	grave
iuvenis-e*	young	juvenile
lenis-e	smooth, mild, gentle	lenity
levis, -e	light (of weight or mood)	levity
omnis-e	all, every	omnivore
senex (gen. senis)*	old, reverend	senile, senator
tristis, -e	sad, gloomy	-----
turpis-e	vile, foul, loathsome	turpitude
verdis, -e	green	verdant

*Both *iunvenis* and *senex* are often used as substantive nouns to mean "young person" and "old person."

These words, to repeat the major point, will be spelled differently from the noun with which they agree if that noun is first or second declension. Thus a "green forest" is *silva verdis*, a "fast horse" is *equus celer* (though we might also say *equus rapidus*), and a "faithful daughter" is *filia fidelis*. Even when both noun and adjective are third declension, we have no guarantee that the same letters will appear at their end. A "sad king" would be *rex tristis*, and a "horrible river" (the Styx of the Underworld, for instance) might be *flumen atrox*.

Frankly, the Roman poets did not like stringing together words with look-alike endings. They felt that a recurrent *–is* or an echoed *–ibus* would sound childishly singsong, like a jingle. They would probably have described an *equus* as *celer* rather than *rapidus* just to avoid doubling the *–us* sound. So you most certainly need to understand the principle of agreeing inflections spelled differently if you ever intend to read the great classical poets, or even the great prose stylists.

To the list above might be added dozens of adjectives of the very familiar form, *terribilis-e, horribilis-e, flexibilis-e*, and so on. These words have generally migrated directly into English with minimal change either to their spelling or their meaning. (Did we just use the word "familiar"? *Familiaris-e* is also on the list, though its meaning often implies blood kinship and not mere familiarity.)

Below is the most common third-declension adjective paradigm, in which masculine and feminine forms are all identical.

	singular			plural		
	M	F	N	M	F	N
nom.	fortis	fortis	forte	fortes	fortes	fortia
gen.	fortis	fortis	fortis	fortium	fortium	fortium
dat.	forti	forti	forti	fortibus	fortibus	fortibus
acc.	fortem	fortem	forte	fortes	fortes	fortia
abl.	forti	forti	forti	fortibus	fortibus	fortibus

Once again, notice that these adjectives follow a pattern that would be called "i-stem" if they were nouns, with the ablative singulars and genitive plurals all preserving that little vowel. Only present participles (see Appendix B below) qualify as third-declension adjectives yet do not regularly display these i-stem characteristics. (Their ablative singular usually ends in *-e* and their genitive plural in *-um*, like mainstream third-declension nouns).

Now we turn to Greek, of which the same general comments may be made and for which a list very like that directly above can be composed. Note, in other words, that while Greek third-declension adjectives tend to cluster around a certain pattern in the nominative (υς-εια-υ), they are far from having a rigid uniformity.

Greek	pronunciation	meaning	derivative
’αληθης-ες	ah-lay-THAYSS	true, not forgotten	alethiometer
βαρυς-εια-υ	bah-REWss	heavy, severe, serious	baritone
γλυκυς-εια-υ	glew-KEWss	sweet (taste)	glycerine
’ελαχυς -εια-υ	eh-lah-HKHEWSS	small, tiny	elachiptera

’ευρυς-εια-υ	euw-REWSS	wide, broad	Europe
‘ηδυς-εια-υ	hay-DEWSS	pleasant, soft, sweet	hedonism
‘ημισυς-εια-υ	HAY-mi-sewss	half, midway	hemisphere
’ιθυς-εια-υ	ih-THEWSS	straight, direct	____
κρατυς-εια-υ	krah-TEWSS	powerful, ruling	theocratic
’οξυς-εια-υ	oks-EWSS	sharp, keen	oxygen
πας, πασα, παν	PAHSS	all, every	pandemic
παχυς-εια-υ	pah-HKHEWSS	thick, dense	pachyderm
πολυς-εια-υ	poh-LEWSS	many, much	polymer
ταχυς-εια-υ	tah-HKHEWSS	quick, fast	tachometer
χαριεις-εσσα-εν	hkhah-REE-ayss	graceful	charity

Notice the number of terms for the "laboratory sciences," especially, derived from these adjectives. The list is well worth memorizing for those whose interests are carrying them in such a direction (and further Greek adjectives should be added). As helpful as this vocabulary can be, however, the declension of the words above might tax the genius of a nuclear physicist—not that the paradigm is difficult overall.

Here is the proper format for most of the adjectives just given. You will notice immediately the peculiar fact that the feminine forms are identical to those of adjectives in the first declension throughout the singular and in most of the plural.

	singular				plural		
	M	F	N		M	F	N
nom.	γλυκυς	γλυκεια	γλυκυ		γλυκεες	γλυκειαι	γλυκεα
gen.	γλυκεος	γλυκειης	γλυκεος		γλυκεων	γλυκεων	γλυκεων
dat.	γλυκει	γλυκειηι	γλυκει		γλυκεσσι	γλυκειηισι	γλυκεσσι
acc.	γλυκυν	γλυκειαν	γλυκυ		γλυκεας	γλυκειας	γλυκεα

We may generalize that the upsilon yields to an epsilon after the nominative singular forms of the masculine and neuter (with the accusative singular raising a slight protest), and that the diphthong –ει runs throughout all feminine forms. You might also be able to predict by now that this is just asking for trouble farther along the evolutionary road—for the weak epsilon stem is a cinch to fuse with surrounding vowels sooner or later and to create new alternatives. We won't go down that road here.

No, the real problem is that several third-declension adjectives had already started to develop their own peculiar habits even in Homer's time. For instance, the feminine forms of πας ("all, every") look entirely first-declension, such as the nominative plural πασαι instead of παντες (used only in the masculine): not even the –ει prefix is added to these endings. Πολυς ("many") does the same thing in the feminine. Although you have been warned about letting your adjectives slip into a declension where they don't belong, it actually looks as though the Greeks were permitting such "decay" from a very early time. Just as Roman bridges and roads outlasted those in Greece, so Roman grammar seems to have proved more resistant to erosion than its Greek counterpart!

A final note on style: Homer often employs the nominative phrase γλυκυς 'υπνος ("sweet sleep") and the dative phrase 'οινοπι ποντωι ("[in] the wine-dark sea"). It would appear, therefore, that even the ancient poet nearest to Greece's purely oral traditions shared the much later Roman inclination to match nouns and adjectives whose endings would not be pronounced exactly the same. (On the other hand, both formulaic expressions above show a distinct fondness for repeated vowel sounds—a side of Homer to which scholars have so far paid little attention.) Hence you must again take heed that agreeing adjectives and nouns often will not share look-alike endings in classical texts. Blind chance would warn us that this must sometimes happen—but the rules of ancient taste tell us that it was actively avoided when possible.

Summary
Third-declension adjectives in both Latin and Greek are like their first/second declension counterparts in that they must draw their endings only from within their declension, regardless of what noun they modify. In the poetry of both languages, furthermore, convention favored avoiding the use of an identically pronounced inflection in words set closely together; so the student must constantly remember that agreeing noun/adjective pairs may not have the same spelling. These adjectives, finally, are prone to have peculiar nominatives.

Exercise Set 5.2

A. Translate the following noun/adjective phrases into Latin. As in Exercise 5.1, make them nominative unless they are preceded by a preposition.

1.	green fields	6.	the vile enemy's
2.	all the dangers	7.	difficult times
3.	because of (propter + acc.) a sad chance	8.	bold laws
4.	in a fierce fire	9.	to a young comrade (dat.)
5.	my rich uncles	10.	with our happy cats

B. Now translate these phrases into Greek.

1.	all memories	6.	of the many tribes
2.	a small number	7.	by the fast dogs (gen.)
3.	the true colors	8.	for the graceful children (dat.)
4.	with sweet wine (dat.)	9.	half of the universe*
5.	with sharp hatred (dat.)	10.	into the wide sea (acc.)

*Make both words nominative. In both Latin and Greek, "half of" is treated as a simple adjective, not as a noun + genitive.

C. Translate into Latin.

1. The boys regarded the bitter wine of their old uncle as poison ("regard as" = *tenêre pro*).

2. My horse's terrible fall before the race was finished (use *ante* + noun & perfect participle) had been a heavy blow.

3. In winter (use *hiems, hiemis*), the fountain's gentle waters will be changed into cruel ice, and the green forests will sit in white sleep.

*Even though "boys" is plural, "uncle" is singular and *suus* must agree with it.

D. Translate into Greek.

1.   The true heart (use θυμος) of a small child will be persuaded by (use δια with acc.: equivalent of Latin's ablative of means) soft words.

2.   The powerful king is holding the city's beloved freedom under ('υπο + dat.) the heavy hand of hubris.

3.   The swift horses were being driven by ('υπο + gen. [same as Latin ablative of agent) the powerful hero along (κατα + acc.) the wide road.

Solo Flight: Below is the first stanza of a famous ode (1.37) by the Roman poet Quintus Horatius Flaccus, or Horace. This stanza masterfully illustrates how a classical poet could sow adjectives in different parts of a line—or even in different lines—without fearing that their "owner" noun would lose them. Can you figure out which adjectives belong to which nouns? (Hint: there are two nouns possessing two adjectives apiece and two nouns possessing one adjective each.)

> Aequam memento rebus in arduîs   [*memento* is an old-fashioned imperative: "remember"]
> Servare mentem, non secus in bonîs   [*secus*: "otherwise"]
> Ab insolenti temperatam   [last word the past participle of *temperare*, "to temper, restrain"]
> Laetitiâ, moriture Deli.   [last two words both vocatives, the former a future participle; would you know
> how to translate it in the famous utterance of gladiators addressing Caesar?
> *Nos morituri te salutamus*!]

III. Noun/Adjective Agreement in the Romance Languages

One of the reasons for this subject's particular importance is its high degree of relevance to modern languages. Noun/adjective agreement is still very much alive, at least in number and gender. (In such tongues as German that retain a case structure, agreement naturally extends to that variable, as well.) Students taking Spanish or French, for instance, typically have trouble with two distinct facets of agreement. One is the very notion itself; yet a little practice accustoms them to the idea that in the phrases like *buenos días* and *Champs Élysées*, the adjective has an "s" because its noun does. What turns out to be far more confusing is why *buenos* has an "o" before the "s" instead of being spelled like *días*, or why *frijoles* are *fritos* instead of *frites*? If the French word for "night" is feminine, then why does *nuit* in the phrase *nuit blanche* ("white [i.e., sleepless] night") not have an "e"—or why does *blanche* not drop its final "e"? The Italian phrase *tutti frutti* looks perfectly reasonable: why cannot all noun/adjective pairs follow its example?

You now know why not. It is because all of these languages inherited the Latin system. Since *día* is masculine in Spanish, obeying a late trend in ancient Latin, its plural form must be teamed with the adjective *buenos*, just as "good poet" in Latin is *poeta bonus*. Yet because the Spanish word for "night"—*noche*—is feminine, the "good" in "good night" shifts to the spelling *buenas*. (The Spanish, with admirable generosity, always wish one another good days and nights, in the plural.) This modern tongue and Italian both possess two distinct groups of adjectives, just like Latin. An "easy book" thus cannot be expressed as *libro facilo* by either of them, because *facilis-e* in Latin is a third-declension adjective, while *liber* (gen. *libri*) is a second-declension noun.

French is rather less taxing in this regard because it has virtually lost any historical awareness of different declensions. All French adjectives of any provenance essentially add an "e" if they are feminine and an "s" if they are plural (though this simplicity is complicated by certain consonants that must change in order to assume the stated additions). For this reason, noun/adjective agreement is notably easier to master in French than in Spanish or Italian. Nouns themselves do not observe any inherited difference between first/second and third declensional endings. A plural noun usually needs just an "s," as in English—the relic of Latin's third-declension nominative plural in *–es* now applied unilaterally.

The table below juxtaposes the inflections used by the three modern languages for Latin adjectives of the first/second and third declensions.

	Italian	Spanish	French
	Italian	**Spanish**	**French**
	adjectives drawn from Latin first/second declension		
	m/f	**m/f**	**m/f**
sing.	buono / buona	bueno / buena	bon / bonne
pl.	buoni / buone	buenos / buenas	bons / bonnes
sing.	bianco / bianca	blanco / blanca	blanc / blanche
pl.	bianchi / bianche	blancos / blancas	blancs / blanches
	adjectives drawn from Latin third declension		
	m/f	**m/f**	**m/f**
sing.	facile / facile	fácil / fácil	facile /facile
pl.	facili / facili	fáciles / fáciles	faciles /faciles
sing.	triste / triste	triste / triste	triste / triste
pl.	tristi / tristi	tristes / tristes	tristes / tristes

This synoptic view is not intended to stir discussion: it merely illustrates what has already been said. Italian and Spanish do not offer more options than French even for first/second declension adjective endings, because the French system, simply using "e" and "s," is able to create four of its own. The real point of departure, then, is that French does not significantly alter inflections in moving from first/second- to third-declension adjectives. The masculine forms of this latter group already have an "e" ending as a relic of their Latin-based spelling: that hardly justifies the conclusion that the French actually recognize these words as being historically distinct. Unless they have studied Latin, French people today most likely consider all adjectives as belonging to a monolithic group.

Summary

*Noun/adjective agreement is simplified in the romance languages inasmuch as nouns no longer possess cases, so that their descriptors do not reflect case; yet all adjectives must still agree with their nouns in number and gender. In Italian and Spanish they must also adhere to a specific group of endings dictated by the old Latin declensions. This means, specifically, that the **buono/bueno** (first/second) type of adjective has endings distinct from the **facile/fácil** (third) type of adjective's.*

Exercise Set 5.3

A. The adjective in each of these pairs has an erroneous ending. Locate the problem and correct it. (The noun's gender will be obvious from its meaning, its ending, or both: remember that these languages have only masculine and feminine nouns.)

1. uomini conosciuto—"known men" (It.)   6. hermanas chica—"little sisters" (Sp.)

193

2. hija amado—"beloved daughter" (Sp.)	7. libro facilo—"easy book" (It.)
3. mari fidèles—"faithful husband" (Fr.)	8. femine grande—"great women" (It.)
4. caballos blanca—"white horses" (Sp.)	9. tantes ainé—elderly aunts" (Fr.)
5. barca belle—"lovely boat" (It.)	10. épouse amoureux—"loving wife" (Fr.)

B. Translate these noun-adjective pairs into the language indicated. Vocabulary is specified in parentheses.
1. strong hands—French (hand: main [f]; strong: fort)
2. poor boys—Italian (boy: ragazzo; poor: povero)
3. big cats—Spanish (cat: gato; big: grande)
4. faithful sisters—Italian (sister: sorore; faithful: fidele)
5. dazzling voice—French (voice: voix [f]; dazzling: éclatant)
6. good mothers—Spanish (mother: madre; good: bueno)
7. happy girlfriend—Italian (girlfriend: amica; happy: felice)
8. professional cooks—Spanish (cook: cocinero; professional: profesional)
9. dear grandmother—French (grandmother: grand'mère; dear: cher)
10. new parts—Spanish (part: parte [f]; new: nuevo)

Solo Flight: Now return to 5.3.B above and change every phrase whose number is plural into the singular, and vice versa for the singulars. (By the way… you should now be able to determine the gender of the Italian noun *vice*: what is it, and how do you know?)

IV. The Use of Articles in the Romance Languages

a) definite articles

Now that you understand the necessity of making nouns and adjectives agree in the romance languages, you are ready to grasp the complexities of the definite and indefinite articles in these tongues. You may think initially that a one-size-fits-all word for "the" and another for "a" should work in these languages just as it does in English; but when you reflect that the articles of romance languages began their evolution as adjectives, you will be able to see why matters are not quite so simple.

Latin has no way to say "a" or "the": neither does Homeric Greek (and neither does Russian, by the way). Later Greek would develop what we call a definite article—the "the" form, termed "definite" because it limits the noun in question to a particular individual. The Greeks accomplished this end by using a demonstrative adjective. The phrase ʽo θεος would have meant "this god" or "that god" early on, but later it simply means "the god." The form of the adjective-become-article would change in case and number along with its noun, so that the nominative plural "the gods" would emerge as ʽοι θεοι. The ancient Greeks never did develop an indefinite article ("a" or "an," "some" in the plural), but the presence of at least one form of article provided later Greek with a new precision which assisted in the rise of Greek philosophy. (It would be fascinating, for instance, to correlate the mere expression ʽo θεος in Plato and subsequent authors to the spread of monotheistic ideas.)

In English, it would sound a bit odd to say, "That man was watching those children," unless you wished to emphasize a certain man and certain children. Yet the evolution of our definite article "the" took just such a course. The same is true of "the" in the romance languages: it grew from the Latin demonstrative adjective meaning "that" or "those." We shall not be studying Latin demonstratives in this text, for their forms are quite archaic at times and thus capable of confusing the novice. Suffice it to say that the nominative singular form of the Latin adjective for "that" is *ille* (masculine), *illa* (feminine), *illud* (neuter); and the nominative plural would run *illi, illae, illa*.

194

Actually, we may ignore the last item of these two triads, since none of the romance languages has a neuter gender. Furthermore, we do not have to worry about any case except the nominative, since the romance languages do not have noun cases. That leaves us with *ille/illa* in the singular and *illi/illae* in the plural. If we trim a little, we will arrive at the definite articles of Italian, Spanish, and French from these four words:

	singular			plural	
	M	**F**		**M**	**F**
Latin	*ille*	*illa*		*illi*	*illae*
Italian	*il*	*la*		*i / gli*	*le*
Spanish	*el*	*la*		*los*	*las*
French	*le*	*la*		*les*	*les*

Notice that *la* is the feminine singular definite article in all three languages. The masculine singular is more troublesome. Italian and Spanish build it from the first syllable of the Latin *ille*, while French chooses the second syllable. In compensation (*en revanche*, as they say), French is very obliging with its plural forms: they are the same for both genders and have no exceptions. Italian and Spanish continue to impose a gender distinction.

A few special cases exist. The major one concerns nouns beginning with a vowel. Italian and French will sensibly handle such nouns in the singular by lopping off the article's final vowel (*la* in Italian, both genders in French) and using "l" with an apostrophe: e.g., *l'aqua, l'amour*. Spanish achieves the same effect by switching from the feminine to the masculine article so that no collision of vowels takes place, even though the noun remains feminine: e.g., *el agua*. In the plural, Spanish and French encounter no problems thanks to the final "s" in all their forms. Italian has to substitute *gli* as the article for the plural forms of both genders before a vowel—which seems to make little sense, for the final "i" is still itself a vowel. The *gl* in Italian, however, is pronounced very like the curious *ll* sound in Welsh: a near-h with the sides of the tongue rolled up against the teeth. (The classic Welsh name "Hugh" is spelled *Llew* in that language; the initial breathing is so heavy that some *ll* Welsh names are rendered into English with an "f," as when "Lloyd" is spelled "Floyd.") Thus the final vowel of *gli* emerges in a very different position from any ensuing vowel, and the necessary separation is created.

Italian also uses *lo* before singular masculine nouns beginning in "st" or "z" (*lo studente*, "the student"; *lo zio*, "the uncle"). These nouns will use the regular *i* as their definite article in the plural (*i studenti, i zii*). Again, only masculine nouns are affected. Spanish uses the *lo* when an adjective becomes a substantive noun (e.g., *lo mejor*, "the best").

These exceptions should not preoccupy you at present. They are not raised in the exercises below. You will have to learn them if you should ever pursue the specific study of one of the romance languages, but here they merely represent a distraction. The main points to remember are in the summary.

Summary
The definite articles of the romance languages are formed from a Latin demonstrative adjective. As such, they must agree with their noun in number and gender (case having disappeared in these more modern tongues). Of course, all of these languages have only masculine and feminine genders. Various adaptations are made when the article ends in a vowel and the noun following it also begins in a vowel.

b) indefinite articles

In most Western languages, the indefinite article—"a" or "an" in English—descends from the cardinal number "one." This is true of English itself: you can see the vestiges of "one" in the word "an." In German, the word *ein* is both the indefinite article and the number one. (In Gaelic, which has no indefinite article, the *an* has rather annoyingly become the definite article! Yet its origin still lies within the word for "one," *aon*.) As we shall see at the end of this chapter, the Latin word for "one" is *unus*. This number (along with the numbers two and three) is actually a declinable adjective. In other words, just as *ille* produced the form *illa* as a feminine singular definite article for Latin's linguistic grandchildren, so *unus* has given *una* to the romance languages as an indefinite article for feminine singular nouns. Below is a contrast of the ways to say "a man" and "a woman" in these tongues—and it is not, in fact, much of a contrast:

Latin	Italian	Spanish	French
unus/una	*un uomo/una femina*	*un hombre/una mujer*	*un homme/une femme*

French replaces the final "a" of the feminine form with an "e" (which is not pronounced *per se*, but which forces an emphatic pronunciation of the preceding "n"). The masculine forms have all been conveniently scaled down to the same short monosyllable—although *uno* is employed before Italian nouns beginning in "st" and "z": *uno studente*, *uno zio*.

That leaves the plural. You might think it laughable that the word for "one" would have a plural form; and, indeed, only Spanish of the three modern tongues above dares to say *unos hombres* and *unas mujeres* to signify "some men" and "some women." Irrational as it may seem, the strategy is at least consistent and easy to remember! Besides, it is not without classical precedent, although most Latin textbooks will not offer a plural form for the adjective *unus-a-um*. Julius Caesar, who is considered an excellent source for authoritative rulings on grammatical issues, uses the plural form *uni* in his *Gallic War*: *qui uni ex Transrhenanis*—"who alone of those across the Rhine…" (4.16). Still, this usage scarcely constitutes an indefinite article.

The truth is that English itself does not have an indefinite article in the plural. There is no single word to say "horses of an indeterminate amount" other than "some"; and "some" remains clearly an adjective rather than an article, though it is indeed indefinite. It might mean "a few," or "many," or really any quantity less than the whole. This final idea—i.e., of being part of the whole—has guided Italian and French in their search for a structure that might function as a plural indefinite article. Instead of using the equivalent adjective for "some" in the plural (*qualchi* in Italian, *quelques* in French), these language opt for what is called the **partitive genitive** in Latin grammar. That is, they say "of so-and-so" to express the idea that a quantity less than the whole is at issue. If you were to say in Italian, "I need some English books," it would emerge something like this: *Mi bisogna dei libri inglesi* (the little word *dei* representing "of" + definite article). If you were to ask for some green beans in French, you might say, *Je voundrais des haricots*. In neither case does any word representing "some" appear: you are literally saying, "I need *of the* English books," and, "I would like *of the* green beans."

This discussion has now carried us into territory considerably more difficult to travel than learning a simple word for "a" or "an." Once again, the student has no compelling need in the present circumstances to understand all of what has just been said. Grasping the general idea behind the indefinite article is achievement enough at this level.

Summary
The modern romance languages essentially use the numeral "one" as their indefinite article in the singular; and, as with the definite article, it has masculine and feminine forms. The plural form is more complicated—at least in

Italian and French, where it requires comprehension of the partitive genitive (and does not really exist as an article).

Exercise Set 5.4

A. Either the article or the adjective is misspelled in the following phrases. Figure out which word's ending is improper, and correct it. As in Exercise 5.3.A, the noun's gender should be obvious.

1. le garçons timides—French (the timid boys)
2. les ragazze piccole—Italian (the tiny girls)
3. los muchachas lindas—Spanish (the pretty girls)
4. la épouse belle (the lovely wife)
5. lo rei potenti—Italian (the powerful kings)
6. las reinas grandas—Spanish (the great queens)
7. la sœur brun—French (the brown-haired sister)
8. le femine fidele—Italian (the faithful women)
9. la agua crystal—Spanish (the crystalline water)
10. gli avi buone—Italian (the good ancestors)

B. Now translate these phrases into the languages indicated.

1. the ugly boys—Italian (boy: ragazzo; ugly: brutti)
2. a divine Muse—French (Muse: Muse; divine: divin)
3. the weary men—Spanish (man: hombre; weary: cansado)
4. the beautiful countesses—Italian (countess: contessa; beautiful: bello)
5. some ancient princes—Italian (prince: principe; ancient: antiquo)
6. an old father—Spanish (father: padre; old: viejo)
7. a happy grandmother—Italian (grandmother: nonna; happy: felice)
8. a famous husband—French (husband: mari; famous: fameux)
9. some young chickens—French (chicken: poule; young: jeune)
10. some strong conquerors—Spanish (conqueror: conquistador; strong: fuerte)

Solo Flight: In his 1894 novel *I Vicerè*, Federico De Robertis coolly traces the hypocrisy and decadence of an aristocratic Sicilian family. About halfway through the story, one of the protagonists is trying to manufacture complaints sufficient to nullify a marriage of which he has tired. He begs and bribes everyone imaginable for sympathetic testimony: "prima di tutti la parentela, il principe, le sorelle, i cognati, gli zii, le cugine; poi gli amici, poi la servitú, poi tutta la città." That's quite a string of nouns! Referring to the information in the previous section, can you identify the number and gender of all nine nouns preceded by definite articles?

V. Substantives

A substantive is an adjective functioning as a noun. This mild shift of function may happen when the adjective's governing noun is so obvious a generality that readers may simply assume its presence: usually a word like "people" or "things." To put it another way, if you can place a phrase like "those who are" or "that which is" before a seemingly free-floating adjective, then you are in the presence of a substantive. In our culture, phrases such as "the poor," "the wealthy," and "the disabled" occur commonly. Biblical translations have made current such categories as "the quick and the dead," "the meek, the suffering, the pure in heart," etc. (Yet in such instances, the substantives almost always originate in Greek and Latin, the two languages through which the New Testament reached English.) The poet John Dryden declared that "none but the brave deserve the fair." In Dryden's day, of course, every school child's elementary education included an immersion in classical languages—and the poem, in

197

any case, was about Alexander the Great!

Latin and Greek literature, frankly, abound in expressions of the substantive variety. This is perhaps inevitable when a tongue has gender- and number-inflections for its adjectives. A word like *nostri* (used innumerable times by Caesar as he recounts his military expeditions) already means "our men" all by itself in Latin, since it is both plural and masculine. Similarly, the Greek phrase τα καλα can only be translated as "the good **things**" since the adjective καλα is neuter plural. (Note the presence of the reaffirming definite article τα before the adjective, as well. We skipped the study of Greek articles since it would have slowed our progress excessively: but weigh the effect in English of THE good things, as in "that which is good," against "good things." The former seems more categorical, does it not? As was suggested above, the emergence of the article after Homer may have helped later Greeks to probe philosophical abstractions.)

Virgil has Aeneas declare to his neighbors as the city of Troy burns down about their heads, *Una salus victîs nullam sperare salutem*: "The only safety for **the vanquished** is to hope for no safety at all." The dative plural word *victîs* refers to all people in dire straits: men, women, and children.

The elegiac poet Propertius plainly has women in mind, on the other hand, when he writes, *Sunt apud infernos tot milia formosarum.* To be exact, only the last word is unequivocally feminine: *formosarum* must be a feminine genitive plural of the adjective *formosus-a-um* ("beautiful, shapely"—the origin of the Spanish word *hermosa* and also of the first name with which Western explorers christened the island of Taiwan: Formosa.) Yet Propertius does mention that "there are so many thousands of **beautiful women**" *apud infernos*—"among those who dwell in the Underworld"; and these latter appear to be male, since the accusative plural *–os* ending is distinctly masculine. Are beautiful female spirits, then, to be found abundantly mingling in the quarters of male spirits? Not at all. The substantive *infernos* actually designates all of the dead, both male and female. It is masculine because first/second-declension adjectives distinguish male and female in most of their inflections, having a common ending only for dative and ablative plurals; and, if even a small minority of a mixed group is male, the Greeks and Romans referred to the whole assembly as such in situations where no shared ending existed. The practice hardly seems fair—but it continues today in the modern romance languages. The substantive is especially apt to draw charges of "cultural sexism" because, as an adjective, it must select one gender out of two or three for its ending.

(Sexism isn't entirely a one-way street, by the way. Only the French ever use their word "ingénue" in its masculine form (i.e., *ingénu*: this happens to figure in the title of one of Voltaire's *Contes Philosophiques*). We always speak of a gullible person as "naïve," which is the adjective's feminine form; and likewise, there is no masculine form for "prima donna," though plenty of males insist on being the star of the show!)

Far and away the preponderance of classical substantives familiar to us, however, employs the neuter gender. An *addendum* is a "thing needing to be added." A *datum* is a "thing given." In Greek, a φαινομενον is a "thing that has been brought to light," a νουμενον is a "thing thought," and a προλεγομενον is a "thing to be read beforehand" (phenomenon, noumenon, and prolegomenon). The Roman statesman and philosopher Cicero entitled one of his greatest treatises *De Finibus Bonorum et Malorum*: "Concerning the Ends of Good and Bad Things" (i.e., "of right and wrong"). The title's plural genitives could also be masculine, but philosophical discourse had already created a convention of speaking and writing about abstractions represented by the neuter gender. Aristotle's *Prior Analytics* and *Posterior Analytics* both employed the neuter plural substantive 'αναλυτικων ("of things dissected," as you might literalize the word). The early sixth-century (BC) Athenian sage Solon very occasionally used καλον and κακον (still without any definite article) in the singular to signify "the good" and "the bad." Two centuries later, Socrates would be speaking fluidly of "good things" and "bad things," employing both words as plural substantives.

Be aware, then, that you can shape a great many of the adjectives just introduced into nouns simply by giving them a certain gender and number. We should observe at this point an extremely curious feature of Greek usage that you need to understand if you are to stay within the boundaries of classical grammar: *neuter plural subjects always use a singular verb.* We cannot possibly determine the reason for this counter-intuitive practice at our far remove—except to say that it is very old, for it also occurs in Sanskrit. It certainly seems to predate the clear emergence of neuter substantives… and yet, the two may be related. That is, perhaps the Greeks had a tendency to view all neuter plural things as "stuff" deprived of personality and individuality—hence fit to be treated as one big bundle. If such were their early conception, the tendency would readily have fed into the creation of neuter substantive terms later on.

The Romans did NOT adopt this odd practice: neuter plural subjects in Latin always have plural verbs. Latin and Greek have few real grammatical differences: this is one.

The romance languages, since their adjectives also designate gender and number, are naturally suited to continue this tradition of producing substantives—and, to some extent, they have done so. Consider how many adjectives-turned-nouns English has drawn from these tongues for various persons or groups of people: elite, ingénue, literati, bravo, attaché, desperado, and so on. No doubt, the volume of such words is somewhat greater than that of those nursed along strictly within the borders of Anglo-Saxon English. Yet it would also be fair to say that no modern Western language employs the substantive as much as the ancients did. Might it be that the Greeks and Romans were eager to generalize before the prod of a new philosophical curiosity, whereas we of today are absorbed by the specifics of late-breaking news about relative trivialities? Speaking in philosophical generality is becoming a lost art, though gross oversimplification is alive and well: so sayeth the cynic!

Summary

A substantive is an adjective functioning as a noun after its governing noun has been suppressed (a noun of necessarily general meaning, like "people" or "thing"). The presence of gender and number indicators in the adjectives of classical and romance languages makes them especially well suited to the creation of substantives.

Exercise Set 5.5

A. Translate these Latin sentences into English. All of them contain several substantives.

1. Omnia scripta* antiquorum non obtinuimus (from obtinêre, "to obtain").
2. Milites intacti,** vobis ("to you" [dat.]) cura superatorum et vulneratorum esse debet.
3. Docta memoramus iuvenes, radices visorum comprehendimus senes, sed invisa (= non visa) optime ("best" [adverb]) scimus liberi.***

*From the 3rd-conjugation *scribo scribere, scripsi, scriptus*—"write."
**If *tango, tangere, tetigi, tactus* means "to touch," what do you think this adjective means?
***Do you remember who "the free ones" are? Children!

B. Translate these Greek sentences into English.

1. Πεφυμενα 'επι χθονι βιον σοφοισι διδωσι.*
2. 'Οι πολλοι ("the many, the masses") βασιλεα κρατεα φιλησουσι; 'ολιγοι και σοφοι 'εν φιλεομενωι (refers to specific king of previous clause) τυραννον σκοπησουσι.
3. Δηλον** 'εστιν 'οτι ("that") λογοι νεων φαρμακα μισει παλαιωι 'ου πεφυκεσαν.

*N.B.: Remember that neuter plural subjects take a singular verb.
**Here the neuter substantive is best translated by the English expression "it is clear" rather than "a clear thing is" (and the "is" would probably be left understood in Greek, either way, rather than written out).

C. All of the words below are adjectives in their original language (and all stem from some variety of participle)— yet in English they have become substantive nouns exclusively. See if you can match each word with the literal English translation of its meaning. Do you know each word's "dictionary" meaning in English?

1.	communiqué	a)	coiled, tightly twisted
2.	bastinado	b)	beginning

3. reverend
4. roué
5. dictum
6. conoscente
7. volute
8. debutante
9. vista
10. Christ

c) (having been) said
d) worthy of being honored
e) anointed
f) beaten (with a cane)
g) (having been) seen
h) knowing
i) communicated
j) turned

Solo Flight: Film titles frequently employ substantives (though perhaps not as frequently now as in the past). See if you can create a list of at least a dozen substantives that appear in the names of movies.

VI. Numbers: Cardinals and Ordinals

A short section on numbers is essential, since the sciences and—especially—mathematics employ so many Latin and Greek numbers in their nomenclature. Both cardinal and ordinal numbers fall into the grammatical category of "adjective." Usually the cardinal number (or numeral) cannot be declined. In Latin, "one" may be treated as an adjective just like the words for "any" and "none," *ullus* and *nullus* (all three sharing the same peculiar genitive and dative singular in *-ius* and *-i*: e.g., *unius* and *uni*). "One" has no plural in most authors, naturally—though Spanish gives *uno* plural forms equivalent to our word "some." "Two" and "three," contrarily, have a plural but no singular. *Centum* (100) is indeclinable as an adjective, but some authors decline it as a noun (e.g., Caesar makes it a masculine plural noun—*centi*—when it substantively represents soldiers or masses of people.) *Mille* is fully declinable as a neuter plural noun of the third declension, where it loses one "l" for some reason (*milia, milium, milibus*, etc.).

As for Greek, the first four numerals and the word "thousand" are declined as regular adjectives. Numerals may have slight differences in spelling from one author and dialect to another (e.g., πισαρες for τεσσαρες).

All ordinals in both languages are regular first/second declension adjectives. The Latin versions of these seem to be much more involved than the Greek in the creation of English derivatives.

Roman Numbers

	cardinal	ordinal	derivative
1	unus-a-um (gen. unius)	primus-a-um	prime
2	duo-duae-duo	secundus-a-um	second
3	tres-tres-tria	tertius-a-um	tertiary
4	quattuor	quartus-a-um	quart
5	quinque	quintus-a-um	quintuplet
6	sex	sextus-a-um	sextagenarian
7	septem	septimus-a-um	September*

200

8	octo	octavus-a-um	October*
9	novem	nonus-a-um	November*
10	decem	decimus-a-um	decimal
11	undecim	undecimus-a-um	-----
12	dodecim	didecimus-a-um	-----
100	centum	centesimus-a-um	centennial
1,000	mille (pl. milia)	millesimus-a-um	millennium

* September was originally the seventh month in the Roman calendar, as October was the eight, and so on. All of these later months were bumped back two spaces after two new summer months were dedicated to Julius Caesar and Caesar Augustus.

Greek Numbers

	cardinal	ordinal	derivative
1	ʽεις, μια, ʽεν	πρωτος-η-ον	prototype
2	δυω (also δυο)	δευτερος-η-ον	Deuteronomy
3	τρεις, τρια	τριτος-η-ον	triskelion
4	τεσσαρες-α	τετρατος-η-ον	tetrad
5	πεντε	πεμπτος-η-ον	pentagon
6	ʽεξ	ʽεκτος-η-ον	hexagon
7	ʽεπτα	ʽεβδομος-η-ον	hebdomedary
8	ʼοκτω	ʼογδοος-η-ον	octopus
9	ʼεννεα	ʼενατος-η-ον	ennead
10	δεκα	δεκατος-η-ον	decade
11	ʽενδεκα	ʽενδεκατος-η-ον	hendecahedron
12	δωδεκα	δωδεκατος-η-ον	dodecahedron
100	ʽεκατον	ʽεκατοστος-η-ον	hecatomb
1,000	χιλιοι-αι-α	χιλιοστος-η-ον	chiliast

Summary

Cardinal numbers are generally not declinable in Latin or Greek beyond the first three (Latin) or four (Greek) and very high numerals like "a hundred" (Latin) and "a thousand" (both). Ordinals are fully treated in both languages as normal first/second-declension adjectives.

Exercise Set 5.6

A. Return to the phrases in Exercise Set 5.2.A and do the following. Replace the adjective used in each phrase with either the cardinal or the ordinal version—whichever makes more sense—of the phrase's number in the exercise. For instance, in Number 1, write "first fields" instead of "green fields" (and instead of "one fields," which makes no sense); or in Number 7, write "seven times" instead of "difficult times" (and instead of "seventh times," which makes no sense).

B. Repeat what you did above in A for Exercise Set 5.2.B, this time in Greek.

Solo Flight: Look up the definitions of all the derivatives given in the two tables above. Some words are quite obscure; yet once you understand how they're put together and what they convey, you can use their conceptual strategy to create further words of the same kind. Try to do this in a many instances as you can. What, for instance, would you call a polygon with eight sides? What about a person who is eighty years old?

VII. Prepositions

The last section of this book's grammatical content is dedicated to what is often the first topic in "classical elements" texts aiming at vocabulary development. The words of the English language that draw upon Latin and Greek prepositions must be practically innumerable, especially since these handy prefixes are constantly being deployed to create yet more words. Certainly being familiar with their original meaning can greatly help the student who covets the ability to take a good guess at a strange term.

Always remember, though, that prepositions are not just isolated mini-words giving one an edge at Scrabble (or on an entrance exam). Their story implies much about the nature of language's evolution. They were pure adverbs at first, floating more or less loosely through prehistoric Latin and Greek sentences even as they often do in Homer's recorded verse. When noun inflections were much more numerous and less equivocal than they would become by the days of writing, one could discern simply by listening to a noun's ending whether it designated the location of an event, whether action were moving around it or away from it, and so on. Adverbs that collected to lend a hint of additional clarity to such situations eventually were said to "govern" a certain case of the noun; and with respect to the noun, they occupied a spot up front ever more frequently. The preposition was born as this loose collaboration evolved from the routine to the mandatory.

Thus it would be putting the cart before the horse to say that the Latin or Greek preposition originally declared a straightforward meaning and then threw its shadow heavily over the following noun. The shade of meaning in question, to repeat, appeared first in the noun's ending: the so-called preposition developed so as to bring out the inflection's colors, dimmed by the forces of time. Even at the high-water mark of classical Latin, some prepositions could still have different meanings depending on the case of the noun that trailed them (e.g., *in* as either "into" [accusative noun] or merely "in" [ablative noun]).

You have learned that the genitive's proper function of possession was never reinforced in classical times—in either Latin or Greek—by a preposition. You know that this is equally true of the dative's proper role as signifying an indirect object. Now you have learned further that, in a few instances, a preposition's sense would not have been fully understood by a Roman or ancient Greek until he or she also heard the following noun's final syllable: knowledge of that noun's case was sometimes needed to determine exactly what the preposition meant.

Rather than viewing certain words and cases as welded together, therefore, you might more accurately picture this scenario: the cases under which the prepositions below are listed describe a general set of circumstances, and the given preposition is called upon to lend nuance. In Greek, especially, these circumstances may be quite diverse.

With that much said in warning against oversimplification, then, here follows a good basic list of Latin and Greek prepositions.

Latin Prepositions

Most of these prepositions have contributed to so many English derivatives that we have abstained from supplying any except in cases where popular usage is often *wrong* (e.g., the confusion of *inter* with *intra*).   The exercises at the end of the section will invite you to discover several derivatives for yourself. Directly below, therefore, we have simply appended common phrases, many of them in Latin and Greek, where these words are usually operating as prepositions.

Preposition	Meaning	Common Word/Prhase
with ablative		
ab / â	away from, by (agent)	*a priori* ([knowledge] from pre-experience)
cum	with (means/instrument)	*cum laude* (with praise)
de	down from, concerning	*de facto* ([taken] from actual deed)
ex / ê	out of, out from	*ex cathedra* (from the chair [of judgment])
prae	in front of, regarding, due to	praecordium (chest area in front of heart)
pro	on behalf of, for	*pro bono* (on behalf of the [public] good)
sine	without	*sine qua non* (without which, not [feasible])
sub	under; coming from under (abl.), approaching from beneath (acc.)	*sub rosa* (under the rose [sign of secrecy])
with accusative		
ad	toward, to, with regard to	*ad valorem* ([pegged] to its value)
ante	before (time or space)	*ante bellum* (before the war)
circum	around	circumlocution (roundabout speech)
contra	against	*contra mundum* (against the world)
inter	between	interstate (between states)
intra	within, among	intravenous (within the veins)
ob	over against, facing; because of	*nihil obstat* (nothing stands against)

per	through, along	*per se* (through [in and of] itself)
post	after, behind	*post hoc, ergo propter hoc* (after this, therefore because of it—logical fallacy)
propter	on account of	(see directly above)
trans	across	trans-oceanic (across the ocean)
super	over, above	super-heated (heated above natural limit)

Greek Prepositions

Here we revert to the book's more typical habit of offering English derivative words—except that these terms all hearken to the sciences, especially medicine. Though Greek prefixes are about as common in our language as Latin ones, the words they adorn tend to belong to specialized fields. Science majors should therefore pay particular attention!

Preposition	Meaning	English derivative
with genitive		
’αντι	instead of, contrary to, against	antidote (given in opposition to)
’απο	from, away from	apoge ([sun's greatest distance] from earth)
’εκ / ’εξ	out of, from	ectopic (out of place)
προ	forward (from)	prothorax (forward section of insect)
with dative		
’εν / ’ενι / ’ειν	in (static location)	entropy (turning in [on itself])
συν	with (means or accompaniment)	syndrome (running along with)
with accusative		
’εις / ’ες	into, toward	esophagus (within eating area)
with various cases		
’αμφι	around, about, on both sides	amphibian (living on both sides)
’ανα	upon, up, along	anaphylaxis (up-and-down guarding)
δια	(along) through, on account of	diaphysis ("through" growth [of bone shaft])
’επι	upon, toward, facing	epilepsy (seizing upon)
κατα	(down) through	cataract (downward rush)

μετα	with, after (space or time)	metastasis (after-stage)
παρα	beside, from alongside	paralysis (near [to death] release)
περι	all around, concerning	pericardium (around the heart)
προς	toward, with reference to	prosthetic (put in place of)
ʽυπερ	over, on behalf of	hypertrophy (over-development)
ʽυπο	under, by means of	hypodermic (under the skin)

Summary

Strictly speaking, there was no such thing as a preposition in Ancient Greek or Latin. Cases bestowed certain functions on nouns and pronouns, and adverbs occasionally helped to elucidate these functions. With time, as the case system began to collapse, the assisting adverbs were viewed as mandatory in some instances and were "preposed" before the affected nouns. Yet remember to let both preposition and noun inflection work together, for the latter can also determine the fully proper translation of the former.

Exercise Set 5.7

A. Work your way through the list of Latin prepositions above and, in every case, propose an English word wherein the preposition appears as a prefix. Also explain how the Latin preposition's basic meaning influences the English word that has evolved from it. Be aware that *cum* will always be transformed into "con-" or "com-" and *prae* into "pre-" as a result of English spelling conventions.

    Example 1: propose—to place or posit "on behalf of"

    Example 2: preposition—a part of speech "put in front of" another, which it is said to govern

B. Now repeat Exercise A with the list of Greek prepositions. Remember that many of your English derivatives will likely belong to various scientific fields.

    Example 1: summary—a concise bringing "together" of all essential elements

    Example 2: hypoglycemia—a level of blood sugar "under" the healthy amount

C. Translate the following sentences (Latin and Greek mixed) into English.

    1. Ob impetum hostium, dux exercitûs suas copias dua milia passuum* ex agrîs ad montes ducere ("to lead") desiderabat.

    2. Post annos quinque, ê partibus remotîs redivero (from *redire* [re + ire], "to return") et tertium librum meum de moribus Britannorum populo Romano dabo.

    3. Illâ ("that") nocte, propter numerum stellarum splendidarum, imperium deorum super omnia esse ("to be") clarum â philosopho dictum est.

    4. Λελεγμενα (λεγω) ʽυπο μαντει γεραιωι περι δεκατωι ʼενιαυτωι πολεμου πολλους ʼεφοβεε.

    5. Μετα ʽηματων ʽεπτα καταβασεα (κατα + βασις, "descent, downward walking") δια ποταμον, ʽοπλιτες πολεας μεγαλας ʼαμφι ποντον σκοπησουσι.

*A mile is expressed in Latin as mille passuum (lit., "a thousand of paces). Recall that the accusative case all by itself can indicate duration (= length) of time or space.

**Just what it looks like—but remove the "re" and find the root of which this is the perfect participle. Do you see how we arrive at the meaning "remote"?

D. Translate into the languages indicated.

    1. Without hope, we shall not remain on the island for (= through) the ten promised* days. (Latin)

    2. With great speed, the seventh son, (though) not having been seen by his father for four years, was called to

the king's home. (Latin)

   3. The demons with three eyes** will be summoned (= called) by the first hero. (Greek)

*Select the appropriate word from *promitto, promittere, promisi, promissus*.

**The genitive 'ομματων τριων, without a preposition, would probably be more authentic—but for the sake of practice, go ahead and write "with" + the proper case.

Solo Flight: This final exercise puts together numbers, adjectives… pretty much everything you have learned. If you need a little help, take a peek at *Iliad* 13.20-26. The selection comes from a unique passage where the sea god Poseidon royally descends from a mountaintop into the sea. Notice how "golden" everything is about him!

τρις μεν 'ορεξατ' 'ιων (present participle, "going"; see Appendix B), το δε τετρατον 'ικετο τεκμωρ ("destination"),

'Αιγας, 'ενθα ("where") δε 'οι (dative: "to/for him") κλυτα δωματα βενθεσι λιμνης ("in the depths of the bay")

χρυσεα μαρμαιροντα (what kind of stone does "marmor" sound like?) τετευχαται, 'αφθιτα 'αιει ("unperishing forever").

'ενθ 'ελθων ("having come") 'υπ' 'οχεσφι τιτυσκετο ("yoked") χαλκοποδ' 'ιππω (dual ending—two horses)

'ωκυπετα (compound adjective, like previous one), χρυσεηισιν 'εθηρηισιν κομοωντε ("crowned with… manes").

χρυσον δ' αυτος 'εδυνε ("he put on" [aorist]) περι χροι, γεντο δ' 'ιμασθλην ("he took the rein")

χρυσειην 'ευτυκτον, 'εου ("his") δ' 'επιβησετο διφρου ("chariot").

ANSWERS TO EXERCISES

Exercise Set 5.1

Answers to **A**: 1. arbores pulchrae 2. feminae altae 3. puerorum parvorum 4. (cum) bono rege 5. mala bella 6. agricolae misero 7. dies calidi (or calidae—f. in earlier Latin) 8. exercitûs multi 9. nocte frigidâ 10. militum nostrorum

Answers to **B**: 1. πολεμος δεινος 2. 'ιπποι μελαινοι 3. βασιλειας 'ετερης 4. 'ενι πολει παλαιαι (= ηι) 5. θυγατερες νεαι 6. 'αλγεα μεγαλα 7. ('εξ) 'αστερος λευκου 8. μαντεσσι ζωοισι 9. τυραννων κακων 10. ('εις) ποιητην 'ελευθερον

Answers to **C**: 1. Vulnerati (or-*ae* for females), leonem album nostrîs minibus tenebamus. 2. Antares rufus multarum stellarum in caelo semper mihi visus est signum bonum. 3. Cumulus magnus foliorum in vias latas urbis vento rapido portatus erat.

Answers to **D**: 1. 'Αλγεα πολα 'εν γαιηισι βασιληος μεγαλου φαινησεται. 2. Θεοι 'ιεροι, και 'ου φοβεομενοι, κουρουσι 'ατυποισι πεφωνηκεσαν. 3. Ω Κλειτε φιλεομενε, 'εξ 'εργων δεινων 'υπο μοιρης καλης 'εχεαι.

Exercise Set 5.2

Answers to **A**: 1. campi (or agri) verdes 2. omnia pericula 3. propter casum tristem 4. in igne feroci 5. mei avunculi divites 6. hostis vilis 7. tempora difficilia 8. leges audaces 9. socio iuveni 10. cum felibus felicibus

Answers to **B**: 1. πασαι μνημαι 2. 'αριθμος μικρος 3. χρωματα 'αληθεα 4. (συν) γλυκει 'οινωι 5. (συν) μισει 'οξει 6. εθνεων πολεων 7. ('υπο) κυνων 'ωκεων 8. παισι (= παιδεσσι) χαριριεσσι 9. χοσμος 'ημισυς 10. ('ενι) ποντον 'ευρυν

Answers to **C**: 1. Pueri vinum acre sui* avunculi senis pro veneno tenebant. 2. Casus terribilis equi mei ante cursum finitum ictus gravis fuerat. (But the Romans would actually have written *ictui gravi* in the dative—"as a heavy blow"—even though we see the phrase as a predicate nominative.) 3. Hieme aquae lenes fontis in glaciem atrocem mutabuntur, et silvae verdes in somno albo sedebunt. (Note that the static "in" uses the ablative, while the "in implying "motion toward" uses the accusative.)

Answers to **D**: 1. Θυμος 'αληθης παιδος 'ελαχεος δια λογοισι (or 'επεεσσι) 'ηδεσσι πεισεται. 2. Βασιλευς κρατυς 'ελευθεριαν φιλεομενην πολιος 'υπο χειρι βαρει 'υβριδος 'εχει. 3. 'Ιποι 'ωκεες 'υπο 'ηρωος κατα 'οδον 'ευρυν 'ηγεοντο.

Exercise Set 5.3

Answers to **A**: 1. conosciuti 2. amada 3. fidèle (but final "e" remains, even with masculine noun: part of root word) 4. blancos 5. bella 6. chicas 7. facile (the adjective descends from Latin 3rd declension: "e" is its nominative singular in all genders) 8. grandi (see #7: the plural in all genders is "i") 9. ainées (plural—and adjectives ending in "é" must still add "e" to make feminine form) 10. amoureuse (all French adjectives ending in masculine –*eux* change to –*euse* to form feminine)

Answers to **B**: 1. mains fortes 2. poveri ragazzi* 3. gatos grandes 4. sorori fideli 5. voix éclatante 6. buenas madres* 7. amiche felici (Italians preserve the "k" sound in the singular *amica* by inserting an "h" in the plural; for some reason, this doesn't happen with the masculine form *amici*, where the –*ci* is actually pronounced "chee" to an English ear) 8. cocineros profesionales 9. chère grand'mère* (French adds the *accent aigu* before the "r" because the terminal "e" changes the quality of the previous one) 10. nuevas partes*

*Word order doesn't really matter here—but very common adjectives are usually allowed to slip before the noun rather than occupying the standard position behind it.

Exercise Set 5.4

Answers to **A**: 1. le > les 2. le > le 3. los > las 4. la > l' 5. lo li 6. grandas > grandes (because *grande* is based on a 3rd-declension adjective) 7. brun > brune 8. fidele > fideli (see explanation in # 6) 9. la > el (because article is followed by a vowel) 10. buone > buoni (*li* becomes *gli* before vowel)

Answers to **B**: 1. i ragazzi brutti 2. une Muse divine 3. los hombres cansados 4. le contesse belle 5. dei principi antiqui 6. un padre viejo 7. una nonna felice 8. un mari fameux 9. des jeunes poules 10. unos conquistadores fuertes

Exercise Set 5.5

Answers to **A**: 1. We have not obtained all the writings (lit., "all things written") of the ancients.. 2. Unharmed (lit., "untouched") soldiers, the care of the defeated and the wounded ought to be to you (= "ought to be yours"). 3. We remember teachings (lit., "things taught") as youths, we understand the roots of the visible (lit., "of things seen") as old men, but we best know the invisible (lit., "things not seen) as children.

Answers to **B**: 1. Things produced upon the land give life to the wise. 2. Many (men, people) will love a powerful king; the few and wise will see in the beloved one (= the king; *present* passive participle because he is still beloved at time of main verb) a tyrant. 3. It is clear that the reasons of the young (= young people) have not produced cures for an ancient hatred.

Answers to **C**: 1. i 2. f 3. d 4. a 5. c 6. h 7. j 8. b 9. g 10. e

Exercise Set 5.6

Answers to **A**: 1. primi campi 2. duo (nom. pl. in all genders) pericula 3. propter casum tertium 4. in igne quarto 5. quinque avunculi mei 6. hostis sextus 7. septem tempora 8. octo leges 9. socio nono 10. cum decem felibus

Answers to **B**: 1. πρωται μνημαι 2. 'αριθμος δευτερος 3. τρια χρωματα 4. (συν) 'οινωι τετρατωι 5. (συν) μισει πεμπτωι (granted, counting off "hatreds" is a little unusual!) 6. 'εξ εθνεων 7. ('υπο) 'επτα κυνων 8. 'οκτω παισι (= παιδεσσι) 9. χοσμος 'ενατος 10. ('ενι) ποντον δεκατωι (if there can be seven seas, why not ten?)

Exercise Set 5.7

Answers to **A**: too many possibilities to list all here, but some examples might be "avert," "contraband," "decline," "intravenous," and "sinecure." The preposition *propter* is alone in prefixing no English words.

Answers to **B**: again, possibilities are innumerable. Consider "antibody," "catatonic," "endemic," "peritoneum," and "synergy."

Answers to **C**: 1. Because of the enemies' attack, the army's leader wanted to lead his troops (for two miles) from the fields toward the mountains. 2. After five years, I shall have returned from remote parts, and I shall give to the Roman people my third book about the customs of the Britons. 3. On that night, because of the number of brilliant stars, the rule of the gods over all things (supply "things": substantive) was said by the philosopher to be clear. (Note that *super* + acc. expresses "over" in a mobile sense, as in "covering"—not in the static sense of "located above.") 4. The things said by the old prophet about the war's tenth year were frightening many (people). 5. After a descent of seven days along the river, the hoplites will see great cities around the sea.

Answers to **D**: 1. Sine spê, in insulâ per (optional: classical Latin would not employ the preposition—just the accusative) decem dies promissos non manebimus. 2. Magnâ cum celeritate, filius septimus, [per] quattuor annos non visus â patre, ad domum regis vocatus est. 3. Δαιμονες συν τρισι 'ομμασι (= 'οματεσσι) 'υπο 'ηρωος πρωτου καλησονται.

Appendix A: Subjunctives

The next topic we would have covered in this text if our introductory parameters had not restricted us would have been the subjunctive mood. Although subjunctives have very nearly wasted away in contemporary English, they remain fairly prominent in the modern romance languages (though under a gradual assault there, as well). For that reason, you should at least be made aware of the subjunctive's existence. Furthermore, if you were to pick up a classical text—either Latin or Greek—and attempt to read it on the basis of this book's preparation, our neglect of the subjunctive mood would be the one deficiency most likely to cause you major problems; so, again, this appendix is offered by way of putting you on alert.

When grammarians talk about "mood," they are not referring to a text's degree of cheer or gloom or tension, as one would expect if the same word cropped up in a literature class. Mood has to do with the speaker's or writer's view of his or her material's connection to reality. (Philosophers employ the word "modality" to refer to the same thing.) If you regard your expressions as mere statements of fact, then their mood is **indicative**. Unknown to you, all of your utterances might unhappily be false—but this is entirely irrelevant in determining mood. Your belief or conviction that you are releasing declarative statements simply reflecting the world as it is causes their mood to be indicative. Almost every verbal formulation in this text appears in the indicative mood. "He called the girl"… ""I will see you tomorrow"… "You had lived in Rome"… all of these short sentences are intended to describe reality as the speaker understands it. Of course, a speaker who should knowingly use the indicative mood when misrepresenting facts would be engaged in what we call lying!

The **imperative** mood is employed, as it were, to shape reality. If a mother urges a child, "Stop wasting your time!" she is clearly not declaring that the child will no longer waste time (though she is implying that she believes the child to be doing so presently). Above all else, she is expressing a strong desire that the waste of time should stop. Imperatives are used to issue orders. We want the real circumstances surrounding us to proceed thus-and-so. We therefore command or exhort those whom we suppose open to persuasion to follow a certain course. In most modern languages, the true imperative only has a second-person form, since ordering yourself in the first person to do something seems a little unhinged, while ordering someone not in your presence (and so out of hearing) to do something seems utterly insane. Nevertheless, Latin and Greek had third-person imperatives, usually employed in legal formulas. We practice such usage, too, as a matter of fact; but we always resort to the verb "let," as in, "Let no one cancel a contract without the other party's consent," or, "Let all signators of this treaty be held accountable for the obedience of their citizens." We generally don't think of such phrasing as imperative because we have grown accustomed to picturing imperative forms as single words: "give," "take," "go," etc. We can even use "let" to make first-person imperatives: for instance, "Let us stand firm."

This final example carries us into direct contact with the **subjunctive**. If the Romans ever had distinct imperative forms for the first person, we have no idea what they were. Latin used the subjunctive, instead, for "I" and "we" orders. *Considerem* might be translated, "Let me think," and *audiamus* might be rendered, "Let us hear." A slightly more accurate English version would probably run, "May I think!" The mood here expresses resolution more than commandment, but the difference between the two is very fine. To this day, however, if you use a subjunctive in a romance language to issue an order when an imperative form is available, your command will be received as more polite. *Parla* in Italian means, "Speak up!" while the subjunctive *parli* would be close to, "Please speak."

This species of subjunctive isn't the true subjunctive, all the same. The Greeks actually had a fourth mood which they reserved for such circumstances. It is called by grammarians (using Latin nomenclature) the **optative**, from *optare*, "to wish". We scarcely need to investigate the reasonable but rather complex distinction between the subjunctive and optative moods in this appendix, so we shall content ourselves with noting that it existed. Prehistoric Latin almost certainly possessed an optative mood, as well, but both its function and its actual sound must have been so near to the subjunctive (for we can plainly discern this to be true in Greek) that the two readily fused.

The true subjunctive talks about **what may or might be or have been**. It is conjectural or conditional. In modern English, we seldom say any longer, "If it should rain today, we'll have the picnic tomorrow." Instead, we blurt out, "If it rains today," in the indicative mood: not a very logical thing to do, since we obviously cannot declare how Mother Nature will behave… but we regard the "if" as shifting the whole utterance into a provisional mode. The Romans and those who speak languages descended from theirs are much more likely to emphasize the distinction by shifting moods. An impromptu Internet search turned up the following statement from an Italian news site—along with its English translation—within seconds: "*Se vogliamo che tutto rimanga come è, bisogna che tutto cambi*! If we want things to stay as they are, everything must change!" Notice that the translation of the Italian subjunctive *vogliamo* is a straightforward indicative "we want" (as opposed to "we may/should want"), while the subjunctive *cambi* ("should change") following *bisogna* (lit., "it is necessary") in Italian produces the somewhat equivocal "must change." What if we were to force the issue with the translator by demanding that he use "it is necessary" instead of "must"? Would we be given "it's necessary that we change" or "it's necessary that we should change"? Almost surely the former: when "should" appears in English these days, we assume it to be a synonym for "ought to" rather than an auxiliary verb conveying a subjunctive notion.

Yet the "it's necessary" construction demands a subjunctive. It does not introduce a statement of fact, but rather a conception of something potential—something merely in the "idea" stage. The Frenchman says, *Il faut qu'elle parte*—"It's necessary that she leave." The translation continues to sound like standard English, but now we can clearly spot a subjunctive in the third-person singular, since the indicative form would be "she leaves." English, therefore, does indeed preserve the subjunctive in a few rare cases. How long will it be, though, before we start to hear, "It's necessary that she leaves," in mainstream speech? On that day, we shall have lost just a little more of the logical finesse that makes language a flexible tool capable of exquisite precision.

At least the use of the subjunctive in modern romance tongues generally makes sense to us with a little thought. We can grasp, for instance, why a purpose clause would employ a subjunctive, as in the sentence, "I climbed the hill so that I might know how many houses were in the valley." "Might" introduces a subjunctive in English. The French would employ the phrase, *afin que je susse*, where the verbal form *susse* is an imperfect subjunctive without any sort of helping verb; and so for the Italians and Spanish.

Yet this sentence has other wrinkles to it. The "were" in "how many houses were" must also be subjunctive in Latin, because it occurs in an indirect question. The romance languages are supposed to follow suit, though contemporary practice has gotten a bit sloppy in that regard. Strictly speaking, English never puts indirect questions into the subjunctive. Granted, you might write, "I asked how his mother might be doing," and not attract too many furrowed brows; but in this case, the original question is understood to have been subjunctive, as well: i.e., "And how might your mother be doing?" In other words, the question does not shift to the subjunctive because it is indirect—it had already assumed that form.

Now consider the following slight alteration of our sentence: "I climbed the hill, so I knew how many houses were in the valley." The "so" clause is now called a result clause, since it expresses a state of affairs that ensued as a result of the former clause's action. The sentence does not tell us whether the climber intended to count all of the valley's houses as he began his ascent or not: it only tells us that he did, in fact, end up noticing their number. There seems to be no sound reason to shift the verb "knew" into the subjunctive this time. Its context is declarative, not potential. To paraphrase Caesar, "I came, I saw, I counted."

The romance languages agree with our reasoning—but the Romans, incredibly, would have disagreed. We cannot really know why they would use the subjunctive mood for result clauses and in a few other cases where a straightforward sequence of temporal events seems to be involved. Possibly, their understanding of the difference between a caused effect and an incidental effect was not as clear as ours. Indeed, we would expect a people who believed implicitly in augury, omens, divination, astrology, and other non-rational connections between events to be a little sketchy about whether the house caught on fire *when* you kicked the dog or *because* you kicked the dog. Perhaps their language, through the use of the subjunctive, was leaving the door open to all possibilities.

At any rate, beware of subjunctives if you proceed further with the classical languages, and even if you pursue the study of their modern descendants. Below is a very, very simple overview of the subjunctive's four tenses in Latin and how they have made the transition (or failed to make it) into Italian, Spanish, and French. Forms differ slightly from one conjugation to the next, but we shall not delve into that subject sufficiently here even to highlight the points of divergence. We shall simply follow the third-declension verb *vendere*, "to sell" (as in "vending machine"). This verb becomes second-declension in all of the modern romance tongues. The paradigms also give only the three singular forms so as to compress the table: "I," "you," and "he/she/it." Personal pronouns have been deleted on the French side to save space, but they remain mandatory in actual usage.

	Latin	Italian	Spanish	French
PRESENT	vendam	venda	venda	vende
	vendas	venda	vendas	vendes
	vendat	venda	venda	vende
IMPERFECT	venderem	venderei	vendiera	vendrais
	venderes	venderesti	vendieras	vendrais
	venderet	venderebbe	vendiera	vendrait
PERFECT	vendiderim	-------	-------	-------
	vendiderîs	-------	-------	-------
	vendiderit	-------	-------	-------
PLUPERFECT	vendidissem	vendessi	vendiese	vendisse
	vendidisses	vendessi	vendieses	vendisses
	vendidisset	vendesse	vendiese	vendît

We can conclude this brief appendix with a couple of fascinating observations. One is that the Latin imperfect subjunctive, formed from the present infinitive (*vendere* in this case), produces what is commonly called the present conditional tense in the modern languages (though Spanish grammars often continue to label it an

211

imperfect subjunctive). The Latin pluperfect subjunctive, formed from the perfect infinitive (here *vendidisse* or the contracted form *vendisse*, "to have sold"), has also passed into the modern tongues; yet in them it has entirely lost its pluperfect force, and is merely treated as an imperfect subjunctive. (In Spanish, it is an alternate imperfect; in Italian and French, certain rules tend to prescribe either the conditional or the imperfect subjunctive in various settings.)

Meanwhile, the Latin perfect subjunctive has no contemporary representative. Perhaps it fell from favor because its spelling so closely resembles the future perfect indicative that later generations failed to perceive any difference. Since the pluperfect has "moved up" temporally in the modern languages to fill the gap, any sort of distant past condition in Italian, Spanish, or French must be created by using auxiliary verbs. "To have" can be slipped into the subjunctive and supplied with a participle in such circumstances, just as we do in English. The French, for instance, would write, "I would have finished," by recurring to the same logic as we do: *j'aurais fini* (with *aurais* being the conditional—or originally the Latin imperfect subjunctive—of the verb *avoir*, "to have").

Appendix B: Participles

Like the subjunctive, participles appear all over the place in classical texts, and would surely be among the biggest roadblocks in the way of a student approaching them with no more than this book as a map. Indeed, one of the reasons that Greek and Latin prose often seems to take up so much less space than English translations of it is that participles convey matter in single words that we can only transport with long phrases.

As was demonstrated very cursorily in Chapter Four, the Greeks were especially well endowed with participles. We reviewed the three kinds ending in -μενος-α-ον, all passive. The **present passive** follows the pattern of λυομενος ("being released"); the **future passive** attaches the same suffix to the standard future stem, as in λυσομενος ("about to be released"); and the **perfect passive**, at which we looked more lengthily, becomes λελυμενος ("having been released," or just "released").

All of these forms can also be made active. Present participles pursue a declension that may remind you of λεων, λεοντος, for they are all third declension with an -ντ stem. The **present active** participle "releasing" would be formed λυων, λυουσα, λυον (genitive λυοντος in all genders). To create a **future active** participle, we would do no more than insert a sigma into the correct point of the present participle: λυσων, λυσουσα, λυσον ("about/ready/intending to release": genitive λυσοντος in all genders). The **perfect active** participle is a bit more challenging, since we again have to build upon the often complex perfect stem. Interestingly, though, this form features a final tau in its stem, which should remind you of the standard Latin perfect passive participle (e.g., *vocatus* or *auditus*). "Having heard" in Greek would be λελυκως, λελυκυια, λελυκος (genitive λελυκοτος in all genders).

Compared to this system, Latin is participle-poor (and recall that we haven't even mentioned the aorist participles of Greek). Latin verbs have a passive participle only in their perfect tense—the *vocatus-a-um* paradigm that you studied in some detail. Present participles are always active; and, as in Greek, they are third-declension adjectives with a "nominative -*n*/genitive -*ntis*" pattern (except that the "n" in the nominative is an -*ns* ending and applies to all three genders this time). "Calling" would be spelled *vocans*; "of the calling woman" would be *feminae vocantis*. "Listening" would be *audiens* in the nominative, and "with the listening king" would read *cum rege audiente* (or *audienti*: these participles are declined as i-stems in older or poetic texts). As for "the king being listened to," we would have to fashion this sort of phrase periphrastically. That is, we would require several words to work our way around the problem, since Latin has no present passive participle.

The future participle is also exclusively active. It is constructed easily by inserting a -*ur* into the stem of the perfect participle. "The girl intending to love" would look like this: *puella amatura* (i.e., *amata* with -*ur* slipped in before the case/number/gender ending). In the immortal hail of the assembled gladiators to Caesar, the Latin runs, *Nos morituri te salutamus*: "We who are about to die salute you!" (Notice that "to die," though intransitive, can have a future participle, since in this tense the participle becomes active.)

Now, there is really no correct way to say "about to be called" in classical Latin. Some grammar books will insist that a curious form called the **gerundive** accomplishes this end. In later, more "decadent" Latin, this appears to be true; but earlier Latin always uses the gerundive with an implicit sense of "needing" or "deserving." The beautiful female name "Amanda" doesn't literally mean "about to be loved," but rather "worthy of being loved." When the crusty old Cato kept badgering the Roman senate with the cry, *Delenda est Carthago*! he wasn't observing that Carthago was about to be destroyed; he was insisting, rather, that it deserved to be destroyed, obviously anxious that it might not be so if his arguments failed to carry the day.

The three English words "present," "perfect," and "future," by the way, are all examples of Latin participles, each of them in the tense that its English meaning signifies. You know what *perfectus* means already. *Praesens* is the word for "being," and *futurus* for "about to be." A further aid to learning the present and future forms would be to memorize Horace's couplet, *Prudens futuri temporis exitum / Caliginosâ nocte premit deus* ("Showing wisdom, the god smothers the result of time to come in misty night"). Indeed, the fourth-declension noun *exitus*, like so many of its brethren in that quaternary group, is built upon the pattern of a perfect participle.

This crash course in participles is altogether too much of a nose-dive to help the true beginner very much. Those who wish to solidify the information above should seek out a more advanced text with (of course) exercises and drills. The greater reason for offering this appendix is to build a critical connection between the Latin present participle's formation and that of its romance equivalents—a connection which carries right over into English from French, giving us an enormous volume of adjectives.

Participles can generate adjectives from almost any verb. This is especially so of active participles, since they are not "shut down" if the verb happens to be intransitive. As has been said, the present participle in Latin is always active. Its fertility in producing verbal adjectives is therefore a wonder to behold—and the production is only beginning when historical Latin leaves off. Italian, Spanish, and French all use the participle's *-nt* stem in making their own present participles, as well as in creating a large stock of substantive nouns from these words. Take the Latin verb *studêre*: "to be zealous for," and hence "to study." (When young people didn't have to go to school, they zealously embraced the chance to do so. The very word for "school" among the Romans—*ludus*—originally meant "game"!) A "studying boy" would be a *puer studens*; and since the participle readily came to represent the noun all by itself (substantively), we have the word *studens*, or "student," evolving. All of Latin's descendant languages employ the same word.

Latin	Italian	Spanish	French	English
studens	studente	estudiente	étudiant	student

Notice that French shifts to an *–ant* ending for the participle even though the Latin verb is second conjugation. This happens uniformly in all French present participles: *-ant* is always their stem (but not necessarily their complete ending: gender and number suffixes may still be added, as in the case of *étudiante*—a female student). English draws a great many of its present-participle derivatives from Latin through French. Consider, for instance, "attendant," "savant," and "resistant," none of which comes from a first-conjugation "a" stem verb in Latin. In the case of "student," however, our word has skipped the French connection and descended to us directly from Latin.

Let us conclude this appendix by continuing the incipient list above ("incipient"—literally "beginning"—is another of those direct descendants from Latin) simply to suggest how very lengthy it can grow. The few French words ending in *-ent*, by the way, are not actually used in that language as participles, though they began as such in Latin.

Latin	Italian	Spanish	French	English
ardens	ardente	ardiente	ardent	ardent
ascendens	ascendente	ascendente	ascendant	ascendant
currens	curriente	corriente	courant	current
dependens	dipendente	dependiente	dependant	dependent (but legal, "dependant")
disputans	disputante	disputante	disputant	disputant
importans	importante	importante	important	important
latens	latente	latente	latent	latent
nascens	nascente	naciente	naissant	nascent
potens	potente	potente	puissant	potent
tenens	tenente	teniente*	tenant	tenant

*Though this word does exist in Spanish, its meaning is not "one who rents." It is a contraction, rather, of the French *lieutenant*—literally "one who holds a place." You may have figured out that we draw much of our military and diplomatic vocabulary from the French (attaché, caisson, brigadier, liaison, etc.), courtesy of Napoleon's vast influence upon the nineteenth century. This influence was of course also felt throughout Europe.

215

Appendix C: Maxims and Proverbs

Selected for Their Relative Simplicity and Insight into the Classical Mind

I. Latin

Authors are listed more or less chronologically, from most to least ancient (with some allowance for their genre's ties to tradition). Proverbs, of course, cannot be dated. Translations are as close to the literal as common sense will permit so that you may better see how the Latin fits together.

Ennius

Benefacta male locata malefacta.	Things done well [but] badly located [are] done badly. *Note the abundance of neuter substantives made from perfect participles.*
Flagiti principium est nudare inter cives corpora.	The beginning of shameful acts is to bare bodies among citizens.

Plautus

Aliquid mali est propter vicinum malum.	Something of misfortune (lit. "the bad") is because of a bad neighbor (= "bad neighbors bring bad luck").

Terence

Homo sum: quidquid humanum est non mihi alienum est.	I am a man: whatever is human is not alien to me.
Nam deteriores omnes sumus licentiâ.	For we are all the worse from (= because of) license.
Nullum est iam dictum quod non dictum sit prius.	Nothing is said now which has not been said before. *"Sit" is the subjunctive of "est."*

Sallust

Divitiarum et formae gloria fluxa et fragilis est, virtus clara aeternaque habetur.	The glory of riches and of form (= beauty) is fluid and fragile, [while] virtue is held [to be] transparent and eternal.
Suus cuique animus ex conscientiâ spem praebet.	To each his own spirit offers hope from [a clean] conscience (= "The innocent always have hope").

Cicero

Consuetudo laborum perpessionem dolorum efficit faciliorem.

The habit of labors makes the blow of griefs easier (= more bearable).

Eodem vitio [est] effusio animi in laetitiâ quo in dolore contractio.

The spirit's effusion in joy is from (= because of) the same flaw [as that] by which [is its] contraction in grief.

Non esse cupidum pecunia est, non esse emacem vectigal est; contentum vero suîs rebus esse maximae sunt certissimaeque divitiae.

Not to be greedy is money; not to be spendthrift is income; indeed, to be content with one's own possessions are [= is] the greatest and most certain riches.

Tota philosophorum vita commentatio mortis est.

The entire life of philosophers is a commentary of (= upon) death.

Livy

Fortuna virtutem sequitur.

Fortune follows virtue. *The verb is deponent: it looks passive but is translated actively.*

Virgil

Labor omnia vincit.

Work conquers all. *Virgil substitutes "amor" as the subject in a different line.*

O passi graviora, deus dabit hîs quoque finem.

O ye having suffered graver things, god will give an end to these things, too. *"Passi" is the perfect participle active of the deponent verb "patior."*

Per medias acies mediosque per ignîs, / Invenêre [=invenerunt] viam.

Through the middle (= midst of) battle lines and through the middle of fires, they have found a way.

Quid non mortalia pectora cogis, auri sacra fames?

What do you not drive mortal breasts [to do], cursed hunger of (= for) gold? *Again, Virgil addresses this exact question to "improbe Amor" in another verse!*

Quidquid erit, superanda omnis fortuna ferendo est.

Whatever will be, all fortune must be overcome by enduring. *The two –nd words are gerunds (verbal nouns corresponding to nouns ending in –ing in English).*

Una salûs victîs nullam sperare salutem.

The only safety for the vanquished [is] to hope in no safety.

Horace

Carpe diem; quam minimum credula postero.

Seize the day; trust in tomorrow as little as possible. *"Postero" (for "postero diei") is dative with a verb of trusting.*

Nullus argento color est avarîs abdito terrîs.

No color is (= belongs to) silver hidden in the greedy earth. *The plural use of "terra" is a poetic convention.*

Prudens futuri temporis exitum / Caliginosâ nocte permit deus.

Showing wisdom, the god smothers the result of time to come in misty night.

Qui metuens vivet, liber mihi non erit umquam.

[He] who will live fearing [= in fear] will not ever be free to me [= to my mind].

Virtûs est vitium fugere et sapientia prima / Stultitiâ caruisse.

Virtue is to flee vice, and the first [i.e., origin of] wisdom is to avoid folly. *The final word is a perfect infinitive, and this unusual verb takes the ablative: lit., "to have been lacking in folly."*

Seneca

Aliena vitia in oculîs habemus, â tergo nostra sunt.

The vices of others we hold in [our] eyes, our own are at [our] back.

Argumentum pessimi turba est.

The crowd is an argument of (= for) the worst [position] (i.e., "The mob always chooses the worst course of action").

Est haec natura mortalium, ut nihil magis placeat quam quod amissum est.

This is the nature of mortals: that nothing pleases [them] more than what has been lost.

Ignoranti quem portum petat nullus ventus suus est.

To him being ignorant of (= who knows not) what port he

Magnum exemplum nisi mala fortuna non invenit.

Miserum te iudico quod numquam fuisti miser.
Nulla dura videtur curatio cuius salutaris
effectus est.
Nulli contigit impune nasci.

Pecuniam nemo sapiens concupivit.
Quae inviti audimus libenter credimus.

Veritatem dies aperit.

seeks, no wind is his own (= blows fair). *"Petat" is subjunctive because it appears in an indirect question.*
[Nothing] if not bad fortune finds a great example (i.e., "Admirable models of behavior wouldn't exist but for the misfortunes that gave them scope to show forth").
I judge you miserable because you have never been miserable.
No cure is seen as (= seems) harsh whose effect is wholesome.

To no one has it happened to be born with impunity (i.e., "No one gets a free pass through life's miseries).
No one [who is] wise has craved money.
The things which we hear unwilling, we willingly believe. *"Quae" is a neuter plural relative pronoun: hence "the things which…".*

Daylight opens the truth.

Tacitus
Omne ignotum pro magnifico est.
Optimus est post malum principem dies primus.

Everything unknown is [taken] for something grand.
The best day after a bad ruler is the first.

Proverbs
Aliud ex alio malum [venit].
Cibi condimentum bonum est fames.
Dies adimit aegritudinem hominibus.

Fallacia alia aliam trudit.
In portu navigo.
In silvestribus dumîs poma non pendent.

Nodum in scirpo quaeris.

Porta itineri longissima est.

Another (= one) bad [comes] from another.
Hunger is a good seasoning of (= for) food,
Daylight (= a new day) removes suffering for people. *Note the very loose use of the dative: the translation "people's suffering" would be defensible.*
Another (= one) lie draws forth another.
I'm sailing in port (i.e., "I'm on Easy Street").
Apples don't grow in woodland underbrush (i.e., "Good things aren't found in bad places").
You're looking for a knot on a reed (i.e., "You seek something where it can't possibly be found").
The door is the longest [part] respecting (= of) a journey (i.e., "The first step is the hardest"). *Again, note the flexible use of the dative, which is best rendered in English as a genitive.*

II. Greek

Authors are again listed chronologically, from most to least ancient. Proverbs, as noted above, are often among the most ancient of matter, yet they appear last since we have scarcely any method of dating them.

Homer

'Ανδρος δε ψυχη παλιν 'ελθειν 'ουτε λειστη /
Ουθ' 'ελετη 'επει 'αρ κεν 'αμειψεται 'ερκος
'οδοντων.
'Ει δ' 'αυ τις 'ραιηισι θεων 'ενι 'οινοπι ποντωι, /
Τλησομαι 'εν στηθεσσιν 'εχων τανυπενθεα θυμον.

'Ευ γαρ 'εγω ταδε 'οιδα κατα φρενα και κατα
θυμον: / 'εσσεται 'ημαρ 'οτ 'αν ποτ' 'ολωληι
'Ιλιος 'ιρη.

For a man's soul [is] not [something] seized or snatched to come back when once it will have changed (= removed itself) from the stronghold of the teeth.
But if some one of the gods should toss [me] in the wine-colored sea, I will endure, having in my breast a much-suffering spirit. *The verb 'ραιηισι is a present subjunctive.*
For well I know these things throughout [my] mind and [my] soul: the day will be when holy Ilium will perish. *The verb 'εσσεται is the future of "to be": 'ολωληι is a subjunctive, even though it only makes sense in English as a future indicative.*

Hesiod

Δικη δ' 'υπερ 'υβριος 'ισχει 'ες τελος 'ελθουσα.

Justice prevails over hubris, arriving in the end.

'Ελπις δ' 'ουκ 'αγαθη κεχρημενον 'ανδρα κομιζει.

For hope does not feed well a needy man. *Κεχρημενον = having been reduced to need.*

Καιρος δ' 'επι πασιν 'αριστος.

There is a best moment for all thing. *Πασιν is a neuter plural substantive.*

Κρυψαντες γαρ 'εχουσι θεοι βιον 'ανθρωποισι.

For the gods hold life concealing (= conceal) with regard to men (dative): i.e., "The gods do not reveal the course of life to mortals."

Παντα 'ιδων Διος 'οφθαλμος και παντα νοησας.

The eye of Zeus [is} seeing all things knowing all things. *Both participles are aorist.*

Τον φιλεοντα φιλειν, και τωι προσιοντι προσειναι.

Be friendly to a friend, and go toward someone going toward you. *The two infinitives can function as imperatives (modern Italian offers the same option).*

Τον φιλεοντ' 'επι δαιτα καλειν, τον δ' 'εχθρον 'εασαι.

Invite a well-wishing person to supper, avoid a hostile one. *See note to previous maxim.*

Solon

'Ει δε πεπονθατε δεινα δι' 'υμετερην κακοτητα, / Μη τι θεων τουτοις μοιραν 'επαμφερετε.

If you have suffered fearful things through your cowardice, do not at all thrust the destiny of (= intended by) the gods upon them.

Δειξει δη μεν 'εμην μανιην βαιος χρονος 'αστοις: / Δειξει 'αληθειης 'ες μεσον 'ερχομενης.

A short time will surely show to the citizens my lunacy: it will show [it], the truth having come into the middle (= out in the open). *The final phrase is genitive to indicative either time or cause or both: this is called a genitive absolute. Latin very frequently uses phrases in the ablative case in exactly the same way.*

Chilon

Γλωττης κρατει, και μαλιστα 'εν συμποσιων.

Rule over the tongue, especially at drinking parties.

'Ουδεις 'ελευθερος μη 'εαυτου κρατων.

No one [is] free not ruling over (= if he does not rule over) himself.

Pitticus

'Αναγκηι 'ουδε θεοι μαχονται.

The gods [themselves] do not fight against necessity.

Herodotus

'Ευπραξιης 'ουκ 'εστιν 'ανθρωποις 'ουδεμια πληθωρη.

Of success there is no sufficiency among men; i.e., "Men can never call it quits after a good run."

'Ουκ 'αμα 'αρχηι παν τελος καταφαινεται.

Every end does not accord with [its] beginning.

Simonides

'Ω ξειν' 'αγγελλειν Λακεδαιμονιοις 'οτε τηιδε / κειμεθα, τοις κεινων 'ρημασι πειθομενοι.

O stranger, report to the Lacedaemonians [the Spartans] that here we lie, obeying their commands. *An epitaph for the 300 Spartans who died defending Thermopylae; note the infinitive again seving as an imperative.*

Socrates

Πασα ψυχη 'ακουσα στερεται της 'αληθειας.

Every soul is deprived of the truth unwilling]ly]. *Στερεω takes a genitive just like our "deprive."*

Πασων 'εγω χρεαιν 'ουκ 'εχω.

Of how many things [first word is a gen. pl neuter substantive] I do not have need! *Said to have been the philosopher's joyful cry upon seeing all the wares displayed in the marketplace.*

Diogenes

'Οι μεγαλοι κλεπται τον μικρον 'απαγουσι.

The big thieves are leading away the little one (with reference to judges rounding up a someone charged with a crime).

Plutarch

το 'ηθος 'εθος 'εστι πολυχρονιον.

Character is habit [held] for a long time. *This line provides an excellent way to remember the distinction between two words both spelled "ethos" when transliterated.*

Proverbs

'Ειπων 'ο θελεις, 'αντακουε 'ο μη θελεις.

Having said what you wish, hear back (= in return) what you don't wish.

Νηθιος παθων γιγνωσκει.
Πολλα ψευδονται ποιηται.
Χαλαπα τα καλα.

A fool learns [by] suffering.
Poets will lie about many things. *Ψευδω is transitive.*
Good things are hard. *Both adjectives are substantives.*

Appendix D: Sample Readings

Rewritten to Ease Translation

These brief excerpts have been so liberally adapted to the level of vocabulary and grammar in the foregoing lessons that they should not be taken as strictly authentic. Nevertheless, by reviewing what you have learned, you should be able to rise to the challenge that they pose. Though further study will certainly be required before the original texts may be read without adaptation, you should feel confident that your foot is firmly through the front door if you can negotiate the paragraphs below. Rome wasn't built in a day!

Latin Authors

Accents have been added where they avert confusion with other possible cases. The bracketed comments intended to assist you directly follow the word or phrase to which they apply.

Julius Caesar, *Bellum Civile*

The following passage is adapted from the opening lines of Julius Caesar's *Bellum Civile*. Here Caesar relates the zeal with which he seeks reconciliation with Pompey, once his close friend, now his chief rival for power over the Roman republic. Naturally, the great general represents himself as the party who desires only peace and takes the initiative in seeking it! Caesar always referred to himself in the third person, by the way, in writing his historical narratives. It gives them the immediacy of an action novel, though this was probably not his motive. (Most likely he was copying the style of Xenophon in the *Anabasis*: see below.)

Bellum cum Pompeio imminebat [from *imminere*, "to threaten, be imminent"]. Mortem civium Romanorum omni modo Caesar vitare desiderabat. Ergo nuntios ad se ["himself"] vocavit et eîs [from "ei," "they"] verba cum magnâ curâ docuit. "Est nobis tempus breve ad pacem faciendam ["making"]," dixit. "Omnia ad hanc ["this"] finem temptabo. Si parvo labore magnas controversias removebimus, omnem Italiam metu liberare poterimus [from "possum," "I am able"]. Mihi semper dignitas rei publicae erit carior ["more dear"] quam ["than"] vita mea."

Continuebat: "Pompeio haec ["these"] verba narrabitis, amici fideles. Ad omnia descendere et omnia facere rei publicae causâ paratus sum. Si Pompeius in suas provincias se movebit et ibi ["there"] exercitum mihi hostilem dimittet ["will dismiss"], pax inter nos erit. Milites omnes in Italiâ ab armîs revocare et civitatem ê [=ex] timore liberare debebit. Libera comitia ["elections"] habenda ["to be held"] sunt et omnis res publica senatui populoque Romano danda ["to be given"] est. Pro bono populi Romani eum imploro, 'O Pompei, ad me advenire ["come to"] debes. Periculum tumultûs solutum ["resolved, relaxed"] erit postquam nos imperatores fidem condicionibus iure [from "ius", "oath"] iuraverimus [from *iurare*, "to swear"].'"

Marcus Tullius Cicero, *De Divinatione*, XIX.43-45

In the first part of this philosophical dialogue, Cicero has allowed his brother Quintus to make the case on behalf of divination, which enjoyed a long and reverend tradition of devoted belief in ancient Italy and was largely upheld by the philosophical school known as Stoicism. By Cicero's day, however, more freely reflective minds were beginning to view such elements of their cultural inheritance as mere superstition. Below we see Cicero, early in his rebuttal, posing Quintus some common-sense questions that undermine the old system and even imply ridicule. (The "rhetorical question," of course, was a very popular form of argument, especially when mild derision is the desired effect.) Marcus stresses to his Stoic brother that the leading luminaries of Stoicism are themselves hardly convinced of the truth behind prognostications, since they supply natural mechanisms for supposedly prophetic events.

Quid physici ["physical scientists"] minus ["less"] dicere debent quam ["than"] res incertae certas significare? Num [begins question expecting negative answer] tu putas, frater, fulmen Iovis [genitive of "Iuppiter"] â Cyclopidibus factum esse in Aetnâ monte? Nam quo modo Iuppiter fulmina tam ["so"] multa iacere potest si unum solum habet? Aut quo modo homines mentem divinam ê fulmine cognoscere possunt? Stoici fulmina esse ventos frigidos ê terrâ eruptos credunt. Quis ["what"] Stoicus ergo crederet ["would believe"] signa deorum ex eo natu ["birth. origin"] naturali venire? Significationem rerum ex eventu raro nobis dat natura?

Et si deus fulmina multa iacit, ut saepe accidit ["as often happens"], quid fulmen significationem veram habet et quid nullam? Quâ re [abl. phrase meaning "on account of what thing, why"] Iuppiter fulmina in medium mare iacit, in quo loco homines ni miracula spectant ni vivere possunt? Quâ re ignes in altissimos montes nullîs virîs habitatos rex deorum iaculat? Quâ re in desertas solitudines? Quâ re in terras gentium sine cognitione ominum [from *omen*, not *omnis*]?

Gaius Sallustius Crispus, *Bellum Catilinae*

Sallust was a contemporary of both Caesar and Cicero, as well as their friend and colleague. The conspiracy of the desperate wastrel Catiline to usurp the rule of Rome posed an extreme danger to the state when Cicero was consul. Rounding up and executing the conspirators was the greatest achievement of the latter's political career—and also its ruination; for Catiline had many influential friends, and Cicero would suffer a brief exile for nipping the *coup d'état* in the bud. The eloquence and persistence of advocates like Sallust did much to redeem his reputation.

The opening lines of this treatise have neither the polish of a Ciceronian style nor the fluid directness of Caesarean one. Sallust's prose can be a bit archaic and clumsy, in comparison. His eloquence consists not so much in ease of reading (or hearing) as in profundity of insight. Even these few lines offer some very perceptive comments about human nature.

Omnîs [note the archaic long "i" in the accusative] homines, qui se ["themselves"] laudant super cetera animalia, summâ labore pugnare debent ne ["that... not"] vitam silentio transeant [subjunctive: "should go through, live"] veluti pecora ["like herd animals"], quae [acc. referring to *pecora*] natura prona atque ventri [dative with following word from verb "obey"] oboedientia [both adjectives modify *quae*] creavit. Sed nostra omnis vis [nom. sing.] in animo et corpore posita est: animi imperio vivimus, sed corporis servitio magis ["more"]; alterum [sc. "condition, state"] nobis cum deîs, alterum cum beluîs [from *belua*: "brute, beast"] commune est. Quo ["wherefore, hence"] mihi bonum videtur ingeni plus ["more"] quam virium [from *vis*, "strength": both genitives must follow the ablative *auxilio* in translation] auxilio gloriam quaerere ["to seek"]. Quoniam ["because"] vita illa quam ducimus [*ducere*, "to lead"] brevis est, memoriam nostri longissimam efficere debemus. Nam divitiarum et formae [=*pulchritudinis*] gloria fluxa atque fragilis est, virtus clara aeternaque habetur.

Sed diu ["for a long time"] magna inter mortalîs [substantive; again note long "i" for acc. pl.] pugna fuit: vi corporis an ["or"] virtute animi res militaris magis procederet ["would [prosper]"]? Nam et ["both... and"] dux bonus consilium ante impetum capit et impetum fortem quoquo ["some kind of"] consilio facere debet. Ita ["thus"] utrumque ["each"] per se non erit utile.

Greek Authors

In these excerpts, considerable adjustments have been made to avoid vocabulary, tenses, and structures not covered in our book. Once again, bracketed matter immediately follows the word or phrase that it is intended to elucidate. The use of definite articles (words for "the"), though un-Homeric, has been preserved, since these will give you further clues as to the case of the nouns they accompany.

Remember also that when neuter plurals are the subject of a Greek sentence, their verb is singular! Two out of the three selections offer examples of this peculiarity.

Herodotus, *Histories*

The dazzling collection of factual records, dubious reports, and legends that ancient Greece's first historian packed into his epic prose work contains, among other things, our oldest account of the Spartans' defense of Thermopylae. This particular excerpt (Book 7, 10E: 1) shortly precedes the story of that immortal stand. Artabanus is advising the Persian king Xerxes not to proceed hastily with his invasion, offering a kind of wisdom that would appeal to any Greek, since it revolves around the notion of *hubris* (i.e., arrogantly forgetting one's vulnerable mortality). Of course, Xerxes ignores the excellent counsel. That's why he is not a Greek!

Artabanus is directly addressing Xerxes throughout the passage.

'Οραεις 'ως ["how, that"] 'ο θεος τα 'υπερεχοντα [from two words meaning "over" and "holding": i.e., "superior"] ζωα κεραυνωι [dative of "thunder"] τυπτει, τα δε σμικρα [=μικρα] 'ουκ 'ουταζει [from verb for "wound"]. Και 'οραεις 'ως 'ες 'οικηματα [neuter form of 'οικος] τα μεγιστα [superlative of μεγας] 'αιει και 'ες δενδρεα τα μακιστα [superlative of μακρος] βαλλει τα βελεα [things thrown, darts] 'εξ 'ουρανου. Φιλεει γαρ 'ο θεος τα υπερεχοντα παντα κολουειν ["punish, chastise"]. 'Ουτω δε και στρατος πολλος 'υπ' 'ολιγου [sc. στρατου] διαφθειρεται ["is destroyed"] 'επεαν ["when"] σφι [dative of "them" with verb] 'ο θεος φοβον 'η ["or"] βροντην 'εμβαλλει. 'Ου γαρ 'εαει [from 'εαω, "I allow"] φρονεειν μεγα [used as an adverb] 'ο θεος 'αλλον 'η 'εαυτον ["except himself"].

New Testament, *The Gospel of John*

The passage below was adapted (i.e., "homerized" somewhat as well as simplified) from the Gospel of John, ch. 10. In particular, a few future tenses have been stirred in with the dominant present tense of Jesus' allegory—this in order to afford a little more practice to the student. Such an "iterative" use of the future as is modeled below is not unusual in popular speech and oral traditions. (In the Scottish English of the Highlands, for instance, one might hear, "He whistles his favorite song every day as he leaves the house," transformed into, "He will be whistling his favorite song every day as he will be leaving the house.")

'Αμην, 'αμην, λεγω 'υμιν, 'ανθρωπος 'ο μη ("that... not") χωρεει δια ("through") της θυρας ("gate") 'εις την 'αυλην ("pen, fold") των προβατων ("sheep"), 'αλλα 'εισβαινει 'αλλαχοθεν ("from elsewhere")— 'εκεινος ("this one") κλεπτης 'εστι και ληστης ("plunderer"). 'Ο δε ("but he who") χωρησει δια της θυρας 'εστι ποιμην ("shepherd") των προβατων.

Τουτωι 'ο θυρωρος ("gatekeeper") την θυρην 'ανοιγει ("opens"), και τα προβατα της φωνης 'αυτου 'ακουει, και τα 'ιδια ("single, individual") προβατα καλεει κατ' ("by") 'ονομα, και 'εξ 'αυλην 'αυτα 'αγει. Και 'οταν ("when") τα προβατα 'εξηγαγε ("has led out"), 'εμπροσθεν ("before") του ποιμνιου (from "ποιμνιον", "flock") βησεται (future of βαινω), και 'εκαστος 'αρνος ("each lamb") 'ακολουθησει (from ακολουθεω, "follow") 'οτι ("because") μανθησεται (=μανθησει) την φωνην του ποιμενος.

Ξενον ("a stranger") δε 'ου μη 'ακολουθησουσι 'οι 'αρνοι, 'αλλα φευξουσι (φευγω, "flee") 'απ 'ανθρωπων 'αλλων, 'οτι 'ου γιγνωσκουσι 'αλλα ["except"] την φωνην του ποιμενος του 'αυτων ("their own").

Dio Cassius on Marcus Aurelius

It shocks most of us now that distinguished Roman legislators and men of letters (Dio was both) would have composed in Greek. The degree to which the Empire's center of gravity had shifted east by the third century A.D. is not widely appreciated. The great Stoic emperor Marcus Aurelius also wrote his *Meditations* in Greek rather than Latin. In *Roman History* 71.33.2, Dio Cassius gives us an account of how thoroughly this extraordinary man devoted himself to the service of others, even though—had he chosen to do so—he might have ruled despotically and encountered little resistance.

Note that the very name "Marcus" is preceded by the definite article "the" on both occasions when it is mentioned. The two perfect tenses in the passage, as well, are aorists in the original, a reminder that the Greeks practically never used the perfect form of most verbs.

'Ο δε Μαρκος χρηματων 'εκ του δημοσιου ["public funds"] 'εδεετο ["needed": always passive in form and used with a genitive], και την βουλην [Greek word for Roman Senate] 'ητηκε (perfect of 'αιτεω: "I ask, petition"]). Το κρατος το 'αυτου ["his own"] λαμβανειν ταδε ["these"] χρηματα 'ηιατο [from 'εαω, "I allow"], βασιλευς γαρ ["for"] μεγας παντοις 'εφαινετο. 'Αλλ 'ο Μαρκος τηι βουληι λελεξε [from λεγω], "Παντα τωι δημωι [dative of possession] 'εστι, και τα χρηματα του θησαυρου και 'εμε 'αυτον ["I myself"]. 'Ουτως 'ουδεν 'ιδιον ["my own"] 'εχω. Και 'εν τηι 'υμετερηι 'οικιηι [feminine form of 'οικος] 'οικεω."

Two for One

The incomparable poetess of Lesbos, Sappho, is most famous for a few verses that describe a lover's adoring paralysis before a lady at a public gathering, probably a dinner. (See Exercise Set 3.2, Solo Flight.) The poem is fragmentary, but its opening stanza survives intact. So celebrated was this work, even in antiquity, that the great Roman lyricist Catullus translated it into Latin. Finding any beautiful poem safely transported from one language to another is a minor miracle, regardless of the era or the languages—and Catullus has pulled off this marvel. Notice the subtle shifts he makes in the original in order to preserve its sense while also allowing himself some latitude in his own tongue.

Not a word of either version has been altered, by the way. For that reason, a very literal (and artless) translation has been supplied across from each line. Both of these stanzas are well worth the labor of memorizing, even though Sappho's dialect is rather peculiar (e.g., aspiration is dropped before several initial vowels that would normally have it).

φαινεται μοι κηνος 'ισος θεοισιν

'ειμμεν' 'ωνηρ, 'οττις 'ειναντιος τοι

'ισδανει και πλασιον 'αδυ φωνει-

σας 'υπακουει.

That one seems to me equal to the gods

To be—that man who across from you

Sits and to [of] you nearby sweetly

Speaking listens.

Ille mi par esse deo videtur—

Ille, si fas est, superare divos—

Qui sedens adversus identidem te

Spectat et audit.

That man seems to me equal to a god—

If it's no sacrilege, to surpass the gods, he—

Who, sitting across, again and again you

Doth watch and hear.

Glossaries

I. **English-to-Latin by Part of Speech**

II. **English-to-Greek by Part of Speech**

III. **Complete English-to-Latin List Alphabetized**

IV. **Complete English-to-Greek List Alphabetized**

V. **Complete Latin-to-English List Alphabetized**

VI. **Complete Greek-to-English List Alphabetized**

I. English-to-Latin by Part of Speech

I. Nouns

The word is listed under its most frequently used English translation. After the Latin form is given, a parenthetic notation supplies information about gender and declension.

Abundance, wealth: copia (f-1)

Age: senectûs, -tûtis (f-3)

Animal, life form: animal, -is (n-3)

Ambush: insidiae (f pl-1)

Anger: ira (f-1)

Answer: responsum (n-2)

Antiquity: antiquitas, -tatis (f-3)

Apple tree: malus (f-2)

Arm (body): bracchium (n-2)

Arms, weapons: arma (n pl-2)

Army: exercitus (m-4)

Attack: impetus (m-4)

Fruit: fructus (m-4)

Arrival: adventus (m-4)

Back: dorsum (n-2)

Back: tergum (n-2)

Baggage: impedimenta (n pl-2)

Bear: ursa (f-1)

Beauty: pulchritudo, -tudinis (f-3)

Bird: avis, -is (f-3)

Blow, slap: ictus (m-4)

Body: corpus, -oris (n-3)

Blood: sanguen, -inis (n-3)

Bone: os, ossis (n-3)

Book: liber (m-2)

Bow (archery): arcus (m-2)

Boy: puer (m-2)

Brain: cerebrum (n-2)

Breath: anima (f-1)

Bridge: pons, -ntis (m-3)

Brother: frater, -tris (m-3)

Bull: taurus (m-2)

Camp (military: castra (n pl-2)

Candor, frankness: candor, -oris (m-3)
Care, concern: cura (f-1)

Cat: feles, -is (f-3)

Fire: ignis, -is (m-3)

Cause, reason: causa (f-1)

Chance, accident: casus (m-4)

Chest, breast: pectus, -oris (n-3)

Citizen: civis, -is (m-3)

City: urbs, -bis (f-3)

Cloud: nubes, -is (f-3)

Comrade, ally: socius (m-2)

Correction: correctio, -tionis (f-3)

Council, advisory body: concilium (n-2)

Counsel, advice: consilium (n-2)

Crime: crimen, -inis (n-3)

Crowd: turba (f-1)

Cypress tree: cupressus (f-2)

Danger: periculum (n-2)

Daughter: filia (f-1)

Day: dies (m/f-5)

Death: mors, -rtis (f-3)

Deed, active group: factio, -tionis (f-3)

Dog: canis, -is (m/f-3)

Eagle: aquila (f-1)

Ear: auris, -is (f-3)

Elbow: ulna (f-1)

Elm tree: ulmus (f-2)

Enemy: hostis, -is (m-3)

Eye: oculus (m-2)

Face, surface: facies (f-5)

Faith: fides (f-5)

Farmer: agricola (m-1)

Father: pater, -tris (m-3)

Fatherland: patria (f-1)

Fear: timor, -oris (m-3)

Ferocity: ferocitas, -tatis (f-3)

Field (cultivated): ager (m-2)

Field (unplowed): campus (m-2)

Fig tree: ficus (f-2)

Fight: pugna (f-1)

Finger: digitus (m-2)

Fish: piscis, -is (m-3)

Flaw, weakness: vitium (n-2)

Flesh: caro, -rnis (n-3)

Flower: flos, -oris (m-3)

Forest, woods: silva (f—1)

Fountain: fons, -ontis (m-3)

Fox: vulpes, -is (f-3)

Friend: amica (f-1)

Friend: amicus (m-2)

Game: ludus (m-2)

Gift: donum (n-2)

God: deus (m-2)

Goddess: dea (f-1)

Gold: aurum (n-2)

Grandfather: avus (m-2)

Gravity, seriousness: gravitas, -tatis (f-3)

Grief, pain: dolor, -oris (m-3)

Hand: manus (f-4)

Happiness: felicitas, -tatis (f-3)

Hatred: odium (n-2)

Head: caput, -pitis (n-3)

Heap, pile: cumulus (m-2)

Heart: cor, -rdis (n-3)

Help, aid: auxilium (n-2)

Hollow, cavity, bay: sinus (m-4)

Home: domus (f-4)

Hope: spes (f-5)

Horn (animal or trumpet): cornu (n-4)

Horror: horror, -oris (m-3)

Horse: equus (m-2)

Hour: hora (f-1)

House: villa (f-1)

Ice: glacies (f-5)

Injury: iniuria (f-1)

Iron, weapon (of iron): ferrum (n-2)

Island: insula (f-1)

Journey, way: iter, -tineris (n-3)

Kind, type: genus, -eris (n-3)

King: rex, -gis (m-3)

Knee: genu (n-4)

Lake: lacus (m-4)

Land, earth: terra (f-1)

Laurel tree: laurus (f-1)

Law: lex, -gis (f-3)

Leader: dux, -cis (m-3)

Leaf: folium (n-2)

Letter (mail): epistola (f-1)

Letter (of alphabet): littera (f-1)

Liberty: libertas, -tatis (f-3)

Life: vita (f-1)

Line (of sight or battle): acies (f-5)

Lion: leo, -onis (m-3)

Light: lux, -cis (f-3)

Lord, master: dominus (m-2)

Love: amor, -oris (m-3)

Man: vir (m-2)

Matter, affair: res (f-5)

Means, way: modus (m-2)

Message, messenger: nuntius (m-2)

Milk: lac, -ctis (n-3)

Mind: mens, -ntis (f-3)

Moon: luna (f-1)

Mother: mater, -tris (f-3)

Mountain: mons, -ntis (m-3)

Mouth, face: ôs, ôris (n-3)

Night: nox, -ctis (f-3)

Noise, loudness: clamor, -oris (m-3)

Nose: nasus (m-2)

Number: numerus (m-2)

Oak tree: quercus (f-2)

Obstacle: impedimentum (n-2)

Part: pars, -rtis (f-3)

Peace: pax, -cis (f-3)

People, population: populus (m-2)

Person, man: homo, -minis (m)

Pine tree: pinus (f-2)

Place: locus (m in sing., n in pl-2)

Poet: poeta (m-1)

Poison: venenum (n-2)

Poplar tree: poplus (f-2)

Port (sea): portus (m-4)

Power: potestas, -tatis (f-3)

Price: pretium (n-2)

Queen: regina (f-1)

Rain: pluvium (n-2)

Reinforcementss (military): auxilia (pl-2)

Repeal, annulment: abrogatio, -tionis (f-3)

River: flumen, -inis (n-3)

Road, way: via (f-1)

Root: radix, -cis (f-3)

Rule, authority: imperium (n-2)

Running, race, track: cursus (m-4)

Sailor: nauta (m-1)

Sea: mare, -is (n-3)

Shame, modesty: pudor, -oris (m-3)

Sheep: ovis, -is (f-3)

Ship: navis, -is (f-3)

Shoulder: umerus (m-2)

Silver: argentums (n-2)

Sister: soror, -ris (f-3)

Size (in quality): magnitudo, -tudinis (f-3)

Size (in quantity): multitudo, -tudinis (f-3)

Sky: caelum (n-2)

Slavery: servitudo, -tudinis (f-3)

Soldier: miles, -litis (m-3)

Son: filius (m-2)

Song: cantus (m-4)

Speech: locutio, -tionis (f-3)

Speed: celeritas, -tatis (f-3)

Spirit, soul: animus (m-2)

Stag, deer: cervus (m-2)

Star: stella (f-1)

Stone, rock: saxum (n-2)

Story: fabula (f-1)

Strength: fortitudo, -tudinis (f-3)

Sun: sol, -lis (m-3)

Tail: cauda (f-1)

Teacher: magister (m-2)

Terror: terror, -oris (m-3)

Time, weather: tempus, -oris (n-3)

Tongue, language: lingua (f-1)

Tooth: dens, -ntis (m-3)

Town: oppidum (n-2)

Troops, wealth: copiae (f pl-1)

Truth: veritas, -tatis (f-3)

Type, kind: species (f-5)

Uncle: avunculus (m-2)

Uproar: tumultus (m-4)

Victory: victoria (f-1)

Vileness: turpitudo , -tudinis (f-3)

Virtue (manliness): virtûs, -tûtis (f-3)

Voice: vox, -cis (f-3)

Wall: murus (m-2)

War: bellum (n-2)

Water: aqua (f-1)

Whale: cetus (m-2)

Wind: ventus (m-2)

Wine: vinum (n-2)

Wolf: lupus (m-2)

Woman: femina (f-1)

Word: verbum (n-2)

Work, deed: opus, -eris (n-3)

World, universe: mundus (m-2)

Year: annus (m-2)

Youth: iuventûs, -tûtis (f-3)

II. Verbs

Verbs with only three principle parts are intransitive: that is, they cannot take a direct object and do not have a passive voice.

Ask: rogo, -are, -avi, -atus (1)

Avoid: vito, -are, -avi, -atus (1)

Be silent: taceo, -êre, tacui (2)

Be strong, worthy: valeo, -êre, tacui (2)

Break, shatter: frango, -ere, fregi, fractus (3)

Break, split: rumpo, -ere, rupi, ruptus (3)

Call, summon: voco, -are, -avi, -atus (1)

Care for, look after: curare, -are, -avi, -atus (1)

Carry: porto, -are, -avi, -atus (1)

Change: muto, -are, -avi, -atus (1)

Choose, wish for: opto, -are, -avi, -atus (1)

Come: venio, -ire, veni (4)

Command: impero, -are, -avi (1)

Conceal: celo, -are, -avi, -atus (1)

Conquer: vinco, -ere, vici, victus (3)

Conquer, overcome: supero, -are, -avi, -atus (1)

Count: numero, -are, -avi, -atus (1)

Do, drive, force: ago, -ere, egi, actus (3)

Do, make: facio, -ere, feci, factus (3)

Deny, refuse: nego, -are, -avi, -atus (1)

Drag, pull: traho, -ere, traxi, tractus (3)

Dwell, live in: habito, -are, -avi, -atus (1)

Efface, destroy: deleo, -êre, delevi, deletum (2)

Fear: timeo, -êre, timui (2)

Feel, perceive: sentio, -ire, sensi, sensum (4)

Fight: pugno, -are, -avi (1)

Fill, fulfill: pleo, -êre, plevi, pletus (2)

Finish: finio, -ire, -ivi, -itus (4)

Fly: volo, -are, -avi (1)

Fortify: munio, -ire, -ivi, -itus (4)

Frighten: terreo, -êre, terrui (2)

Give: do, -are, dedi, datus (1)

Go: eo, ire, ivi (4)

Guard, watch over: custodio, -ire, -ivi, -itus (4)

Hang: pendeo, -êre, pependi, pensus (2)

Have, possess: habeo, -êre, habui, habitus (2)

Hear: audio, -ire, -ivi, -itus (4)

Hit, slap: pulso, -are, -avi, -atus (1)

Hold: teneo, -êre, tenui, tentus (2)

Hope (for): spero, -are, -avi (1)

Join, put together: iungo, -ere, iunxi, iunctus (3)

Kill: neco, -are, -avi, -atus (1)

Know, be certain of: scio, -ire, -ivi, -itus (4)

Laugh: rideo, -êre, risi (2)

Lay waste, devastate: vasto, -are, -avi, -atus (1)

Lead, bring: duco, -ere, duxi, ductus (3)

Leave, depart: relinquo, -ere, reliqui, relictus (3)

Lie down: iaceo, -êre, iacui (2)

Lose: perdo, -ere, perdidi, perditus (3)

Love: amo, -are, -avi, -atus (1)

Mix: misceo, -êre, miscui, mixtus (2)

Move: moveo, -êre, movi, motus (2)

Order: iubeo, -êre, iussui, issus (2)

Owe, ought: debeo, -êre, debui (2)

Please: placeo, -êre, placui (2)

Praise: laudo, -are, -avi, -atus (1)

Prepare: paro, -are, -avi, -atus (1)

Press, squeeze: primo, -ere, pressi, pressus (3)

Prohibit, forbid: veto, -are, -avi, -atus (1)

Put, place: pono, -ere, posui, positus (3)

Punish: punio, -ire, -ivi, -itus (4)

Rejoice: gaudeo, -êre, gavisus sum (2)

Remain, stay: maneo, -êre, mansi (2)

Report: nuntio, -are, -avi, -atus (1)

Rule over: domino, -are, -avi, -atus (1)

Sail: navigo, -are, -avi (1)

Save, preserve: servo, -are, -avi, -atus (1)

Say, speak: dico, -ere, dixi, dictus (3)

Seek, ask: peto, -ere, petivi, petitus (3)

Seize, attack: occupo, -are, -avi, -atus (1)

Send: mitto, -ere, misi, missus (3)

Shine: splendeo, -êre, splendidi (2)

Shout: clamo, -are, -avi, -atus (1)

Show: monstro, -are, -avi, -atus (1)

Sit: sedeo, -êre, sedi (2)

Sleep: dormio, -ire, -ivi (4)

Stand, be still: sto, stare, steti (1)

Swear, take an oath: iuro, -are, -avi (1)

Take, seize: capio, -ere, cepi, captus (3)

Teach: doceo, -êre, docui, doctum (2)

Tell: narro, -are, -avi, -atus (1)

Think, reflect: cogito, -are, -avi, -atus (1)

Think, calculate: puto, -are, -avi, -atus (1)

Try, attempt: tempto, -are, -avi, -atus (1)

Wait for: exspecto, -are, -avi, -atus (1)

Walk: ambulo, , -are, -avi (1)

Wander, go astray: erro, -are, -avi (1)

Want, desire: desidero, -are, -avi, -atus (1)

Warn: moneo, -êre, monui, monitus (2)

Watch, observe: specto, -are, -avi, -atus (1)

Wound: vulnero, -are, -avi, -atus (1)

Write: scribe, -ere, scripsi, scriptus (3)

III. Adjectives

All, every: omnis-e

Bad, wicked: malus-a-um

Beautiful: pulcher-chra-chrum

Big, great: magnus-a-um

Black, dark: niger-gra-grum

Bold, daring: audax (gen. audacis)

Bright, shining: candidus-a-um

Broad, wide: latus-a-um

Cold: frigidus-a-um

Cruel, horrible: atrox (gen. atrocis)

Difficult: difficilis-e

Easy: facilis-e

Faithful: fidelis-e

Famous, bright: clarus-a-um

Fast, swift: rapidus-a-um

Few: paucus-a-um

Fierce: ferox (gen. ferocis)

Free: liber-a-um

Full: plenus-a-um

Good, upright: bonus-a-um

Green: verdis, -e

Happy: felix (gen. felicis)

Hard, tough: durus-a-um

Healthy: sanus-a-um

Heavy: gravis, -e

High, tall, deep: altus-a-um

His/her/their own: suus-a-um

Hot, warm: calidus-a-um

How much/many: quantus-a-um

Left (side): sinister-tra-trum

Light: levis, -e

Long, extensive: longus-a-um

Many, much: multus-a-um

Middle: medius-a-um

My: meus-a-um

New: novus-a-um

Old, reverend: senex (gen. senis)

Other, the rest: ceterus-a-um

Our: noster-tra-trum

Pale: pallidus-a-um

Red: rufus-a-um

Rich: dives (gen. divitis)

Right (side): dexter-tra-trum

Sad, wretched: miser-a-um

Sad: tristis, -e

Sharp, bitter: acer-acris-acre

Shining, brilliant: splendidus-a-um

Short, brief: brevis-e

Sick, ill: aeger-gra-grum

Slow, late: tardus-a-um

Small: parvus-a-um

Smooth, gentle: lenis-e

So much/many: tantus-a-um

Strong, brave: fortis, -e

Swift: celer-is-e

True, genuine: verus-a-um

Vile, foul: turpis-e

White: albus-a-um

Worthy, noble: dignus-a-um

Young: iuvenis-e

Your (singular): tuus-a-um

Your (plural): vester-tra-trum

IV. Prepositions

Across: trans (acc.)

After, behind: post (acc.)

Against: contra (acc.)

Around: circum (acc.)

Away from, by (agent): ab / â (abl.)

Before (time or space): ante (acc.)

Before, in front of, regarding: prae (abl.)

Between: inter (acc.)

Down from, concerning: de (abl.)

In, on, at: in (abl.)

Into: in (acc.)

Out of, out from: ex / ê (abl.)

On account of: propter (acc.)

On behalf of, for: pro (abl.)

Over, above: super (acc.)

Through, along: per (acc.)

Toward, to, with regard to: ad (acc.)

Under; coming from under: sub (abl.)

Up against, facing; because of: ob (acc.)

With (means/ instrument): cum (abl.)

Within, among: intra (acc.)

Without: sine (abl.)

II. English-to-Greek by Part of Speech

I. Nouns

Army: στρατος (m-2)

Beginning: 'αρχη (f-1)

Bird: 'ορνις, -ιθος (m/f-3)

Blood: 'αιμα , -ατος (n-3)

Body: σωμα, -ατος (n-3)

Book: βιβλος (f-2)

Boy: κουρος (m-2)

Bull: ταυρος (m-2)

Cause: 'αιτιον (n-2)

Chaos, wild disorder: χαος (n-3)

Chest, breast: στηθος, -εος (n-3)

Child: παις, παιδος (m/f-3)

Child (either sex): τεκνον (n-2)

Citizenry, common people: δημος (m-2)

City: πολις (f-3)

Cloud: νεφος, -εος (n-3)

Color: χρωμα, -ατος (n-3)

Companion, friend: 'εταιρος (m/f-1/2)

Custom, habit: 'εθος , -εος; also'ηθος (n-3)

Daughter: θυγατηρ, -ερος (f-1)

Dawn: 'ηως, -οος (f-1)

Day: 'ημαρ, 'ηματος (n-3); also 'ημερα (f-1)

Death: θανατος (m-2)

Deed, action (on stage): δραμα, -ατος (n-3)

Dog: κυων, κυνος (m/f-3)

Dream: 'ονειρος (m-2)

Drug, medicine: φαρμακον (n-2)

Earth (planet): γαια (f-1)

Earth (soil): χθων. –ονος (f-3)

End, purpose: τελος, -εος (n-3)

Fate, destiny: μοιρα (f-1)

Father: πατηρ, -ερος (m-3)

Fear, terror: φοβος (m-2)

Fire: πυρ, -ος (m-3)

Fish: 'ιχθυς, -υος (m-3)

Footsoldier: 'οπλης, 'οπλιτις (m-3)

Forgetfulness, oblivion: ληθη (f-1)

Freedom: 'ελευθερια (f-1)

Gap, space, gulf: χασμα, -ατος (n-3)

General, commander: στρατηγος (m-2)

Gift, portion: δοσις (f-3)

Gift: δωρον (n-2)

Girl: κουρη (f-1)

God: θεος (m-2)

Goddess: θεα (f-1)

Grief, sorrow: πενθος, -εος (n-3)

Hand: χειρ, -ος (n-3)

Hatred: μισος , -εος (n-3)

Hero: 'ηρως, -ωος (m-3)

Home, domicile: 'οικος (m-2)

Honor, glory: κυδος, -εος (n-3)

Horse: ‘ιππος (m-2)

Hubris, arrogance: ‘υβρις. –ιδος (f-3)

Hurt, pain: ’αλγος , -εος (n-3)

Island: νησος (m-2)

Joy: χαρμα, -ατος (n-3)

Judgment: κρισις (f-3)

King: βασιλευς, -ηος (m-3)

Kingdom: βασιλεία, accent on third syllable (f)

Knowledge: γνωμη (f)

Lesser god, luck: δαιμων, -ονος (m-3)

Life (specific): βιος (m-2)

Life (general): ζωη (f-1)

Light, brilliance: φαος, -εος (n-3)

Lion: λεων, λεοντος (m-3)

Love: ’ερως, -ωτος (m-3)

Maiden, virgin: παρθενος (f-2)

Main room: μεγαρον (n-2)

Man: ανηρ, ’ανδρος (m-3)

Measure: μετρος (m-2)

Memory: μνημη (f-1)

Moon: μην, -νος (m-3)

Mother: μητηρ, -ερος (f-3)

Mouth, face: στομα, -ατος (n-3)

Name: ’ονομα , -ατος (n-3)

Nature, Creation: φυσις (f-3)

Need (goods, money): χρημα, -ατος (n-3)

Night: νυξ, νυκτος (f-3)

Number, tally: ’αριθμος (m-2)

Old man: γερων, -οντος (m-3)

Opinion, teaching: δογμα, -ατος (n-3)

Origin, birth: γενεσις (f-3)

Pain, suffering: παθος, -εος (n-3)

Path, road, way: ‘οδος (m-2)

Person, man: ’ανθροπος (m-2)

Pilot, helmsman: κυβερνητης (m-1)

Place: τοπος (m-2)

Plan, scheme: σχημα, -ατος (n-3)

Poet: ποιητης (m-1)

Power: κρατος, -εος (n-3)

Prophet(ess): μαντις (m/f-3)

Queen: βασίλεια, accent on second syllable (f);

        also βασιλις, -ιδος (f-3)

Race (descent): γενος, -εος (n-3)

Race (tribe): ’εθνος , -εος (n-3)

Release: λυσις (f-3)

River: ποταμος (m-2)

Sea: πελαγος, -εος (n-3)

Sea: ποντος (m-2)

Seed: σπερμα, -ατος (n-3)

Skin: δερμα, -ατος (n-3)

Sleep: ’υπνος (m-2)

Son: ‘υιος, gen. both ‘υιου and ‘υιεος (m-3)

Soul, spirit: ψυχη (f-1)

Spouse: ποσις (m/f-3)

Star: ’αστηρ, -ερος (m-3)

Stone: πετρος (m-2)

Story, lore: μυθος (m-2)

Thunder: βροντη (f-1)

Time: χρονος (m-2)

Tree: δενδρος (n-3)

Turn (in direction), style: τροπος (m-2)

Tyrant, ruler: τυραννος (m-2)

Universe, arrangement: κοσμος (m-2)

Wall: τειχος, -εος (n-3)

War: πολεμος (m-2)

Water: 'υδωρ, 'υδατος (m-3)

Wind: 'ανεμος (m-2)

Wine: 'οινος (m-2)

Witness: μαρτυρος (m-2)

Woman: γυνη (f-3)

Word, lore: 'επος , -εος (n-3)

Word, pattern: λογος (m-2)

Work, task: 'εργον (n-2)

Wrath, rage: μηνις (f-3)

II. Verbs

Accompany: 'ομιλεω

Arrange: τασσω

Believe: νομιζω

Call, summon: καλεω

Carry, bear: φερω

Change, answer: 'αμειβω

Die: θνησκω

Do, perform: πρασσω

Dread: ταρβεω

End, complete: τελευταω

Frighten: φοβεω

Fear: ταρβεω, φοβεομαι

Hear, listen: 'ακουω

Hold, have: 'εχω

Judge: κρινω

Know, learn: γιγνωσκω

Lead, drive: 'αγω

Lie, be false: ψευδω

Like, love: φιλεω

Live: ζωω

Make, cause: τευχω

Make, fashion: ποιεω, τευχω

Move, go, withdraw: χωρεω

Persuade: πειθω

Produce, bring forth: φυω

Rejoice, be healthy: χαιρω

Release, loosen: λυω

Remember: μιμνησκω

Rule: κρατεω (with gen.)

Run, flow: 'ρεω

Say, read, collect: λεγω

See: 'οραω

Send, escort: πεμπω

Signal, mark out: σημαινω

Show, bring to light: φαινω

Speak, utter: φωνεω

Stop, cease: παυω

Suffer: πασχω

Suppose, imagine: δοκεω

Take, seize: λαμβανω

Think, notice: νοεω

Throw: βαλλω

Turn, direct: τρεπω

Walk: βαινω

Watch, look at: σκοπεω

III. Adjectives

All, every : πας, πασα, παν

Ancient: παλαιος-α-ον

Bad, wicked: κακος-η-ον

Beloved, friendly: φιλος-η-ον

Big, great, mighty: μεγας, -γαλα, -γαλον

Black, dark: μελας, -λαινα, -λαινον

Clear, obvious: δηλος-η-ον

Enemy, hostile: 'εχθρος-η-ον

Equal, even, level: 'ισος -η-ον

Few: 'ολιγος -η-ον

Foolish, stupid: 'ατοπος-η-ον

Free, independent: 'ελευθερος

Frightening, "terrific": δεινος-η-ον

Good, right: καλος-η-ον

Graceful: χαριεις-εσσα-εν

Half, midway: 'ημισυς-εια-υ

Heavy, severe: βαρυς-εια-υ

Holy, sacred: 'ιερος-η-ον

Living, alive: ζωος-η-ον

Many, much: πολυς-εια-υ

New, young: νεος-α-ον

Old: γεραιος-η-ον

One, lone: μονος-η-ον

Other: 'αλλος-η-ον

Pleasant, soft, sweet" 'ηδυς-εια-υ

Powerful, ruling: κρατυς-εια-υ

Quick, fast: ταχυς-εια-υ

Red: 'ερυθρος -η-ον

Self, same: 'αυτος -η-ον

Sharp, keen: 'οξυς-εια-υ

Similar: 'ομοιος-α-ον

Small, tiny: 'ελαχυς -εια-υ

Small, paltry: μικρος-η-ον

Straight, direct: 'ιθυς-εια-υ

Straight, correct: 'ορθος -η-ον

Sweet (taste): γλυκυς-εια-υ

Thick, dense: παχυς-εια-υ

True, unforgettable: 'αληθης-ες

True, real: 'ετυμος -η-ον

Wide, broad: 'ευρυς-εια-υ Wise: σοφος-η-ον

White, bright: λευκος-η-ον

IV. Prepositions

Above, for the sake of: 'υπερ (gen.)

Along under, during: 'υπο (acc.)

Among, amid: μετα (dat.)

Around, about, concerning: περι (gen., dat,, acc.)

Around, about, on both sides: 'αμφι (gen./acc.)

Because of, during: δια (acc.)

Beside, at: 'επι (dat.)

Beside, near: παρα (dat.)

By, from under: ῾υπο (gen.)

Down along/through, according to: κατα (acc.)

Down from, below: κατα (gen.)

Forward (from): προ

From, away from: ᾿απο (gen.)

From before, in sight of: προς (gen.)

From the side, beside: παρα (gen.)

In, on: ᾿εν / ᾿ενι / ᾿ειν (dat.)

Instead of, contrary to, against: ᾿αντι (gen.)

Into, toward: ᾿εις / ᾿ες (acc.)

Into the midst of: μετα (acc.)

On, at, by: προς (dat.)

On, upon: ᾿επι (gen.)

Out of, from: ᾿εκ / ᾿εξ (gen.)

Over, beyond: ῾υπερ (acc.)

Through: δια (gen.)

Through (upward): ᾿ανα (acc.)

To the side of, along: παρα (acc.)

To, toward, up against: προς (acc.)

Under: ῾υπο (dat.)

Up to, against: ᾿επι (acc.)

Upon, up, along: ᾿ανα (dat.)

With: μετα (gen.)

With (means or accompaniment): συν (dat.)

III. Complete English-to-Latin List
Alphabetized

A

Abundance, wealth: copia (f-1)

Across: trans (acc.)

After, behind: post (acc.)

Against: contra (acc.)

Age: senectûs, -tûtis (f-3)

All, every: omnis-e

Ambush: insidiae (f pl-1)

Anger: ira (f-1)

Animal, life form: animal, -is (n-3)

Answer: responsum (n-2)

Antiquity: antiquitas, -tatis (f-3)

Apple tree: malus (f-2)

Arm (body): bracchium (n-2)

Arms, weapons: arma (n pl-2)

Army: exercitus (m-4)

Around: circum (acc.)

Ask: rogo, -are, -avi, -atus (1)

Avoid: vito, -are, -avi, -atus (1)

Attack: impetus (m-4)

Arrival: adventus (m-4)

Away from, by (agent): ab / â (abl.)

B

Back: dorsum (n-2)

Back: tergum (n-2)

Bad, wicked: malus-a-um

Baggage: impedimenta (n pl-2)

Be silent: taceo, -êre, tacui (2)

Be strong, worthy: valeo, -êre, tacui (2)

Beautiful: pulcher-chra-chrum

Because of: ob

Bear: ursa (f-1)

Beauty: pulchritudo, -tudinis (f-3)

Before (time or space): ante (acc.)

Before, in front of, regarding: prae (abl.)

Between: inter (acc.)

Big, great: magnus-a-um

Bird: avis, -is (f-3)

Black, dark: niger-gra-grum

Blow, slap: ictus (m-4)

Body: corpus, -oris (n-3)

Bold, daring: audax (gen. audacis)

Blood: sanguen, -inis (n-3)

Bone: os, ossis (n-3)

Book: liber (m-2)

Bow (archery): arcus (m-2)

Boy: puer (m-2)

Brain: cerebrum (n-2)

Break, shatter: frango, -ere, fregi, fractus (3)

Break, split: rumpo, -ere, rupi, ruptus (3)

Breath: anima (f-1)

Bridge: pons, -ntis (m-3)

Bright, shining: candidus-a-um

Broad, wide: latus-a-um

Brother: frater, -tris (m-3)

Bull: taurus (m-2)

C

Call, summon: voco, -are, -avi, -atus (1)

Camp (military): castra (n pl-2)

Candor, frankness: candor, -oris (m-3)

Care, concern: cura (f-1)

Care for, look after: curare, -are, -avi, -atus (1)

Carry: porto, -are, -avi, -atus (1)

Cause, reason: causa (f-1)

Cat: feles, -is (f-3)

Change: muto, -are, -avi, -atus (1)

Choose, wish for: opto, -are, -avi, -atus (1)

Come: venio, -ire, veni (4)

Command: impero, -are, -avi (1)

Conceal: celo, -are, -avi, -atus (1)

Conquer: vinco, -ere, vici, victus (3)

Conquer: overcome: supero, -are, -avi, -atus (1)

Count: numero, -are, -avi, -atus (1)

Cause, reason: causa (f-1)

Chance, accident: casus (m-4)

Chest, breast: pectus, -oris (n-3)

Citizen: civis, -is (m-3)

City: urbs, -bis (f-3)

Cloud: nubes, -is (f-3)

Cold: frigidus-a-um

Comrade, ally: socius (m-2)

Correction: correctio, -tionis (f-3)

Council, advisory body: concilium (n-2)

Counsel, advice: consilium (n-2)

Crime: crimen, -inis (n-3)

Crowd, masses: turba (f-1)

Cruel, horrible: atrox (gen. atrocis)

Cypress tree: cupressus (f-2)

D

Danger: periculum (n-2)

Daughter: filia (f-1)

Day: dies (m/f-5)

Death: mors, -rtis (f-3)

Deed, active group: factio, -tionis (f-3)

Deny, refuse: nego, -are, -avi, -atus (1)

Difficult: difficilis-e

Do, drive, force: ago, -ere, egi, actus (3)

Do, make: facio, -ere, feci, factus (3)

Dog: canis, -is (m/f-3)

Down from, concerning: de (abl.)

Drag, pull: traho, -ere, traxi, tractus (3)

Dwell, live in: habito, -are, -avi, -atus (1)

E

Eagle: aquila (f-1)

Ear: auris, -is (f-3)

Easy: facilis-e

Efface, destroy: deleo, -ère, delevi, deletum (2)

Elbow: ulna (f-1)

Elm tree: ulmus (f-2)

Enemy: hostis, -is (m-3)

Eye: oculus (m-2)

F

Face, surface: facies (f-5)

Faith: fides (f-5)

Faithful: fidelis-e

Famous, bright: clarus-a-um

Farmer: agricola (m-1)

Fast, swift: rapidus-a-um

Father: pater, -tris (m-3)

Fatherland: patria (f-1)

Fear: timor, -oris (m-3)

Fear: timeo, -ère, timui (2)

Feel, perceive: sentio, -ire, sensi, sensum (4)

Ferocity: ferocitas, -tatis (f-3)

Few: paucus-a-um

Field (cultivated): ager (m-2)

Field (unplowed): campus (m-2)

Fierce: ferox (gen. ferocis)

Fig tree: ficus (f-2)

Fight: pugna (f-1)

Fight: pugno, -are, -avi (1)

Fill, fulfill: pleo, -ère, plevi, pletus (2)

Finger: digitus (m-2)

Finish: finio, -ire, -ivi, -itus (4)

Fire: ignis, -is (m-3)

Fish: piscis, -is (m-3)

Flaw, weakness: vitium (n-2)

Flesh: caro, -rnis (n-3)

Flower: flos, -oris (m-3)

Fly: volo, -are, -avi (1)

Forest, woods: silva (f—1)

Fortify: munio, -ire, -ivi, -itus (4)

Fountain: fons, -ontis (m-3)

Fox: vulpes, -is (f-3)

Free: liber-a-um

Friend: amica (f-1)

Friend: amicus (m-2)

Frighten: terreo, -ère, terrui (2)

Fruit: fructus (m-4)

Full: plenus-a-um

G

Game: ludus (m-2)

Give: do, -are, dedi, datus (1)

Go: eo, ire, ivi (4)

Gift: donum (n-2)

God: deus (m-2)

Goddess: dea (f-1)

Gold: aurum (n-2)

Good, upright: bonus-a-um

Grandfather: avus (m-2)

Gravity, seriousness: gravitas, -tatis (f-3)

Green: verdis, -e

Grief, pain: dolor, -oris (m-3)

Guard, watch over: custodio, -ire, -ivi, -itus (4)

H

Hand: manus (f-4)

Hang: pendeo, -êre, pependi, pensus (2)

Happiness: felicitas, -tatis (f-3)

Happy: felix (gen. felicis)

Hard, tough: durus-a-um

Hatred: odium (n-2)

Have, possess: habeo, -êre, habui, habitus (2)

Head: caput, -pitis (n-3)

Healthy: sanus-a-um

Heap, pile: cumulus (m-2)

Hear: audio, -ire, -ivi, -itus (4)

Heart: cor, -rdis (n-3)

Heavy: gravis, -e

Help, aid: auxilium (n-2)

High, tall, deep: altus-a-um

His/her/their own: suus-a-um

Hit, slap: pulso, -are, -avi, -atus (1)

Hold: teneo, -êre, tenui, tentus (2)

Hollow, cavity, bay: sinus (m-4)

Home: domus (f-4)

Hope: spes (f-5)

Hope (for): spero, -are, -avi (1)

Horn (animal or trumpet): cornu (n-4)

Horror: horror, -oris (m-3)

Horse: equus (m-2)

Hot, warm: calidus-a-um

Hour: hora (f-1)

House: villa (f-1)

How much/many: quantus-a-um

I

Ice: glacies (f-5)

In, on, at: in (abl.)

Inner life, spirit: animus (m-2)

Injury: iniuria (f-1)

Into: in (acc.)

J

Join, put together: (v) iungo, -ere, iunxi, iunctus (3)

Journey, way: iter, -tineris (n-3)

K

Kill: neco, -are, -avi, -atus (1)

Kind, type: genus, -eris (n-3)

King: rex, -gis (m-3)

Kingdom: regnum (n-2)

Knee: genu (n-4)

Know, be certain of: scio, -ire, -ivi, -itus (4)

L

Lake: lacus (m-4)

Laugh: rideo, -êre, risi (2)

Land, earth: terra (f-1)

Laurel tree: laurus (f-1)

Lay waste, devastate: vasto, -are, -avi, -atus (1)

Law: lex, -gis (f-3)

Lead, bring: duco, -ere, duxi, ductus (3)

Left (side): sinister-tra-trum

Leave, depart: relinquo, -ere, reliqui, relictus (3)

Leader: dux, -cis (m-3)

Leaf: folium (n-2)

Letter (mail): epistola (f-1)

Letter (of alphabet): littera (f-1)

Liberty: libertas, -tatis (f-3)

Lie down: iaceo, -êre, iacui (2)

Life: vita (f-1)

Line (of sight or battle): acies (f-5)

Lion: leo, -onis (m-3)

Light: levis, -e

Light: lux, -cis (f-3)

Long, extensive: longus-a-um

Lord, master: dominus (m-2)

Lose: perdo, -ere, perdidi, perditus (3)

Love: amor, -oris (m-3)

Love: amo, -are, -avi, -atus (1)

M

Man: vir (m-2)

Many, much: multus-a-um

Matter, affair: res (f-5)

Means, way: modus (m-2)

Message, messenger: nuntius (m-2)

Middle: medius-a-um

Milk: lac, -ctis (n-3)

Mix: misceo, -êre, miscui, mixtus (2)

Mind: mens, -ntis (f-3)

Moon: luna (f-1)

Mother: mater, -tris (f-3)

Mountain: mons, -ntis (m-3)

Mouth, face: ôs, ôris (n-3)

Move: moveo, -êre, movi, motus (2)

My: meus-a-um

N

New: novus-a-um

Night: nox, -ctis (f-3)

Noise, loudness: clamor, -oris (m-3)

Nose: nasus (m-2)

Number: numerus (m-2)

O

Oak tree: quercus (f-2)

Obstacle: impedimentum (n-2)

Old, reverend: senex (gen. senis)

On account of: propter (acc.)

On behalf of, for: pro (abl.)

Order: iubeo, -êre, iussui, issus (2)

Other, the rest: ceterus-a-um

Out of, out from:ex / ê (abl.)

Over, above: super (acc.)

Owe, ought: debeo, -êre, debui (2)

Our: noster-tra-trum

P

Pale: pallidus-a-um

Part: pars, -rtis (f-3)

Peace: pax, -cis (f-3)

People, population: populus (m-2)

Person, man: homo, -minis (m)

Pine tree: pinus (f-2)

Place: locus (m in sing., n in pl-2)

Please: placeo, -êre, placui (2)

Poet: poeta (m-1)

Poison:venenum (n-2)

Poplar tree: poplus (f-2)

Port (sea): portus (m-4)

Power: potestas, -tatis (f-3)

Power (authority, command): imperium (n-2)

Praise: laudo, -are, -avi, -atus (1)

Prepare: paro, -are, -avi, -atus (1)

Press, squeeze: primo, -ere, pressi, pressus (3)

Price: pretium (n-2)

Prohibit, forbid: veto, -are, -avi, -atus (1)

Put, place: pono, -ere, posui, positus (3)

Punish: punio, -ire, -ivi, -itus (4)

Q

Queen: regina (f-1)

R

Rain: pluvium (n-2)

Red: rufus-a-um

Reinforcements (military): auxilia (pl-2)

Rejoice: gaudeo, -ēre, gavisus sum (2)

Remain, stay: maneo, -ēre, mansi (2)

Repeal, annulment: abrogatio, -tionis (3)

Report: nuntio, -are, -avi, -atus (1)

Rich: dives (gen. divitis)

Right (side): dexter-tra-trum

River: flumen, -inis (n-3)

Road, way: via (f-1)

Root: radix, -cis (f-3)

Rule, authority: imperium (n-2)

Rule over: domino, -are, -avi, -atus (1)

Running, race, track: cursus (m-4)

S

Sad, wretched: miser-a-um

Sad: tristis, -e

Save, preserve: servo, -are, -avi, -atus (1)

Say, speak: dico, -ere, dixi, dictus (3)

Sail: navigo, -are, -avi (1)

Sailor: nauta (m-1)

Sea: mare, -is (n-3)

Seek, ask: peto, -ere, petivi, petitus (3)

Seize, attack: occupo, -are, -avi, -atus (1)

Send: mitto, -ere, misi, missus (3)

Shame, modesty: pudor, -oris (m-3)

Sharp, bitter: acer-acris-acre

Sheep: ovis, -is (f-3)

Shine: splendeo, -ēre, splendidi (2)

Shining, brilliant: splendidus-a-um

Short, brief: brevis-e

Shout: clamo, -are, -avi, -atus (1)

Show: monstro, -are, -avi, -atus (1)

Ship: navis, -is (f-3)

Shoulder: umerus (m-2)

Sick, ill: aeger-gra-grum

Silver: argentums (n-2)

Sister: soror, -ris (f-3)

Sit: sedeo, -ēre, sedi (2)

Size (in quality): magnitudo, -tudinis (f-3)

Size (in quantity): multitudo, -tudinis (f-3)

Sky: caelum (n-2)

Slavery: servitudo, -tudinis (f-3)

Sleep: dormio, -ire, -ivi (4)

Slow, late: tardus-a-um

Small: parvus-a-um

Smooth, gentle: lenis-e

So much/many: tantus-a-um

Soldier: miles, -litis (m-3)

Son: filius (m-2)

Song: cantus (m-4)

Speech: locutio, -tionis (f-3)

Speed: celeritas, -tatis (f-3)

Spirit, soul: animus (m-2)

Stag, deer: cervus (m-2)

Stand, be still: sto, stare, steti (1)

Star: stella (f-1)

Stone, rock: saxum (n-2)

Story: fabula (f-1)

Strength: fortitudo, -tudinis (f-3)

Strong, brave: fortis, -e

Sun: sol, -lis (m-3)

Swift: celer-is-e

Swear, take an oath: iuro, -are, -avi (1)

T

Tail: cauda (f-1)

Take, seize: capio, -ere, cepi, captus (3)

Teach: doceo, -êre, docui, doctum (2)

Teacher: magister (m-2)

Tell: narro, -are, -avi, -atus (1)

Terror: terror, -oris (m-3)

Think, reflect: cogito, -are, -avi, -atus (1)

Think, calculate: puto, -are, -avi, -atus(1)

Through, along: per (acc.)

Time, weather: tempus, -oris (n-3)

Tongue, language: lingua (f-1)

Tooth: dens, -ntis (m-3)

Toward, to, with regard to: ad (acc.)

Town: oppidum (n-2)

Troops, wealth: copiae (f pl-1)

True, genuine: verus-a-um

Truth: veritas, -tatis (f-3)

Try, attempt: tempto, -are, -avi, -atus (1)

Type, kind: species (f-5)

U

Uncle: avunculus (m-2)

Under; coming from under: sub (abl.)

Up against, facing: ob (acc)

Uproar: tumultus (m-4)

V

Victory: victoria (f-1)

Vile, foul: turpis-e

Vileness: turpitudo , -tudinis (f-3)

Virtue (manliness): virtûs, -tûtis (f-3)

Voice: vox, -cis (f-3)

W

Wait for: exspecto, -are, -avi, -atus (1)

Wall: murus (m-2)

Walk: ambulo, , -are, -avi (1)

Wander, go astray: erro, -are, -avi (1)

Want, desire: desidero, -are, -avi, -atus (1)

Warn: moneo, -êre, monui, monitus (2)

Watch, observe: specto, -are, -avi, -atus (1)

Water: aqua (f-1)

War: bellum (n-2)

Water: aqua (f-1)

Whale: cetus (m-2)

White: albus-a-um

Wind: ventus (m-2)

Wine: vinum (n-2)

With (means/ instrument): cum (abl.)

Within, among: intra (acc.)

Without: sine (abl.)

Wolf: lupus (m-2)

Woman: femina (f-1)

Word: verbum (n-2)

Work, deed: opus, -eris (n-3)

World, universe: mundus (m-2)

Worthy, noble: dignus-a-um

Wound: vulnero, -are, -avi, -atus (1)

Write: scribe, -ere, scripsi, scriptus (3)

Y

Year: annus (m-2)

Young: iuvenis-e

Your (singular): tuus-a-um

Your (plural):nvester-tra-trum

Youth: iuventûs, -tûtis

IV. Complete English-to-Greek List
Alphabetized

A

Above, for the sake of: 'υπερ (gen.)

Accompany: 'ομιλεω

All, every: πας, πασα, παν

Along under, during: 'υπο (acc.)

Among, amid: μετα (dat.)

Ancient: παλαιος-α-ον

Army: στρατος (m-2)

Around, about, concerning: περι (gen., dat., acc.)

Around, about, on both sides: 'αμφι (gen./acc.)

Arrange: τασσω

B

Bad, wicked: κακος-η-ον

Because of, during: δια (acc.)

Beginning: 'αρχη (f-1)

Believe: νομιζω

Beloved, friendly: φιλος-η-ον

Beside, at: 'επι (dat.)

Beside, near: παρα (dat.)

Big, great, mighty: μεγας, -γαλα, -γαλον

Bird: 'ορνις, -ιθος (m/f-3)

Black, dark: μελας, -λαινα, -λαινον

Blood: 'αιμα , -ατος (n-3)

Body: σωμα, -ατος (n-3)

Book: βιβλος (f-2)

Boy: κουρος (m-2)

Bull: ταυρος (m-2)

By, from under: 'υπο (gen.)

C

Call, summon: καλεω

Carry, bear: φερω

Cause: 'αιτιον (n-2)

Change, answer: 'αμειβω

Chaos, wild disorder: χαος (n-3)

Chest, breast: στηθος, -εος (n-3)

Child: παις, παιδος (m/f-3)

Child (either sex): τεκνον (n-2)

Clear, obvious: δηλος-η-ον

Citizenry, common people: δημος (m-2)

City: πολις (f-3)

Cloud: νεφος, -εος (n-3)

Color: χρωμα, -ατος (n-3)

Companion, friend: 'εταιρος (m/f-1/2)

Custom, habit: 'εθος , -εος; also'ηθος (n-3)

D

Daughter: θυγατηρ, -ερος (f-1)

Dawn: 'ηως, -οος (f-1)

Day: 'ημαρ, 'ηματος (n-3); also 'ημερα (f-1)

Death: θανατος (m-2)

Deed, action (on stage): δραμα, -ατος (n-3)

Die: θνησκω

Do, perform: πρασσω

Dog: κυων, κυνος (m/f-3)

Down, along/through, according to: κατα (acc.)

Down from, below: κατα (gen.)

Dream: 'ονειρος (m-2)

Dread: ταρβεω

Drug, medicine: φαρμακον (n-2)

E

Earth (planet): γαια (f-1)

Earth (soil): χθων. –ονος (f-3)

End, complete: τελευταω

End, purpose: τελος, -εος (n-3)

Equal, even, level: 'ισος -η-ον

F

Fate, destiny: μοιρα (f-1)

Father: πατηρ, -ερος (m-3)

Fear: ταρβεω, φοβεομαι

Fear, terror: φοβος (m-2)

Few: 'ολιγος -η-ον

Fire: πυρ, -ος (m-3)

Fish: 'ιχθυς, -υος (m-3)

Foolish, stupid: 'ατοπος-η-ον

Footsoldier: 'οπλης, 'οπλιτις (m-3)

Forgetfulness, oblivion: ληθη (f-1)

Forward (from): προ

Free, independent: 'ελευθερος

Freedom: 'ελευθερια (f-1)

Frighten: φοβεω

Frightening, "terrific": δεινος-η-ον

From, away from: 'απο (gen.)

From before, in sight of: προς (gen.)

From the side, beside: παρα (gen.)

G

Gap, space, gulf: χασμα, -ατος (n-3)

General, commander: στρατηγος (m-2)

Gift, portion: δοσις (f-3)

Gift: δωρον (n-2)

Girl: κουρη (f-1)

God: θεος (m-2)

Goddess: θεα (f-1)

Good, right: καλος-η-ον

Graceful: χαριεις-εσσα-εν

Grief, sorrow: πενθος, -εος (n-3)

H

Half, midway: 'ημισυς-εια-υ

Hand: χειρ, -ος (n-3)

Hatred: μισος , -εος (n-3)

Hear, listen: 'ακουω

Heavy, severe: βαρυς-εια-υ

Hero: 'ηρως, -ωος (m-3)

Hold, have: 'εχω

Holy, sacred: 'ιερος-η-ον

Home, domicile: 'οικος (m-2)

Honor, glory: κυδος, -εος (n-3)

Horse: 'ιππος (m-2)

Hostile, enemy: 'εχθρος-η-ον

Hubris, arrogance: 'υβρις. –ιδος (f-3)

Hurt, pain: 'αλγος , -εος (n-3)

I

In, on: 'εν / 'ενι / 'ειν (dat.)

Instead of, contrary to, against: 'αντι (gen.)

Into, toward: 'εις / 'ες (acc.)

Into the midst of: μετα (acc.)

Island: νησος (m-2)

J

Joy: χαρμα, -ατος (n-3)

Judge: κρινω

Judgment: κρισις (f-3)

K

King: βασιλευς, -ηος (m-3)

Kingdom: βασιλεία, accent on third syllable (f-1)

Know, learn: γιγνωσκω

Knowledge: γνωμη (f-1)

L

Live: ζωω

Living, alive: ζωος-η-ον

Lead, drive: ’αγω

Lesser god, luck: δαιμων, -ονος (m-3)

Lie, be false: ψευδω

Life (specific): βιος (m-2)

Life (general): ζωη (f-1)

Light, brilliance: φαος, -εος (n-3)

Like, love: φιλεω

Lion: λεων, λεοντος (m-3)

Love: ’ερως, -ωτος (m-3)

M

Make, cause: τευχω

Make, fashion: ποιεω

Maiden, virgin: παρθενος (f-2)

Main room: μεγαρον (n-2)

Man: ανηρ, ’ανδρος (m-3)

Many, much: πολυς-πολλη-υ

Measure: μετρος (m-2)

Memory: μνημη (f-1)

Moon: μην, -νος (m-3)

Mother: μητηρ, -ερος (f-3)

Mouth, face: στομα, -ατος (n-3)

Move, go, withdraw: χωρεω

N

Name: ’ονομα , -ατος (n-3)

Nature, Creation: φυσις (f-3)

Need (goods, money): χρημα, -ατος (n-3)

New, young: νεος-α-ον

Night: νυξ, νυκτος (f-3)

Number, tally: ’αριθμος (m-2)

O

Old: γεραιος-η-ον

Old man: γερων, -οντος (m-3)

On, at, by: προς (dat.)

On, upon: ’επι (gen.)

One, lone: μονος-η-ον

Opinion, teaching: δογμα, -ατος (n-3)

Origin, birth: γενεσις (f-3)

Out of, from: ’εκ / ’εξ (gen.)

Other: ’αλλος-η-ον

Over, beyond: ‘υπερ (acc.

P

Pain, suffering: παθος, -εος (n-3)

Path, road, way: ‘οδος (m-2)

Person, man: 'ανθροπος (m-2)

Persuade: πειθω

Pleasant, soft, sweet: 'ηδυς-εια-υ

Pilot, helmsman: κυβερνητης (m-1)

Place: τοπος (m-2)

Plan, scheme: σχημα, -ατος (n-3)

Poet: ποιητης (m-1)

Power: κρατος, -εος (n-3)

Powerful, ruling: κρατυς-εια-υ

Produce, bring forth: φυω

Prophet(ess): μαντις (m/f-3)

Q

Queen: βασίλεια, - ειας, accent on second syllable (f-1); also βασιλις, -ιδος (f-3)

Quick, fast: ταχυς-εια-υ

R

Race (descent): γενος, -εος (n-3)

Race (tribe): 'εθνος , -εος (n-3)

Red: 'ερυθρος -η-ον

Rejoice, be healthy: χαιρω

Release: λυσις (f-3)

Release, loosen: λυω

Remember: μιμνησκω

Rule: κρατεω (with gen.)

Run, flow: 'ρεω

River: ποταμος (m-2)

S

Say, read, collect: λεγω

Sea: πελαγος, -εος (n-3)

Sea: ποντος (m-2)

See: 'οραω

Seed: σπερμα, -ατος (n-3)

Self, same: 'αυτος -η-ον

Send, escort: πεμπω

Sharp, keen: 'οξυς-εια-υ

Show, bring to light: φαινω

Signal, mark out: σημαινω

Similar: 'ομοιος-α-ον

Skin: δερμα, -ατος (n-3)

Sleep: 'υπνος (m-2)

Small, tiny: 'ελαχυς -εια-υ

Small, paltry: μικρος-η-ον

Son: 'υιος, gen. both 'υιου and 'υιεος (m-3)

Soul, spirit: ψυχη (f-1)

Speak, utter: φωνεω

Spouse: ποσις (m/f-3)

Star: 'αστηρ, -ερος (m-3)

Straight, correct: 'ορθος -η-ον

Straight, direct: 'ιθυς-εια-υ

Stone: πετρος (m-2)

Stop, cease: παυω

Story, lore: μυθος (m-2)

Suffer: πασχω

T

Take, seize: λαμβανω

Thick, dense: παχυς-εια-υ

Think, notice: νοεω

Through: δια (gen.)

Through (upward): 'ανα (acc.)

Throw: βαλλω

Thunder: βροντη (f-1)

Time: χρονος (m-2)

U

Under: 'υπο (dat.)

Universe, arrangement: κοσμος (m-2)

W

Walk: βαινω

Wall: τειχος, -εος (n-3)

War: πολεμος (m-2)

Watch, look at: σκοπεω

Water: 'υδωρ, 'υδατος (m-3)

White, bright: λευκος-η-ον

Woman: γυνη, -αικος (f-3)

Word, lore: 'επος , -εος (n-3)

Word, pattern: λογος (m-2)

Witness: μαρτυρος (m-2)

Work, task: 'εργον (n-2)

Wrath, rage: μην

Suppose, imagine: δοκεω

Sweet (taste): γλυκυς-εια-υ

To the side of, along: παρα (acc.)

To, toward, up against: προς (acc.)

Tree: δενδρος (n-3)

True, unforgettable: 'αληθης-ες

True, real: 'ετυμος -η-ον

Turn, direct: τρεπω

Turn (in direction): style: τροπος (m-2)

Tyrant, ruler: τυραννος (m-2)

Up to, against: 'επι (acc.)

Upon, up, along: 'ανα (dat.)

Wide, broad: 'ευρυς-εια-υ

Wise: σοφος-η-ον

Wind: 'ανεμος (m-2)

Wine: 'οινος (m-2)

With: μετα (gen.)

With (means or accompaniment): συν (dat.)

V. Complete Latin-to-English List Alphabetized

You should know parts of speech in English; but in case you find them more difficult to identify in Latin, they are indicated parenthetically just before the definition. Do not confuse "n" for "neuter" when it appears to the right of the colon. Here it means "noun.

A

Ab / â: (prep+abl) away from, by (agent)

Abrogatio, -tionis (f-3): (n) repeal, annulment

Acer-acris-acre: (adj) sharp, bitter

Acies (f-5): (n) line (of sight or battle)

Ad: (prep+acc) toward, to, with regard to

Adventus (m-4): (n) arrival

Aeger-gra-grum: (adj) sick, ill

Ager (m-2): (n) field (cultivated)

Ago, -ere, -egi, -actus (3): (v) do, drive, force

Agricola (m-1): (n) farmer

Albus-a-um: (adj) white

Altus-a-um: (adj) high, tall, deep

Ambulo, -are, -avi (1): (v) walk

Amica (f-1): (n) friend

Amicus (m-2): (n) friend

Amo, -are, -avi, -atus (1): (v) love

Amor, -oris (m-3): (n) love

Anima (f-1): (n) breath

Animal, -is (n-3): (n) animal, life form

Animus (m-2): (n) inner life, spirit

Annus (m-2): (n) year

Ante: (prep+acc) before (time or space)

Antiquitas, -tatis (f-3): (n) antiquity

Aqua (f-1): (n) water

Aquila (f-1): (n) eagle

Arcus (m-2): (n) bow (archery)

Argentums (n-2): (n) silver

Arma (n pl-2): (n) arms, weapons

Atrox (gen. atrocis): (adj) cruel, horrible

Audax (gen. audacis): (adj) bold, daring

Audio, -ire, -ivi, -itus (4): (v) hear

Auris, -is (f-3): (n) ear

Aurum (n-2): (n) gold

Auxilia (n pl-2): (n) reinforcements (military)

Auxilium (n-2): (n) help, aid

Avis (f-3): (n) bird

Avunculus (m-2): (n) uncle

Avus (m-2): (n) grandfather

B

Bellum (n-2): (n) war

Bonus-a-um: (adj) good, upright

Bracchium (n-2): (n) arm (body)

Brevis-e: (adj) short, brief

C

Caelum (n-2): (n) sky

Calidus-a-um: (adj) hot, warm

Campus (m-2): (n) field (unplowed)

Candidus-a-um: (adj) bright, shining

Candor, -oris (m-3): (n) candor, frankness

Canis, -is (m/f-3): (n) dog

Cantus (m-4): (n) song

Capio, -ere, cepi, captus (3): (v) take, seize

Caput, -pitis (n-3): (n) head

Caro, -rnis (n-3): (n) flesh

Castra (n pl-2): (n) camp (military)

Casus (m-4): (n) chance, accident

Cauda (f-1): (n) tail

Causa (f-1): (n) cause, reason

Celer-is-e: (adj) swift

Celeritas, -tatis (f-3): (n) speed

Celo, -are, -avi, -atus (1): (v) conceal

Cerebrum (n-2): (n) brain

Cervus (m-2): (n) stag, deer

Ceterus-a-um: (adj) other, the rest

Cetus (m-2): (n) whale

Circum: (prep+acc) around

Civis, -is (m-3): (n) citizen

Clamo, -are, -avi, -atus (1): (v) shout

Clamor, -oris (m-3): (n) noise, loudness

Clarus-a-um: (adj) famous, bright

Cogito, -are, -avi, -atus (1): (v) think, reflect

Concilium (n-2): (n) council, advisory body

Consilium (n-2): (n) counsel, advice

Contra: (prep+acc) against

Copia (f-1): (n) abundance, wealth

Copiae (f pl-1): (n) troops, wealth

Cor, -rdis (n-3): (n) heart

Cornu (n-4): (n) horn (animal or trumpet)

Corpus, -oris (n-3): (n) body

Correctio, -tionis (f-3): (n) correction

Crimen, -inis (n-3): (n) crime

Cum: (prep_abl) with (means/instrument)

Cumulus (m-2): (n) heap, pile

Cupressus (f-2): (n) cypress tree

Cura (f-1): (n) care, concern

Curare, -are, -avi, -atus (1): (v) care for, look after

Cursus (m-4): (n) running, race, track

Custodio, -ire, -ivi, -itus (4): (v) guard, watch over

D

De: (prep+abl) down from, concerning

Dea (f-1): (n) goddess

Debeo, -êre, debui (2): (v) owe, ought

Deleo, -êre, delevi, delet (2): (v) efface, destroy

Dens, -ntis (m-3): (n) tooth

Desidero, -are, -avi, -atus (1): (v) want, desire

Deus (m-2): (n) god

Dexter-tra-trum: (adj) right (side)

Dico, -ere, dixi, dictus (3): (v) say, speak

Dies (m/f-5): (n) day

Difficils-e: (adj) difficult

Digitus (m-2): (n) finger

Dignus-a-um: (adj) worthy, noble

Dives (gen. divitis): (adj) rich

Do, -are, dedi, datus (1): (v) give

Doceo, -êre, docui, doctum (2): (v) teach

Dolor, -oris (m-3): (n) grief, pain

Domino, -are, -avi, -atus (1): (v) rule over

Dominus (m-2): (n) lord, master

Domus (f-4): (n) home

Donum (n-2): (n) gift

Dormio, -ire, -ivi (4): (v) sleep

Dorsum (n-2): (n) back

Duco, -ere, duxi, ductus (3): (v) lead, bring

Durus-a-um: (adj) hard, tough

Dux, -cis (m-3): (n) leader

E

Eo, ire, ivi (4): (v) go

Epistola (f-1): (n) letter (mail)

Equus (m-3): (n) horse

Erro, -are, -avi (1): (v) wander, go astray

Ex / ê: (prep+abl) out of, out from

Exercitus (m-4): (n) army

Exspecto, -are, -avi, -atus (1): (v) wait for

F

Fabula (f-1): (n) story

Facies (f-5): (n) face, surface

Facilis-e: (adj) easy

Facio, -ere, feci, factus (3): (v) do, make

Factio, -tionis (f-3): (n) deed, active group

Feles, -is (f-3): (n) cat

Felicitas, -tatis (f-3): (n) happiness

Felix (gen. felicis): (adj) happy

Femina (f-1): (n) woman

Ferocitas, -tatis (f-3): (n) ferocity

Ferox (gen. ferocis): (adj) fierce

Ferrum (n-2): (n) iron, weapon (of iron)

Ficus (f-2): (n) fig tree

Fides (f-5): (n) faith

Fidelis-e: (adj) faithful

Filia (f-1): (n) daughter

Filius (m-2): (n) son

Finio, -ire, -ivi, -itus (4): (v) finish

Flos, -oris (m-3): (n) flower

Flumen, -inis (n-3): (n) river

Folium (n-2): (n) leaf

Fons, -ontis (m-3): (n) fountain

Fortis, -e: (adj) strong, brave

Fortitudo, -tudinis (f-3): (n) strength

Frango, -ere, fregi, fractus (3): (v) break, shatter

Frater, -tris (m-3): (n) brother

Frigidus-a-um: (adj) cold

Fructus (m-4): (n) fruit

G

Gaudeo, -êre, gavisus sum (2): (v) rejoice

Genu (n-4): (n) knee

Genus, -eris (n-3): (n) kind, type

Glacies (f-5): (n) ice

Gravis, -e: (adj) heavy

Gravitas, -tatis (f-3): (n) gravity, seriousness

H

Habeo, -êre, habui, habitus (2): (v) have, possess

Habito, -are, -avi, -atus (1): (v) dwell, live in

Homo, -minis (m-3): (n) person, man

Hora (f-1): (n) hour

Horror, -oris (m-3): (n) horror

Hostis, -is (m-3): (n) enemy

I

Iaceo, -êre, iacui (2): (v) lie down

Ictus (m-4): (n) blow, slap

Ignis, -is (m-3): (n) fire

Impedimenta (n pl-2): (n) baggage

Impedimentum (n-2): (n) obstacle

Imperium (n-2): (n) power (authority, command)

Impero, -are, -avi (1): (v) command

Impetus (m-4): (n) attack

In: (prep+abl) in, on, at

In: (prep+acc) into

Iniuria (f-1): (n) injury

Insidiae (f pl-1): (n) ambush

Insula (f-1): (n) island

Inter: (prep+acc) between

Intra: (prep+acc) within, among

Ira (f-1): (n) anger

Iter, -tineris (n-3): (n) journey, way

Iubeo, -êre, iussui, issus (2): (v) order

Iungo, -ere, iunxi, iunctus (3): (v) join, put together

Iuro, -are, -avi (1): (v) swear, take an oath

Iuvenis-e: (adj) young

Iuventûs, -tûtis (f-3): (n) youth

L

Lac, -ctis (n-3): (n) milk

Lacus (m-4): (n) lake

Latus-a-um: (adj) broad, wide

Laudo, -are, -avi, -atus (1): (v) praise

Laurus (f-1): (n) laurel tree

Lenis-e: (adj) smooth, gentle

Leo, -onis (m-3): (n) lion

Levis, -e: (adj) light

Lex, -gis (f-3): (n) law

Liber, -bri (m-2): (n) book

Liber-a-um: (adj) free

Libertas, -tatis (f-3): (n) liberty

Lingua (f-1): (n) tongue, language

Littera (f-1): (n) letter (of alphabet)

Litterae (f pl-1): (n) letter (message)

Locus (m in sing., n in pl-2): (n) place

Locutio, -tionis (f-3): (n) speech

Longus-a-um: (adj) long, extensive

Ludus (m-2): (n) game

Luna (f-1): (n) moon

Lupus (m-2): (n) wolf

Lux, -cis (f-3): (n) light

M

Magister, -stri (m-2): (n) teacher

Magnitudo, -tudinis (f-3): (n) size (in quality)

Magnus-a-um: (adj) big, great

Malus (f-2): (n) apple tree

Malus-a-um: (adj) bad, wicked

Maneo, -êre, mansi (2): (v) remain, stay

Manus (f-4): (n) hand

Mare, -is (n-3): (n) sea

Mater, -tris (f-3): (n) mother

Medius-a-um: (adj) middle

Mens, -ntis (f-3): (n) mind

Meus-a-um: (adj) my

Miles, -litis (m-3): (n) soldier

Miser-a-um: (adj) sad, wretched

Misceo, -êre, miscui, mixtus (2): (v) mix

Mitto, -ere, misi, missus (3): (v) send

Modus (m-2): (n) means, way

Moneo, -êre, monui, monitus (2): (v) warn

Mons, -ntis (m-3): (n) mountain

Monstro, -are, -avi, -atus (1): (v) show

Mors, -rtis (f-3): (n) death

Moveo, -êre, movi, motus (2): (v) move

Multitudo, -tudinis (f-3): (n) size (in quantity)

Multus-a-um: (adj) many, much

Mundus (m-2): (n) world, universe

Munio, -ire, -ivi, -itus (4): (v) fortify

Murus (m-2): (n) wall

Muto, -are, -avi, -atus (1): (v) change

N

Narro, -are, -avi, -atus (1): (v) tell

Nasus (m-2): (n) nose

Nauta (m-1): (n) sailor

Navigo, -are, -avi (1): (v) sail

Navis, -is (f-3): (n) ship

Neco, -are, -avi, -atus (1): (v) kill

Nego, -are, -avi, -atus (1): (v) deny, refuse

Niger-gra-grum: (adj) black, dark

Noster-tra-trum: (adj) our

Novus-a-um: (adj) new

Nox, -ctis (f-3): (n) night

Nubes, -is (f-3): (n) cloud

Numero, -are, -avi, -atus (1): (v) count

Numerus (m-2): (n) number

Nuntio, -are, -avi, -atus (1): (v) report

Nuntius, -i (m-2): (n) message, messenger

O

Ob: (prep+acc) up against, facing; because of

Occupo, -are, -avi, -atus (1): (v) seize, attack

Oculus (m-2): (n) eye

Odium (n-2): (n) hatred

Omnis-e: (adj) all, every

Oppidum (n-2): (n) town

Opto, -are, -avi, -atus (1): (v) choose, wish for

Opus, -eris (n-3): (n) work, deed

Os, ossis (n-3): (n) bone

Ôs, ôris (n-3): (n) mouth, face

Ovis, -is (f-3): (n) sheep

P

Pallidus-a-um: (adj) pale

Paro, -are, -avi, -atus (1): (v) prepare

Pars, -rtis (f-3): (n) part

Parvus-a-um: (adj) small

Pater, -tris (m-3): (n) father

Patria (f-1): (n) fatherland

Paucus-a-um: (adj) few

Pax, -cis (f-3): (n) peace

Pectus, -oris (n-3): (n) chest, breast

Pendeo, -êre, pependi, pensus (2): (v) hang

Per: (prep+acc) through, along

Perdo, -ere, perdidi, perditus (3): (v) lose

Periculum (n-2): (n) danger

Peto, -ere, petivi, petitus (3): (v) seek, ask

Pinus (f-2): (n) pine tree

Piscis, -is (m-3): (n) fish

Placeo, -êre, placui (2): (v) please

Plenus-a-um: (adj) full

Pleo, -êre, plevi, pletus (2): (v) fill, fulfill

Pluvium (n-2): (n) rain

Poeta (m-1): (n) poet

Pono, -ere, posui, positus (3): (v) put, place

Pons, -ntis (m-3): (n) bridge

Poplus (f-2): (n) poplar tree

Populus (m-2): (n) people, population

Porto, -are, -avi, -atus (1): (v) carry

Portus (m-4): (n) port (sea)

Post: (prep+acc) after, behind

Potestas, -tatis (f-3): (n) power

Prae: (prep+abl) before, in front of, regarding

Pretium (n-2): (n) price, value

Primo, -ere, pressi, pressus (3): (v) press, squeeze

Pro: (prep+abl) on behalf of, for

Propter: (prep+acc) on account of

Pudor, -oris (m-3): (n) shame, modesty

Puer (m-2): (n) boy

Pugna (f-1): (n) fight

Pugno, -are, -avi (1): (v) fight

Pulcher-chra-chrum: (adj) beautiful

Pulchritudo, -tudinis (f-3): (n) beauty

Pulso, -are, -avi, -atus (1): (v) hit, slap

Punio, -ire, -ivi, -itus (4): (v) punish

Puto, -are, -avi, -atus (1): (v) think, calculate

Q

Quantus-a-um: (adj) how much/many

Quercus (f-2): (n) oak tree

R

Radix, -cis (f-3): (n) root

Rapidus-a-um: (adj) fast, swift

Regina (f-1): (n) queen

Regnum (n-2): (n) kingdom

Relinquo, -ere, reliqui, relictus (3): (v) leave, depart

Res (f-5): (n) matter, affair

Responsum (n-2): (n) answer

Rex, -gis (m-3): (n) king

Rideo, -êre, risi (2): (v) laugh

Rogo, -are, -avi, -atus (1): (v) ask

Rufus-a-um: (adj) red

Rumpo, -ere, rupi, ruptus (3): (v) break, split

S

Sanguen, -inis (n-3): (n) blood

Sanus-a-um: (adj) healthy

Saxum (n-2): (n) stone, rock

Scio, -ire, -ivi, -itus (4): (v) know, be certain of

Scribe, -ere, scripsi, scriptus (3): (v) write

Sedeo, -êre, sedi (2): (v) sit

Senectûs, -tûtis (f-3): (n) age

Senex (gen. senis): (adj) old, reverend

Sentio, -ire, sensi, sensum (4): (v) feel, perceive

Servitudo, -tudinis (f-3): (n) slavery

Servo, -are, -avi, -atus (1): (v) save, preserve

Silva (f-1): (n) forest, woods

Sine: (prep+abl) without

Sinister-tra-trum: (adj) left (side)

Sinus (m-4): (n) hollow, cavity, bay

Socius (m-2): (n) comrade, ally

Sol, -lis (m-3): (n) sun

Soror, -ris (f-3): (n) sister

Species (f-5): (n) type, kind

Specto, -are, -avi, -atus (1): (v) watch, observe

Spero, -are, -avi (1): (v) hope (for)

Spes (f-5): (n) hope

Splendeo, -êre, splendidi (2): (v) shine

Splendidus-a-um: (adj) shining, brilliant

Stella (f-1): (n) star

Sto, stare, steti (1): (v) stand, be still

Sub: (prep+abl) under, coming from under

Super: (prep+acc) over, above

Supero, -are, -avi, -atus (1): (v) conquer, overcome

Suus-a-um: (adj) his/her/their own

T

Taceo, -êre, tacui (2): (v) be silent

Tantus-a-um: (adj) so much/many

Tardus-a-um: (adj) slow, late

Taurus (m-2): (n) bull

Tempto, -are, -avi, -atus (1): (v) try, attempt

Tempus, -oris (n-3): (n) time, weather

Teneo, -êre, tenui, tentus (2): (v) hold

Tergum (n-2): (n) back

Terra (f-1): (n) land, earth

Terreo, -êre, terrui (2): (v) frighten

Terror, -oris (m-3): (n) terror

Timeo, -êre, timui (2): (v) fear

Timor, -oris (m-3): (n) fear

Traho, -ere; traxi, tractus (3): (v) drag, pull

Trans: (prep+acc) across

Tristis, -e: (adj) sad

Tumultus (m-4): (n) uproar

Turba (f-1): (n) crowd, masses

Turpis-e: (adj) vile, foul

Turpitudo, -tudinis (f-3): (n) vileness

Tuus-a-um: (adj) your (singular)

U

Umerus (m-2): (n) shoulder

Ulmus (f-2): (n) elm tree

Ulna (f-1): (n) elbow

Urbs, -bis (f-3): (n) city

Ursa (f-1): (n) bear

V

Valeo, -êre, tacui (2): (v) be strong, worthy

Vasto, -are, -avi, -atus (1): (v) lay waste, devastate

Venenum (n-2): (n) poison

Venio, -ire, veni (4): (v) come

Ventus (m-2): (n) wind

Verbum (n-2): (n) word

Verdis, -e: (adj) green

Veritas, -tatis (f-3): (n) truth

Verus-a-um: (adj) true, genuine

Vester-tra-trum: (adj) your (plural)

Veto, -are, -avi, -atus (1): (v) prohibit, forbid

Via (f-1): (n) road, way

Victoria (f-1): (n) victory

Villa (f-1): (n) house

Vinco, -ere, vici, victus (3): (v) conquer

Vinum (n-2): (n) wine

Vir (m-2): (n) man

Virtûs, -tûtis (f-3): (n) virtue (manliness)

Vita (f-1): (n) life

Vitium (n-2): (n) flaw, weakness

Vito, -are, -avi, -atus (1): (v) avoid

Voco, -are, -avi, -atus (1): (v) call, summon

Volo, -are, -avi (1): (v) fly

Vox, -cis (f-3): (n) voice

Vulnero, -are, -avi, -atus (1): (v) wound

Vulpes, -is (f-3): (n) fox

VI. Complete Greek-to-English List Alphabetized

Again, parts of speech are indicated parenthetically just before the definition. Remember not to confuse "n" for "neuter" when it appears to the right of the colon (where it signifies "noun").

A

'Αγω: (v) lead, drive

'Αιμα, -ατος (n-3): (n) blood

'Αιτιον (n-2): (n) cause

'Ακουω: (v) hear, listen

'Αλγος, -εος (n-3): (n) hurt, pain

'Αληθης-ες: (adj) true, unforgettable

'Αλλος-η-ον: (adj) other

'Αμειβω: (v) change, answer

'Αμφι: (prep+gen/acc) around, about, on both sides

'Ανα: (prep+acc) through (upward)

'Ανα: (prep+dat) upon, up, along

'Ανεμος (m-2): (n) wind

'Ανηρ, 'ανδρος (m-3): (n) man

'Ανθροπος (m-2): (n) person, man

'Αντι: (prep+gen) instead of, contrary to, against

'Απο: (prep+gen) from, away from

'Αριθμος (m-2): (n) number, tally

'Αρχη (f-1): (n) beginning

'Αστηρ, -ερος (m-3): (n) star

'Ατοπος-η-ον: (adj) foolish, stupid

'Αυτος-η-ον: (adj) self, same

B

Βαινω: (v) walk

Βαλλω: (v) throw

Βαρυς-εια-υ: (adj) heavy, severe

Βασιλεία, accent on third syllable (f-1): (n) kingdom

Βασίλεια, -ειας, accent on second syllable (f-1); also
 βασιλις, -ιδος (f-3): (n) queen

Βασιλευς, -ηος (m-3): (n) king

Βιβλος (f-2): (n) book

Βιος (m-2): (n) life (specific)

Βροντη (f-1): (n) thunder

Γ

Γαια (f-1): (n) Earth (planet)

Γενεσις (f-3): (n) origin, birth

Γενος, -εος (n-3): (n) race (descent)

Γεραιος-η-ον: (adj) old

Γερων, -οντος (m-3): (n) old man

Γιγνωσκω: (v) know, learn

Γλυκυς-εια-υ: (adj) sweet (taste)

Γνωμη (f-1): (n) knowledge

Γυνη, -αικος (f-3): (n) woman

269

Δ

Δαιμων, -ονος (m-3): (n) lesser god, luck

Δεινος-η-ον: (adj) frightening, "terrific"

Δενδρος (n-3): (n) tree

Δερμα, -ατος (n-3): (n) skin

Δηλος-η-ον: (adj) clear, obvious

Δημος (m-2): (n) citizenry, common people

Δια: (prep+acc) because of, during

Δια: (prep+gen) through

Δογμα, -ατος (n-3): (n) opinion, teaching

Δοκεω: (v) suppose, imagine

Δοσις (f-3): (n) gift, portion

Δραμα, -ατος (n-3): (n) deed, action (on stage)

Δωρον (n-2): (n) gift

Ε

’Εθνος, -εος (n-3): (n) race (tribe)

’Εθος, -εος; also ‘ηθος (n-3): (n) custom, habit

’Εις / ’ες: (prep+acc) into, toward

’Εκ / ’εξ: (prep+gen) out of, from

’ελαχυς-εια-υ: (adj) small, tiny

’Ελευθερια (f-1): (n) freedom

’Ελευθερος -η-ον: (adj) free, independent

’Εν / ’ενι / ’ειν: (prep+dat) in, on

’Επι: (prep+gac) up to, against

’Επι: (prep+dat) beside, at

’Επι: (prep+gen) on, upon

’Επος, -εος (n-3): (n) word, lore

’Εργον (n-2): (n) work, task

’Ερυθρος-η-ον: (adj) red

’Ερως, -ωτος (m-3): (n) love

‘Εταιρος (m/f-1/2): (n) companion, friend

’Ετυμος-η-ον: (adj) true, real

’Ευρυς-εια-υ: (adj) wide, broad

’Εχθρος-η-ον: (adj) hostile, enemy

’Εχω: (v) hold, have

Ζ

Ζωη (f-1): (n) life (general)

Ζωος-η-ον: (adj) living, alive

Ζωω: (v) live

Η

‘Ηδυς-εια-υ: (adj) pleasant, soft, sweet

‘Ημαρ, ‘Ηματος (n-3); also ‘ημερα (f-1): (n) day

‘Ημισυς-εια-υ: (adj) half, midway

‘Ηρως, -ωος (m-3): (n) hero

’Ηως, -οος (f-1): (n) dawn

Θ

Θανατος (m-2): (n) death

Θεα (f-1): (n) goddess

Θεος (m-2): (n) god

Θνησκω: (v) die

Θυγατηρ, -ερος (f-3): (n) daughter

I

Ἱερος-η-ον: (adj) holy, sacred

Ἰθυς-εια-υ: (adj) straight, direct

Ἱππος (m-2): (n) horse

Ἰσος-η-ον: (adj) equal, even, level

Ἰχθυς, -υος (m-3): (n) fish

K

Κακος-η-ον: (adj) bad, wicked

Καλεω (v) call, summon

Καλος-η-ον: (adj) good, right

Κατα: (prep+acc) down, along/through, according to

Κατα: (prep_gen) down from, below

Κοσμος (m-2): (n) universe, arrangement

Κουρη (f-1): (n) girl

Κουρος (m-2): (n) boy

Κρατεω (with gen.): (v) rule

Κρατος, -εος (n-3): (n) power

Κρατυς-εια-υ: (adj) powerful, ruling

Κρινω: (v) judge

Κρισις (f-3): (n) judgment

Κυβερνητης (m-1): (n) pilot, helmsman

Κυδος, -εος (n-3): (n) honor, glory

Κυων, κυνος (m/f-3): (n) dog

Λ

Λαμβανω: (v) take, seize

Λεγω: (v) say, read, collect

Λευκος-η-ον: (adj) white, bright

Λεων, λεοντος (m-3): (n) lion

Ληθη (f-1): (n) forgetfulness, oblivion

Λογος (m-2): (n) word, pattern

Λυσις (f-3): (n) release

Λυω: (v) release, loosen

M

Μαντις (m/f-3): (n) prophet(ess)

Μαρτυρος (m-2): (n) witness

Μεγαρον (n-2): (n) main room

Μεγας, -γαλα, -γαλον: (adj) big, great, mighty

Μελας, -λαινα, -λαινον: (adj) black, dark

Μετα: (prep+acc) into the midst of

Μετα: (prep+dat) among, amid

Μετα: (prep+gen) with

Μετρος (m-2): (n) measure

Μηνις (f-3): (n) wrath, rage

Μην, -νος (m-3): (n) moon

Μητηρ, -ερος (f-3): (n) mother

Μικρος-η-ον: (adj) small, paltry

Μιμνησκω: (v) remember

Μισος, -εος (n-3): (n) hatred

Μνημη (f-1): (n) memory

Μοιρα (f-1): (n) fate, destiny

Μονος-η-ον: (adj) one, lone

Μυθος (m-2): (n) story, lore

N

Νεος-α-ον: (adj) new, young

Νεφος, -εος (n-3): (n) cloud

Νησος (m-2): (n) island

Νοεω: (v) think, notice

Νομιζω: (v) believe

Νυξ, νυκτος (f-3): (n) night

Ο

'Οδος (f-2): (n) path, road, way

'Οικος (m-2): (n) home, domicile

'Οινος (m-2): (n) wine

'Ολιγος-η-ον: (adj) few

'Ομιλεω: (v) accompany

'Ομοιος-α-ον: (adj) similar

'Ονειρος (m-2): (n) dream

'Ονομα, -ατος (n-3): (n) name

'Οξυς-εια-υ: (adj) sharp, keen

'Οπλης, 'οπλιτις (m-3): (n) footsoldier

'Οραω: (v) see

'Ορθος-η-ον: (adj) straight, correct

'Ορνις, -ιθος (m/f-3): (n) bird

Π

Παθος, -εος (n-3): (n) pain, suffering

Παις, παιδος (m/f-3): (n) child

Παλαιος-α-ον: (adj) ancient

Παρα: (prep+dat) beside, near

Παρα: (prep+acc) to the side of, along

Παρα: (prep+gen) from the side, beside

Παρθενος (f-2): (n) maiden, virgin

Πας, πασα, παν: (adj) all, every

Πασχω: (v) suffer

Πατερ, -ερος (m-3): (n) father

Παυω: (v) stop, cease

Παχυς-εια-υ: (adj) thick, dense

Πειθω: (v) persuade

Πελαγος, -εος (n-3): (n) sea

Πεμπω: (v) send, escort

Πενθος, -εος (n-3): (n) grief, sorrow

Περι: (prep+gen) about, concerning

Περι: (prep+dat/acc) around, about

Πετρος (m-2): (n) stone

Ποιεω: (v) make, fashion

Ποιητης (m-1): (n) poet

Πολεμος (m-2): (n) war

Πολις (f-3): (n) city

Πολυς-πολλη-υ: (adj) many, much

Ποντος (m-2): (n) sea

Ποσις (m/f-3): (n) spouse

Ποταμος (m-2): (n) river

Πρασσω: (v) do, perform

Προ (prep): (prep+gen) forward from, from before, in sight of

Προς: (prep+acc) to, toward, up against

Προς: (prep+dat) on, at, by

Πυρ, -ος (m-3): (n) fire

Ρ

'Ρεω: (v) run, flow

Σ

Σημαινω: (v) signal, mark out

Σκοπεω: (v) watch, look at

Σοφος-η-ον: (adj) wise

Σπερμα, -ατος (n-3): (n) seed

Στηθος, -εος (n-3): (n) chest, breast

Στομα, -ατος (n-3): (n) mouth, face

Στρατηγος (m-2): (n) general, commander

Στρατος (m-2): (n) army

Συν: (prep+dat) with (means or accompaniment)

Σχημα, -ατος (n-3): (n) plan, scheme

Σωμα, -ατος (n-3): (n) body

T

Ταρβεω: (v) dread; fear (also φοβεομαι, "frightened of")

Τασσω: (v) arrange

Ταυρος (m-2): (n) bull

Ταχυς-εια-υ: (adj) quick, fast

Τειχος, -εος (n-3): (n) wall

Τεκνον (n-2): (n) child (either sex)

Τελευταω: (v) end, complete

Τελος, -εος (n-3): (n) end, purpose

Τευχω: (v) make, cause

Τοπος (m-2): (n) place

Τρεπω: (v) turn, direct

Τροπος (m-2): (n) turn (in direction)

Τυραννος (m-2): (n) tyrant, ruler

Y

'Υβρις, -ιδος (f-3): (n) hubris, arrogance

'Υδωρ, 'υδατος (m-3): (n) water

'Υιος, gen. both 'υιου and 'υιεος (m-3): (n) son

'Υπερ: (prep+acc) over, beyond

'Υπερ: (prep+gen) above (static), for the sake of

'Υπνος (m-2): (n) sleep

'Υπο: (prep+acc) along, under, during

'Υπο: (prep+dat) under (static)

'Υπο: (prep+gen) by (agency), from under

Φ

Φαινω: (v) show, bring to light

Φαος, -εος (n-3): (n) light, brilliance

Φαρμακον (n-2): (n) drug, medicine

Φερω: (v) carry, bear

Φιλεω: (v) like, love

Φιλος-η-ον: (adj) beloved, friendly

Φοβεω: (v) frighten

Φοβος (m-2): (n) fear, terror

Φυσις (f-3): (n) nature, Creation

Φυω: (v) produce, bring forth

Φωνεω: (v) speak, utter

X

Χαιρω: (v) rejoice, be healthy

Χαος, -εος (n-3): (n) chaos, wild disorder

Χαριεις-εσσα-εν: (adj) graceful

Χαρμα, -ατος (n-3): (n) joy

Χασμα, -ατος (n-3): (n) gap, space, gulf

Χειρ, -ος (n-3): (n) hand

Χθων, -ονος (f-3): (n) earth (soil)

Χρημα, -ατος (n-3): (n) need (goods, money)

Χρονος (m-2): (n) time

Χρωμα, -ατος (n-3): (n) color

Χωρεω: (v) move, go, withdraw

Ψ

Ψευδω: (v) lie, be false

Ψυχη (f-1): (n) soul, spirit

Printed in Poland
by Amazon Fulfillment
Poland Sp. z o.o., Wrocław